S0-CFU-067

THE POPULAR SCIENCE ILLUSTRATED ALMANAC FOR HOME OWNERS

A man builds a fine house; and now he has a master, and a task for life; he is to furnish, watch, show it, and keep it in repair the rest of his days.

—Ralph Waldo Emerson

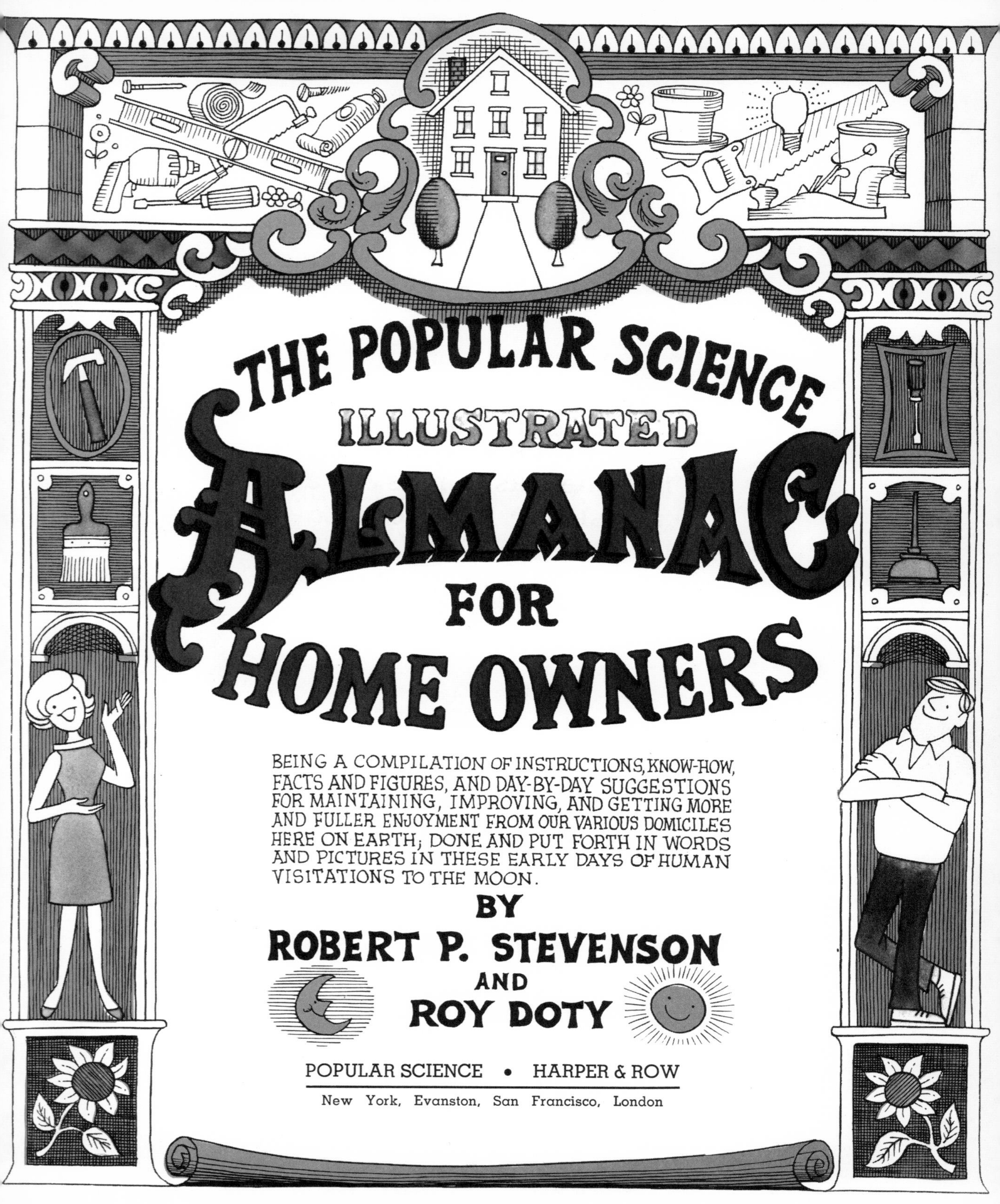
THE POPULAR SCIENCE
ILLUSTRATED
ALMANAC
FOR
HOME OWNERS
BEING A COMPILATION OF INSTRUCTIONS, KNOW-HOW, FACTS AND FIGURES, AND DAY-BY-DAY SUGGESTIONS FOR MAINTAINING, IMPROVING, AND GETTING MORE AND FULLER ENJOYMENT FROM OUR VARIOUS DOMICILES HERE ON EARTH; DONE AND PUT FORTH IN WORDS AND PICTURES IN THESE EARLY DAYS OF HUMAN VISITATIONS TO THE MOON.
BY
ROBERT P. STEVENSON
AND
ROY DOTY
POPULAR SCIENCE • HARPER & ROW
New York, Evanston, San Francisco, London

A calendar, a calendar! look in the almanack; find out moonshine.
—Shakespeare, in *A Midsummer Night's Dream*

Popular Science Publishing Company, Inc.
A Times Mirror Subsidiary

Library of Congress Catalog Card Number: 72-83027
SBN: 06-014106-9

Designed by Jeff Fitschen

Manufactured in the United States of America

To the
Next Generation of
Home Owners . . .
those really great
Youngsters who are
now concerned with
so many other
Important Things

To Our Patrons

There's usually a right time for everything. But how many of us know the right time—that is, the *best* time—for doing the various jobs that should be done in and around our home? This book sets down the right times for a lot of these varied activities. In that respect your Almanac is unique. You can buy many do-it-yourself guides to home repairs and improvement, and you should own several of them. This book is the first one to tell you *when* to do those chores.

The key to the physical well-being of any home is preventive maintenance. To keep your house in good shape, you must engage in a continuous battle with destructive forces that try to waste it away. The Almanac gives you the best times to get in some of your best licks in the battle—if timing makes any difference, which sometimes, of course, it doesn't.

For timing of lawn and garden activities we have consulted some of the foremost horticultural experts. We have also consulted all the signs, portents, and omens we could locate in a stack of old almanacs. Because our grandparents had far more work than we, yet managed to do everything reasonably well and on time, we wanted to see if any of the signs they often lived by might help us too. Maybe you believe in signs. More likely you don't. But the way we figure it, we might as well have them on our side—just in case they do have significance.

This Almanac, then, suggests the best seasonal timing we have been able to determine for various home chores. The timing can be made to apply throughout the United States, and much of Canada. Fortunately, horticultural timing is usually a range over several days; it is not necessarily tied to a single date. Times given are especially suitable for the northeastern states, more or less. This was done because we had to have a *base* timing period. If you live in another area, you determine the approximate timing for your area from the first-frost and final-frost maps of the U. S., described, respectively, under dates of February 8 and September 20. Through the Almanac, you also will find occasional spaces to jot down your own seasonal chores not mentioned in the book—or better done at a time other than the date suggested.

Besides a program of seasonal home-upkeep activities, the Almanac includes others that might be done at any time of the year. So far as possible we have spaced the latter between those events that are logically tied to seasonal or specific dates. The result is a calendar of activities leisurely paced through the entire year. For one year, we'll work right along with you to bring you up even with home and yard duties that you may have neglected. Yours then will be a happy, happy home—spick and span, every nail in place, no creaking stairs, no holes in the wall, every rose healthy and bugfree, everything as houseshape as it can be.

All you'll have to do thereafter is keep this Almanac handy as a reminder of what you ought to be doing, or planning to do, on whatever date you happen to pick it up. Skeptical? Will such a program really work? Well . . . perhaps not, human nature being what it is. But it's a fine dream, anyway! Whether it comes true is up to you.

It is fair to say, I think, that preparation of this book has taken a lifetime. It is based partly on what I have learned in living in a dozen homes. It is also based on what I have learned in my work-a-day world at *Popular Science,* this year celebrating its 100th anniversary—the magazine with which I have been associated for the final quarter of that century, most of the time concerned with the preparation of do-it-yourself reports.

When the idea for this Almanac was first

suggested, I resolved that, above all else, it must be a happy book, that it must reflect the living joy that ought to be found in any home—the center of the entire world for those who dwell there. Along with practical information, I resolved to include some material just because it was lighthearted, interesting, or appropriate to the date. Consequently, you will find the Almanac salted (and sugared) with many just-for-reading tidbits—historical facts, poems, jokes, and inspirational readings, the sort of thing that was scattered through almanacs of old.

I was also resolved that this Almanac must *look* happy. For that reason, I invited Roy Doty, the famous cartoonist, to become my collaborator—to be not only the illustrator but co-author, as well; for I hoped that some of Roy's abundant *joie de vivre* in his everyday associations might carry even beyond his witty and delightful drawings. I have not been disappointed.

Before signing off, I ask you, the readers of this Almanac, to note that I address you as "home owners"—not "homeowners." I do so for what I believe are good reasons. To me, the first term carries the connotations and overtones of happiness that I hope will endure right down to the final period of this book. It describes *you.* The combined form is a special favorite of banks and insurance companies—and to me it suggests dire and distressing situations: frightful fire losses, eight percent mortgages, million-dollar damage suits, and the like. Sound the combined word aloud, running the words and sounds together, and it becomes even worse—"ho-moaners." Not so! Home owners are a *happy* breed, not moaners. Let's have no more home-owners. Webster's, please copy!

ROBERT P. STEVENSON
July, 1972

January

Early Anglo-Saxons had good cause to call this coldest month of the year Wulf Monath. Hungry wolves then came boldly out of the forests to roam villages and farms for food. Owners of homes nowadays, even as in those olden times, find January appropriate for strengthening their defenses and for reviewing the problems of keeping the wolf from the door. Frost on the windowpanes reminds us that it is a month mostly for warm indoor activities, although the January thaw, which often comes in the final days, may prompt you to undertake a few gardening jobs, perhaps some necessary pruning.

January got its name from Janus, in Roman mythology the two-headed god of doors and gates and the beginning of things. When first set up as a time period, January came after December, and February was the final month of the year. In 46 B.C., Julius Caesar picked up January and February and moved them both ahead of all other months of the original ten-month Roman calendar. Caesar also fixed the length at 31 days.

January 1

New Year's Day

Today in History: By an old English custom, husbands on New Year's Day gave their wives money to buy enough pins for a year. Hence, the phrase "pin money." The custom died out with the coming of machine-made pins. A surprise renewal of the custom in your own home could lead to all sorts of happy things in your family relationships.

In 1862, the first U.S. income tax became effective: 3 percent on incomes over $800.

In 1863, near Beatrice, Nebraska, Daniel Freeman took up the first homestead under the Homestead Act, effective that day.

Poor Richard's Advice to Drinkers

There are more old drunkards than old doctors.

Drink does not drown care, but waters it, and makes it grow faster.

Take counsel in wine, but resolve afterwards in water.

Wish not so much to live long, as to live well.

One today is worth two tomorrows.

Keep your mouth wet, your feet dry.

You can't trust your own eyes. This illustration has no point other than to convince you of that, but owners of this Almanac will find within it lots of *useful* facts, too.

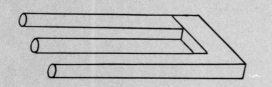

Is Your Home Secure?

This day, the first one of the ancient Wolf Month, is appropriate for making sure modern "wolves" cannot break into your home. Do all doors and windows have strong latches and locks in good condition? Locks have improved a great deal lately and you may want to consider replacing yours. What about basement windows? It might not be amiss to install iron bars such as you find in some older homes. Does

your front door have a chain? A chain on the back door is a good idea, too. And what about one-way viewers that let you see who is outside without opening the door? More homes should have them.

Home fire insurance had its beginnings on this day in 1735 in Charleston, S.C. The Friendly Society for the Mutual Insurance of Houses Against Fire accepted its first subscriptions. Do you have enough fire insurance now? Rising real estate prices lately have often outstripped coverage. Make a note to consider increasing yours next time the policy is renewed.

January 2

Are You a Good Money Manager?

This is a good day to adopt the two-headed pose of Janus, the Roman god for whom January is named. The backward-looking head could think about assembling the data needed for the annual duty of income-tax reporting. Your Government keeps issuing new publications to help you. So why not write a postal today asking for the latest list? The address: Superintendent of Documents, U.S. Government Printing Office, Washington, D.C. 20402.

The second head of Janus, the forward-looking one, might look to the future and begin planning a family budget. A budget is a financial system whereby you set aside money on a regular basis to meet future obligations. The system saves you money. Instead of paying a carrying charge for items bought on time, you save your money, possibly at interest, and pay cash when you have enough.

To put your family on a budget, you need to know how much money comes in and roughly where it goes. So apportion your annual income among your various obligations on a monthly basis. A typical apportionment would include the expected monthly cost of the following:

Food, clothing, housing, health, education, contributions, transportation, personal (haircuts, candy, cigarettes, etc.), recreation, cleaning, home help, gifts, insurance, savings, income taxes (state and federal), dues, and debts.

You should also keep a record of actual expenditures. Thus, at the end of the year, you will know how much you actually spent for each item—and what you have saved toward the things you need or want.

Your Government offers a guide, with forms, to help you in this program. It's called "A Guide to Budgeting for the Family," Home and Garden Bulletin No. 108. Write to the Superintendent of Documents, U.S. Government Printing Office, Washington, D.C. 20402.

Today in History: For the security they enjoyed in their homes against Indians resisting the encroachments of white men, colonial Americans owed a great deal to a man born on this day in 1647—Nathaniel Bacon. When the Virginia governor refused to act against the Indians, Bacon assembled the settlers, drove back the red men, and later threw out the governor, in the first major American uprising against British rule, in 1676—just a century before the Declaration of Independence.

The unit for wallcoverings is the roll. It usually contains about 36 square feet. Compensate for matching and waste, and your yield will be about 30 square feet.

Bird pecks in lumber? Lumber graders sometimes refer to certain marks in wood as bird pecks, and that's exactly what they mean. A small hole or patch of distorted grain results when birds peck through the growing cells. The mark is often shaped like a carpet tack, with the point toward the bark.

January 3

Today in History: "There is no place more delightful than home." That's a quotation from one of the orations of Marcus Tullius Cicero, famous Roman orator born on this day in 160 B.C.

In 1831, the first building and loan association (the Oxford Provident Building Association) was organized in Frankford, Pa.

You Need a Home Guide Book

Begin assembling the information you need to make your personal Home Guide Book. Do you have wiring diagrams and maintenance instructions for all your household appliances? When was the house painted? What type and brand of paint was used? Do you know the model number of your automatic washer? Could you find the instruction book for your rotary mower—right now? Where's the warranty for your air conditioner? Are those important sales slips and receipts filed along with all your guarantees and warranties? How long ago were the roof shingles put on? What color are they? What brand?

You might simply collect all such facts into file folders. Many people do. A looseleaf notebook may be better. Get a packet of reenforcing rings for the holes you'll punch in warranties and instruction sheets for orderly filing. Index tabs might be a good idea, too.

You may say, if you are a man, that making such a Home Guide Book is a waste of time in your case. Perhaps so. You undoubtedly could get along well without it. But what about the lady of the house? Does she know all the helpful and useful facts that you may carry in your head? Such a book also would be of great value to the next owner of your house—in the event you are transferred to another city.

Handy can opener. You will always be able to pry open a flat can of shoe polish—without looking for a knife—if you cement a large washer into a saw kerf cut horizontally into the end of your polishing brush.

Safeguard a door at the head of basement stairs by installing a chain latch high enough to be out of the reach of toddlers.

To keep nuts from loosening, drip clear shellac on the bolt threads just before final tightening. Only a little extra wrench pressure is needed to loosen the nut.

Grow bamboo on your home grounds? In the south, a small planting will provide a supply of no-cost garden stakes.

Time of the "Wolf Moon." American Indians, like early peoples of Europe, knew January as the month of the "Wolf Moon." Then, famished packs grew bold around the wigwams and the music of their night howls echoed through the frozen woodlands. Few wolves remain today.

January 4

Today in History: On Jan. 4, 1850, the Skaters' Club of the City and County of Philadelphia was organized. It was one of the first clubs of this nature.

In 1885, the first appendectomy was performed by Dr. William W. Grant in Davenport, Iowa. The patient lived until 1919.

Disposed of your Christmas tree—safely? Remember: its dried branches and needles will burn with almost explosive speed.

Remove broken or dead limbs from mature pecan trees at this time. This is usually the only annual pruning necessary if the trees were properly trained while young.

Where the final spring frost comes about January 30, you can plant some early vegetables now, especially hardy ones.

Make Your Own Ice Skating Rink

Polyethylene film makes it possible to have an ice skating rink in just about any backyard. Level ground is best, but—as a drawing shows—you can also locate one on sloping land. Ice two inches thick is enough.

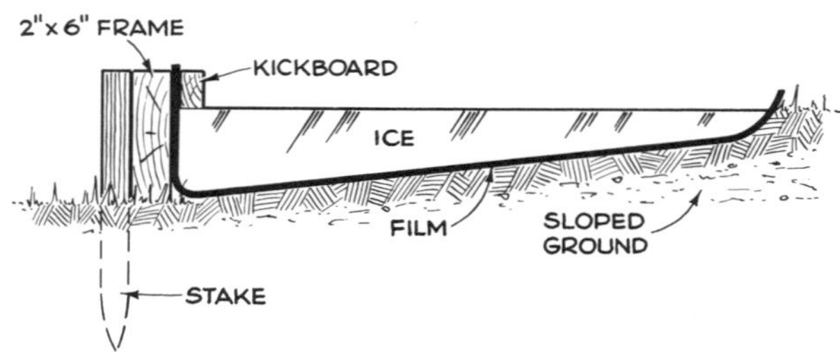

Cross-section of homemade ice rink.

Buy clear or white translucent four-mil polyethylene. Avoid the black type; it might damage your lawn grass. A single large sheet may do the job, but if not available choose film as wide as possible. Lap the joints an inch or so. Seal the joints by freezing ice across them, running cold water slowly over them while the temperature is below freezing. Run the film edge up the frame of boards staked around the rink area. Clamp the film in place with a kickboard nailed in place. If your ground is frozen at this time of year, thaw a spot with a blow torch so you can drive in restraining stakes. Alternately, pile up concrete blocks to hold the wood frame in place.

Flood the rink with a garden hose. If the temperature is very low, you can use a heat tape to protect the outside faucet and the water passing through the hose.

In the spring remove the film before the grass under it starts to grow. Fold the film loosely and store it in a dark place until next season. Pressure-sensitive plastic tape will patch any tears.

Paint a radiator while it's moderately warm and the finish will last longer. Heat tends to bake the paint on.

January 5

Is It Time to Prune Roses?

For those of you who live in the still frozen North, the answer to that question is no. But for residents of the warmer regions of the South and much of California, this is the right time to prune established roses of most varieties.

Their habits of growth divide roses into two main classes—climbing roses, all of which require some kind of support, and bush roses. Climbing roses are used largely to create landscaping effects; bush roses are usually grown for cutting.

Most roses benefit from pruning twice a year—during the dormant season and again, perhaps just lightly, immediately after blooming. Dormant pruning ideally should be timed in the spring after the last killing frost and just before new growth starts. Pruning wounds will then heal over in minimum time. Certain varieties tend to die back if pruned too far in advance of when new growth starts.

This means that pruning should be timed before the end of January in warmer parts of California, in the humid coastal regions of the northwest, and in regions immediately adjoining the Gulf of Mexico. As spring advances northward, the proper rose pruning time advances just ahead of it. As a general guide, you might time your local pruning a week or so after the average date for your last killing temperature (32 degrees) in the spring. Maps elsewhere in this book will give you a clue to that date if you do not already know it.

Prune with sharp tools—pruning shears and perhaps a fine-toothed saw for cutting dead canes. Remove all dead wood first from bush roses, cutting an inch or so below the dark colored areas. Make all cuts to a cane or to a strong outward-facing bud. Do not leave bare stubs. After you have removed dead material, cut out all weak growth and any canes or branches growing toward the center of the bush. If two branches cross, remove the weaker. Finally, shape the plant by cutting the strong canes to a uniform height. Where severe winters kill most of the top growth, just save all of the live wood you can.

Watch for cankered canes and remove them all. Cankers occur commonly in plants that have been weakened by black spot (on the leaves), winter injury, or poor nutrition. Cankers first appear as small reddish spots on the stem. They enlarge and eventually encircle the cane, causing it to die. Disinfect pruning tools with alcohol after use on a cankered shoot.

Prune hardy ramblers sparingly in the spring. Removal of too much wood will reduce production of flowers. But do remove all dead canes and weak branches. Save the main pruning until after the plant has flowered.

Today in History: In 1885 on January 5, the first railroad piggyback operation began. It involved horses, however, and not motor trucks. Wagons loaded with farm produce were rolled onto flat cars at Albertson's Station, Long Island, N.Y. Other cars carried horses and a coach the teamsters. Train arrived at Long Island City at 6:30 a.m., a ferry carried the wagons across the East River at 7 a.m. to the markets in New York City.

Better check your furnace filters. They take a beating at this time of year. They probably need cleaning or replacing.

Some plants won't thrive in the warm climates of the U.S. because they do not undergo the necessary chilling experience of a period of dormancy or sleep Included are cherries, lilacs, and peonies. Winter sleep is simulated for tulips by keeping the bulbs in cold storage before planting.

The earliest wallpapers were flocked patterns produced in England a few years after Columbus set sail for America.

January 6

Doctor's Rx: More Home Humidity

Winter colds and other respiratory ailments are often traceable to a dry home atmosphere. In these cases, doctors are prescribing more humidity. Research and development engineers have introduced a number of

recent improvements in their continuing search for the ideal humidifier. Even if you already have a humidifier, it may be advisable to update it.

Atmospheric dryness is likely to be at its worst in your home at this time of year. A dry atmosphere picks up moisture from wherever it can grab it. The results are soon evident. Cracks open up or widen in the house woodwork. Furniture becomes wobbly. Homes heated by a hot-air system normally have the worst dryness problem.

Two types of humidifiers are available—self-contained units that you locate where you wish, and accessories that you install in the ducts of a heating system. In the latter, humidity and heated air circulate together. Self-contained humidifiers are built to look like a piece of furniture. You must add water to the reservoir in some; in others, a plumbing connection is made so that the water is replenished automatically, just as happens in a heating-duct humidifier. Check out the new ones at the showroom of a local heating contractor.

Today in History: A farm crop surplus was ordered destroyed to improve prices on Jan. 6, 1639. The Virginia General Assembly decreed that all bad parts of the year's tobacco crop and half of the good be burned. Prices for tobacco were so low that "planters could not subsist by it . . . or pay their debts."

January 7

Today in History: The first U.S. seed business was organized on Jan. 7, 1784 by David Landreth, of Philadelphia. Farm and garden seeds previously had come from Europe.

Do You Receive Garden Catalogs?

Have you thought about the garden seeds you will need this year? Are your grounds not yet fully planted with trees, shrubs, and flowers? You can find many suggestions and ideas in the annual garden and nursery catalogs appearing soon. Send off postals today asking for them. Choose from these:

W. Atlee Burpee, Philadelphia, Pa. 19132; Clinton, Iowa 52732; or Riverside, Calif. 92502. Vegetables, flowers, fruit and nut trees.

Dutch Mt. Nursery, Augusta, Mich. 49012. Wide variety of shrubs and trees.

Gurney Seed & Nursery Co., Yankton, S.D. 57078. Vegetables, flowers, trees.

Kelly Bros., Dansville, N.Y. 14437. Vegetables, flowers, fruit trees.

J. E. Miller Nurseries, Canandaigua, N.Y. 14424. Fruit, nut and shade trees.

Musser, Indiana, Pa. 15701. Evergreen trees and shrubs.

Natural Development Co., Bainbridge, Pa. 17502. Organic fertilizers, vegetables, flowers.

George W. Parks Seed Co., Greenwood, S.C. 29646. Flowers, vegetables.

Clyde Robin, P. O. Box 2091, Castro Valley, Calif. 94546. Wild flowers, seeds.

Savage Farm Nursery, P. O. Box 125, McMinnville, Tenn. 37110. Trees, shrubs, plants, vines.

R. H. Shumway, Seedsman, Rockford, Ill. 61101. Fruits, flowers, vegetables.

Stark Bros., Louisiana, Mo. 63353. Fruits and shade trees.

Stern's Nurseries, Geneva, N.Y. 14456. Plants, flowers, trees, shrubs.

Stokes Seeds, Box 548, Buffalo, N.Y. 14240. Flowers and vegetables.

Wayside Gardens, Mentor, Ohio 44060. Flowers, trees, shrubs.

Western Maine Forest Nursery Co., Fryeburg, Me. 04037. Evergreens.

Your Own Reminders

Week of Jan. 1–7

January 8

Today in History: A price regulation law effective Jan. 8, 1777, in Rhode Island limited charges that could be made for supplies bought for the Revolutionary Army.

Snow Removal Equipment Ready for Use?

What's the condition of your snowthrower —if you own one? You may need it again at any moment. Last time you used it did you clean off all the dirty snow and other slop? After the machine was clean and dry, did you apply oil to all the friction points? This is a good program to follow immediately after every use.

And what about your snow shovel? Can you find it in a hurry? Do you have one that's Teflon-coated? The coating makes the work a lot easier.

January 9

How to Prevent Roof Ice Dams

Progress sometimes creates problems. Ice dams on the roofs of modern homes are an example. When cold periods come, our heating systems increase their output. Heated air reaches the underside of the house roof in the attic. Unless an efficient layer of insulation interferes, the warm air melts any snow on the roof, often aided by a warming sun.

The snow melt courses downward toward the gutters. In many modern homes, you find the gutters at the outer edge of a wide roof overhang. The temperature under this overhang may be far below freezing. The result is obvious. When the snow melt flows on the overhang, it freezes again. Ice chokes the gutters. A sheet of ice slowly climbs the roof. More and more water comes from the melting snow. The ice dam holds it back. Seeking an escape, the water quickly finds cracks in the roofing and seeps down into the house, perhaps down into an outside wall without being observed.

Rust stains around nail heads, paint peeling and blistering, and swelling and buckling of siding are some of the signs that moisture has been going down through the walls.

A minimum of six inches of insulation on the attic floor or under the roof will prevent escape of most of the heat that creates the problem. A strip of roll roofing or metal flashing placed along the lower edge before the finished roofing is applied will keep water from seeping down into the house at that level. But no construction methods completely forestall dams.

Today in History: The first balloon flight carrying a presidential order took off in Philadelphia at 10:16 a.m. on Jan. 9, 1793, in the presence of President George Washington and other officials. The balloonist, Jean Blanchard, carried a Washington directive that he be permitted "to descend in such places as circumstances may render most convenient." The balloon landed in New Jersey about 15 miles from the start of the flight.

Electric heating cable offers a simple way to keep ice dams from forming. Right now—today—you can take preventive measures if you have previously had the problem at this time of year. Buy a piece of cable to run the length of each gutter, plus at least three feet more. Some cables come with built-in thermostats that turn the cable on automatically when the temperature drops to about freezing. These are convenient but not essential.

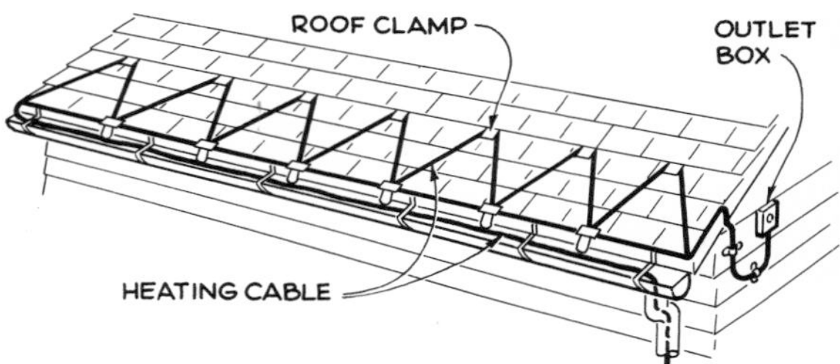

Heating cable on roof prevents ice dams from forming.

For quickest protection simply lay the cable in the bottom of the gutter and carry one end to an outdoor-type extension cord plugged in where you have an outlet. You might install the cable in a more workmanlike and efficient way by stapling the cable to strips of wood lath, all of equal length. The wood keeps the heat from being dissipated through a metal gutter. The strips also make it easy to fold and store the cable in the spring.

Where ice dams are a more difficult problem you may prefer to use the cable by zigzagging it across the overhanging part of the roof, back along the gutter, and carrying the free end down the downspout. In making the zigzags, allow the cable to loop below the roof to provide a heated drip point.

Install a weatherproof outlet for connecting the cable. Let the cable or connecting cold lead loop downward before entering the box to keep water from following the lead into the box. Manufacturers also recommend that you ground metal gutters and downspouts with a driven ground bar.

January 10

What Fertilizers Do You Need?

That's a good question to consider at this time of year. In this busy world, the time for applying the proper ones to your lawn, trees, shrubs, flowers, and vegetable garden will be here before you know it. And let there be no doubt about it: You must have fertilizers to get the most out of owning a home. Soil in its natural state rarely is fertile enough for the best growth of plants.

A soil test is the only way to learn exactly what your ground needs. Your county agent can tell you how to have this test made if you do not already know. It will show you what fertilizer is needed and how much to apply.

For greatest economy, buy fertilizer for its weight of nutrients, not for its total weight.

The primary-nutrient content of a fertilizer mixture is indicated by a series of three numbers. The numbers show the percentage of nitrogen, phosphoric oxide, and potash in that order. A mixture 5-10-5 contains 5 percent of total nitrogen, 10 percent of available phosphoric oxide, and 5 percent of soluble potash.

The relative proportions of primary nutrients in a fertilizer mixture determine the suitability of the mixture for specific soils and plants. Lawn fertilizers usually are highest in nitrogen. Fertilizers for vegetables may be highest in phosphoric oxide. It usually is wasteful, and may even be harmful, to use the wrong type of fertilizer.

Fertilizers of several grades may contain the same proportions of primary nutrients. For example, 5-10-5 and 6-12-6 are both composed of one part of nitrogen, two parts of phosphoric oxide, and one part of potash, though 6-12-6 contains the higher percentage of these nutrients.

Fertilizers having the same proportions of primary nutrients generally can be used interchangeably. It usually is only necessary to alter the rate of application so the desired amounts of primary nutrients are applied to the area being fertilized.

Frequently the price per pound of the nutrients in mixtures containing a high percentage of nutrients may be lower than the price per pound of nutrients in fertilizer mixtures containing a lower percentage. For example, 1 pound of 10-20-10 contains the same amount of nutrients as 2 pounds of 5-10-5, yet an 80-pound bag of 10-20-10 may cost only a third more than an 80-pound bag of 5-10-5.

Today in History: On Jan. 10, 1946, a radar signal was bounced off the moon from Belmar, New Jersey, by the Army Signal Corps. Echo received 2.4 seconds later.

A snow-covered shrub is beautiful but the weight can cause a lot of damage, especially to evergreens. Shake heavy, wet snow off the branches of your trees and shrubs as soon as possible after it falls, hopefully before it freezes.

January 11

Today in History: Life insurance had its beginnings in Philadelphia on Jan. 11, 1759. A company was incorporated to provide annuities for Presbyterian ministers, their widows, and their children.

Organize Your Family Records

The welfare of your family depends on a surprisingly long list of valuable papers and documents. You should keep them all in a place safe from theft and fire. All adult members of the family should know where to find them in an emergency.

Husband and wife could profitably spend one of these wintry evenings making an inventory of the documents and recording where they are kept. The advantages of making this a joint task are obvious. If one spouse dies, the other will know more about how to keep the household running and where to turn for any required help.

To guide you in organizing your documents and to make the job easier, four pages of forms are presented in the back of this book as Appendix D. Make your first record right on those pages. Plan then to take the book and have Xerox or other copies made. Alternately, you might make copies of the forms first, before you begin filling in the required information.

The forms were adapted from an informative pamphlet, "Guide to Organizing Your Valuable Family Papers," published in California by the Extension Service. California residents can get a copy by writing to Public Affairs, 90 University Hall, University of California, Berkeley, Cal. 94720.

It is advisable to have two separate storage centers for your papers—a safe deposit box in a local bank and a storage container at home, preferably fireproof and theftproof. You might consider the purchase of a home safe. Many people have them.

Your most important papers and records should go into a bank safe deposit. But keep copies or records of them in a safe place at home. In most states a safe deposit box is legally sealed for a time after the owner or coowner dies. Place a copy of your four-page family document inventory into the safe deposit. Keep another at home.

Wills should go into the safe deposit with a copy at home. Reverse the procedure for insurance policies, keeping only a record of the policy numbers in the bank vault. For convenience, you will want savings-account bankbooks at home, but keep the book number in the bank. Keep birth certificates in the bank with photographic copies at home. Burial instructions and the location of a cemetery lot should remain at home. Make an inventory of household possessions and keep a copy of it in both storage sites. Cancelled checks and income tax reports can be stored at home, but just about everything else—bonds, stock certificates, property deeds, car titles, and marriage records, for instance—should go into the bank.

January 12

Today in History: John Hancock was born on Jan. 12, 1737. As president of the Continental Congress, he was the first to sign the Declaration of Independence—and he did so in a bold script. That's the origin of our saying about signing your "John Hancock" when you sign your name.

Do You Have a Property Map?

You may already have learned how much time a repairman can waste—at your expense—probing for the buried necessities on your property! For that reason you should make and keep a plot plan showing exact locations of septic tanks or sewerage lines, water lines, a well if you have one, and buried power lines.

You can probably place the locations of all of these necessities directly on the plot survey map that you should already have among your important documents, usually as an adjunct to your property deed. If the survey map already is cluttered with information, trace off the outline and start another map for just such things as your utilities. Keep this to scale and it will prove invaluable over the years. Should you sell the property, turn this map over to the buyer. If *you* should be the buyer, demand such a map. It's important. Keep it in or with your Home Guide Book. See January 3.

Plant ranunculus (buttercup) bulbs in warm climates at any time from mid-December until the middle of April. You'll then have masses of (usually yellow) flowers from May to July.

Residents of California coast counties who now are thinking about spring planting may want to know that their State Extension Service offers a booklet on shrubs especially for their area. Ask the county agent for "Shrubs for Coast Counties in California."

January 13

Prune Many Shade Trees Soon

Any pleasant day at this time of year is a good time for maintenance pruning of many shade trees. Choose a day when the temperature is above freezing. Cutting frozen wood may cause excessive damage to the part that remains.

Although deciduous trees can be pruned at any time of year, you can see the problems better in midwinter. A few weeks from now—in late winter and early spring—some trees will lose sap profusely from pruning cuts.

If needle-leaf evergreens are pruned just before growth begins in spring, new foliage will grow rapidly, soon covering the pruning cuts and giving the tree a pleasing appearance.

Corrective pruning while a tree is small will make it unnecessary to undertake difficult and

> **Today in History:** The Jan. 13, 1906 issue of *Scientific American* carried the first advertisement for a radio receiver. Hugo Gernsback offered the "complete outfit" for $7.50.

expensive pruning in later years. Each year, check your trees for:

Dead, dying, or unsightly parts.

Sprouts growing at or near the base of the trunk of the tree.

Branches that grow from another branch back toward the center of the tree.

Crossed branches. Disease and decay can enter through abrasions where they rub. Remove one branch.

Vee crotches. These split easily, especially in storms. Remove one of the trunks if it is possible to do so without ruining the appearance of the tree. Make two cuts as shown in the sketch. (On most trees the main branches should be spaced far apart on the trunk and should make a wide angle with it—even as much as 90 degrees.)

Nuisance growth. Cut away branches that will interfere with electric or telephone lines, that shade street lights, that block the view at street corners or driveways. Prune out branches that shut off desirable breezes. Cut off low limbs that may hamper lawn cutting.

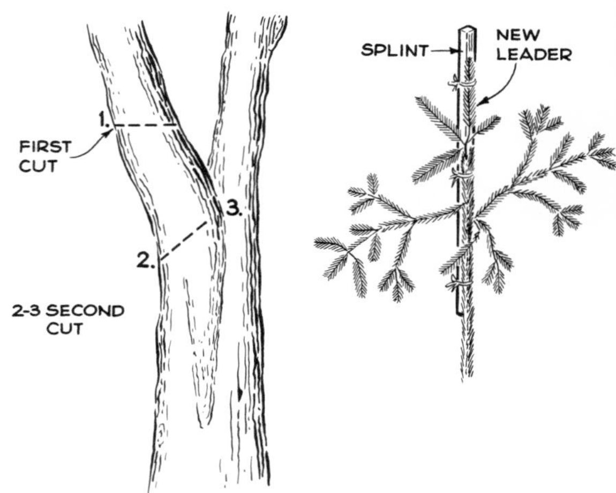

Two cuts for pruning a vee crotch (*left*); how to tie a splint to the leader of an evergreen branch (*right*).

Remove growth to improve the shape of the tree.

Be sure to treat all pruning cuts with a tree-wound antiseptic. Buy this in either a spray or spread-on form from a garden shop or hardware store.

Never cut the central leader from a needle-leaf evergreen. If a leader is broken or lost on a young tree, you can help develop a new central stem by tying a small pole or splint so it rises straight up from the broken leader. See the accompanying sketch. Then select a pliable branch in the upper whorl of growth, bend it upward, and tie it to the splint. Remove the splint in a year or so after the branch has taken over as the new central trunk.

Deer don't like 'em. If you live in a region where deer damage lawn plantings ask your county agent for a list of deer-resistant ornamental shrubs.

January 14

Today in History: The trademark Celluloid was registered on Jan. 14, 1873. This man-made material was one of the first plastics. Early in this century it was the fashion for men to wear stiff white collars made of it.

Tips on Repairing Plastics

Our modern world is full of plastic products. Some of them occasionally develop breaks, tears, or holes—and the need for repairs faces us. With some types, this is an easy task; with others it is almost impossible.

Excellent cements are available for patching items made of sheet vinyl. These were developed primarily for patching swimming-pool liners (they work even under water) and covers. They can also be used for repairing other products made of vinyl. The cement usually comes as part of a kit containing instructions and patching material made of sheet vinyl. You will find the kits at hardware, department, and pool-supply stores.

The liquid supplied with the kits is a solvent for vinyl. Use a little of it on a clean cloth or tissues to remove traces of dirt around the damaged area. Then abrade the area lightly with fine sandpaper or steel wool. Remove dust and wipe the surface again with solvent before applying a coating of the liquid and a patch cut large enough to extend at least an inch beyond the tear or break. Apply a clamp or heavy weight over the patch and leave for several hours. Acetone and methyl ethyl ketone are solvents for such plastics as vinyl, polyethylene, and polypropylene.

For repairing rips and tears in the other common sheet plastic—polyethylene—a good bet is a pressure-sensitive tape, although such a repair may not be very durable. Use a cloth tape or a clear polyethylene tape 10 mil thick and an inch or two wide. The clear tape may be less noticeable on some surfaces.

If feasible, heat-bonding of ripped polyethylene edges may be better than tape. By this procedure, the edges are overlapped and a source of heat (a clothes iron, for example) applied until the two materials soften and bond together. In the early days of home freezing of foods, this procedure was introduced to seal the plastic containers.

For repairs to other plastic materials, ask your hardware dealer if he knows of anything suitable. Manufacturers are continuing to search for cements and glues that will work well.

How thick is a mil? You often encounter this term as a thickness measure for plastic sheet. One mil is one-thousandth (.001) of an inch. This page is about .2 mil thick.

Your Own Reminders

Week of Jan. 8–14

January 15

Time to Plant Early Vegetables?

You bet it is—in some of the southernmost parts of the U.S. Even in much of those mild climates, however, you should restrict your planting largely to produce that can withstand a little frost.

For the list of vegetables you Southerners or Southern Californians can plant safely around this date, please refer to the spring frost-free map given with the entry for February 8. On that map locate the areas where the final spring frost occurs about January 30. You will find that these areas include a good portion of Florida, the delta below New Orleans, narrow strips along the Gulf Coast to the west, and sizeable regions in southern California, especially along the coast as far north as San Francisco.

So, if you are fortunate enough to dwell within one of those regions, what should you do next? There are many warm-weather activities you might turn to (to the envy of people still freezing in the North) but the subject now at hand is growing vegetables—if you want to eat better at less cost. Turn the pages to Appendix E at the back of the book. On this, find the column headed January 30. Go down the column and what do you learn? That around this date (January 15) you can safely plant the following vegetables:

Beets, broccoli (plants), Brussel sprouts (plants), cabbage (plants), carrots, cauliflower (plants), celery and celeriac, chard, chives, collards, cornsalad, upland cress, dandelion, endive, kale, kohlrabi, leek, lettuce, mustard, onion seed or sets, parsley, garden peas, peppers (plants), potatoes, radishes, salsify, shallot, sorrel, spinach, and turnips.

In this same column, you will also note that you can add other vegetables very soon, about February 1. Among these are beans, both lima and snap; sweet corn, eggplant, New Zealand spinach, and tomatoes. But wait at least until February 15 for cucumbers, muskmelons, okra, black-eye peas, sweet potatoes, and watermelon. But even for the later vegetables, you can improve your time by preparing the ground now.

Those who live farther north can learn from the foregoing how to suit their vegetable gardening to the season. Refer to the map to see what date the final frost can be expected where you live, and then refer to Appendix E at the back of the book. On this Appendix, find the column that coincides with your final frost date. Mark the column. Refer to it when you want to know when it is time to plant what.

If you'd like more facts about this simple vegetable timing system, as well as other helpful information about raising your own vegetables, write to the Superintendent of Documents, U.S. Government Printing Office, Washington, D.C. 20402 and ask for Home and Garden Bulletin No. 9, "Suburban and Farm Vegetable Gardens."

Today in History: Dr. Lee DeForest patented the three-element vacuum tube for radio use on Jan. 15, 1907. He had announced it on Oct. 20, 1906.

House plants get dusty in midwinter. Every week or so, take them to the kitchen sink and wash glossy leaves with water. Spray hairy-leaved plants with a fine mist and let dry in the shade.

Raise your own figs? They thrive in quite a broad belt across the southern U. S., although even there trees and bushes are frequently frozen back by severe winter cold or early-fall and late-spring freezes. If winter temperatures are frequently below 10° F. in your area, you would do better to forget about them, however. But providing winter protection will enable you to grow them beyond their usual northern limits. Plant them while dormant in a location where they are shielded from winter winds or plant them in containers and move them indoors for the winter. Check your state extension service for information about planting and care.

January 16

Today in History: A patent was granted on Jan. 16, 1877 to Halcyon Skinner and Alexander Smith for a power loom to weave Axminster carpets.

How to Meet a Carpet Emergency

Carpet manufacturers make the following points about what to do when something has been spilled on a carpet or rug:

1. Wipe up the staining material at once.
2. Use a detergent. Never use soap, ammonia, or any cleaning preparation intended for hard surfaces. These products might damage carpet fibers. Mix your solution weak, say about a teaspoon of light-duty detergent and a teaspoon of white vinegar to a quart of warm water. Never use hot water for carpet cleaning.
3. Blot the area with a sponge dipped in the detergent solution. Don't rub the spot. Sponge the spot lightly. Don't soak it. Avoid getting the back of the carpet wet. It delays the surface drying and can cause a carpet to mildew.

The above three-step procedure is a safe way to remove stains caused by beverages, washable inks, or other water-soluble substances. Animal stains can be removed by this process, too.

For other carpet stains, try one of these cleaning methods:

Use a solvent cleaner (a commercial home dry-cleaning product) to remove butter, grease, oil, hand cream, milk or cream, ballpoint ink, and hair oil stains. Soak a sponge in the cleaner

and blot the stain. Be careful not to rub it. Then blot again with absorbent facial tissues or paper towels. Repeat the cleaning process if the stain still shows.

Detergent solutions and solvent cleaners can be used for the removal of coffee, tea, milk, gravy, eggs, sauces, salad dressing, ice cream, and chocolate stains. Sponge the area first with detergent solution (several times if necessary) and then apply the solvent cleaner.

To remove gum, paint, shellac, glue, heavy grease, lipstick, crayon, or candy, apply the solvent cleaner first and follow with detergent solution. Use a tissue to absorb moisture. Repeat the process until the area is clean.

If a spot resists home cleaning, special treatment is probably required by a professional. Call him before you fray the carpet fibers with repeated treatment.

Is your new carpet shedding? That often seems to happen. Actually, there is nothing to worry about. Short fibers that were buried in the face of the carpet during manufacturing operations are merely working their way to the surface. Shedding, or fluffing, gradually decreases and in time disappears.

Keep house plants well watered at this time of year if your home atmosphere tends to be dry.

Plant spring-flowering bulbs in mid-January in states south of a line from South Carolina to southern California. Tulip, hyacinth, crocus, and narcissus grow well in this region.

January 17

Today in History: Benjamin Franklin, born on this day in 1706, gave good advice for modern do-it-yourselfers: "God helps them that help themselves." He scattered many other wise sayings through his *Poor Richard's Almanac,* published every year from 1733 to 1758. See samples herewith.

Poor Richard's Advice to Home Owners

Don't throw stones at your neighbor's if your own windows are glass.

Three removes is as bad as a fire.

When the well's dry, we know the worth of water.

A quarrelsome man has no good neighbors.

Love your neighbor, yet don't pull down your hedge.

An old man in the house is a good sign.

Pray don't burn my house to roast your eggs.

At the workingman's house hunger looks in, but dares not enter.

An egg today is better than a hen tomorrow.

Fish and visitors stink after three days.

Never take a wife till thou hast a house (and a fire) to put her in.

A house without woman and firelight
Is like a body without soul or sprite.

Rhymes from Poor Richard

Those who in quarrels interpose
Must often wipe a bloody nose.

What is a butterfly? At best
He's but a caterpillar dressed.

He that whines for Glass without G
Take away L—and that's he.

Hide not your talents.
They for use were made:
What's a sundial in the shade?

Quarrels never could last long,
If on one side only lay the wrong.

If you would have guests merry with cheer,
Be so yourself, or at least so appear.

I never saw an oft-removed tree,
Nor yet an oft-removed family,
That throve so well as those that settled be.

Early to bed and early to rise
Makes a man healthy, wealthy and wise.

Poor Richard's Wisdom About Women

Let thy maid-servant be faithful, strong, and homely.

Keep your eyes wide open before marriage, half shut afterwards.

Man, dally not with other folks' women or money.

January 18

It's Time to Cut Firewood

In the olden days, country people cut next season's supply of firewood at this time of the year. They were motivated by two things. First, they had few other pressing chores at this time of year. And second, and most important, dormant trees have less sap in them. If cut now, wood will have seasoned well and be ready for burning when next autumn arrives. So you may want to look now to what you can do along the same line. Perhaps you have a tree that ought to come down. Or perhaps a neighbor does. If so, he might listen to a cutting-on-shares proposal from you. Considering the increasing prices asked for firewood, you and a group of neighbors might want to rent a truck and a chainsaw and proposition a farmer or woodlot owner about cleaning up his fallen and dead trees. A shares deal could be made appealing in that case, too, for the owner could sell his share of the wood at a good profit with no work involved.

Be careful when you fell a tree. Know which way it will fall, and get out of the way as soon as it starts to tip.

For wood of the best burning qualities, be guided by the accompanying rhyme.

Rhyme for a Happy Hearthside

Oak logs will warm you well
  If they're old and dry.
Larch logs of pinewood smell
  But the sparks will fly.
Beech logs for Christmas time,
  Yew logs heat well.
'Scotch' logs it is a crime
  For anyone to sell.
Birch logs burn too fast,
  Chestnut scarce at all.
Hawthorn logs are good to last
  If you cut them in the fall.
Holly logs will burn like wax,
  You should burn them green.
Elm logs like smouldering flax,
  No flame to be seen.
Pear logs and apple logs
  They will scent your room.
Cherry logs across the dogs
  Smell like flowers in bloom.
But ash logs, all smooth and gray,
  Burn them green or old;
Buy up all that come your way,
  They're worth their weight in gold.

—Old English folk rhyme

Today in History: An X-ray machine was exhibited on January 18, 1896 at the Casino Chambers in New York City. X-rays had been discovered just the year before by Roentgen.

January 19

Today in History: A patent was issued to Ezra Daggett and his nephew, Thomas Kennet, on Jan. 19, 1825 to "preserve animal substances in tin." Seafood was being canned as early as 1819.

Why Not Preserve Some of Your Food?

The canning anniversary mentioned in today's historical note makes this an appropriate date to consider that question. For years, most people have preferred the convenience of commercially frozen and canned foods to the work and expense of home freezing and canning. But attitudes have been changing lately, especially among the young, who dream of a more self-sufficient life. Increasing costs at the store have made home food preservation economically attractive.

Anyone who likes to garden has taken the first step toward eating better and more economically. A home refrigerator with even minimum freezing space can be used for some of the surplus—which a good garden always produces. Freezing supplies—recommended containers, wrap, and tape—are readily available and inexpensive. The information you need is contained in the 47 pages of Home and Garden Bulletin No. 10, "Home Freezing of Fruits and Vegetables" from the Superintendent of Documents, U.S. Government Printing Office, Washington, D.C. 20402.

Similar information about canning is available from the same source. It's Home and Garden Bulletin No. 7, "Home Canning of Fruits and Vegetables," a 30-page book.

Other available pamphlets tell how to freeze or can meats and poultry.

In citrus regions, better plan to apply nitrogen fertilizers soon to home citrus trees. Apply five to ten pounds of calcium nitrate, ammonium nitrate, or ammonium sulfate to each tree before the spring rains end. A good plan: Divide the total amount of fertilizer into four lots. Apply one part now, and the rest at monthly intervals just before irrigation or watering.

Use a few drops of glycerin to lubricate rotary egg beaters, meat choppers, and other kitchen utensils that have cogs.

In the Southwestern U.S., place names that include "Alamo" and "Alameda" come from the Spanish. Alamo is the Spanish name for the cottonwood tree. Alameda is a groove of cottonwoods.

Tired of scraping snow and ice from your car's windshield every morning? Cover it with a sheet of plastic secured by magnets.

January 20

Today in History: Inauguration Day for U.S. Presidents every four years on Jan. 20 began in 1937. Previous inaugurations had been held on March 4.

Prune Fruit Trees Soon

Annual pruning of fruit trees is now due if you have not already done it. Pruning usually is recommended during dormancy—in the fall, after the leaves have fallen; during the winter, or in early spring before growth starts.

The purpose of pruning is to develop or shape a tree so it will have maximum strength in its framework branches to support a load of fruit. Ideally, a fruit tree of bearing age should be low headed. All its main branches should leave the trunk at a wide angle. It should have a single trunk at ground level and about six main branches. The latter should be spaced six to ten inches apart on the trunk, with the spacing so that none is directly above or opposite another. The lowest branch should emerge about a foot from the ground on the southwest side. In the northern latitudes, this position will protect the trunk from sunscald.

When planting, cut a young tree back to about 30 inches from the ground, making the cut just above a strong bud. This heading will induce low branching. During the tree's growth period, prune it just enough to produce the low head. Thereafter, annual pruning should be aimed at retaining the desired shape. Remove sprouts and sub-branches needed to accomplish this. Also remove diseased, injured, broken, or down-growing branches. Thin out the tops to allow sunlight to reach the leafy areas of lower branches. Leaves always should shield the main trunk and the branches themselves. Apply tree dressing to all cut surfaces of an inch or more diameter.

January 21

Are Your Electric Circuits Marked?

A shipshape home should have a chart or labels in or near the fuse or circuit-breaker box to show exactly what each circuit involves.

You may have some labels already in place—the heating plant (if it requires electricity), the automatic washer, the refrigerator, the dishwasher, perhaps a water pump if you live away from the city mains. Each of these ordinarily demands, and should have, a circuit to itself, usually one of twenty amps. Beyond these, as new circuits were added for one reason and another, no one may have bothered to affix labels.

To correct this, turn on all lights in the house and out. Get a small lamp, one with a bulb you're sure is good. Then screw out one fuse or trip one circuit breaker switch. (When you install a new fuse, your best advice is to turn off the main house switch first, for safety. Because you can't do this for our present checkup, screw out the fuse carefully, holding only the outer rim.)

Now return to the main house area and locate what lights are out. With your lamp determine which outlets no longer give juice. Make a record.

You may be able to put labels immediately adjoining or on a specific fuse or circuit switch. If there's too little space, place a number or letter key there—and a corresponding one on a master chart placed inside the door of the circuit box or in the immediate vicinity. Make a second copy of the master chart for the household records book described January 3.

For a really neat setup, you might use a modern label maker. Make a game of it—and get your youngsters to help. A pre-schooler might

A time-lag fuse is a convenience for some house circuits. It permits a temporary overload. You might use one on a circuit where you plug in power tools or a motor-driven appliance. Some motors may draw as much as 30 amperes for a second while starting but run on as little as 6. These motors could blow a 20-ampere fuse. The time-lag fuse permits the temporary overload.

learn to spell C-I-R-C-U-I-T instead of C-A-T. There's no way of knowing what such early electrical conditioning might lead to—a Twenty-first Century electrical wizard perhaps.

When you have determined the limits of your first circuit, screw in the first fuse or flip the switch to "on." Then, in succession, do the same thing for each circuit on the panel.

Today in History: The first atomic-powered submarine, the Nautilus, was launched at Groton, Connecticut, January 21, 1954.

In the deep south and the coastal areas of Southern California, plant seeds of flowers indoors for transplanting into outdoor beds about March 15.

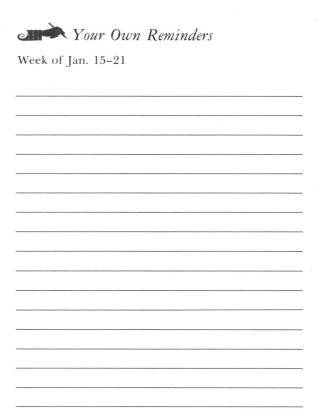

Your Own Reminders

Week of Jan. 15–21

January 22

All Your Doors Have Guards and Stops?

Doors constantly opened and closed against a wall can make your home look old before its time. So why not take a little time today to check out the door situation in your home, especially the kick guards and wall stops?

Every door that swings to a wall should have a stop in good condition to keep the knob from damaging the wall. Rubber-tipped stops that screw into the baseboard behind the door are the most common solution. Hardware stores also offer at least two other devices for achieving

the desired result. One is a replacement for the pin of the door hinges. Projecting arms limit the door swing. Concave rubber guards also are available for attaching to the wall to cushion the knob.

Kickplates across the bottom of all outside doors look much better than the scuffing that comes from the shoes of those who use their feet to help their hands open the doors. These kick-guards come in attractive brass or aluminum. A grille across the lower half of a screen or storm door extends the life of the screening and glass and protects children from cuts.

Plant Irish potatoes soon in the southern states.

Gardens can be spaded in the southern latitudes across the U.S. at any time now.

January 23

Time to Prune Summer-Flowering Shrubs

Now that the new year is well under way, you might like to undertake a chore that will take you outdoors for part of a day. The job: pruning summer-flowering shrubs.

Shrubs that bloom in mid or late summer produce their flowers on growth of the same season; that is, wood that develops after spring arrives. (In contrast, spring-flowering shrubs grow blossoms on wood that developed during the previous season.) Horticulturists agree that the only proper time to prune most summer-flowering shrubs is during the dormant season, the winter months.

Summer-flowering shrubs include abelia, aesculus, amorpha, buddleja, callicarpa, caryopteris, ceanothus, colutea, elsholtzia, genista tinctoria, hibiscus syriacus, hydrangea, florists varieties; hydrangea snowhill, hydrangea paniculata, hypericum, lespedeza, ligustrum, potentilla, rosa, hybrid tea; sorbaria, spiraea anthony waterer, spiraea billiardi, spiraea bumalda, spiraea japonica, symphoricarpos, vitex.

Among these are some that grow in the shape of a mound—snowhill hydrangea and the summer blooming spiraeas. As the first step with these, thin out the weakest canes, cutting them off at the base. Next, cut back the remainder of the canes to varying heights so the flowers develop at varying heights, hopefully covering the entire mound. To accomplish this, it usually is necessary to lop off from a third to two-thirds of each cane. Make each cut just above a bud.

Peegee hydrangea will produce longer stems and larger flower heads if weak wood is first removed and the older flower-bearing heads are cut back to two or three nodes.

Rose of Sharon, treelike in habit, can be treated much like one. Thin out weak wood. Cut the remainder back about one-third.

Several late-flowering shrubs continue to produce flowers up to frost. On these, new wood does not mature and is likely to winter kill. Such shrubs include buddleja, callicarpa, caryopteris, elsholtzia, hypericum, lespedeza, and vitex. Except for callicarpa, it usually is best to cut back all of these plants to a foot or so from the ground in late winter. Thin out the weakest trunks of callicarpa, remove the dead wood and cut away the part that has bloomed. This usually will be sufficient for callicarpa, but it may be advisable to cut the plant back to about a foot from the ground every few years for complete renewal. Ceanothus, genista tinctoria, hydrangea paniculata, and sorbaria may be cut back severely each winter. Removing old flower heads is all you need to do to most of the other shrubs listed.

Dormant sprays are due now along the southern fringe of the U.S. and in southern California—if you haven't already applied them. See the entries for January 26 and February 10.

If you have a citrus tree on a lawn, feed it nitrogen through a foliage spray to avoid overstimulating the grass. Mix two heaping tablespoons of urea (one ounce) per gallon of water. Do not exceed the amount recommended. Apply the spray now and later, whenever a slight yellowing of leaves indicate a need for nitrogen.

Apartment dwellers: Want a tree on your balcony next summer? Try Japanese Maple, Hop Hornbeam, Foster Holly in a tub.

January 24

Today in History: One of our modern ecological problems dates back to this day in 1935. Beer was first offered for sale in cans on Jan. 24, 1935.

Your Home Recycling Center

The need to recycle cans and other household rubbish has now become a part of our way of life. So you might as well do what you can to make the job easier.

You may already know about the kitchen appliances you can buy to help with the job—the under-counter compacters. These do a fine job of creating small parcels out of big ones. But if you do not want to go that route, the homemade devices shown here will be a big help.

You store your accumulating newspapers in the baler, then bind them into a neat package when the baler is full. Make it of 1/2″ or 5/8″ fir plywood. Size the bottom to your folded newspaper. Place cord through the opposite slots before you put in the first papers. When the

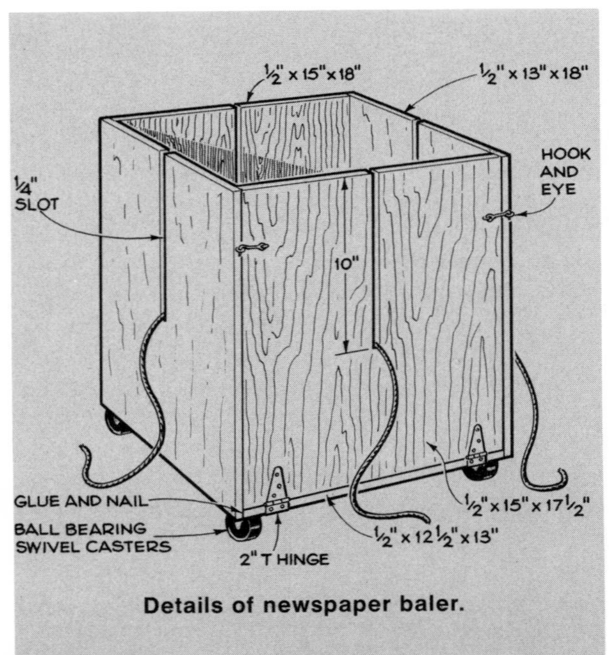

Details of newspaper baler.

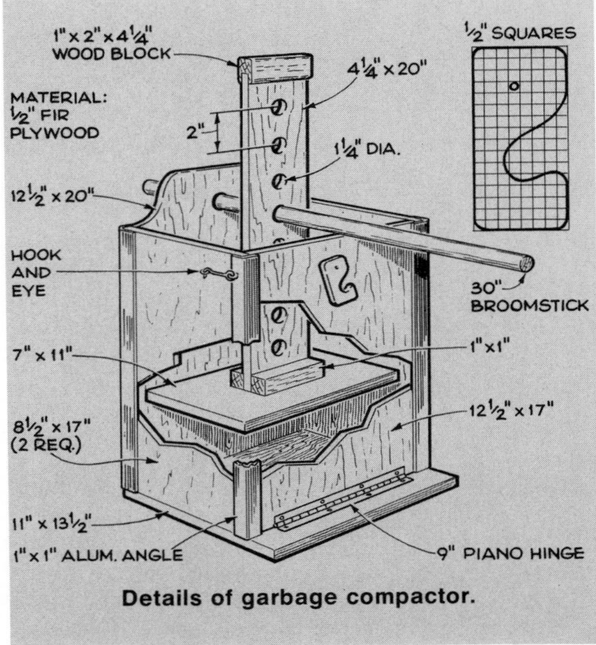

Details of garbage compactor.

bundle has been tied up, drop the hinged front to remove it.

The compacter is intended for the packaging material that reaches the kitchen in such great volume—boxes, cartons, bags. Make it just a trifle shorter than the grocery bags you use in it. Swivel the plywood hook over the handle to keep the pressure on between loads. Drop the hinged front to remove the compacted waste material. Restrict the compacter to waste paper and cardboard, and you will wind up with a bundle ready for recycling.

Some home owners have tried to cobble together a lever-equipped can crusher, but such a device is not really needed. Rinse the cans and soak off paper labels. Equip your kitchen with a good can opener—the type that cuts out the entire end of the can, perhaps electrically operated. Remove both ends and flatten the can by stepping on it. You cannot remove the ends of some cans. Hammer these flat.

Collect the flattened cans and lids in cartons or bags that your groceries come in. Separate cans according to type, depending on the instructions put out by your local recycling organization. Do not include aerosol cans with your recycled material. Do not puncture them or throw them into a fire. Dispose of them along with your garbage.

Return all returnable bottles to the store where you bought them. Be fair about it. Do not buy them at one store and return them to another. Collect nonreturnable bottles in cartons for delivery to the local salvage center. Remove the little metal ring that stays on the neck of a bottle with a twist-off cap. Separate your bottles by color—white, green, brown.

Plastic containers should go out along with your garbage.

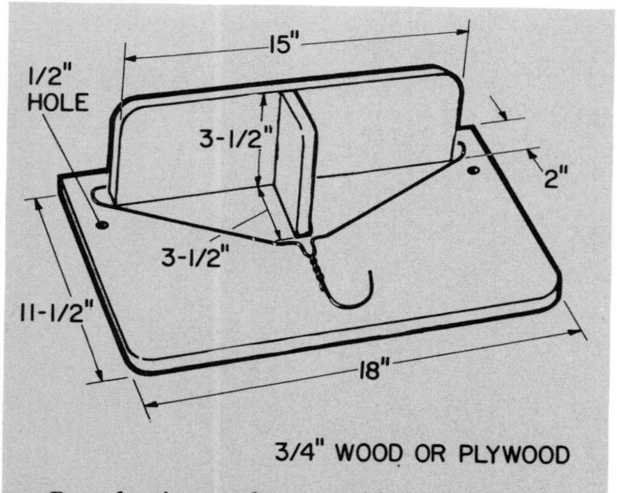

Recycle wire coat hangers with the help of this rack, made from 3/4″ wood or plywood. Hang the rack on a closet wall. Store hangers on it. When it's full, take the hangers back to the cleaner for reuse.

Check Out Automatic Dryer Vent

In many households, automatic dryers have now fully replaced clothes lines, but this useful appliance has not always been installed properly.

Vent it to the outdoors, never into a crawl space or attic. The shorter the vent the better. You can use metal ducting or, in some areas, a flexible ducting. Manufacturers recommend a maximum length of 16 feet for aluminum, including two elbows. Deduct two feet for each additional elbow, and don't exceed a total of four. Flexible ducting, where permitted, should be restricted to about half the length allotment for aluminum.

Keeping the vent short lessens the chance of lint buildup. Any vent should be cleared of lint about once a year—today, for instance. Avoid using screws to join sections of ductwork, for they can create lint buildup if allowed to project into the duct area. Venting into a crawl space or attic will deposit piles of lint and create a fire hazard.

After each use, remove and clean the lint filter. Once a year—again, today—disconnect the dryer, remove the service panels, and vacuum out the accumulated lint, especially around the heater box and motor.

January 25

Today in History: Robert Burns, the Scottish poet, was born on Jan. 25, 1759.

Home's not merely four square walls,
Though with pictures hung and gilded;
Home is where Affection calls—
Filled with shrines the Heart hath builded.

—Charles Swain "Home"

Your Home: A Happy Place

To make a happy fireside clime
To weans* and wife,
That's the true pathos** and sublime
Of human life.

—Robert Burns "The True Pathos"

Parents must spend much time, energy, and money running a home. It's a tough job. But take time to play, too. Building happy memories for children in their younger years should pay off in the long run.

Give thought to improvements that will make your home a better place for play through the years—space for hobbies, a supply of games, a pool table, musical instruments, a badminton court, perhaps a swimming pool.

*Young children **Experiences

Good Rules for Buying Fruits and Vegetables

Buy only what's in season. Although many fruits and vegetables are available throughout the year, most have seasons of peak supply, perhaps spread over several months. Quality is best at these times and prices are often lower. Check your newspapers for U.S. Department of Agriculture reports on what produce is currently in abundant supply.

Buy only what you can use promptly. All fruits and vegetables are perishable. A modern refrigerator makes it possible to keep these products a reasonable time. Know how much you can refrigerate properly and use without waste.

Be skeptical of bargain prices. They may result because the produce already has been on hand in the market too long. Unless the lower prices come about because of a current seasonal abundance, you may not get a bargain.

Don't buy on size alone. Fruits and vegetables of supersize are not necessarily the best quality. The smaller may have a better taste. Fruit that seems heavy for its size is sometimes a good buy.

Demand freshness. Know the characteristic signs—a bright, lively color and crispness. Avoid produce that shows wilt and decay.

Handle with care—or not at all. In the long run, you (the customer) often wind up paying the grocer's loss for spoilage and waste caused by handling. In other words: Pinch today and you'll pay tomorrow.

January 26

Your Garden Sprayers and Dusters

How are you fixed for garden sprayers and dusters? It's a rare home that can't use at least one or two. Your season for needing one will soon arrive—if it hasn't already. As you can see in the accompanying chart, the time for dormant spraying of shrubs and small trees is now at hand in the southern states.

For control of flies, mosquitoes, ants, bees, wasps, and other annoying insects in a limited way, a few aerosol bombs may suffice. Or you might buy pesticide dusts in disposable plastic squeeze containers or plunger cartons for the same purpose.

But for more extensive and economical spraying, a plunger-operated sprayer or duster is usually a better bet. One of these may be all you need to protect the average home flower and small-scale vegetable garden. Operating the plunger with one hand as you hold the body with the other propels a stream or mist of liquid insecticide or a cloud of dust. These hand pumps are available in various forms.

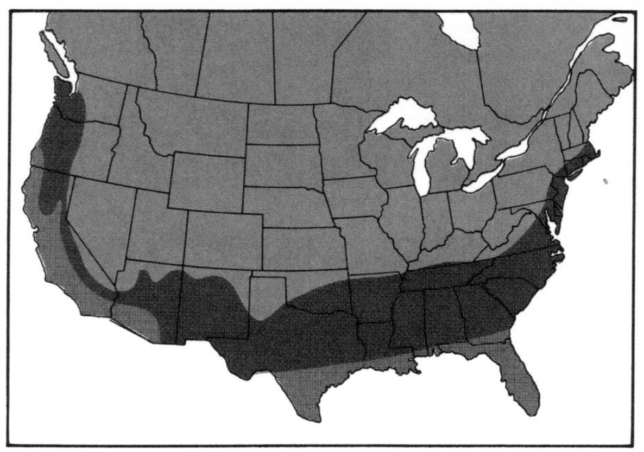

Determine the shading of the area you live in on this map. Then follow the corresponding bar on chart.

To reach the tops of your shrubs and small trees you will need a compressed-air sprayer, one with a carrying handle or a shoulder strap. Tanks range from 1½ to 5 gallons. Some sprayers have adjustable nozzles to provide a range of droplet sizes. The pressure built up by hand pumping can propel the insecticide to the tops of fairly high shrubs and ornamental and fruit trees. To handle larger quantities of spray material you can buy bucket, barrel, and wheeled sprayers powered by traction or one-cylinder gasoline engines. There are also spray outfits for making use of the water pressure supplied by a garden hose. These are useful only in areas that can be reached by the garden hose.

Crank-operated knapsacks and powered wheel machines are available for large-scale application of insecticide dusts. These usually are

Today in History: Dishonest baby sitters? An insurance policy issued on Jan. 26, 1950, covered baby sitters available through the Missouri State Employment Service. The policy bonded each sitter up to $2500 for fraud and dishonesty.

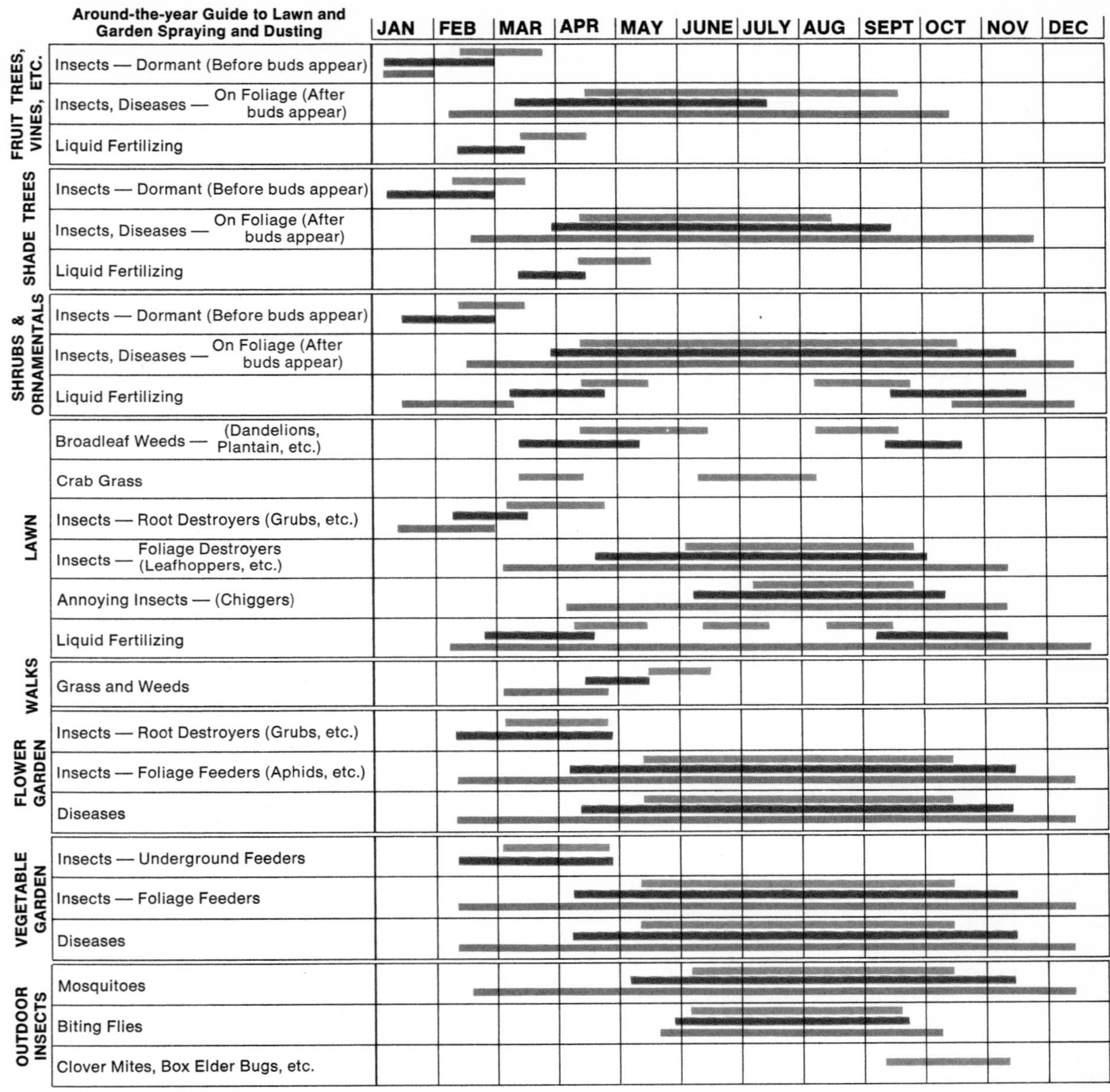

most useful in truck gardening or farming.

If you already own the equipment you need, better make sure now that it is clean and ready for use. Were all parts cleaned after the last use, especially the nozzles and screens? Is there a coating of oil on all parts that might rust? Plunger-operated sprayers may lose compression. When this happens, pull the handle out as far as possible and squirt oil in the air hole at the end of the pump cylinder. Gaskets that seal the tanks of pressure-operated sprayers deteriorate and require replacement after a few years.

Otherwise you lose pressure, or you can't build it up. Better check yours now.

As you can see in the accompanying chart sprayers and dusters are needed—somewhere in the U.S. and Canada—during every month of the year. The chart is intended only as a general guide to timing. Your state Extension Service can provide specific information for your area.

The chart was adapted from a full-color Spray/Dust Timetable copyright 1962 by H.D. Hudson Co., 154 East Erie St., Chicago, Ill. 60611. Write to Hudson for information about the spraying and dusting equipment the company manufactures.

January 27

Today in History: Thomas A. Edison received a patent for the incandescent lamp bulb on Jan. 27, 1880. Later in the same year, Oct. 1, he opened a factory in Menlo Park, New Jersey, to make the bulbs. By the time the factory moved to Harrison, New Jersey, on April 1, 1882, more than 130,000 bulbs had been made.

Your Choice in Incandescent Bulbs

Incandescent light bulbs for household use have been developed into a wide assortment of shapes, colors, sizes, and wattages since Thomas A. Edison introduced the first one in 1880. You now can select a special bulb for the use you have in mind.

The most commonly used bulbs come in three finishes—inside frost, inside white (silica coated), and clear. Well-shielded fixtures are required for both inside frost and clear bulbs. The inside white finish (a milky-white coating) produces a diffused, soft light and helps reduce bright spots in shields. In addition to standard shapes, clear bulbs also come in decorative shapes for use in chandeliers and simulated candles. Dimmer switches make it possible to vary the output of any bulb.

Three-way bulbs are another refinement to Edison's invention. These must go into three-way sockets. They offer three lighting levels. You can also buy such special purpose items as silver-bowl bulbs, spotlight bulbs, floodlight bulbs, and tinted bulbs. Silver-bowl bulbs are standard bulbs with a silver coating on the outside of the rounded end. Use them with the base up to direct light upward to the ceiling or a reflector. You have a choice of 60, 100, 150, and 200 watts.

As the name suggests, a spotlight directs light in a narrow beam for lighting a particular object. Floodlights spread intense light over a wider area. Bulbs with a parabolic shape (PAR bulbs) are made resistant to rain and snow for use outdoors. Floodlights come in tints to provide illumination in a variety of colors as well as white.

For special effects, you can choose ordinary bulbs with inside coating that produce tints of colored light. Another choice: bulbs in decorative shapes—globe, flame, cone, mushroom, and tubular. These come in either tinted or clear glass.

Your Own Reminders

Week of Jan. 22–28

January 28

Facts About Fluorescents

Fluorescent light bulbs have advantages over incandescents, and you may want to use them at several locations in your home. You understand, of course, that fluorescents must go into fixtures that contain the necessary accessories. When current is turned on, an electric arc jumps from one end of the tube to the other, producing ultraviolet light. This light causes the tube's inner coating (phosphor) to fluoresce, or glow brilliantly. The longer the tube, the higher the wattage. Fluorescents also come in circular form, especially suitable for kitchen or bathroom use.

A consumers service report from the U.S. Department of Agriculture recommends that only deluxe tubes be bought for home use. An "x" in the color-coding letters on the tube indicates that it is a deluxe one. Ask your dealer to order deluxe tubes for you if he doesn't have them on hand. A deluxe warm white tube (WWX) gives a flattering light, can be used with incandescent light, and does not distort colors any more than incandescent light does. A deluxe cool white tube (EWX) simulates daylight and goes nicely with color schemes of green and blue.

For maximum light output keep the tube and its reflector clean and dust-free. When it is necessary to change a tube or remove it, twist the tube a quarter turn until the end pin will slip down out of the end holders. Reverse this to put in a new tube. If a tube seems insecure or moves from side to side, loosen the screws holding the end holders to the fixture and move the holders inward.

The little can-like starter is responsible for many fluorescent troubles—blinking, slow starting, or failure to start. Press it lightly and twist to remove. Make sure the wattage of the replacement matches the wattage of the bulb being used. Lamp makers suggest installing a new starter with every second bulb replacement.

Fluorescent bulbs are sensitive to temperature between 70 and 80 degrees F. Below that, light output falls rapidly. Cool breezes blowing around the fixture may cause irregular operation of the tube. This peculiarity makes fluorescents a bad choice for illumination in some areas of your home.

January 29

Replacing Fuses Correctly

Everyone in your family should know what to do when an overload causes a fuse to blow or a circuit breaker to trip. Today is as good a time as any to call them all together for a review of the procedures. But first you ought

to make sure your panel is labeled and that you have a supply of replacement fuses of the appropriate amperages.

Lighting circuits in a home usually are protected by 15-ampere fuses. Major appliances mostly require 20-ampere circuits although a few—for instance an automatic dryer—need 30-amperes and an electric range may go as high as 70. Heavier wire may be used in 20-ampere than in 15-ampere circuits. This leads to the first rule that you should drill into the mind of each family member—replace a blown fuse with one of the same amperage. No substitutions! Reason: a 20-ampere fuse in a circuit rated for 15 could permit dangerous overheating of the lighter wire (No. 14) often found there.

Make sure you have a record of the proper amperage for each circuit. Sketch the fuse layout on a sheet of paper. Mark the amperage on each one. Relate the appropriate amperage to your circuit-labeling system. Cement the sketch to the inside or outside of the box door.

When a fuse blows, your labeling system will lead you directly to it—and tell you the replacement amperage required. Fuses are all marked, of course, and the blown one will show what replacement is needed. But if someone has goofed in the past your records could catch it.

When a fuse blows, first try to determine the cause of the failure. If the fuse blew when you plugged in or turned on an appliance, disconnect it before replacing the fuse. Impress this rule on other members of the family. Ask them to remind you when you come home to check out the appliance for a suspected short or take it to a repairman.

Second step in the replacement procedure should be to turn off the main house switch at the fuse box. Then replace the blown fuse—and turn on the main switch. Throw the blown fuse into the refuse can. If you are dealing with a circuit breaker, you will find the lever midway between the "on" and "off" signs. Just push it to "on."

Store replacement fuses in a convenient container near the fuse box. Make sure everyone knows where they are.

January 30

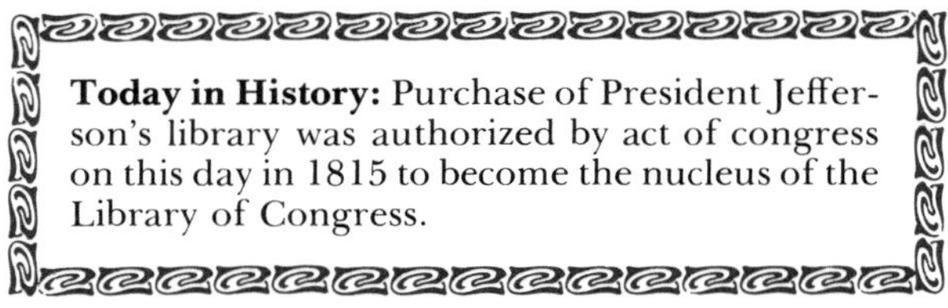

Today in History: Purchase of President Jefferson's library was authorized by act of congress on this day in 1815 to become the nucleus of the Library of Congress.

Home Owner's Five-Foot Shelf*

Anyone can make a bookcase. Just stack up bricks and boards. In it, keep such useful books as those in the list below. Each book in the list was carefully chosen to provide additional how-to information for the calendar home maintenance chores suggested in the book you now are reading—the Popular Science Illustrated Almanac for Homeowners. The list:

America's Handyman Book
By The Staff of Family Handyman
Charles Scribner's Sons, 597 Fifth Avenue
New York, N.Y. 10017, $8.95

Basic Handyman's Book
By George Daniels
Harper & Row, 10 East 53rd Street
New York, N.Y. 10022 $5.95

Complete Book of Home Improvement
By Darrell and Frances Huff
Popular Science Publishing Co.
P.O. Box 226, Manhasset
New York 11030, $11.95

Complete Book of Home Repairs
By Jackson Hand
Popular Science Publishing Co.
P.O. Box 226, Manhasset
New York 11030, $8.95

---

* Our list of books useful to homeowners still measures somewhat less than 5 feet. But keep looking. You'll find 'em.

The Complete Homeowner
By Robert Schwartz & Hubbard Cobb
Macmillan Company, 866 Third Avenue
New York, N.Y. 10022, $5.95

Electronics for Everybody
By Ronald Benrey
Popular Science Publishing Co.
P.O. Box 226, Manhasset
New York 11030, $6.95

Encyclopedia of Gardening
Edited by Norman Taylor
Houghton Mifflin Company
Boston, Mass., $12.95

Formulas, Methods, Tips and Data for Home and Workshop
By Kenneth M. Swezey
Popular Science Publishing Co.
P.O. Box 226, Manhasset
New York 11030, $7.95

Home and Workshop Guide to Sharpening
By Harry Walton
Popular Science Publishing Co.
P.O. Box 226, Manhasset
New York 11030, $1.95

Home Guide to Plumbing, Heating, Air Conditioning
By George Daniels
Popular Science Publishing Co.
P.O. Box 226, Manhasset
New York 11030, $1.95

Homeowner's Complete Outdoor Building Book
By John Brimer
Popular Science Publishing Co.
P.O. Box 226, Manhasset
New York 11030, $7.95

How to Be Your Own Home Electrician
By George Daniels
Popular Science Publishing Co.
P.O. Box 226, Manhasset
New York 11030, $1.95

How to Build Cabinets for the Modern Kitchen
By Robert P. Stevenson
Arco Publishing Company,
219 Park Ave. South
New York, N.Y. 10003, $7.50

How to Do Your Own Wood Finishing
By Jackson Hand
Popular Science Publishing Co.
P.O. Box 226, Manhasset
New York 11030, $1.95

How to Fix Almost Everything
By Stanley Schuler
M. Evans & Company
E. Washington Square
Philadelphia, Pa. 19105, $4.95

How to Work with Tools and Wood
By Robert Campbell & N. H. Mager
Pocket Books, 1 West 39th Street
New York, N.Y. 10018, $1.25 paperback

The Unhandy Man's Guide to Home Repairs
By Barbara & Richard O'Neill
Macmillan Company, 866 Third Avenue
New York, N.Y. 10022, $6.95

January 31

Today in History: First U.S. satellite was launched in 1958—and what visitors to Cape Kennedy now call "bird watching" began. That's the local term for watching a satellite take off.

Odd Facts About Owls

Great horned owls always are up and about their business of mating early in the year. In wild regions all over the U.S., you are apt to hear the mating calls of these large owls at this time of year. The young hatch in March.

Many people collect owl-shaped objects as decorative items for their homes. This has reached the proportions of a fad. At least that is the report we have from Ingraham Industries, Bristol, Connecticut 06010, the people who make owl clocks—a source which, understandably enough, is prejudiced in favor of promoting such a fad. To that end, their public relations man (Donald Moffitt) has assembled these strange facts about owls:

Ancient Persians believed that a mama owl always laid two eggs—one of which, if eaten, could cure baldness while the other caused unwanted hair to fall away. But how to know which was which?

In rural districts of England, some people still believe that owl broth cures whooping cough.

Pliny the Elder wrote in his "Natural History" that owls hatch upside down because of the weight of their beaks.

Owl coins were minted in Athens about 500 B.C.

The Greeks gave the owl its reputation for wisdom. They made it the sacred bird of Athena, goddess of wisdom.

Owls range in size from less than five inches to more than two feet long. Ornithologists have named more than 200 kinds.

From earliest times, owls were thought to be able to foretell the future.

Ancient Egyptians put mummified owls in tombs to bring the dead person good luck on his way to the next world.

From Peru, the art world has gained a rich heritage of pre-Columbian owl jugs, owl vases, and owl-shaped agricultural instruments thought to involve the owls' protection for crops.

Sioux warriors sometimes painted an owl on their shields as protection from arrows fired by other Indians.

A craze for owl drinking cups swept Europe during the sixteenth and seventeenth centuries. They ranged from exquisite gold containers to stoneware beer mugs.

The owl's eyesight at night is exceptionally acute, but it also has ears so good that it can hunt in utter darkness by hearing alone.

The owl's name apparently came from its distinctive cry. In Latin, it was "ulula," which gave us the word "ululate," meaning to wail or howl. In old English, the name became "ule" and later "owle."

Are young children likely to unhook a window screen from the inside of a high window and fall out? Drive a screw into the sill behind the arm of the hook so the hook cannot be removed from the eye without using a screwdriver.

February

February, the year's shortest month, brings the first stirrings of spring. Anglo-Saxons called it Sol Monath in recognition of the northward swinging sun and lengthening days. Nowadays garden catalogs arrive in all their colorful glory and gardeners dream and plan for the growing season ahead. Outdoors, it's a time for serious pruning.

Earliest calendars had no February. Numa, a legendary Roman king, added January and February to the old ten-month Roman calendar. Julius Caesar dropped one day, Augustus took away another, giving February its present 28. In leap year it regains a day.

February derives its name from the Latin verb "to purify." At the mid-month festival of Lupercalia, the old Romans purified themselves for the start of a new year in March. February for many years was the final month of the year.

The month has two major holidays—Lincoln's birthday, the 12th, and Washington's birthday, the 22nd. Ash Wednesday, beginning of Lent, also may fall during the month.

February 1

Let's Have a Home Lube Day

Several dozen points of friction throughout your home need occasional lubrication. So why not have an annual lube day? That way you'll get all the points taken care of at once. A day at this time of year, when you may be confined indoors, is a fine time to select.

Have on hand several kinds of lubricant—a light oil in a squeeze container, a heavier machine oil (No. 20) in a squirt can, a commercial stick lubricant, a container of powdered graphite, and an aerosol spray lubricant containing fluorocarbon (check the label when you buy). A candle stub or piece of paraffin can sometimes be used in place of stick lube.

Starting at the top of the house, get out any summer fans stored in the attic. Put a drop or two of light oil in the reservoir (if there is one); otherwise on the blade shaft. Do you have a built-in attic fan? Lube it now—the motor (if required) and the fan shaft—and you will not need to climb into the hot attic next summer. Your heavy oil probably will be right for this.

Turn next to the doors on the upper floors. Apply a drop of light oil to the hinges of the swinging doors after first taking out pins and cleaning them. Blow graphite into door locks. Rub stick lube on latches.

Apply light oil to sash locks and window cranks (if you have them). Use a stick lube on casement and jalousie channels, working the window to spread it. Use the spray lube on the channels of double-hung windows and the channels of combination storms and screens.

The spray is also the thing for tracks of sliding closet doors and sliding furniture doors, as well as drawer slides. A stick lubricant, candle, or paraffin might also be used.

Use the spray lubricant, too, in medicine cabinet doors and for a sliding shower door. Give the moving surfaces of plumbing fixtures a light shot of graphite oil. Apply light oil to the toilet-seat hinge.

Go through all rooms of the first floor, oiling all friction points as indicated. Use spray lubricant on the sliding parts of drapery traverse rods and all moving parts of Venetian blinds if you have them.

Rub stick lubricant on friction catches in the kitchen cabinets. Then think about all of the appliances. Should you lubricate any of them? The instructions should tell you—and how to go about it. Give special attention to the kitchen exhaust fan.

In the basement or utility room give the oil-burner motor, circulation pump or blower their semiannual drop or two of oil. Don't overlube. While you are in the basement (if that is where you keep your tools) give thought to applying

Today in History: The first auto insurance policy was issued on Feb. 1, 1898, to Truman J. Martin, Buffalo, N.Y., by Travelers Insurance Company. The fee was $11.25 for liability ranging from $5,000 to $10,000.

light oil to all of their metal surfaces to foil rust.

Storm-door snubbers on the exterior doors can use stick lubricant on the sliding surfaces and light oil in the mechanism. The tracks of overhead garage doors should have lubricant, too, although you may want to delay this until warmer weather. Use heavy oil on rollers and pulleys, graphite on tracks.

February 2

The Origins of Groundhog Day

You know the old saying. Everyone does. If the groundhog sees his shadow on February 2, we'll have six more weeks of winter. If the day is overcast, without sunshine, the worst of winter has passed.

Early immigrants brought this tradition from Europe. In Germany, the badger was supposed to break its hibernation to take a forecasting look at the skies. In America, German immigrants transferred this belief to the groundhog. In England, people for centuries have been reciting this rhyme on February 2:

If Candlemas Day be fair and bright
Winter will have another flight;
But if it be dark with clouds and rain,
Winter is gone and will not come again.

In the Roman Catholic Church, February 2 has long been celebrated as Candlemas Day. Candles to be used during the remainder of the year are blessed. The festival honors the purification of the Virgin Mary after the birth of Jesus. In two Pennsylvania communities—Quarryville and Punxsutawney—local clubs have developed elaborate ceremonies of fun and nonsense to pay tribute each year on this day to the supposed weather forecasting abilities of the groundhog, also variously called woodchuck or whistle pig.

Meanwhile, the groundhog—no prophet, anyway—usually is still hibernating on February 2 and entirely unconcerned with all the fuss.

Today in History: A patent for waterproof boots—Wales Patent Arctic Gaiter—was issued on Feb. 2, 1858, to Thomas Wales, of Dorchester, Mass. Galoshes anyone?

Never thin odorless paint with turpentine. That will give it an odor again.

When comparing the prices of resilient floor tiles, be sure to consider the thickness. It should be marked on the container.

For rooms which adjoin one another, use companion wallcovering patterns. These are patterns designed and colored to go together. Each is quite different from the other, and each can stand on its own merits, but each enhances the other.

Lawn grass is the biggest crop grown in any community.

February 3

Annual Pruning of Citrus Trees

Removal of green leaves from citrus reduces the ability of the trees to bear fruit. A moderate annual thinning of mature trees, therefore, will reduce the crop but should improve the quality and size of the fruit. In general, however, it is best to confine pruning of mature trees to removal of dead and broken limbs.

Cut away enough growth from the center of the tree to facilitate fruit picking and control of pests and disease. Citrus trees normally produce long vigorous suckers. Remove them if they are not well placed, but leave them when possible to build up the tree. If left alone, they tend to fill the center and top of the tree with a tangle of growth.

Do not remove low-hanging branches. They bear fruit within easy reach and shade the ground so weeds do not grow. The ideal tree has a skirt of foliage right down to the ground.

Lemons need more pruning usually than oranges. It may be desirable to remove or cut back some of the more vigorous shoots from young lemons.

Fill an empty squeeze-type plastic bottle with water and keep it in the glove compartment to clean sticky fingers. You also can keep this type of plastic bottle handy to squirt water on your windshield on mud-spattering days if you don't have an automatic windshield washer, or if it is temporarily empty.

Watch for first snowdrop blossoms. Mild weather now may bring them out any time—even in the north. If you have none of these lovely harbingers of spring, plan to plant some bulbs next fall.

Prune a quince tree while it is dormant. Remove dead branches, branches that rub others. Removal of a few older branches may be necessary to thin out the top and admit sunlight. Removal of old growth stimulates new growth on which the fruit forms.

February 4

Today in History: A patent was granted on Feb. 4, 1913, to Louis Henry Perlman of New York City for a major automobile improvement—the demountable tire-carrying rim.

Keep Road Salts Washed off Car

Frequent washing of a car is important during the winter to remove the salts and other chemicals used on icy and snowy roads. Yet how many of us do it? Subzero temperatures make it an unpleasant task to do at home—and we may not get around to visiting the local car-wash establishment. As a result, by the time spring comes the salts may have started rust action under the car and on the wheels and attacked the finish on the body.

You are more apt to do the job regularly, say once a week during the worst slush season, if you have a hot-water faucet available for hooking up your garden hose. Why not install both a cold and hot-water faucet inside your garage?

While you are at it, a mixing faucet is a good idea. You'll then have water available, either hot or cold, for regular car washing throughout the year. Install shelves on the garage wall and store all your cleaning, polishing, and waxing supplies there. Hang a hose on an adjacent holder and you'll be all set, summer and winter.

In the winter, the important thing is to wash away the salts. With hot water available through your hose, a very few minutes will suffice for the task—even in cold weather. As you coil up the hose, be sure to drain out all the water to avoid freeze-bursting it.

If your garage stands away from the house, and is unheated, place the water lines underground—below frost depth for your area. In any installation, use freeze-free faucets—the type that cuts off the water back where freezing is unlikely to occur. In a detached garage, you might also coil heat tape around the pipes to a point below the frost line.

Check trees and shrubs for storm damage and plan repairs before new growth starts. Saw off broken branches and cover cut surfaces with tree wound dressing.

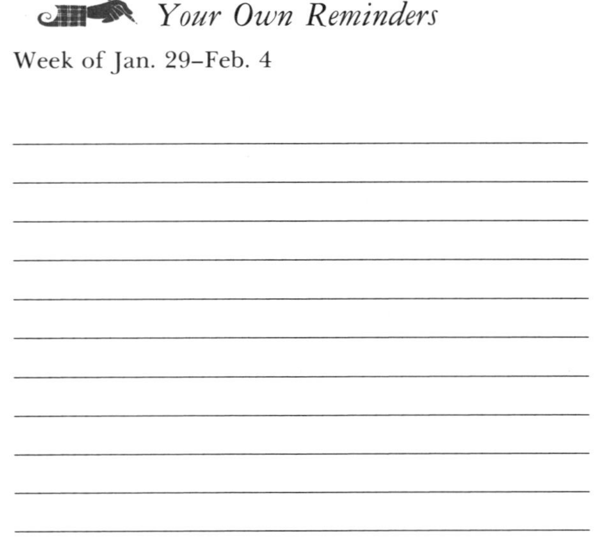

Your Own Reminders
Week of Jan. 29–Feb. 4

February 5

Today in History: An ordinance was adopted in Baltimore on Feb. 5, 1817, permitting Rembrandt Peale and others to make and distribute coal gas "to provide for more effectually lighting the streets, squares, lanes, and alleys of the city of Baltimore."

A Gas Lamp Outside Your Home?

Taking a cue from today's historical note, you might want to consider installation of a modern gas lamp at the front of your home or on a patio. The lamps and poles are available from a number of manufacturers in a variety of styles and you can choose one to suit the architectural period of your home—Colonial, Victorian, or modern.

Instead of a conventional lamp with gas burning through mantles, you might want to think about something newer—a dramatic outdoor gas torch light. The free flame burns through a bed of volcanic rock contained in a metal bowl, 14 inches across, set atop a pole. The dancing flame is pleasant to watch as you relax on the patio during the evening. The torch works even in a high wind. One maker has given his product appropriate names—the Olympic and the Roman Torch.

Gas lamps operate on either natural or LP gas, but in buying the equipment you must be careful to specify which type of orifice you want. A gas lamp can be equipped with an electric eye device to lower the flame during the day. Unless the lamp is equipped with automatic ignition, you usually are advised not to turn it off completely.

Your gas company can probably show you suitable lamps or suggest a local source. If not, write to the Gas Appliance Manufacturers Association, 1901 North Fort Myer Drive, Arlington, Va. 22209. Arrange with the gas company to make the installation.

February 6

Water Shut-offs Labeled?

Would the lady of the house know how to shut off the water supply if the automatic washer began to leak or a faucet refused to turn off? Such emergencies can occur in the best-run household. Why not prepare for them right now?

Most homes have a valve, in basement or utility room, to shut off all water from the street main. Shut-off valves also may be found in both hot and cold water lines below or near sinks, lavatories, tubs, showers, and water-supplied appliances. The latter shut-offs also may be found in the water lines some distance away, perhaps in the basement.

If you don't already know the location of all your shut-offs, locate them now, as an indoor cold-day activity, and apply a label to each distant one telling what it controls. Shipping tags make good labels for this purpose. When you have each valve tagged, take all adults and teen-age children on a tour and demonstrate what to do in case water must be turned off in a hurry.

February 7

Insect Egg Hunt

Are tent caterpillars or gypsy moths a problem in your neighborhood? You can help control these insect pests by organizing a community egg hunt at this time of the year. The many eyes of your posse will make quick and sure work of locating egg masses of both insects and destroying them before they hatch and set out on a trail of rampage through the trees and shrubs of your neighborhood.

Look for tent-caterpillar eggs especially on wild cherry trees, but also pay attention to limb and twig crotches of apple, peach, plum, and other fruit trees. Cover an area as broad as possible. Adult caterpillars wander widely and may spread to your trees from a neighbor's land. That's why community control measures are advisable.

When you locate the first egg mass of the tent caterpillar—a large number of cylindrical eggs glued together in a band about twigs of the host tree—call all your searchers together to see what they are looking for. Do the same for the first example of gypsy moth eggs. The latter are laid in clusters—often of oval shape—containing 400 or more eggs, all covered with brownish hairs. They look like small pieces of chamois. Look for them on tree branches and trunks and on fences and stone walls.

When possible, break or cut off the twig or branch on which the eggs of either pest are found. Destroy twig and eggs by burning. When it is not possible or desirable to remove the egg mass in this way, soak gypsy moth eggs with a creosote solution. Simply rub tent caterpillar eggs from the limb, catching them in a tin can for later disposal by fire.

If you suspect your refrigerator isn't airtight, test it this way: place strips of paper between the seal and jam of the door. Close it. If the strips come out easily, the seal is too loose.

For destroying gypsy moth eggs, dilute creosote with kerosene or fuel oil. Add a little lamp black to the solution and you'll mark treated spots so conspicuously that you won't skip any. Don't apply creosote or oil to a painted surface; a permanent stain will result. Scrape off eggs from such surfaces into a container of oil.

Tent caterpillars are found over many states. Gypsy moths, accidentally introduced into the U.S. in 1869, are restricted to northeastern states. Government agencies have been trying to head off the pest's threatened spread to forest and shade trees in the Midwest and South. The voracious caterpillars strip all leaves from trees they attack. They can kill pines and hemlocks in a single year. Two successive years of defoliation will kill most deciduous trees.

Extend your search for gypsy moth eggs to the under surfaces of any trailers or camping vehicles that have visited the infested areas of the Northeast the previous season. Camping often coincides with the time—in July and August—when adult moths are seeking suitable spots to deposit eggs. Consequently, eggs have been found on camping vehicles hundreds of miles away from where they were deposited. Your own vehicle may transport the insect into an area where it has never been a pest before.

You can plant new roses at any time in southern regions where the temperature never dips below 10 degrees. See May 4.

If a green manure crop was planted last fall as a prelude to spring lawn seeding in the southern and lower middle regions of the U.S., better turn it under soon. Delay lawn seeding from four to six weeks thereafter.

Spray note: It's time now in northern areas to spray maples for bladder gall mite, plums and cherries for black knot, peaches for leaf curl.

Don't plant outdated seeds in your garden. It's poor economy. Old seeds often germinate poorly. Use seeds with this year's date.

A few step shelves are handy space savers around any home. Use them on closet floors, on shelves, in kitchen cabinets. Make them of three pieces of scrap wood.

February 8

Spring Is on its Way!

Those of us in the ice-bound North who are tired of winter can now rejoice. Spring is on its way. On the accompanying map, this date —February 8—marks an irregular line across the southern United States. At its eastern end, after spanning the broad midriff of Florida in the Tampa area, the line takes to the water, crosses the northeastern corner of the Gulf of Mexico, makes a landfall just east of New Orleans, and then generally follows the natural curves of the shore line before plunging across the Rio Grande River west of Brownsville, Texas.

Now, before anyone has a chance to induce a premature attack of spring fever, let's all be sure what the February 8 line means. You must remember two things about it, both having to do with the fact that the date and the line are merely a general guide. February 8 has been the average date of the last 32-degree (F) temperature (or frost) along the indicated line in weather records kept for more than a quarter of a century.

In some years, the last frost on that date may have occurred north of the line—and still might. In some years also, there has been frost south of the line on February 8—and there still might be.

This possible variation continues to hold true with other dates as you travel up the map with the advancing spring. The date given for each line is a *mean*, or average, date. It's not for sure —just a guide.

The people in the Weather Bureau and other government services who had a hand in compiling the map would also have us say to you that:

"Caution should be used interpolating on this generalized map. Sharp changes in the mean date may occur in short distances due to differences in altitude, slope of land, type of soil, vegetative cover, bodies of water, air drainage, urban heat effects, etc."

The foregoing advice leads naturally to another map fact that you must know if you are to get the most benefit from the frost lines. At various places, you will find the words "Before" and "After" used in connection with a date. These tell you whether the mean freeze date comes before or after the date printed on the line. As an example, see the small circled area marked "Before Feb 8" in the middle of Florida. Check a large-scale map of Florida and you'll find that this small circle coincides with the mid-Florida lake region. This water apparently keeps temperatures higher and has the effect

Today in History: A patent was granted to Simon Willard of Boston, Mass., on Feb. 8, 1802, for "an improvement in a time-piece"—the home accessory that we now know as a banjo clock.

When Spring Comes to the Eastern United States

When Spring Comes to the Western United States

of giving the lake region an earlier spring than some areas a few miles to the southward.

Later in the season these regional temperature variations leave behind many islands of cold weather in the mountains of the middle states as spring temperatures advance generally northward.

Not only must spring fight its way up the map; it must make an even stronger effort to climb the mountains. And it's interesting to note that in doing the latter, spring often advances sideways. So who's perfect? Spring obviously isn't. But spring gets there just the same.

You'll see on the map that frosts may have occurred south of the February 8 line only a few days ago. Today's line represents a northward advance of just a few miles. But it shows that spring is slowly gathering its strength. From now on, it will advance up the map with steadily advancing speed.

So that our Almanac can suggest appropriate seasonal chores for wherever you happen to live, we have divided the map into latitudinal regions where you can expect the spring temperature conditions to be about the same, south to north. Note now in which region you live—and remember the Roman numeral that applies to it. When you encounter the numeral on the pages that follow, you will know that the suggested activity applies generally to your area. If you live toward the southern edge of the region you may want to anticipate the given date by a few days, even up to a week earlier. If you live toward the northern boundary of your region, you should normally delay a few days after the given date. In using the map, remember, too, to take into account the effects produced by altitude, water, and other factors on local temperatures. Such variants may delay the arrival of spring as much as a week or ten days within a space of only a couple of miles. If you don't already know whether such variations prevail in your area, ask some of the older gardeners.

Spring generally reaches the northern borders of the U.S. around May 20 or 30. But, as you may note on the map, frost possibility remains in the higher parts of the Rockies for still another month.

What about the states of Hawaii and Alaska? The foregoing applies to the continental U.S. and Canada only. Hawaii is tropical, with no freezes at all except in the mountains above 3,000 to 4,000 feet. Along the southern coastal regions of Alaska, spring comes at about the same time that it does in the lower parts of Region IV of the continental states, that is around April 30 or May 15. Protected inland valleys may have their final frosts around June 15 up to about latitude 66 degrees. Northward, frost occurs during every month of the year. The mountains of Alaska have a snow cover most of the year, of course, as well as freezes almost every month.

Sprinkle 10-6-4 fertilizer around established boxwood. Do the same around lilacs that are growing on sandy soil.

Don't be too hasty about pruning back citrus trees that have been damaged by frost. Allow time for new growth to show the extent of the damage. By pruning too early, you may remove branches that will come back.

Drain collected sediment from a humidifier.

See the map with April 2. If you find your frostfree date is about April 1, start seed of flowers indoors soon.

Some summer-flowering bulbs should be started in pots or flats soon. Popular ones include tuberous rooted begonia, canna, dahlia, gladiolus, lily, and caladium. One good source of information about planting times and cultivation: "Summer Flowering Bulbs," Home and Garden Bulletin No. 151, available from Superintendent of Documents, Government Printing Office, Washington, D.C. 20402.

You need not feel boxed in, even in a one-room apartment. Wallcoverings with scenic designs or many contemporary geometrics give the illusion of space.

February 9

Today in History: An act of Congress on Feb. 9, 1870, authorized the establishment of the U.S. Weather Bureau. Responsibility for gathering weather information was assigned to the Signal Corps of the War Department. In 1891, everything was transferred to an agency in the Department of Agriculture called the Weather Bureau.

Your Home Weather Instruments

Every home needs certain instruments to keep track of, or help predict, the weather. Thermometers record indoor and outdoor temperatures, hygrometers let you know the state of your indoor humidity, and barometers

(by recording atmospheric pressure) indicate approaching weather changes.

You can buy all three instruments mounted on a single wall plaque in a style to suit your home furnishings—traditional, Colonial, or contemporary. Some people also like to have an indoor-outdoor thermometer. This enables you to read both temperatures from inside the house. Lacking that, you can mount an outdoor thermometer so it can be read through a window.

Another type of thermometer that gardeners find useful gives three readings—the present outdoor temperature and the high and the low maximums since the last setting. With this, there's no guessing about how low the mercury dropped on a certain morning while you still were asleep.

Some people also like to record inches of rainfall. They do this with a rain gauge. A volunteer weather observer in your area can probably tell you where to get one—and how to use it.

February 10

Spraying Due Soon for Scale Insects

Wherever you live, scale insects attack the trees, shrubs, vines, flowers, and fruits that you enjoy. They are flakelike and live by sucking the juices from the host plant. Practically all scales are protected by a hard shell under which they live. Most are so small that you may not realize they are living insects. The young move about, but the adults usually remain stationary.

The ones you may hear most about include San Jose scale, juniper and pine-leaf scales, oyster-shell scale, black scale (on citrus), cottony scales, scurfy scale, and terrapin scale. Whatever kind of plant you try to grow, indoors or out, more than likely you will eventually find that a particular scale is attracted to it.

An oil spray or lime-sulfur spray just before the outdoor host plants start growth in the spring is the most common and successful method of control. These are known as dormant or delayed-dormant sprays.

Check the Spray Chart presented on January 26 and the Spring Map on February 8 and you will see that right now is a target time for this outdoor dormant spray in the middle belts of the U.S. The target time already has passed in the southernmost fringe of the U.S. and in southern California, generally Zone I on the Spring Map.

So far as humans are concerned, oil sprays are one of the safest you can use, and they do not adversely affect trees and shrubs during the period of full dormancy. Applied to the eggs and larvae of insect pests, the oil kills by smothering. Oil sprays generally are divided into two classes—dormant (or delayed dormant) and summer. Summer oil sprays are formulated so as to cause the least possible damage to evergreens and deciduous trees in leaf.

Besides scale insects, oil sprays help control mites, scab, plant bugs, mealy bugs, thrips, newly-hatched aphids, and the eggs of coddling and other moths, leaf rollers, and cankerworms. One application, therefore, is likely to do a lot of good.

Fruit growers in the Pacific northwest commonly prefer to apply oil sprays during the spring before any green appears in the buds—about now for the most part. Later spraying is avoided because of possible damage to the buds.

Delayed-dormant spraying is more the rule, however, for deciduous fruit trees in the northeastern states—the spraying being timed when the buds have begun to swell, or even break. At that time, a higher kill of winter eggs of all pests is usually obtained. A fungicide may be applied along with the oil spray. Dormant spraying is usually recommended for a day when the air temperature is above 40 degrees.

Your state Extension Service can give you specific information about what is effective in your area—and when to apply it.

Shopping reminder: First of the new crop of asparagus should appear soon at your markets. Your grocer also should have a good supply of winter-sweetened parsnips about now.

Furnace filters may need changing. Better check them this week.

February 11

Today in History: The Pennsylvania Hospital in Philadelphia was opened on Feb. 11, 1752. It was supported by Benjamin Franklin.

On Feb. 11, 1880, Judge Jesse Fell demonstrated in his home in Wilkes-Barre, Pa., that it was possible to burn anthracite (hard coal) and heat a home with it. Previously, anthracite had been considered only as a curious black rock with little or no value.

Do You Have a Home First Aid Kit?

Accidents do happen, and you may be called upon at any moment, night or day, to give first aid to a member of your family or a visitor. You will make the best job of it if you take these two steps:

First, make sure one or more members of the family group have training in first aid. If such training is lacking in your household, why not see if a course isn't given as part of the adult education program at your local school?

Second, have on hand the equipment you may need in an emergency. The National Safety

Council suggests that a home kit should include:

Individual package-type sterile dressings (2″ × 2″ and 4″ × 4″) for open wounds and burns.

Roller bandages for fingers (1″ × 5 yds.) and for holding dressings in place (2″ × 5 yds.).

Roll of adhesive tape Bandaids (various sizes).

Bath towels or bed sheets, which can be cut and used as needed.

Triangular bandage (37″ × 37″) for a sling or dressing, or as a covering. Blanket.

Safety pins, blunt-tip scissors, tweezers, measuring spoons, eye dropper and wooden tongue blades.

Splints (1/4″ thick, 3 1/2″ wide, 12″-15″ long) for broken arms and legs (plywood is fine).

Square of moleskin. A "cold pack." Snakebite kit.

Alcohol for cleansing and sterilizing. A bar of mild soap for cleansing of wounds, scratches and cuts.

Aspirin. Papercups. Flares. Flashlight (batteries kept separate).

First-aid manual.

Remember that first aid is just that. Call for professional help as soon as possible. Post these telephone numbers near your phone: Your physician, your police department, your fire department.

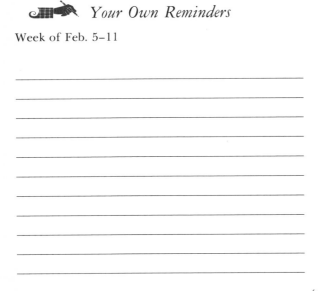

Your Own Reminders

Week of Feb. 5–11

February 12

Today in History: Abraham Lincoln, born Feb. 12, 1809, in a log cabin near Hodgenville, Ky., was the first U.S. president born outside the boundaries of the original 13 states.

How the Moon Helped Abe Lincoln Win a Court Case

In Abraham Lincoln's day, weather almanacs were important reading in almost every household. Issued annually, these small booklets contained monthly calendars with information of considerable value to persons who lived close to nature—when the sun would rise and set each day, for instance, and when the moon was in which phase and when it would set. A calendar of this kind once helped Lincoln win an important court case. In fact, it saved his client from hanging.

The story begins while Lincoln was a young man in the Illinois village of New Salem, clerking in the local store and reading law books in his spare time. Responding to a challenge, Abe floored the town strong man, Jack Armstrong, in a wrestling match. The two then became friends, and Lincoln often visited the Armstrong home after Jack married.

Years later, while Lincoln was in the midst of his debates with Stephen A. Douglas, Mrs. Armstrong came to him and pleaded that he defend her son William, accused of killing a young man named Metzker in a drunken fight.

At the trial, witnesses fixed the time of the fatal fight at about 11 o'clock on the night of August 29. A witness named Allen swore that he saw Armstrong strike the fatal blow. Cross-examining, Lincoln asked Allen how he could see so clearly at that time of night.

"By the moonlight," Allen replied.

"Well, was there light enough to see everything that happened?" Lincoln continued.

"The moon was about in the same place that

the sun would be at 10 o'clock in the morning and was almost full," Allen said.

Bringing forth a calendar, Lincoln called the attention of the court and the jury to the date of August 29–30, 1857. On the night of August 29, the calendar showed, the moon was only slightly past its first quarter. At 11 o'clock, it would have given little light for it was low in the sky and had set at seven minutes after midnight.

The jury acquitted Armstrong.

Quotations From Lincoln's Writings

Abraham Lincoln loved his home and his family. Leaving Springfield, Ill., on February 11, 1861—one day before his 52nd birthday anniversary—he said goodby to his friends and neighbors in the following brief address as he set off for Washington to assume the Presidency:

"To this place, and the kindness of these people, I owe everything. Here I have lived a quarter of a century, and have passed from a young to an old man. Here my children have been born, and one is buried. I now leave, not knowing when or whether ever I may return, with a task before me greater than that which rested upon Washington. Without the assistance of that Divine Being who ever attended him, I cannot succeed. With that assistance, I cannot fail. Trusting in Him who can go with me, and remain with you, and be everywhere for good, let us confidently hope that all will yet be well. To His care commending you, as I hope in your prayers you will commend me, I bid you an affectionate farewell."

Other memorable Lincoln statements:

"A house divided against itself cannot stand."

"With malice toward none; with charity for all; with firmness in the right, as God gives us to see the right, let us strive on to finish the work we are in; to bind up the nation's wounds; to care for him who shall have borne the battle, and for his widow, and his orphan—to do all which may achieve and cherish a just and lasting peace among ourselves, and with all nations."

February 13

Get Your Garden Plans Made

Wherever you live, it's time now to take positive steps toward the vegetable and/or flower garden you hope to have this season. When your outdoor planting date is about six weeks away, you should plant flats of seeds indoors. You can also order garden manure, right now. And above all, you can plan your garden on paper.

Line out on paper the boundaries of the plot you expect to plant, making it at least approximately to scale. Then put in lines representing

where you'll plant what. Past experience is your best guide to how long a row, or how much area, you'll want of a vegetable or flower. Lacking this experience, let the instructions on the seed package, or in garden books, be your guide. In making your plan, remember that you can often plant some crops in rows between other crops, and that you can make later plantings where early plantings have already been harvested. Let your plan include the times for various plantings.

In the north, better spray the lawn again at this time for control of snow mold.

February 14

Today in History: February 14 is St. Valentine's Day, a festival for lovers that dates back hundreds of years. How did the date become associated with lovers? One theory is that the custom arose from a widely held belief in the Middle Ages that birds began mating on February 14. In "Parliament of Foules," Chaucer wrote about the date like this:

For this was Seynt Valentyne's day,
When every foul cometh ther to choose his mate.

Maple Sap Is Flowing Now

A sweet thought for St. Valentine's Day: If the trees on your property include a maple tree of fair size, why not sample one of nature's sweets—maple sap? Sugar maples are traditionally tapped each year in northeastern states as a source of delectable maple sugar and syrup, but any kind of maple yields a delicious sap.

Choose a tree with a trunk at least eight inches in diameter, preferably larger. Drill a hole straight into it for about two inches, sizing the hole for the "spile" you have ready. In New England, spiles are hollow metal tubes that are driven into the drilled holes to carry the sap into a pail suspended on the spile. You can make one by removing the pith from a six-inch length of elderberry wood.

A surprising amount of sap will flow from a single tap—several gallons, in fact. So suspend a large pail under the spile overnight.

Cool the collected sap in your refrigerator and use it as a refreshing drink. Or, as an experiment for the delight of the youngsters in the house, put it into a large pan atop the stove and start it slowly boiling. As the water evaporates, syrup is left behind. The longer the syrup boils, the more concentrated it becomes. You won't want to produce any great amount of syrup this way, but you and your family can have a lot of fun with it.

When you have all the sap you want, remove the spile, whittle a wooden plug and drive it into the hole. The tree will soon heal itself.

Old English superstition: It's bad luck to bring snowdrops into the house before Valentine's Day if unmarried girls in the house hope to be married before the end of the year.

February 15

Today in History: Cyrus McCormick, inventor of the grain reaper, was born on Feb. 15, 1809. His machine greatly reduced hand labor in harvesting grain.

Set Out New Muscadine Grape Vines

Vines of muscadine grapes can be set out any time during the dormant season. These grapes thrive in the region shown by the shaded area of the map. Protect the roots from drying out until the plant is in the ground. Plant about two inches deeper than the vine grew in the nursery. Prune the vine to one strong stem before planting. Shorten the stem to six or eight inches when the vine is in the ground.

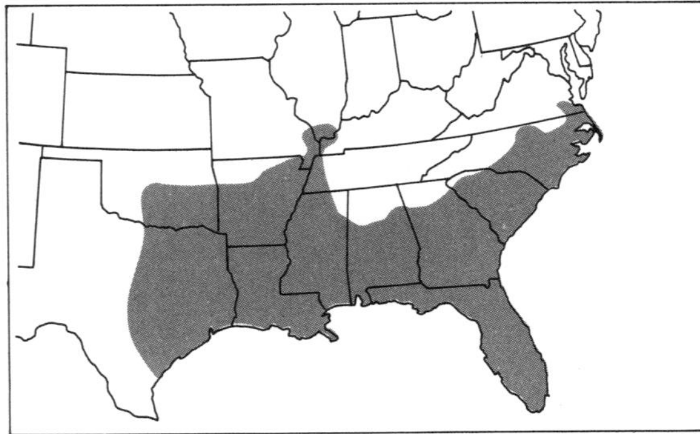

Shaded area shows region where muscadine grapes thrive.

Plant flowering crabapples. The ground should be free of frost now in the middle latitudes of the U.S. As soon as you can dig the hole is an ideal time to plant flowering crabapple trees on your lawn. All species should be planted while dormant.

Flowering crabapples demand a winter rest. They need about 50 cumulative days of under 45 degrees to break their dormancy. Because of this, many varieties do not grow well where winters are mild.

February 16

Let's Build a Bluebird House

Book critic Lewis Gannett once wrote that "a man who never sees a bluebird only half lives." On that basis, very few of us now are more than half alive. A century or more ago John Burroughs asked: "Yonder bluebird with the earth tinge on his breast and the sky tinge on his back—did he come down from heaven?" Throughout his writings, that famous nature chronicler frequently expressed his delight at the physical beauty and plaintive "disembodied voice" of this once-common harbinger of spring,

Sally laughs at everything you say. Why? Because she has fine teeth.—Poor Richard

now so rare that even country dwellers seldom see it.

Henry David Thoreau loved bluebirds, too, and in 1838 made them the subject of one of his poems. It begins:

In the midst of the poplar that stands by our
  door
We planted a bluebird box
And we hoped before the summer was o'er
A transient pair to coax.

The Thoreau nesting box was very successful. On several occasions he mentions it in his Journals for the years that followed.

Building and putting up a nesting box is no guarantee that bluebirds will consent to live on your property. But why not give it a try? You may have to war constantly with house sparrows, for they are of a size to enter the hole that suits the bluebird. A hole no larger than that suggested in the accompanying plans, however, thwarts every attempt of starlings to usurp the box. So why not have a nesting box in place, just in case a "transient pair" comes along? Locate it in a spot as isolated as possible, on a tree or post five to twelve feet from the ground, facing a lawn or other open area to the east or south.

The nesting box shown here couldn't be easier to make. Use any wood 3/4″ thick. Only straight saw cuts are required. Cut one piece 4 1/2″ by 4 1/2″ (bottom), two pieces 6″ by 9 3/4″ (sides), one piece 4 3/8″ by 9 3/4″ (front), one piece 4 1/2″ by 14″ (back), and one piece 7 1/2″ by 8″ (roof). The entrance hole should be 1 5/8″ in diameter and is located 2″ from the top of the front piece to the center of the hole. No perch is needed. Let the roof project at the front and sides. Use 6-penny coated or aluminum nails.

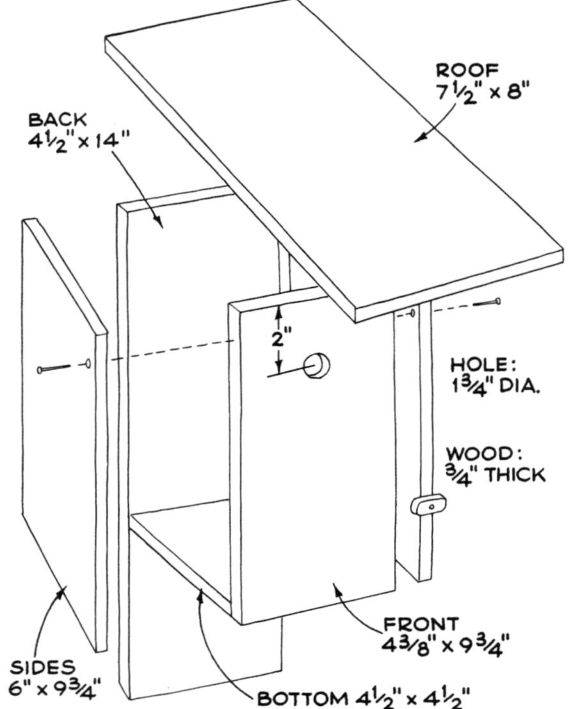

Nesting box for bluebirds.

The projection of the back at the bottom provides space to attach the box against a post or tree. When a post is the proper height, you can also rest the bottom of the box on the post top; nails through the lower part of the back will then hold the box to the post.

Drill oversize holes through the sides for nails that serve as pivots for lifting up the front for cleaning the box. A small turnbutton on the edge of one side will keep the front closed.

Stain the box if you wish, or just let it weather. Do not paint it.

Today in History: A patent was granted Feb. 16, 1937 to Dr. Wallace Hume Carothers for the invention of nylon. It was assigned to DuPont.

Late winter is the time to apply a zinc spray to the leaves of citrus. Mix one ounce of zinc sulfate and one ounce of washing soda per gallon of water. Three to five gallons is enough for most mature trees.

February 17

Order Nursery Stock Soon

Do you like to get valuable items free? Mail-order nurserymen often send along a bonus plant or two to the thoughtful customer who places his order early—in the supplier's slack season. So why not get out the catalogs now and send off your order? The stock will be shipped for arrival at the proper planting time in your region. Meanwhile, as soon as the ground thaws, you can dig the holes the stock will require.

Spring is a good time to propagate citrus trees by budding, especially satsuma tangerines.

February 18

Today in History: Alessandro Volta was born on Feb. 18, 1845, in Como, Italy. He invented the electric battery. The volt is named for him.

Are Your Electrical Cords Safe?

Safety associations urge that home owners check all electrical cords twice a year. So today let's review what this involves. Six months hence, your Almanac will remind you to make the year's second checkup.

Sound reasons can be listed for this program. Electrical codes apply in all regions, and inspectors certify that home wiring meets safety regulations up to the wall outlets. As manufactured, electrical appliances or lamps carry approval of the Underwriters' Laboratories (UL). But the connections from the wall outlets to the appliances—the flexible cords—are *your* responsibility.

As first installed, the cords more than likely are fully safe. But the wear and tear of constant use can bring about conditions dangerous to you and other members of your family.

When it is necessary to replace a cord, select one designed to do the job you want done. Make it a rule to choose a cord with replacement wire of the same size, or heavier, and insulation equal to or better than the old cord. And remember always to look for the UL label when you buy a length of cord, a cord set, or an appliance with cord attached.

In your semiannual checkup, go over each cord for visible breaks in the insulating covering. If you find a break, do not delay making repairs. Disconnect the cord from the outlet first. If a fabric cord covering is frayed, use matching thread to wrap the frayed section. When you discover worn spots in a rubber or plastic cord, separate the conductors and wrap each one separately from end to end of the break with plastic electrical tape. Finally, tape the two together with the same type of tape. Or you can wrap the wires separately with rubber tape and end up with a wrapping of friction tape.

When an actual break occurs in one of the conductors, replace the entire cord. The national electrical code requires that flexible cords "be used in continuous lengths without splice or tap." If a cord is too short, do not splice it. Get a new one that is long enough—but no longer than necessary.

In your initial cord review, ask yourself whether some cords are longer than they need be. Or are you using several extension cords? Both situations indicate that your home may need additional convenience outlets. The electrical code stipulates that flexible cord should not "be used as a substitute for the fixed wiring of a structure." The code also prohibits running cords "through doorways, windows, or similar openings." Install fixed wiring and outlets.

A cord run under a rug is a fire hazard. Again, this can be avoided by proper additions to the house wiring.

In addition to inspecting each cord throughout its length, check the plug at one end and the connections to the lamp or appliance at the other. Insecure or loose connections at the screws are hazardous. Make sure they are tight and properly insulated. If you do not have the time to make the necessary repair now, take the cord or appliance out of service. Affix a tag to it:

NOT TO BE USED UNTIL REPAIRED.

Grow your own vegetable plants—tomato, cabbage, head lettuce, etc.? Seed your flats now in Spring Regions III and IV. And how about starting some flowers indoors? See the April 2 map. Start seedlings if your frostfree date is about April 15.

Your Own Reminders

Week of Feb. 12–18

February 19

Today in History: The phonograph was patented on Feb. 19, 1878, by Thomas A. Edison. The first recording on the cylinder machine was "Mary Had a Little Lamb."

Plant Vegetables Now in California?

The answer to that question depends on where you live in the state. Lying north and south, California spans so many degrees of latitude that planting times within its borders can vary almost as much as for the U.S. as a whole. The altitude range of its deserts and mountains also results in seasons moving vertically (or sideways) as well as north and south. Nevertheless, agricultural scientists in the state have managed to tabulate planting times that you can go by. This table is given at the back of the book as Appendix K.

Vegetables listed are divided into cool-weather and warm-weather crops. Run your finger down that column and you will find that a good number of cool-weather crops can be planted at about this time of the year. But since the climate may vary even in small sections of the state, you should bear in mind that planting dates are only approximate.

Californians can get cultivation and other details about crops listed in the table. Obtain a copy of "Home Vegetable Gardening" (Circular 499) from the Extension Service or county agent.

Spring meadow saffron, glory-of-the-snow, crocus, winter aconite, dwarf iris, and snowflake are among the spring-flowering bulbs that can be expected to blossom soon. Plant some next fall if you have none.

Prune American bunch grapes in the northern areas where low winter temperatures sometimes damage the vines. Cut away damaged canes and shape up uninjured ones for fruiting. See November 23 for details.

February 20

Moisture Condensing in the Attic?

Does your home have a moisture problem? The cold weather now is a good time to find out. Visit whatever unfinished attic space you have. Look over the rafters. Put your finger to the ends of roofing nails protruding through the sheathing. Peer into the dark recesses along the eaves.

Chances are you will find moisture, perhaps frozen into frost or icicles. You may even find a lot of it.

Where does the moisture come from? From each of the many moisture-producers in any home—a shower bath, a steaming teakettle or cooking pot, your clothes and dish washers, moisture in the basement (in many homes), or from bare ground in a crawl space. Excess moisture may even come from a humidifier installed for the comfort and health of the house occupants when the air is deemed too dry.

Warm air inside a house absorbs moisture as vapor. Open a bottle of perfume in a room where the air is still and you soon will find you can detect the fragrance in every part of the room. Water vapor spreads uniformly throughout a house in the same way. Vapor equalizes its pressure by moving from an area of high concentration to one of lower concentration.

In winter, cold air outside a house holds much less moisture than the warm air inside. The vapor pressure inside is greater than out. Water vapor inside therefore seeks to find its way to the cold outdoor air. The water vapor exerts an outward pressure just like steam.

When the moisture-laden air comes into contact with cold outer surfaces of a house, it first loses heat. It then loses moisture through condensation. In the attic, the wood sheathing of an uninsulated roof may be so cold that ice or frost forms on it, exactly as frost forms on the freezing coils of a refrigerator.

Any signs of condensation in an attic indicate that all is not well elsewhere in the house.

Older homes seldom had a condensation problem. They were so loosely built that the exchange of inside and outside air through cracks and around doors and windows removed excessive water vapor. When there is no insulation, outside walls are relatively warm and condensation may not occur.

Condensation develops when improved building practices keep warm moist air from leaking out of the house. This condensation may occur *within* the walls of a house that has insulation without a vapor barrier. Common visible evidences are water spots on the walls and ceilings, peeling exterior paint, and deterioration of structural materials. A vapor barrier is now commonly installed inside the insulation in new construction to prevent such damage.

What can you do right now if you discover attic condensation? Ventilate. What about the attic itself? If it is open and unheated, louvers and vents should remain open all year—in the summer to remove excess heat and in the winter to carry away water vapor and prevent its condensation. If all attic vents are already open, perhaps you need to add more. A rule of thumb: For gable roofs, have a square foot of inlet and a square foot of outlet ventilation area for each 300 square feet of attic floor; for flat roofs, double the ventilation area. Keeping the roof area colder will also help prevent ice dams.

Simply opening a window occasionally, or at night while you are asleep, will also help keep excess household moisture under control. Just let it out—like the cat. You may also want to consider ventilating fans—in the attic, bathrooms, and kitchen—if you do not already have them, or improved ones if they are not now doing their job.

Vent kitchen and bathroom fans to the outside, not into the attic. Laundry equipment also should be vented. After the laundry is done, the house should be aired out.

February 21

Let's Think About Pesticides

Misuse of pesticides has helped create some of our ecological problems. There's no doubt about that. Yet we still need some pesticides and there is no good reason we should not use them if we do so in a safe manner.

Whatever you do, keep in mind—all the time—one fact: Pesticides kill! Certain pesticides are just as likely to fulfill that function against you, or one of your children, as against the insect pests that prompt you to buy the stuff.

Before you buy, check the label. Make sure the pesticide is intended for the pest you want to control. Make sure, too, that you will be able to apply it in a safe manner.

What you buy depends on your problem. Through this book you will find many suggestions that it's time to spray for this or that. Find out what to use from your state Extension Service. Recommendations keep changing, often for the better ecologically.

Store pesticides in well-labeled containers, where children or pets cannot reach them. Do not place them near food or feed. Do not store them under the sink, in the pantry, or in the medicine cabinet.

Always leave pesticides in the original containers. Be sure the labels remain on them. If a pesticide is marked "POISON," it will have an antidote statement on the label. Read it. In case of accident, take the container with you when seeking medical assistance.

Read the label and determine the right amount of the right pesticide to use. Overdosage may leave a harmful residue on fruits and vegetables.

Be careful not to get pesticides on food, dishes, or cooking utensils. Remove pets and their food and water pans before applying pesticides. Keep people, particularly children, away from areas where you are mixing or applying pesticides. Dilute or mix sprays outdoors or in a well ventilated place.

When the label warns against it, be sure to avoid breathing pesticidal dusts or mists. Keep your face away from, and to one side of, the cap when opening a container.

Handle liquid concentrates and oil-base sprays as though they were flammable.

Place poison bait out of reach of children and pets. (Baits for rats, ants, and roaches account for a high percentage of the cases of accidental swallowing of pesticides by children under 12 years of age.)

Do not use a pesticide in the home if the label says a gas mask is required in its application.

In handling any pesticide, avoid prolonged contact with the skin. Use protective equipment if the label recommends it. Avoid excessive contamination of clothing when spraying.

Do not use your mouth to blow out clogged lines, nozzle tips, or other equipment parts, or to siphon a pesticide from a container.

When spraying or dusting pets, be sure pesticide is labeled for such use.

Do not smoke while handling pesticides. Wait until you have washed your hands.

Apply pesticides only to the plants listed on the label.

Do not apply pesticides near dug wells where they might contaminate the drinking water.

Wash with soap and water and change clothing immediately if you spill a pesticide concentrate on skin or clothing. If you get a concentrate in your eyes, flush them with plenty of water for 15 minutes and get medical attention.

If you accidentally swallow some pesticide, or if you feel ill effects after using it, call your physician at once. Read the label to him, naming the active chemical ingredient. Follow any antidote instructions on the label.

Today in History: The Washington Monument was dedicated on Feb. 21, 1885. The cornerstone had been laid on July 4, 1848.

February 22

Hail to George W! It's Still His Birthday

The COMPLEAT DISSENTER

Poor George Washington! There's a problem again about his birthday. When he was born in 1732, the old-style (O. S.) calendar was still in use and the future hatchet boy made his debut on February 11. Then they changed the calendar, and George's birthday became February 22, the holiday we long have celebrated.

Now that holiday is in peril. Advocates of three-day weekends—a fine practice, indeed!—have gotten everyone to agree that there'll be a Presidents' Day, a floating date, to create a three-day weekend between Lincoln's Birthday (February 12) and Washington's.

So what do we do about February 22? Forget it? Not much! Let's celebrate it—and Presidents' Day too. The more the merrier when it comes to raising a cheer—or a glass—to a very, very remarkable man.

February 23

Prune Established Clematis Vines

Late winter or early spring is the time to prune a well established Sweet Autumn or Japanese Clematis (*Clematis paniculta*) for complete renewal of the top. This is one of several late-blooming vines that kill back somewhat, even in mild winters. So before full spring arrives cut it almost to the ground. From this stump will grow as great or even greater vine coverage than you had the previous year. If the vine is used as a porch screen, the growth will be effective by July 15 in the Northeast.

Silvervine Fleeceflower (*Polygonum aubertic*) is another vine that may be treated this way.

February 24

Repairing Window Shades

A window shade should move up firmly and without delay when you give the pull cord a tug. A coiled spring inside revolves the roller when centrifugal force releases and holds out the pawls at the flat-pin end. If the shade moves sluggishly, the spring needs retensioning. Take down the entire shade by first slipping the flat pin from its locking bracket and then pull the round pin free. Roll the fabric up completely by hand and put the shade back in its brackets. If you then find it too tight, take it down again and unroll a few turns of the fabric.

While you have it down, check the pawls to see that they work freely. Apply a dry lubricant to them every year or so. If a shade won't roll up at all, the spring probably is broken. Find out by removing the end cap and pulling out the entire spring assembly. A new roller is the best repair for a broken spring. A good idea: keep an entire roller on hand for parts.

If a bent round pin causes a roller to wobble, straighten it with pliers or substitute a nail of about the same diameter and length. Withdraw the pin slightly or replace it with a long nail if a new or substitute roller doesn't quite reach between existing brackets on a window. When a shade works in brackets on the outer face of a window casing, you can reset one of the brackets to suit the roller's length. When a roller is too long for a particular window, saw off some of the round-pin end and replace the end cap and pin on the new end surface. Use a razor blade (or utility knife) and a straightedge to trim enough from one side of the shade so it will fit between the end caps of the shortened roller.

For a shade inside the casing, measure the opening and subtract one-eighth of an inch to find the tip-to-tip dimension (including the end pins). For an installation outside the casing, measure the opening and add three inches for an overlap at each side. To determine the length of shade needed, measure the window opening from top to bottom and add eight inches. Attach a new shade to the roller with a strip of tape.

February 25

Replacing Wood Tool Handles

Here is a useful cold-day activity for this time of year. Well-stocked hardware stores have a new handle to fit the tool that needs attention. Take along the old one, or even the entire tool, to help you find a match. However, you must expect to do some trimming for a snug fit.

The handle replacement procedure is much the same for hammer, hatchet, axe, or sledge. Saw off the broken handle close to the tool head. Then try to tap the handle end out of the eye. If you can't, drill into the eye several times with a metal bit and then work out the remaining wood. Never burn out the old handle stump.

Trim the new handle with plane, rasp, or sander until you can drive it into the eye. Drive-fitting will leave a slight glaze on high spots, showing where to trim it further.

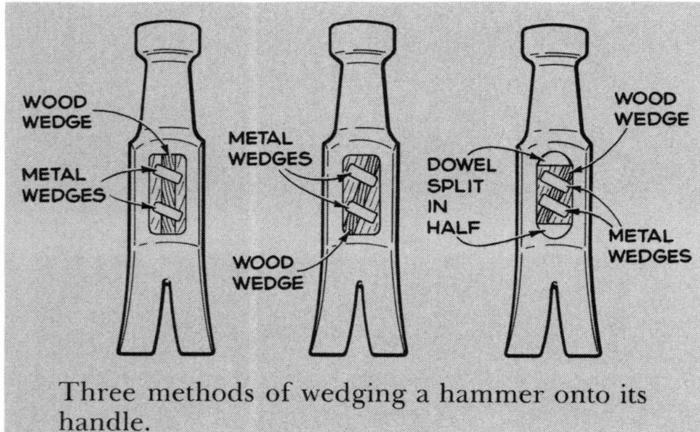

Three methods of wedging a hammer onto its handle.

Before you drive the handle in finally, decide which wedging method you will use. See the sketches. Make a saw kerf about 1½ inches deep into the end of the handle for the wooden wedge. Some dealers include wood and metal wedges free with new handles. If not, you may be able to use the old metal ones and shape a wooden wedge from a piece of hardwood. Drive it in, cut it off flush, and then drive in the metal wedges with a mallet. When the tool has a rounded tapered eye, saw a suitable dowel lengthwise, then fit and glue each half into the opening as shown in the sketch. Insert wood and metal wedges as described for the other heads.

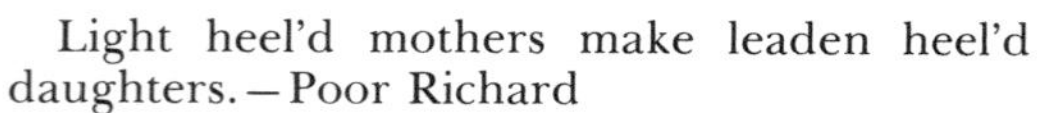

Light heel'd mothers make leaden heel'd daughters.—Poor Richard

Your Own Reminders

Week of Feb. 19–25

February 26

Time to Force Forsythia and Other Plants Indoors

You can bring an advance touch of spring into your home right now if you have a forsythia bush or two. Cut a bouquet of the bud-bearing canes, put the stems into a large vase

filled with water in a warm part of the house, and in about a week the yellow blossoms will begin to develop. For a succession of blossoms, make new cuttings every ten days until the shrub begins to bloom outdoors.

The dormant period is the approved time for pruning forsythia. So you can prune as you cut the bouquets. Old wood should all be thinned out of this shrub every two or three years in order to encourage new growth within the bush. Remove new growth as necessary to open up the center.

Other blossoms that you can force this way include flowering quince, pussy willow, redbud, magnolia, apple, pear, cherry, and peach.

Today in History: William F. Cody, who gained fame as Buffalo Bill, was born Feb. 26, 1846, in Scott County, Iowa.

February 27

Today in History: Henry Wadsworth Longfellow, one of America's first great poets, was born on Feb. 27, 1807, in Portland, Maine.

A SHADOW

I said unto myself, if I were dead,
What would befall these children? What would be
Their fate, who now are looking up to me
For help and furtherance? Their lives, I said,
Would be a volume wherein I have read
But the first chapters, and no longer see
To read the rest of their dear history,
So full of beauty and so full of dread.
Be comforted; the world is very old,
And generations pass, as they have passed,
A troop of shadows moving with the sun;
Thousands of times has the old tale been told;
The world belongs to those who come the last,
They will find hope and strength as we have done.

—Henry W. Longfellow (1875)

Renew Leggy Rhododendrons and Azaleas

Do you have a rhododendron or some azaleas that have become too tall and leggy? You can renew the top by pruning during the winter or very early spring before growth starts.

Spread the renewal over several years. The first year select about a third of the trunks, spacing them throughout the plant. Cut these back to about eight inches or a foot from the ground. Dormant buds below will send up new growth. The next year do another third of the plant, and so on.

Interested in adding a magnolia to your plantings? Better buy and plant it soon.

February 28

Dig or Buy Winter-Sweetened Parsnips

Winter-sweetened parsnips should be available in your vegetable markets soon if not now. The flavor of this root vegetable greatly improves with prolonged exposure to temperatures below 40 degrees. Oldtimers accomplished this by leaving their crop right in the ground over winter, a practice you might want to adopt nowadays. Plant seed this spring and your crop will be ready for digging a year from now. Dig up all the roots before the tops start to grow.

Salsify, or oyster plant, is another easily-grown garden root crop that you can treat the same way.

February 29

This is Leap-Year Day

Single girls take heed. This is the day for you to go after that man you do not have. It is a rare day indeed. Normally, it comes only each four years—in those years that can be divided evenly by four. But there is an exception to that rule: the years that begin a new century. Only the century years that you can divide by 400 are leap years. That means that the year 2000 will come up as a leap year, whereas the year 1900 was not.

Leap years were added to the calendar year to make the calendar year approximately equal to the solar year.

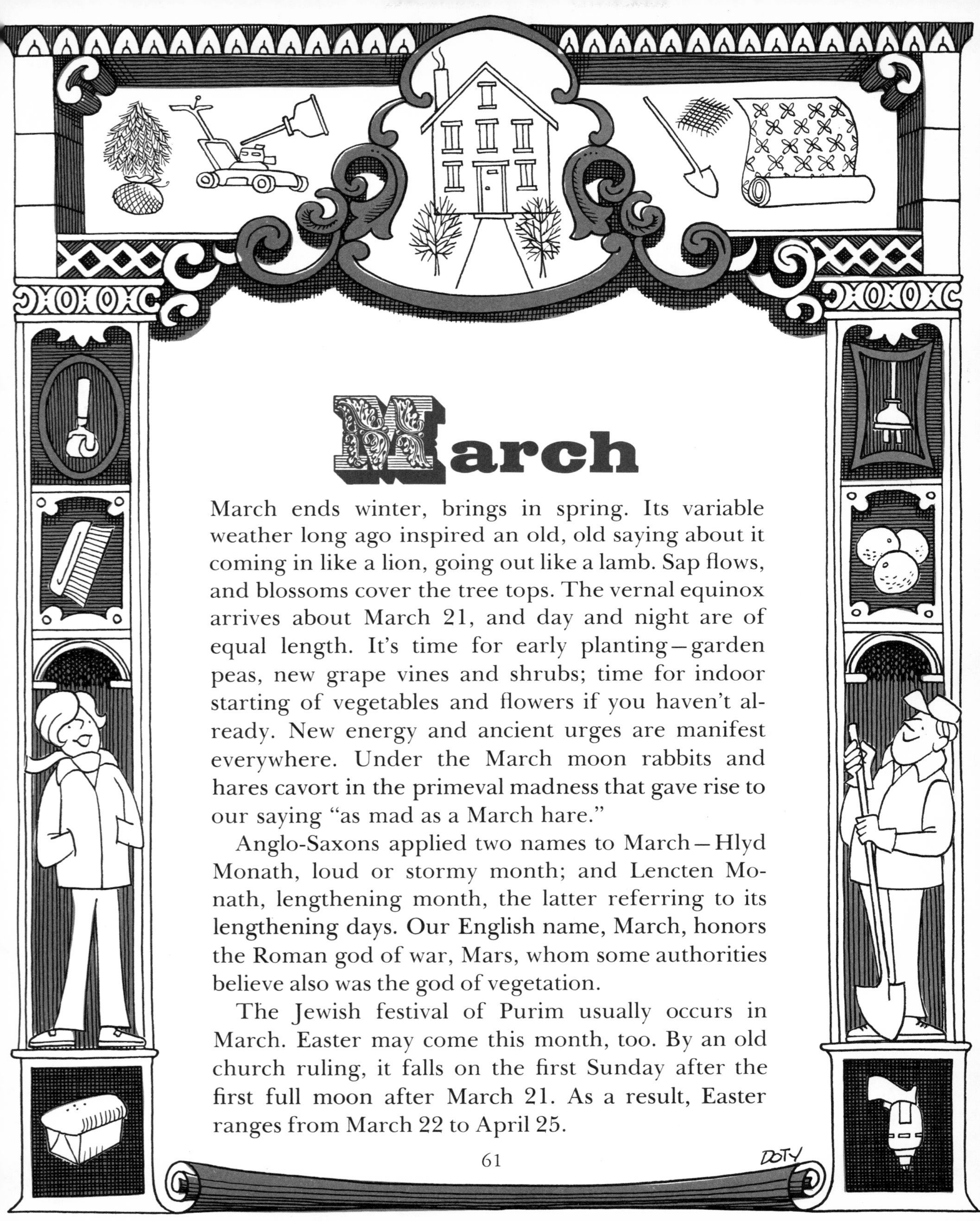

March

March ends winter, brings in spring. Its variable weather long ago inspired an old, old saying about it coming in like a lion, going out like a lamb. Sap flows, and blossoms cover the tree tops. The vernal equinox arrives about March 21, and day and night are of equal length. It's time for early planting—garden peas, new grape vines and shrubs; time for indoor starting of vegetables and flowers if you haven't already. New energy and ancient urges are manifest everywhere. Under the March moon rabbits and hares cavort in the primeval madness that gave rise to our saying "as mad as a March hare."

Anglo-Saxons applied two names to March—Hlyd Monath, loud or stormy month; and Lencten Monath, lengthening month, the latter referring to its lengthening days. Our English name, March, honors the Roman god of war, Mars, whom some authorities believe also was the god of vegetation.

The Jewish festival of Purim usually occurs in March. Easter may come this month, too. By an old church ruling, it falls on the first Sunday after the first full moon after March 21. As a result, Easter ranges from March 22 to April 25.

March 1

Choosing Trees for the Curbside

The space between the sidewalk and curb in front and perhaps also the side of your house is an important part of your living environment. Trees and shrubs there can screen out undesirable sights and muffle street noises. A local governmental agency may select and care for plantings there. If not, it's up to you—as part of the general landscaping of your property.

A good street tree is one that gives shade and ornamentation, does not interfere with vehicular or pedestrian traffic, and stays healthy. A street tree must be tough. It must withstand adverse effects of automobile and industrial fumes, lawn mowers, sewer and utility lines, and sidewalk and street paving. The health of a tree depends on the extent and effectiveness of its feeder roots. Some trees have such extensive root systems that you should keep them away from water and sewer lines. Among these are red and silver maples, willow, elm, and poplar.

What trees can you safely plant in this hostile strip of ground? Your local parks department, if you have one, can probably help. Or your county agent.

Today in History: An act of Congress on March 1, 1872 authorized establishment of Yellowstone National Park.

Apply a dressing of well-rotted manure around grape vines to keep up the organic matter in the soil.

Figs can be propagated by cuttings taken in late winter from the previous season's growth. Make cuttings 8 to 10 inches long, making the base cut just below a joint or node. Plant in the garden or a container with only the top bud showing. Water sparingly.

March 2

Tips on Taking Care of Electrical Cords

Are the electrical cords in your home receiving the care they deserve? The treatment they get while in use—and in storage—has an important bearing on how long they will remain safe. (See February 18.) It's a good idea to check up on this and see that everyone understands the rules.

Have you arranged so that the cords are stored in a cool, dry place? Are all kinks straightened out before they are wound loosely on a holder? Perhaps you'll want to put up a suitable holder. This might be a large thread spool or an

adhesive-tape spool, nailed on a closet wall; large rounded wooden pegs, or two large hooks. Wind cords loosely to protect the fine wires of the conductors and lengthen the useful life of the cords. Wrapping cords tightly may loosen the connections and eventually break the insulation and wires.

To protect cords while in use, keep them free of kinks, knots, and sharp bends, which tend to break the fine wires and insulation. Avoid cutting or scraping the insulation over sharp edges. Keep cords free of oil or grease. These are harmful to rubber insulation and covering.

Keep the cord out of a vacuum cleaner's path. On an upright vacuum cleaner, loop the cord loosely and hang it from the top hook of the cord holder when not in use.

Overheating may soften the insulation or cause it to stiffen or crack. Keep cords away from heaters and heated appliances. Do not set a hot pan on or close to an appliance cord. When ironing, avoid touching the cord with the heated iron. Be sure the appliance is cool if you wrap the cord around it.

Today in History: This is Texas Independence Day. While Santa Ana was besieging the Alamo, a conference of Texans on March 2, 1836, declared Texas independent of Mexico.

March 3

Is Your Flashing Adequate?

Flashing on the exterior of a house has one important function: to keep out rain and melting snow. If flashing is missing at any point where good construction practice calls for it, moisture may seep in and eventually cause wood decay. Sheet copper and aluminum are commonly used. Aluminum is the least expensive. It also is nonstaining.

Why not make it a custom each March to check over all of your house flashing before the April rains come?

On a roof, flashing should go around any openings—a chimney and bathroom or other vent pipes. It also is frequently placed in the valleys at the juncture of two roof slopes at right angles to each other. A strip of flashing along the lower edge of a roof under the first course of finish roofing helps keep water from backing up under the roofing if ice dams form in the winter. Flashing also is called for where a shed roof meets the siding of the main house.

Today in History: An act of Congress signed by President Hoover on March 3, 1931, designated "The Star Spangled Banner" as the national anthem. Francis Scott Key wrote the words during the War of 1812. See the entry for September 14 in your Almanac if you'd like to review the words of this inspiring song.

In the latter case, the flashing should fit up under the bottom edge of the first row of siding; the lower edge of flashing should spread over the finish roofing for several inches. At a chimney the upper edge of flashing should be embedded in the chimney mortar. Inspect flashing at this spot periodically to see that the mortar has not crumbled away, allowing water to go behind the flashing. Repairs can be made with a bituminous roofing cement.

March 4

Today in History: On March 4, 1801, the first President was inaugurated in the new capital city of Washington, D.C. He was Thomas Jefferson. March 4 continued as inauguration day until 1937.

California adopted plant quarantine legislation on March 4, 1881 to control shipments of fruit and fruit trees. The act was aimed at an insect (*Phylloxera vastatrix*) that had infested Sonoma Valley grapevines and at the San Jose scale (see February 13) and the codling moth, the latter both serious apple pests.

Rules for Home Landscaping

Will you put in new shrubs or other plantings this spring? Before you do, it may pay you to review some of the principles of good landscaping.

Landscaping should improve the natural setting of your home. Without landscaping, the contrasts between the horizontal lines of the ground and the vertical lines of the house are too abrupt. Landscaping makes use of shrubs and trees to give a gradual transition between nature and home. The irregular shapes of plant material break the straight lines of house and ground.

When planning your landscaping, approach the house as a unit. While you may intend to install only portions of the landscaping now, design the job as a whole.

Keep in mind that most plants look best in groups of three or more. This does not apply to accent shrubs or large shade trees.

You may use many kinds of trees and shrubs, but select those that are harmonious when used together. Relate their mature size to the size of your home. Use very low plantings for a ranch house, taller ones for a two-story house. Below windows, put in plantings that never will grow above the sills.

Corner plantings provide transition between the sharp vertical corner of the house and open space beyond. Extend the planting beyond the corner to give an appearance of greater width. Use a grouping curved around the corner. At corners use trees or shrubs that will grow higher than the eaves.

The front entrance is often a good place to use an unusual plant that will create a focal point for your home. If you have a large porch or entrance area, you may wish to use several potted trees or shrubs. Potted perennials, changed seasonally, can provide vivid splashes of color.

Your Own Reminders

Week of Feb. 26–March 4

March 5

Choosing the Right Trees

Trees must be carefully chosen to fit the landscaping described yesterday. Perhaps your home is a new one and you still need to evolve a landscaping plan. Or maybe you already have a plan but still need to fill in some of the details. Either way, this March day is a fine time to make some decisions so you can order what you will plant this spring.

The trees you choose, first of all, must suit the region in which you live. No banana trees in Maine. A local nursery is one of your best sources. If you order by mail, buy from a mail-order house that starts the trees in a climate similar to yours. Stick to trees that are *reliably* hardy in your area. Trees native to the North may die in summer heat in the South. Trees planted north of their adapted range are sure to be killed when an especially severe winter comes along.

Know where you will plant a tree before you buy it. After deciding to stick to trees hardy in your area, this is your most important rule: Will the tree's mature height suit the spot where you set it? And what about its form? A spreading form may be okay in an open area. Tall slim trees are best along a driveway or between the sidewalk and curb. And avoid trees with undesirable characteristics—objectionable fruit or nut droppings on walkways, susceptibility to specific diseases or insect attacks, blossoms with nose-turning odors.

Growth rate is another factor to consider. Some trees grow rapidly, giving shade and screening in only a few years. They reach maturity quickly, then decline. Will this decline and need for removal affect you? Plant a tree with a 40-year life expectancy when you are 25, and you may lose its shade just as you retire at 65.

Because curbside trees have special problems, they need their own day in this Almanac. See the entry for March 1.

Today in History: A patent was issued on March 5, 1872, to George Westinghouse for a "triple air brake" for railroad trains. His original brake, patented April 13, 1869, caused each car to brake later than the one ahead of it. The new version corrected this fault.

If you notice leaf yellowing on such plants as pyracantha, roses, or gardenia, apply a little iron sulfate.

March 6

You Can Patch Torn Wallpaper

If you have wallpaper in your home, what's its condition? Does it look beat up from tears and smudges that don't come off? If you saved part of a roll when it was put on—always a good idea—you still may be able to get more service from it by applying patches over the torn or dirty areas.

The secret of an inconspicuous wallpaper patch is a torn edge, not one cut with scissors. Tearing usually leaves a thin edge that you can paste down so it is hardly noticeable at a distance.

Select an area in your spare roll where the design will match that of the spot you want to cover. Tear out this area in any shape that happens to result. Test fit it to the wall to make sure you see where you must place it. Then apply wallpaper paste (or white glue) thinly to the back of the patch. Position it carefully so that the design of the patch matches the original paper exactly. Press it down firmly by drawing the edge of a ruler outward toward all edges. Remove all excess paste immediately with a moist sponge. The patch will soon dry.

You may find that the original paper on the wall has faded or otherwise changed color or tone from the patch. But give the latter time and it will gradually blend in.

March 7

Today in History: A patent for the telephone was granted on March 7, 1876, to Alexander Graham Bell. Bell was born on March 3, 1842, in Edinburgh, Scotland.

Luther Burbank was born on March 7, 1849. He developed many new plants.

Want to Plant Boxwood?

Early spring, just after the ground thaws enough for easy digging, is a logical time to plant boxwood. At that time, the shrub should still be dormant.

Although many consider boxwood mostly a southern shrub, it will thrive surprisingly far north. Common and English box grow best in Zone 7 of the U.S. plant hardiness map. (See Appendix B.) Japanese box grows to the north in Zone 6 and the even hardier Korean box does nicely in the southernmost parts of Zone 5. Zones 4 and lower are too cold and Zone 10 is too hot for any box varieties. Boxwood culture is almost impossible in regions where temperatures drop to 10 below zero.

Water a new planting thoroughly. Direct a slow flow of water under the crown. Continue watering until the ball is wet through. Build a low ridge around the plant to conserve water.

Shade the box for a year after planting, using a lattice that cuts off about half the light. Place the lattice at least 10 inches from the foliage.

March 8

Plan Now to Plant Evergreens

Make plans now for planting or transplanting any evergreens that you want as ornamental or foundation plantings. One of the best times of the year for doing this is in the spring just after the frost is out of the ground.

That time has now arrived in the South and along both coasts—in Spring Zones I and II and some parts of III. The ground has thawed, and is workable, as much as a month before the date of the final killing frosts.

The reason for planting early: you want the plant to develop the strongest possible root system before hot weather sets in. All evergreens give off water throughout the year. Unless a good root system has developed, hot weather may damage the young tree.

This applies to both narrow-leaved and broad-leaved evergreens. Narrow-leaved evergreens include pine, spruce, fir, juniper, arborvitae, and false cypress. Horticulturists divide broad-leaved evergreens into two groups. All members of each group have the same cultural requirements. The ericaceous group includes such plants as rhododendron, andromeda, and mountain laurel. Many azaleas lose their leaves each winter but their care is the same as for this group of broad-leaved evergreens. Most of this group require cool, acid soil, high in humus.

The second group, the non-ericaceous group, will do well in less acid soil. This group includes Oregon-grape, American holly, and boxwood. Your county agent can give you information about testing the soil where you want to place any of these plants.

To plant, dig a hole at least a foot greater in diameter than the balled roots of the evergreen. Place at the same depth the plant grew in the nursery. Never add fertilizer or fresh manure to the soil returned to the hole. Root injury may result. For shallow-rooted plants such as azaleas, add two or three inches of mulch after planting. Water well, soaking fully around the ball.

Flower blight is one of the most damaging diseases of camellias. It was first reported in 1938 near San Francisco. It has now spread out of California to Oregon, Georgia, Louisiana, North Carolina, South Carolina, Florida, Texas, Virginia, and probably other southern states. Your county agent can tell you how to overcome it.

Seed of some perennials (pinks, delphiniums, and columbines) can be sown in cold frames in the North for blooms later this year.

Dormant pruning of roses is now overdue in the northern parts of Spring Region I. See January 5.

The danger of a spring frost has just about passed for those who live in Region I. See the February 8 map.

Bush fruits such as raspberries, blackberries, dewberries, blueberries, currants, and gooseberries might be planted as soon as the ground can be worked in regions where such fruits thrive. In some cases, locally suitable varieties must be chosen.

March 9

Does Your Toilet Tank Leak?

Water constantly drains out of the toilet tanks and down through the toilet bowls in some homes—and no one is the wiser. How about yours?

To test for such leakage, dry off the inner surface of the toilet bowl above the rear edge of the trapped water, using a wad of tissues. Then press a dry piece of tissue against that surface, being careful to place it above the level of the trapped water. Does the tissue soon become damp? Yes? Then you're losing water from the tank. A faint humming sound also may indicate leakage.

The water may be escaping either through the flush system or the water-supply system in the tank. Check the flush system first. Is there a slimy coating on the rubber stopper that drops into the discharge opening when the toilet is flushed? Wipe off the slime. Also shut off the water to the tank, flush it, and clean the sloping inner surface of the opening with a soapy cloth. Then rub the inner face with emery cloth to remove any built-up scale and make the seat smooth again. Next, make sure the rubber stopper is not deformed (replace it if so) and that it drops squarely into the flush opening. Finally, put the toilet back into service—and give the bowl the tissue test again.

If water still is flowing, check out the water-inlet system, the one controlled by the float ball that rises and falls with the changing water level in the tank. (Note that the water charge in the tank can be varied by bending the float-ball arm either up or down. However, do not let the level rise so high that water flows into the top of the open overflow pipe—the large pipe to which the flush-opening stopper is suspended. That, in itself, would permit a constant loss of water.)

Holes sometimes rust through the float ball and let it become water-logged. In that condition, it may not be shutting off the inlet valve located at the end of its arm. Replacement of such a ball is usually best.

When float pressure fails to shut the inlet valve, the washer may be worn, its seat pitted, or the plunger jammed by rust or scale. To change washers turn out the thumbscrews that hold the plunger lever and lift the plunger out of the cylinder along with the lever assembly. Inspect leather shutoff pad on plunger's end and leather ring in groove around its middle. Check linkage holes for out-of-round wear. Look into the valve to inspect the seat for scale or roughness.

If the inlet-valve seat is rough, it can be reached for smoothing with fine emery cloth by unscrewing the valve body. If smoothing doesn't help and the leather ring or pad on the end of the plunger is worn, unscrew the entire assembly from the flange at the bottom of the tank and replace it. Some plungers have leather end washers that can be changed like faucet washers. On this type, a center washer is used instead of a ring.

Today in History: A patent for artificial teeth was granted to Charles M. Graham, of New York City, on March 9, 1822.

Fertilize young grape plants now. Apply half a pound of 5-10-5 around each plant. Begin about six inches from the plant and apply in a ring several feet wide. Plants in sandy soil may need more nitrogen. When the plant is fully established, after about four years, double the amount of fertilizer applied at this time of the year.

Prune currants and gooseberries each spring to keep the bushes vigorous. Cut away all stems four years or more older.

Apply plenty of water to new citrus trees set out this year.

Start flower seedlings at once if you live in the southern half of the U.S. See the April 2 map.

March 10

Do Your Floors Sag?

If you don't already know, you can quickly find out whether a wood floor sags in the middle. Tack a strong cord to the floor near one wall. Stretch it as taut as you can and tack it to the floor at the opposite wall. Do your fingers slip under the string at the center of the room without touching it? They will in many homes.

Doors that are difficult to open and close, distorted baseboards, and cracked walls and ceilings are also usually signs of floor settling.

Floors develop sags for several reasons. The joists may be too light for the distance they span. The central girder on which the joists rest also may be too light or this girder, if made of wood, may have shrunk enough to cause the sag. Posts or columns supporting the girder may have settled because the footings under them were inadequate for the load.

When you can get underneath—as in an unfinished basement or crawl space—an adjustable steel post will enable you to raise the floor to its original level. These posts, which operate as screw jacks, are available from hardware stores in several lengths. If you wish, you can use the post only to raise the floor and then install a wood post in place of it.

A firm base is required for the new support. The usual basement floor will do nicely. But if there's any doubt about it, the concrete should be broken away, the ground excavated, and a new broad-based concrete footing poured. Build this to a height of about three inches above the original floor. Keep new concrete damp for a week or so to cure it.

When you want to raise sagging joists, place a heavy beam across about six of them and center the jack post under it. This beam could be made of two lengths of three-by-eights, one on top of the other. Set the jack post in place and plumb it with a level held vertically against the side. Turn the jack post up slowly, a quarter turn every day until the floor sag has been removed. A girder can be raised in the same way, but you won't need a supporting beam under it, of course. When the girder has been made level, you may find that the original posts along its length need hardwood shims at the top to make everything snug.

Fertilize mature pecan trees about this time. Broadcast fertilizer evenly from the trunk to two or three feet beyond the branch spread. Use 1½ pounds of ammonium sulfate for each inch of trunk diameter, measured a foot above the soil line.

Watch pines for sawflies and spray when you see them.

Watch winter-mulched perennial flowers. As soon as growth starts, remove the mulch. Plan to apply a new one later in the season.

Boxwood needs lots of water—the equivalent of an inch of rain every ten days. Starting now, make up any deficiency in rainfall by watering every ten days. Continue until midsummer.

Replace furnace filters now if clogged.

March 11

Order Manure Soon for Garden Plot

In areas where you can buy animal manure, it is not too early to contract for a load to be delivered for use on a garden plot.

As in the old days, horse manure can be one of the best. Horses have increased in numbers lately and a riding stable in your vicinity may be a source of supply, sometimes even without cost except for carting. Chicken farms also may offer manure free.

Stable manure varies in quality depending on the bedding used. Avoid sawdust bedding if you can; the unrotted wood waste can be harmful to a garden by encouraging fungus growth. Straw or peat moss beddings are best.

Whatever manure you get, compost it before use. Put it in piles, apply water, and mix soil with it as you turn it every week or so. Mix poultry manure with an equal bulk of oil as you work it over. The piles are ready for use when no longer warm to the touch at the center.

Treat rabbit manure the same as poultry manure. Sheep manure is available in bags, dried and shredded. Use it sparingly.

Check your frostfree date. If it has passed you can plant tubers of the fragrant tuberose in the southern latitudes. Plant new ones each year for reliable blooms.

Encourage bushy growth by nipping the tops of snapdragon and stock plants in the warmer regions.

New citrus and avocado trees can be planted now in coastal and low desert areas.

Along California and southern coasts you can begin planting seed of flowering annual vines.

Spray spruce trees for gall aphids before new growth appears.

Your Own Reminders

Week of March 5–11

March 12

Your Guide to Concrete Blocks

Concrete blocks are handy for many repairs and improvements within and around a home. Common shapes and sizes are shown in the accompanying illustrations. Other units are available with smooth surfaces, rounded corners, raised patterns, and in various colors. The common blocks are referred to as measuring 8″ × 8″ × 16″. That is finished measurement (including the mortar joints). The actual blocks measure less. Use the 8″ × 8″ × 16″ figure for your computations.

Blocks are usually designated as *heavyweight* or *lightweight. Heavyweight* masonry is made with portland cement, sand, gravel, or crushed stone. *Lightweight* masonry is made with expanded aggregate such as clays, shales, slags, cinders, or pumice.

STRETCHER 8"x 8"x16" (TWO CORE)

CORNER 8"x 8"x 16" (THREE CORE)

PARTITION 4"x 8" x 16"

HALF HIGH STRETCHER 8"x 4" x 16" (TWO CORE)

SPLIT BLOCK 4"x 4" x 16" (ONE FACE ROUGH)

HALF UNIT 8"x 8"x 8"

DOUBLE BEVEL FACE 8"x 8"x 16" (THREE CORE)

Today in History: A steam engine, made in England, was put into service on March 12, 1775, at the Schuyler copper mine at North Arlington, N.J., to pump water from the mine.

In building a masonry wall, the corners are laid first and a chalk line stretched tightly between the corners to serve as a guide for the wall. A full bed of mortar is placed on the footing or foundation for the first course of block, then each succeeding course has mortar placed on the top edges of each block and on the ends. A solid block usually caps the top of each exposed wall. The fresh mortar joints are compressed with a masonry jointer or a 5/8-inch round bar for uniform appearance and tight joints.

Mortar for laying up concrete block is made by using 1 part masonry cement and between 2 and 3 parts of damp, loose mortar sand. Mix thoroughly with just enough clean water to give desired workability. Mix only that amount of mortar to be used at one time. Mortar that is partly set should be discarded, and a new batch mixed.

March 13

Root-Prune Conifers Soon

As soon as frost is out of the ground—in late winter or early spring—it's time to root-prune coniferous foundation plantings if these evergreens are immature stages of such forest trees as red cedars or junipers, Japanese false-cypress, arborvitae, pines, spruces, or firs—as many are. Root pruning, practiced each year as soon as the trees become established, will help keep them from growing too tall for their situation. Sever the lateral roots by thrusting a spade full length vertically into the ground in a circle around the trunk. Make the circle about one-third of the way in from the outside foliage line to the trunk. Root pruning tends to dwarf the plant.

You can do this, however, only if you begin the annual chore while the planting is still not foundation height. Actually, it's better to plant dwarf types in the first place.

Today in History: The figure of Uncle Sam first appeared on March 13, 1852, in a cartoon published in the New York Lantern, a comic weekly. Frank Bellew was the cartoonist.

Treat the soil around yew to control the taxis weevil.

It's top-shearing time for pittospurums grown as a tall hedge in California and elsewhere. Take from two to six inches off the top to form a bushy growth.

March 14

Time to Dig Flower Beds?

In the southern latitudes, the proper time is now—for you will be able to plant seeds or set out plants soon. For a bed where you never have grown flowers before, you should have done the preliminary digging last fall—as described in the entry for September 30.

At the spring spading, work peat moss, sand, fertilizer, and lime into the soil. A soil test will show you exactly what fertilizer and lime is needed.

For ordinary garden soil, use a 1- to-2-inch layer of peat moss and a 1-inch layer of unwashed sand—from building-supply yards.

Where trailing blackberries thrive, tie the new vines in a spiral to stakes six feet tall.

In northern states, the recommended time for planting grapes is at hand. See October 30.

Shopping reminder: Freshly-dug potatoes which are not quite mature are designated as "new" potatoes. These are on the market in late winter or early spring. Best use of new potatoes is boiling or creaming.

If your soil is heavy clay, use twice this amount of peat and sand. By adding peat and sand to the soil each time you reset the plants, you can eventually improve even poor subsoil to make a good garden soil. You can use well-rotted compost instead of peat moss.

Add a complete fertilizer such as 5-10-5 at the last spading. Use at a rate of 1½ pounds (3 rounded cups) per 100 square feet. Add ground limestone at a rate of 5 pounds (7 rounded cups) per 100 square feet.

Rake the soil surface smooth. After raking, the soil is ready for seeding or planting with started plants.

Add organic matter to the beds each year—either peat moss or compost.

March 15

Today in History: This is the Ides of March. The ides was a day near the middle of the month in the old Roman calendar—the 13th of all months except March, May, July, and October, when it fell on the 15th. Caesar was assassinated on this day in 44 B.C.

When Should You Establish a Lawn?

Depending on where you live and the type of grass you choose, the answer to that question might be any of the four seasons except winter. Lawns are established in two ways: by sowing seed or by planting vegetative grasses (spot or strip sodding, sprigging, or stolonizing). Some vegetative planting may be done in either spring or summer.

Spring planting, either by seed or vegetative method, is best done early enough so that the lawn is well established before hot summer weather begins. Soil preparation can begin as soon as frost is out of the ground. For an indication of when this may occur in your area, see the spring frost map with the February 8 entry. Planting can follow as soon as the ground is ready. (In the South, you may want to plant a green manure crop—crimson clover, hairy vetch, winter rye, or ryegrass the fall before spring lawn seeding. Turn it under four to six weeks before seeding or planting the lawn.)

The U.S. Department of Agriculture recommends that seed for the following type of grasses be sown only in the spring: bahiagrass, at the rate of 2 to 3 pounds per 1000 square feet; bermudagrass, 2 to 3; blue gramagrass (unhulled), 1 to 1½; buffalograss (treated), ½ to 1; carpetgrass, 3 to 4; centipedegrass, 2 to 3; and Japanese lawngrass (hulled), 1 to 2. Ryegrass seed, either domestic or perennial, may be sown in either spring or fall.

In vegetative planting, the Department recommends sodding of buffalograss only in the spring. Vegetative planting may be used in either spring or summer for bermudagrass, carpetgrass, centipedegrass, or zoysia.

For the kinds of grasses best suited to growing conditions in your area see Appendix A. Also consult your county agent for this information and best planting procedures. The U.S. Department of Agriculture has a helpful booklet, *Better Lawns.*

March 16

Do Your Evergreens Need Fertilizer?

The period during March and April in northern areas is the proper time for fertilizing any evergreens that show poor color or that haven't made the proper growth. Fertilizing later in the year may stimulate late growth that will be susceptible to winter injury. A soil test will indicate what your evergreens need.

If a soil is low in phosphorous and potassium, apply 1 pound of 5-10-10 fertilizer to each 10 square feet. If you prefer to use a fertilizer designed especially for broad-leaved evergreens, be sure some of the nitrogen content (the first number in the formula) is available as water-soluble, natural, or synthetic organic sources for a gradual release of nitrogen during spring and early summer. Too much nitrogen late in the year will result in late twig growth—and winter kill.

How old is steam heat? The year 1845 seems a likely date. In that year, a steam system was installed in the Eastern Hotel in Boston. Coils of pipe diffused the heat.

Well-placed shade trees can reduce summer room temperature of a frame house in a dry climate by as much as 20 degrees.

March 17

Today in History: John J. Montgomery made a 600-foot flight in a glider on March 17, 1884, from a hill near Otay, Calif. He later became known as "The Father of Gliding."

Plant Garden Peas Now in Many Areas

In the Northeast, it long has been a tradition that garden peas should be planted on St. Patrick's Day. Government researchers agree that for best success with this tasty green vegetable you should heed the old tradition in a good part of the U.S.

Garden peas are a cool-weather crop. Summer plantings are doomed to failure. Peas sometimes are planted in the fall, but yields seldom are as good as you get from spring seeding. Several successive plantings may be made at ten-day intervals.

The U.S. Department of Agriculture lists garden peas among eight very hardy vegetables that may be put into the ground from four to six weeks before the final spring frost in any area. Others are broccoli, cabbage, lettuce, onions, potatoes, spinach, and turnips. Another half dozen—beets, carrots, chard, mustard, parsnips, and radishes—may be planted from two to four weeks before the final frost.

For the regions where peas and many of these other vegetables should be in the ground by this time, check the spring frost map given with the February 8 entry in this book. Find the frost-free date for your area. Then refer to this date in the column headings for Appendix E in the back of the book. If your frost date is April 20 or earlier, today's a good time for garden peas. To the southward, you could have planted them earlier—even in January if you wished.

What is shamrock? The national flower of Ireland may be any one of several three-leaved plants, but a small clover is usually considered the true shamrock.

March 18

Plant Ground Covers Now

Early spring is the best time to plant ground covers in most localities. This timing allows the plants to become well established before winter, giving them a better chance to withstand hard freezes.

Ground covers often are a better choice than grass for some parts of the lawn. Once established, they require minimum care. What you

might choose depends to a considerable extent on where you live. Refer to Appendix B, the plant hardiness map, in the back of this book and note the zone in which you live.

Knowing this, you can then select suitable ground covers from the following list:

Barrenwort, zones 4 to 8; bearberry, 2 to 9;

bugleweed, 5 to 9; capeweed, 9 and 10; coral-berry, 3 to 9; cotoneaster, 5 to 10; cowberry, 5 to 9; creeping lilyturf, 5 to 10; creeping thyme, 5 to 10; crownvetch, 3 to 7; daylily, 3 to 10; dichondra, 9 and 10; dwarf bamboo, 6 to 10; dwarf hollygrape, 6 to 9; dwarf lilyturf, 7 to 10; dwarf polygonum, 4 to 10; English ivy, 5 to 9; germander, 6 to 10; goldmoss stonecrop, 4 to 10; ground-ivy, 3 to 9; heartleaf bergenia, 5 to 10; honeysuckle, 5 to 9; iceplant, 10; Japanese holly, 6 to 10; Japanese spurge, 5 to 8; juniper, depending on variety, 3 to 10; memorial rose, 5 to 9; moss sandwort, 2 to 9; periwinkle, 5 to 10; St. Johnswort, 6 to 10; sand strawberry, 6 to 10; sarcococca, 6 to 10; South African daisy, 9 and 10; strawberry geranium, 7 to 9; wandering Jew, 10; weeping lantana, 8 to 10; winter-creeper, 5 to 10; wintergreen, 5 to 7.

Your Own Reminders

Week of March 12–18

March 19

Spring Salads from the Wild

Let's think today about Euell Gibbons, author of *Stalking the Wild Asparagus* and other books devoted to the proposition that we can all eat better by gathering some of our foods from the fields and woodlands. One of the wild foods

he extols—wintercress—is now abundant and ready for picking. It may grow almost anywhere, but you will find its smooth and rounded green leaves in greatest abundance and vigor along brooks and ditches. Warm and sunny periods throughout the winter trigger it into lush growth, and at this time of the year in the middle latitudes of the U.S. wintercress offers a green salute to the approaching spring.

Gather it now, while its leaves are small and young. Later wintercress becomes bitter. Use it in fresh salads or as boiling greens, seasoned with salt and pepper and perhaps vinegar. Some people know it as mustard greens—and it does happen to be a member of the wild mustard family.

Before long, or even now in the southernmost parts of the country, you can gather a second wild crop that has high food value—dandelion leaves, all of them loaded with the vitamins that bring health and happiness to you and your family. Gather these, too, while they are young, and use them in salads or as boiled greens.

Borrow or buy one of Euell Gibbons' "Stalking" books and you will discover many other wild crops that will give your family good and healthful eating, as well as lighten your food budget.

March 20

Check Your Lawn and Garden Tools

Grass is beginning to green up over a considerable portion of the country at this time of year and—probably before you know it—you will soon need the tools and other equipment you use to keep your grounds in order. Is everything in good condition, ready for use? An hour or two devoted right now to checking everything, in the comfort of your shop area, would be time well spent.

What about your power mower? You should have cleaned it up last fall at the end of the season. If you didn't, get it out and clean all the dried grass and other gunk from its surfaces, top and bottom, and from its working parts. After all the metal is clean, wipe the surfaces with a light oil. Or you may want to apply a rustproofing paint to selected areas.

Does the mower need sharpening? There's no reason you shouldn't undertake this yourself, preferably at least once a year. But if you want someone else to do it, there never will be a better time than now to deliver it to a pro—before all of the last-minute-doers have the same idea. You may also want the pro to do engine work at the same time, a tune-up perhaps; an oil change before grass cutting begins is also in order. See your instruction manual.

In addition to the mower, you may also own powered trimmers, electric perhaps. Clean these up, oil them, check out the cords for

breaks, and make any needed repairs.

Spades, shovels, hoes and other edged gardening tools need periodic sharpening. Use a flat file. Scour off any rust and oil the metal surfaces. Pay attention, too, to the handles. Taping the area of a slight split, for instance, may keep the handle in good service for years.

Plant watermelons now in the South.

March 21

Any Insect Screens Need Repairs?

The time is approaching when insect hordes once again will make screening necessary in windows and doors. Before you need them, and while cold weather still is probably keeping you indoors anyway, why not see if any of your screens need repairs?

You might discover the need for any of three types of repairs—patching, refastening the mesh along one or more edges, or complete screening replacement.

A straight break in metal screening can be pulled and held together by weaving a strand of fine wire back and forth across the break. Pull a strand out of the cut edge of a spare piece of screening. You can also apply a patch of new screening. Cut a rectangular or square patch slightly larger than the hole or break. With your pliers pull out one or two strands of wire adjoining all four edges. Then bend the projecting wire ends at 90 degrees to the face of the patch. Apply this patch over the break so that the projecting ends pass through the screen you are repairing. Then simply crimp the projecting ends flat—and your patch is complete.

But maybe you have fiberglass screening. With care, you can fuse a fiberglass patch on this type of plastic screening by using the edge of a hot iron.

When human hands or animals have pushed screening loose along one edge, particularly in screen doors, place a block of wood on each side of the screening an inch from the frame. Then clamp the blocks to the screen with a large C-clamp that straddles the frame. Use the C-clamp as your handle to pull the edge of the screen into place for refastening, either by tacking it under wooden molding or by placing it under beading in the slot found in aluminum screens.

Stapling is the most convenient fastening method when you replace screening on wood frames although you may prefer a hammer and No. 8 tacks. Stretch the screening taut before fastening. One way to do this: Attach the screening to one end of the frame as it rests on sawhorses. Place screening the length of the frame (before cutting the screening), clamp a weight to the uncut end while you staple or tack along the inner edge of the frame at that end. Then cut off the new length of screening adjoining the fasteners. For metal frames, cut the new screening to size and fasten the edges by clamping them under the plastic spline that presses into the frame slot. Yanking the spline from the slot allows you to remove the old screen. Drive the spline back into place with a thin piece of wood or metal.

Why can you cut grass without impairing its ability to form new leaves? There's an interesting reason: each leaf grows from the lower part of the stem, not the tip. Trees, shrubs, and flower plants grow from the tip.

March 22

Outdoor Furniture Ready for Spring?

Why not get ready now for some of the loafing you'll probably want to do when spring fever hits you a few weeks from now? Take a look at your outdoor furniture and see what maintenance it needs. Perhaps there's a chair you took out of service last season because it needed repairs. Carry the chair to your shop area and repair it now. Reglue any loose joints you find in any wood-framed furniture.

Will any or all of the furniture need painting? You probably can get this done before your outdoor living season arrives—if you await a day mild enough to do it outdoors. Apply paint indoors only if you can have lots of ventilation.

Remove corrosion from aluminum parts with damp soap pads and a household cleanser. When dry, apply an aluminum preservative recommended by your hardware store.

Wirebrush rust from wrought iron and then clean up the area with fine steel wool before painting. To prevent further rusting, apply an anticorrosive primer, one or two thin coats of indoor-outdoor type enamel, or one that's intended for metals.

Enamels designed for painting machinery may be used. They come in attractive colors and dry to a low sheen. These enamels can take expansion and contraction due to summertime temperature changes. They produce a tough, durable finish that adheres exceptionally well.

If you want to restore the original color to weathered redwood furniture, apply a redwood finish. For other wood outdoor furniture, if a natural finish is desired, rag on a penetrating wood sealer designed for outdoors.

Replace canvas or other coverings that need it—and you'll then be all set to give in comfortably, out in the yard, when an attack of spring fever seems imminent a few weeks—or days—from now.

March 23

Plant Fruit Trees in the Coldest States

Wherever you live, one time to plant fruit trees is early spring while they are still dormant. Spring is the recommended time for states where winter temperatures dip very low. Included are North and South Dakota, Montana, Wyoming, Nebraska, Idaho, eastern Oregon, Washington, and the higher elevations of Colorado and New Mexico. If you have any doubts about your region, your county agent can advise you about when and what to plant.

Only hardy varieties can be successful in the cold regions. Even these must have special care

Today in History: A patent was granted on March 23, 1880, to John Stevens, of Neenah, Wis., for a "grain-crushing mill." His invention produced a superior wheat flour.

to overcome cold and drought. In the northern Great Plains, fruit trees must have protection from the prevailing west winds, the hot drying south winds in the summer, and the cold north winds in winter. Buy young trees only from local nurseries.

Planting procedure is generally the same as described for fall planting under date of October 20.

Subtropical and tropical plants such as hibiscus and bougainvillea can be set into the ground now in all semitropical areas.

In regions where dewberries grow, tie the canes in a spiral form to stakes six feet high.

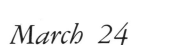

March 24

Signs of Carpet Beetles

At this time of the year, you may find small beetles about one-eighth inch long on the inside of windows. Take a close look. They may be ladybird, or ladybug, beetles, mostly orange with black spots. These are beneficial—great aphid eaters—and you have nothing to worry about. But if the beetles you see are the same shape and size as lady beetles, but all black or mottled black, brownish, and white, you are looking at carpet beetles. Somewhere in the house, their stubby larvae are at work. You can find the larvae in dark, undisturbed locations at about anytime of the year. Cast-off hairy skins of the larvae and sand-like pellets are signs of an infestation. The larvae leave no webbing such as the larvae of clothes moths do.

Adult carpet beetles do no harm. The larvae feed on a variety of natural materials or the products made from such materials—hair, feathers, wool, fur, horn, dried animal products, pollen, and occasionally certain spices and cereal products. The larvae on occasion attack synthetic fibers such as nylon and Dacron, especially if food has been spilled on them. Damage done by carpet beetle larvae often is attributed to clothes moth larvae.

Good housekeeping practices and applying protective treatments to susceptible items will keep a home free of infestation. To eliminate an infestation you must treat the premises with insecticides that effectively kill insects. For a heavy infestation, get the services of a pest-control firm.

If you clean thoroughly, you will deprive the larvae of some of their food supply. At the same time you will remove insects and their eggs.

Home rug makers may spread carpet beetles. Woolen scraps exchanged with a neighbor or friend who is hooking or crocheting a rug may carry along the larvae, especially if the scraps have been stored in a dark closet.

Clean often enough to prevent lint and hair from accumulating.

In cleaning, give close attention to rugs and carpets, draperies, upholstered furniture, radiators, and the surfaces behind them, corners, cracks, baseboards, molding, and all other parts of the house that may have hard-to-reach and hard-to-clean cracks and crevices.

Deserted bird nests are often breeding spots for carpet beetles. Adult beetles may fly from them into the house.

Besides cleaning rugs and carpets frequently, rotate them occasionally. Insects often feed under heavy pieces of furniture where cleaning is inconvenient.

After vacuum-cleaning, promptly dispose of the sweepings. They may contain larvae, eggs, or adult insects. These could transfer infestation from one place in the home to another.

If an infestation is suspected in wall-to-wall carpeting, pull it up around the edges and treat the underside and the pad with a five percent methoxychlor solution. Re-lay the carpet and lightly spray its upper surface.

From now until a week into April is a good time in Spring Zone 4 for applying a dormant oil spray to rhododendron and azaleas for control of scale insects.

Don't delay planting sweet peas in the middle and northern regions. They need cool weather for best growth.

Spray locusts with malathion in early spring to kill borers under the bark. Also spray holly for red mite.

In southern states, you might like to adorn your grounds with Mexican shell flower (or tiger flower), a favorite in ancient Mexico. Bulbs should be planted in the spring. Where winters are mild, they can be left in the ground and divided every three or four years.

March 25

It's Pruning Time—for Many Shrubs

Wherever you live, you can give your shears and other pruning equipment considerable use at this time of year. American holly, evergreens, foundation shrubs, and boxwood are among the plantings that you may want to trim or cut back.

Coniferous evergreens used as foundation plantings or hedges are due about now for one of their two annual shearings—the second coming in June or early July. And take note that shearing is the word. Use a sickle—or a heavy pruning knife used like a sickle—to shear feathery types such as junipers, arborvitaes, and retinisporas. With these tools you can create a more graceful shape than the bald and shorn effect that often follows use of hedge clippers. Shear away an inch or two, about half of the previous year's growth. This increases the number of growing points, causing more twigs to develop and the shrub to become denser.

When the hedge is of spruce, hemlock, or yew, you'll need to cut each shoot individually. For this, you can use clippers.

And speaking of shearing, you may see some of your neighbors shearing their azaleas soon after blooming. Not all horticulturists recommend this. They point out that it makes the top very dense and spoils the natural gracefulness of the plant.

Boxwood and holly, two old-time favorites in the milder latitudes of the U.S., should both receive your attention now. Prune holly before growth starts if you did not prune it enough last Christmas—the preferred pruning time. Winter injury occurs when boxwood is grown north of its normal range. If leaves appear scorched and fine outer twigs dead, shear the shrub lightly just below the injury. Sometimes an entire branch may be killed. Remove it all—right back to live wood. New growth will soon fill in the space.

Rhododendron and laurel seldom need real

pruning, but this is a good time to check them over and remove any dead or exceptionally long branches.

Do you have some shrubs that you prize largely for the bright color of their bark in winter—for instance red osier dogwood? If so, you can assure a good supply of bright twigs for next winter by pruning now. You'll find the brightest winter color on the youngest twigs exposed to the sun.

You can safely cut back all of the plant almost to the ground each year if you will not miss its foliage during the summer. If you would rather have some foliage, cut from a third to a half of the canes each year, making the cuts 6 to 12 inches from the ground.

Spring also is the time to prune hardy vines like wisteria, bittersweet, and trumpet creeper. For a treelike form, keep the plant to a single stem. Induce branching by pinching the top buds when the stem is six or seven feet tall. Remove weak branches each spring and cut back the rest to three or four buds.

Your Own Reminders

Week of March 19–25

____

____

____

____

____

____

____

____

____

____

____

____

____

____

____

March 26

Repairs to Countertopping

Plastic laminates on kitchen counters, bathroom vanities, and other work surfaces will last for years and years with normal use. But accidents do happen and the need for repairs develop. Today might be the time to check yours.

Light scratches or cuts. Use fine steel wool or crocus cloth to gently work out the scratch. Wetting the fine abrasive with water will help it work. Charge a small buffing wheel with jeweler's rouge and drive it with an electric drill to work over the area. Buffing may require ten minutes or more.

Deep scratches or burns. When the damage is too deep to be polished out, touch up the depression with India ink. This is available in a range of colors. Choose one to match the laminate. Apply several times to fill the scratch. You can make such repairs also with stick shellac of a matching color. Apply it and smooth it flush with a putty knife heated with a torch. Sand the repair lightly and apply furniture wax.

Bubble in laminate. This may show up because someone skimped on the adhesive in bonding the laminate to its base. If the underside of the base material (probably 3/4-inch plywood or composition material) is accessible, drill two or more holes up through the base, being careful not to go through the laminate. Then put the tip of a squeeze glue container to the holes and squeeze all the adhesive you can up into the space between the laminate and the upper surface of the base. Plug the holes and apply a smooth and heavy weight to the laminate until the adhesive has had a chance to set.

Damage to self-edge. The edges of many counters are covered with the laminate used on the top. If this edging becomes extensively damaged, you may be able to obtain a few scrap pieces of the original laminate and replace the damaged edge. Warm the damaged area with a torch or heat lamp to soften the adhesive. Pry off the strip or chisel it away. Cut a new strip slightly oversize and cement it in place, letting it project a bit at the top and at any corner. Dress down the overhanging edges with a file.

Major damage. A deep burn or gouge can also be repaired by cutting out a piece of the laminate and then inserting a matching patch. Kitchen-cabinet shops often can supply scraps of laminate with the same pattern as yours. If you do a kitchen or bath countertopping job, be sure to save a few pieces for just such repairs as this.

Outline the area with a grease pencil. Note whether joints can be concealed in the pattern. Adjust the outline to suit. Then cut an edge around the damaged part with a sharp wood chisel and mallet. Hold the chisel so the beveled edge faces the damage, thus assuring a crisp, straight-sided cutout.

Heat the piece to be removed with a torch to make the adhesive let go. When hot, the laminate can be pried away from the core by inserting a broad chisel under its edge.

Brush contact cement onto the core and allow it to dry for the time recommended by the manufacturer. If the wood soaks it in, apply a second coat. Be sure to brush it out to the edges of the opening. Also apply adhesive to bottom of the patch.

Drop the patch carefully in place. Once it makes contact, the adhesive grips immediately, leaving you no chance to adjust the piece or slide it around to improve fit.

Use stick shellac and patience to fill in the thin joint around the patch. Heat the putty knife often with a torch.

March 27

Roll a Lawn? Experts Say No

Frost-heaving of the ground during the winter leaves a rough surface on many lawns, and you will see some people out with a water-filled roller at this time of year smoothing it down. Lawn experts usually will tell you that this may not be a good practice. The heavy

roller compacts the soil, making it just so much more difficult for grass roots to develop. It's better to leave the lawn alone. After a few weeks, and the first mowing or two, the surface will be level.

A roller has its best use when moles have been at work or the lawn surface has become rutted while still soft in the spring. But the environs of your home can probably benefit from a general clean-up now. Have winter snows broken or cracked limbs of some trees and shrubs? Prune them off, making clean cuts and applying a wound dressing to all cuts that have a diameter of a half inch or more.

The lawn may look better if raked in its entirety. Clean off dead material remaining in garden areas and flower beds. Don't be too hasty, however, about uncovering perennial flowers, especially in the northern areas. Some of the materials can be composted. Package up the rest for your disposal service.

Today in History: A patent was granted on March 27, 1855, to Dr. Abraham Gesner for a process that produced oil from bituminous shale and cannel coal. It was called "kerosene."

March 28

Plant Nasturtiums, Protect Peonies Now

Here are two garden tasks that are well timed at this time of the year:

In all areas where you can work the soil, select your least fertile tract, spade it, moisten it if necessary, and plant nasturtium seed for late spring and summer bloom. In fertile soils, these plants grow mostly to leaves.

If trees or shrubs grow near peonies, dig up a strip of ground now between the flowers and shrubs or trees. Dig at least three feet away from the peonies and a foot or more deep. This will limit growth of the tree roots that might interfere with the flowers.

March 29

Grow Your Own Breakfast Fruit

Citrus fruits can be grown successfully in a surprisingly extensive part of the U.S., especially if you will take the trouble to protect trees from frost. New trees should be planted in the spring as soon as possible after the danger of frost has passed. This will allow them to become well established before the hot periods of summer.

Oranges, grapefruit, lemons, and tangerines can be grown in Florida, Texas, Arizona, and California. Louisiana grows satsuma tangerines south of New Orleans near the Mississippi River. A few oranges also are grown in Louisiana.

Some tangerines are grown near the Gulf coast of northwest Florida, Alabama, and Mississippi. Trees in these areas must be protected from freezes to survive. An occasional satsuma tree is found in southern Georgia where frost protection is given.

Lemons are the least cold resistant of citrus trees. Grapefruit is less cold resistant than oranges. Oranges are less cold resistant than satsuma tangerines. Citrus trees in marginal climates are more likely to survive if planted on the south side of structures which protect them from the north winds. Also, protection from frosts as well as freezes will aid survival.

Cold-tender plants are sometimes protected by building a cover for the plant and supplying heat inside. If the cover is made of plastic, care must be taken not to let the plastic touch the tree. Foliage of cold-tender plants in contact with plastic during a freeze will be killed.

If you live on the northern limits of the citrus belts, you may be able to grow satsumas if nothing else. These will stand more cold than other citrus varieties and will mature where summers are relatively cool.

March 30

Today in History: In Alaska, this is a holiday, Seward Day. On March 30, 1867, Secretary Seward signed a treaty with Russia whereby the latter ceded the territory to the U.S. for $7,200,000.

Make Your Own Sourdough Starter

In the early days of Alaska, bread making at home was a necessity. Food supplies came only once or twice a year. Many localities received supplies only when a steamer could navigate river or lake during the few months of summer thaw. Orders placed the year before required careful selection with close attention to keeping qualities. Yeast became deactivated in a short time and could deteriorate entirely en route. Ordinary yeast plants, sensitive to the extreme cold, refused to grow. Sourdough starter was a perfect solution.

Sourdough was a yeasty starter for leavening hotcakes, waffles, muffins, bread, and even cake. Bread could not be made without it, so the starter became a precious possession.

To make your own nowadays, use glass or pottery containers. Never use a metal container or leave a metal spoon in the starter. A good starter contains only flour, water, and yeast. It has a clean, sour milk odor. The liquid will separate from the batter when it stands several days, but this does not matter. If replenished every few days with flour and more water, the starter keeps fresh. If starter is not to be used

for several weeks, freeze or dry it to keep it from spoiling. In the dried form the yeast goes into a spore stage which will keep inert for a long time like old-fashioned yeast foam. Water and warmth bring the yeast back to the active stage.

Recipe: Mix well—2 cups flour, 2 cups warm water, 1 package dry yeast or 1 yeast cake. Place in a warm place or closed cupboard overnight. In the morning put ½ cup of the starter in a scalded pint jar with a tight cover and store in the refrigerator or a cool place for future use. This is sourdough starter. The remaining batter can be used for pancakes, waffles, muffins, bread, or cake immediately.

Commercial sourdough starters now on the market are dried and powdered. Adding water brings them to life. Growing, the yeast gives off a carbon dioxide gas which forms bubbles in the dough. The lactic acid bacteria changes starch and sugar to lactic acid, giving the dough a sour odor. Soda is added to react with the acid to form more gas which makes the batter lighter. If too much soda is added, the product is brownish when baked. If too little soda is used, the product tastes sour. Add the soda just before baking. In any sourdough recipe it is most helpful to reserve one tablespoon of the liquid to dissolve the soda. Add this to the batter last, mix thoroughly, and bake. Never add soda to the starter, as it kills the yeast.

Harden (toughen) indoor plants before moving outdoors. Withhold water and lower the temperature for two weeks before the proper time for moving outdoors. Lettuce and cabbage plants can be toughened to withstand frost; tomatoes and peppers cannot.

Keep tab on strawberries. Remove most of the winter mulch (clean straw or hay) when new growth starts. Leave a light covering and let the plants grow through it.

March 31

Do You Have the Tools You Need?

This is a fine day to consider whether you have on hand the tools required to keep your house in order.

But first, a moment of truth.

Are you qualified to undertake *major* repairs? Do you have a natural facility in the use of tools? Do you enjoy conquering a contrary dishwasher? Would you rather take on a repair job than go to the movies? If you can answer such questions with an enthusiastic "yes," then you probably already have a shopful of tools. If you don't, you will be sure to acquire them eventually.

However, you may prefer to leave major improvements and repairs to the professionals. This would make you one of a very large group of very smart people. That group does—and should—include most of us. For major work, we ought to call in the pros. But even so, we ought to be ready for the minor fixes—those for which we must pay too heavily in both money and inconvenience if we always rely on outside help.

Minor repairs you are most apt to face involve only a few operations—making holes in wood, sawing wood, driving and removing screws, turning nuts on and off bolts, and perhaps cutting wire and metal. To do all of these

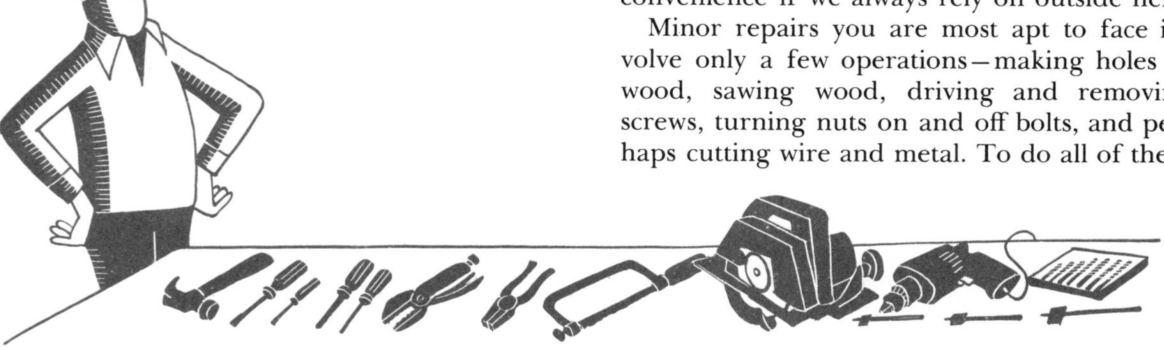

things—and quite well, too—you need just a few well-chosen tools.

A hammer must surely head the list. Get yourself the man-sized hammer the professional carpenter uses—a 16-ounce claw, preferably one with a fiberglass handle, made by a well-known company.

To prepare for removing and driving screws, lay in four screwdrivers—two of the standard-bit type for slot-headed screws (one medium size and one very small); and two of the four available sizes of Phillips drivers—the smallest (No. 1) and the second largest (No. 3).

For tightening and loosening bolts and nuts choose an open-end wrench with an adjustable jaw—say one about eight inches long. A pair of pliers, the kind called slip-joint pliers, will also help you turn things, and the cutter slot in one jaw will cut wire when necessary. A small hacksaw will put you into the metal-cutting business.

A 26-inch eight-point crosscut handsaw, with Teflon S coating, is the least expensive good answer to cutting wood. But if you see any great amount of wood sawing in your future, better jump right to a portable circular saw. The power tool is your best insurance for straight and square cuts, never easy with a handsaw.

For making holes in wood, a brace and a couple of auger bits—say 1/4 and 1/2 inch—will get you by in many cases. When you must make a hole of a different size, buy a bit to suit. An electric drill? Sure. But you'll be going beyond actual necessity. If you decide to plunge, however, better go all the way and choose a variable speed, reversible unit. With this, get a set of spade bits for wood, a selection of high speed drills for metal, and you will be equipped for solving hole-making problems for years to come.

Beginning the second year after planting a fig tree or bush, head it back after frost danger has passed and before growth has started. Remove a third to a half of the annual growth.

Leaves of colchicum should be appearing now. Sprinkle a pinch of low nitrogen fertilizer (5-10-5) around each plant.

Today in History: Americans had their first experience with daylight saving time on March 31, 1918, when clocks were set one hour ahead. World War I was then going on.

April

Nature comes completely awake in April. The grass grows green. Early flowers spring up. Buds unfold on trees and shrubs, reminding us that April may have received its name from a Latin verb meaning "to open."

If you can find the time, it's great just to sit in the sun and think of outdoor pleasures. The baseball season opens soon—even for the Little League. Yard cleanup is due. Oversize trout are biting—somewhere. Is the mower ready? Digging of garden plots can't wait much longer. You have so much to do and enjoy. Why does this good month have *only* 30 days?

Its historical anniversaries and religious days are plentiful. Four of our wars began in April—the Revolution, the Civil War, the Spanish-American War, World War I. Jewish Passover celebrates the exodus from Egypt. In most years, the month brings three important Christian days—Palm Sunday, Good Friday, and Easter.

The ancient custom of exchanging gifts of eggs at Easter is appropriate to the month, for eggs represent the new life that returns to the natural world at this season.

April 1

Today in History: This is All Fools' Day. By an old tradition, the day isn't complete unless you send someone on a fool's errand—or go on one yourself.

Time to Graft Fruit Trees

If you enjoy gardening, you can get a real kick out of fruit-tree grafting. Develop the varieties you want on a tree that is already well started. You can have two or more varieties on the same tree. Bridge grafting can be used to repair mouse or mower damage on the lower trunk of a tree.

In many areas the best time for grafting has now arrived, or will soon. Choose a warm day when the trees are beginning to break dormancy. Garden supply stores have the wax needed. Find instructions in a good garden book.

 *Your Own Reminders*

Week of March 26–April 1

April 2

Let Flowers Brighten Your Home

Some flowers come up and bloom year after year. These are the perennials. Others must be planted anew each year. These are the annuals—and the time has come now, in all parts of the country, to do something about it if you want to share in the beauty that such annual flowers can bring.

In most of the country it is still much too early to put either plants or seed of most annual flowers outdoors. But those of you who live in the still-frigid North can begin preparing the ground where you want flowerbeds. You can also lay in your supply of seeds. And you can actually plant certain flower seeds just as soon as you can prepare the soil. Included are baby's breath, cornflower, gaillardia, globe-amaranth, phlox, poppy, cleome, stock, strawflower, summer-cypress, sweet alyssum, and sweetpea.

When to Plant Flowers

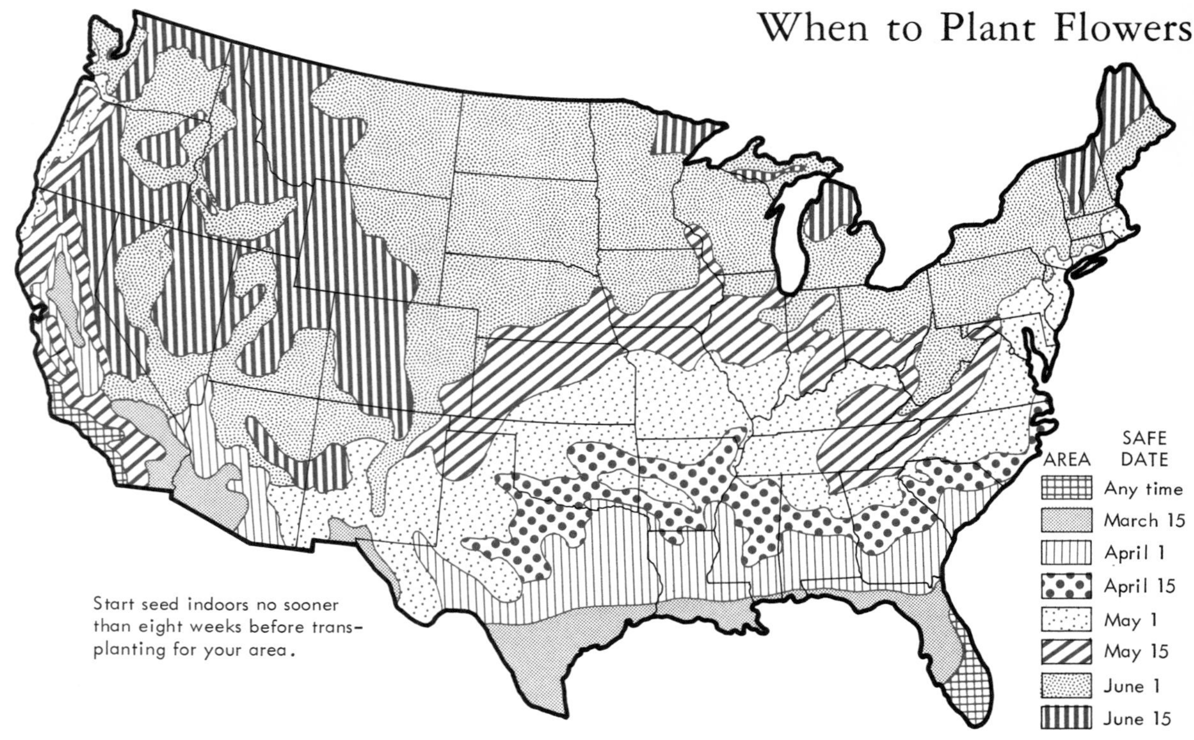

Do not be hasty, however, about actual planting of other flowers. Time this by the dates you find on the accompanying map. Trying to rush the season can only bring poor results. Seed will not germinate, and plants may be set back if the soil has not had a chance to warm up.

The dates and regions shown on this map are roughly the same as the dates and regions you will find on the spring map with the February 8 entry. The latter map, however, gives much more detailed information about local variations in temperatures, and its final-frost dates are averages. The dates on the accompanying map, on the other hand, have a generous leeway so that gardeners are not likely to lose valuable seedlings to a frost that comes later than average.

It is unwise to start seedlings indoors any sooner than eight weeks before you can safely transplant them outdoors. Large plants are more difficult to transplant satisfactorily. If anything, err on the short side of eight weeks.

Refer to Appendix C for information about when to plant and how to cultivate common annual flowers. This chart came from Home and Garden Bulletin No. 91, "Growing Flowering Annuals," available from the Superintendent of Documents, U.S. Government Printing Office, Washington, D.C. 20402.

Today in History: The first motion picture theater was opened on April 2, 1902, in a Los Angeles tent. First pictures shown included "New York in a Blizzard." The show cost a dime and lasted about an hour.

In Spring Zone IV, spray arborvitae now for juniper scale.

Plan to spray firethorn for scab at budbreak, as well as ten and 20 days thereafter.

April 3

Plant a Quince Bush?

In blossom in the spring, a quince bush is an attractive ornamental for an open spot in the yard in most areas of the U.S. The blossoms are big—a delicate rosy pink. Those fortunate enough to know the delights of eating quince honey, a spread made from the fruits, will have a second good reason for wanting to plant one.

The quince grows slowly. At maturity, a tree as a rule stands no more than 15 feet high. For that reason you may want to buy a three-year-old. But if you want it to develop into a bush form rather than a tree, a one-year plant is a good choice. You can then top it to a height of 10 or 12 inches to induce branching near the ground.

A good time to plant is during the spring while the tree is still dormant. Plant as you would an apple tree.

Dormant pruning of roses is due now in most of Spring Region II. See January 5 for the details.

April 4

Do Small Outside Paint Jobs

Wooden structures outdoors will make a better appearance during the coming growing season if you take care of their paint needs now. Check especially flower boxes, trellises, gates, fences, perhaps a dog house. Annual repainting may not be needed, but check at this time of year to see. Use trim or other non-chalking paint on such structures.

Some ground covers used in the warm parts of the country need trimming or mowing after they finish flowering in the spring.

April 5

Prune Spring-Flowering Shrubs Now? Probably Not

Should you prune spring-flowering shrubs just after they blossom? Many people will tell you yes. But listen to these arguments against the practice:

Pruning, to be successful, should be done *at once* after the flowers fade. But do you have the time, or opportunity, to make a daily check on your shrubs? If you delay, you may do more damage than good.

Moreover, while the shrub is in leaf it is difficult to see the framework and determine which shoots or branches should be removed.

So why not wait until your shrubs are dormant? For a fuller discussion of the subject, see December 4.

Watch the condition of magnolia blossoms during this period. Any pruning that is required should be done immediately after flowering. The plants are in their condition of most active growth then and wounds will heal best.

Training is always better than pruning for this class of plants, however. Large pruning wounds do not heal readily. If a bud starts to form in a place where a branch will be undesirable, rub it off with your thumb as soon as you notice it. Prune only when this practice has not been followed.

April 6

Today in History: On April 6, 1918—during the days of World War I—the American's Creed was adopted by Act of Congress. The statement was written by William Tyler Page.

THE AMERICAN'S CREED

I believe in the United States of America, as a government of the people, by the people, for the people; whose just powers are derived from the consent of the governed; a democracy in a republic; a sovereign nation of many sovereign states; a perfect union, one and inseparable; established upon those principles of freedom, equality, justice and humanity for which American patriots sacrificed their lives and fortunes.

I therefore believe it is my duty to my country to love it, to support its constitution, to obey its laws, to respect its flag, and to defend it against all enemies.

Yellow is relatively rare among flowering trees. Consider cornelian cherry, golden chain, and golden-rain tree for color change.

Colonial housewives sometimes used sassafras bark to dye their woolen cloth an orange or brown color.

April 7

Today in History: William Wordsworth, nature poet, was born on April 7, 1770, at Cockermouth, England. Many have thrilled to the famous first stanza of one of his poems:

I wandered lonely as a cloud
That floats on high o'er vales and hills,
When all at once I saw a crowd,
A host, of golden daffodils;
Beside the lake, beneath the trees,
Fluttering and dancing in the breeze.

Raising Daffodils

Some gardeners will tell you that Wordsworth's daffodils really were trumpet narcissus—single blossoms of a deep yellow color.

But by whatever name you know them, these long-stemmed beauties give a hearty welcome to spring—after they are once established.

Few flowers are easier to grow than daffodils. Locate the bulbs at random on the lawn or in a woodland area if you have one. Daffodils are a good choice for a shaded spot because, like many wild flowers, they develop and bloom before the tree canopy leafs out. In a lawn area, you can mow around them the first few times, then cut off the foliage after it dies down.

Since the bulbs constantly multiply, you should divide daffodils periodically. Smaller blossoms are a sign that division is needed. Divide the clumps in the spring after blossoming —while the dead foliage is still attached and you can locate and dig the bulbs. Some gardeners break the clustered bulbs apart, put them away to dry, and replant them in the fall, about five inches deep. But others say a dormant period is unnecessary and replant bulbs at once.

A light sprinkling of 5-10-5 fertilizer before growth starts in the spring should be helpful. But many gardeners give daffodils no care whatsoever, and they continue to thrive, year after year.

What is a jonquil? Certain garden experts say that this name is correctly applied only to one distinct species (*N. jonquilla*). This plant usually has several blossoms on a single stem—small golden-yellow flowers with medium to short cups. The foliage is nearly round, and rushlike.

If you planted new peonies last fall, keep them well watered through this first season.

The first dwarf iris may bloom soon in your area if they haven't already. Their blooming season continues through April and May. If you have none, you might like to visit a commercial iris garden to make choices for planting in the late summer.

Remove winter soil covering from raspberries in northern regions. It's also time to uncover grapes that have been protected in the same way.

April 8

How to Have a Minigarden

No outdoor yard space for a vegetable garden? Then use containers inside the house, on a patio or terrace, even on the balcony of an apartment house. A surprising number and variety of vegetable crops can be harvested

in that way—on a small scale. Container gardening indoors also helps you get a jump on the outdoor gardening season by starting plants for transplanting.

You can get all the details of this happy making practice from Home and Garden Bulletin No. 163, "Minigardens for Vegetables," available from the Government Printing Office, Washington, D.C. 24002.

The bulletin suggests the use of such containers as plastic or clay pots, an old pan, a plastic bucket, a bushel basket, a plastic bag, a wire basket, or a wooden box. You might also use a five-gallon plastic trash can on a patio, and plastic laundry baskets can be lined with sheet plastic. Provide drainage by spacing 1/4-inch holes around the sides near the bottom (but not on the bottom). Improve drainage by putting a half inch of coarse gravel in the bottom of the container. Wood containers will last longer if painted inside and out with a wood preservative. Garden centers have soil substitutes especially prepared for such gardening. Or you can mix your own, using garden soil.

Scallions, chives, radishes, leaf lettuce, miniature tomatoes (Tiny Tim), parsley, and peppers are among the plants you can grow to maturity in containers. Others can be started for later transplanting.

Your Own Reminders

Week of April 2–8

Your own indoor gardening mixture can be mixed like this: To one bushel each of horticultural grade vermiculite and shredded peat moss, add 14 ounces of ground limestone (preferably dolomitic), 4 ounces of 20 percent superphosphate, and 8 ounces of 5-10-5 fertilizer. Mix thoroughly. Add a little water, if desired, to reduce the dust while mixing.

April 9

Fertilize Established Lawns Soon

It's time for the first of three or four applications of fertilizer to established lawns of bluegrass, fescues, and other cool-season grasses —those that grow most in spring and fall and are dormant or semidormant in summer. Don't overfertilize now—just enough to keep the grass growing well. Fertilize again about a month hence.

If you seeded a new lawn two to four weeks ago, better apply a light application of nitrogenous fertilizer at this point.

And while you're in the fertilizing business, consider any ground covers you have. Scatter organic fertilizer while the foliage is dry. Brush it to the ground with a broom.

Had a lot of Japanese beetles in recent years? If so, this is the ideal time to declare microbe warfare on the grubs now developing at the roots of your lawn grass. See May 23 for the details.

Better check whether now isn't the best time for applying an oil spray in Zone II for controlling scale insects. See January 26 and February 10.

Spray ash trees with malathion for flower gall after the buds swell but before new growth starts.

Check Appendix E for the vegetables you can now safely plant in Region III.

April 10

Time for First Lawn Mowing?

The time to mow your lawn is best determined by observing the growth of the grass. For most lawns made up of cool-season grasses, a cutting height of 1½ to 2 inches is recommended. Mow it when the grass has no more than doubled in height, perhaps even before.

Mowing to a 2-inch height keeps down weeds. Crabgrass can be reduced by the shading effect of tall grasses on the crabgrass seedlings.

Grass grows at a variable rate during the season. You may need to mow every three or four days during fast-growing periods in spring and fall. In the summer, mowing every ten days may be sufficient. An automatic once-a-week schedule, therefore, is seldom satisfactory. Do not let the grass grow overtall and then clip it back. This is a shock to the plants and may necessitate removal of the cut grass. Normally, you can leave clippings on the lawn.

Warm-season grasses, particularly bermudagrass, require closer mowing than most cool-season grasses. For a fine quality turf, cut bermudagrass frequently to a height of ⅝ inch or less. Other warm-season grasses such as zoysia, centipedegrass, carpetgrass, and St. Augustinegrass should be mowed to 1 inch.

Keep your mower sharp enough to cut the grass cleanly without bruising or tearing the leaves. In hot summer weather, it's usually best to cut cool-season grasses at full 2 inches. Rest the mower on a concrete walk or floor to adjust the cutter height.

Today in History: The basic patent for the safety pin was granted on April 10, 1849, to Walter Hunt, of New York City. He sold his rights to this universally useful invention for a mere $100.

Pull weeds and grass from around iris plants. Loosen the soil surface, being careful not to damage the root.

Remove winter mulch from spring bulbs where frost is no longer a threat to new growth.

In southern states where roses are now blooming, remember to keep dead flowers removed. Cut the stems at a point two buds above the main stem. This will extend the blooming period.

In southern areas start new poinsettias now from cuttings. Make them 12 to 18 inches long, poke a hole in the ground where you want to make the planting, and thrust three-fourths of the cuttings length into the ground. Leave two eyes above the surface. Press the soil down firmly around the plant.

April 11

Drain Water Away from House

What happens to all of the water that falls on your house during rains? Where does it go? During the next hard rain, why not don your raincoat and boots and circle the house, taking a look for yourself? You might be surprised at what you find.

Poor drainage around a house is a primary cause of wet basements. Sometimes, simply by carrying rain and ground water away from the outside walls, a wet-basement problem can be solved.

Consider the roof runoff first. Do the gutters and downspouts do the job they should do in a real downpour? That's a big point to check on your rainy-day inspection. Does each gutter have enough pitch to avoid overflow along its length? If a downspout carries water from an upper to a lower roof, is the downspout from the latter overburdened? If so, a downspout from the upper roof directly to the ground or an additional downspout from the lower roof may solve the problem. Keep all drainage within the gutter system, not dripping or overflowing from it.

What happens when the runoff reaches the ground? Does it simply spill out on the ground? Or do underground pipes carry it to a sewer or dry well? If the latter, note during your rainy-day inspection whether some of the runoff backs out of the joint where the downspout goes into the sewer line. This could indicate that the underground line is clogged or that a dry well has finally filled up and needs re-digging. See June 25.

If the roof runoff spills out of the downspout on to the ground and you have a wet basement, you should plan to make an underground connection to a municipal storm sewer or to your own dry well. A splash block cast from concrete may also be a satisfactory solution. These are sometimes available readymade from garden centers or building supply houses. A splash block has a gutter depression to carry water three feet or more away from the downspout.

When a home is located on a hillside, obviously you do not want surface runoff coursing down the hill against its upper side. Be sure the water is channeled to either side and around the house. When the foundation was built, tiles should have been installed to divert underground water in the same way.

Remove side buds on peonies as soon as they are visible. This will allow the terminal bud on the tip of each stem to develop into a showy blossom. Pull the side buds out with your fingers.

If you notice leaf yellowing on such plants as pyracantha, roses, or gardenia, apply a little iron sulfate.

April 12

Time to Divide Some Perennials

Clumps of perennial flowers should never go longer than three years without dividing. Unless divided, the clump will grow poorly and produce few flowers.

Horticulturists do not always agree about when to do this. One recommendation: make the divisions in the spring—about this time—in the North; make the divisions in the early fall in the South. Another recommendation: divide fall-blooming perennials (such as chrysanthemums) in the spring (now) but divide spring and summer bloomers in late August and September. Better ask a gardening friend what the prevailing practice is in your particular region.

To make the division, dig up the entire clump and clean off all soil. Select only vigorous side shoots, the outer part of the clump. This is the part that will grow best. Discard the center of the clump.

Divide the plant into clumps of three to five shoots each. Be careful not to overdivide; too small a clump will not give much color the first year after replanting.

Stagger plant division so that the whole garden will not be done over at the same time; a good rotation will give you a display of flowers each year.

Do not put all the divisions back into the same area that the original plant came out of. That would be too many plants in a given area; there would be poor air circulation around them.

Discard extra plants, give them to friends, or plant them elsewhere in your yard.

In the northernmost areas you should make plans at once to plant any new evergreens—or it will be too late to do it this spring. See March 8.

The chance of a spring frost has almost passed now for those who live in Region II. See the February 8 map. Spading for a vegetable garden is overdue.

April 13

Extra Screen for Combination Windows

Combination storm windows and screens are great labor savers, and most of the newer homes have them. At the proper time in the spring (about now perhaps) you go through the house, sliding both glass inserts to the top (or bottom if you want summer ventilation through the top of the window) and pulling the screen insert in place. You then are all set for the summer; no need to climb a ladder to interchange separate storm windows and screens as in the old way. The glass inserts also are easily removable for easy and safe washing.

Combinations usually have two storm inserts and one screen, working in three tracks. This has a drawback if you like to open a double-hung window at both top and bottom for better summer ventilation. As a solution, why not buy an extra screen insert? At this time of year, you can then remove and store both glass inserts, install the extra screen insert, and screening then covers the full window.

While you're switching from storm to screen inserts is a good time to brush off and cleanse all surfaces of the window units. Remove the inserts and wash them thoroughly with a household detergent. Before replacing the inserts, also cleanse the frames, paying close attention to the channels to make sure any corrosion is removed.

Take down storm windows and install screens if you still make this switch twice a year. Brush the screens well first and wash them with detergent water.

April 14

Choose Paint to Improve Lighting

In the spring, home owners often think about redecorating, especially repainting those rooms where the old paint or wall covering may have become dingy. Next time you get such an urge, remember that the color and finish of the walls, ceilings, wood floors or floor coverings, and large drapery areas will help determine whether the room is satisfactorily lighted.

White surfaces, of course, reflect the greatest amount of available light. Light tints of colors reflect light next best. Somber color tones absorb much of the light that falls upon them and reflect little light.

If a large room gets plenty of daylight, you probably can use fairly strong color. Light tints on walls make a small room seem larger.

Whatever the room size, try to keep colors within the 35 to 60 percent reflectance range, as shown in the accompanying table. Ceilings should have reflectance values of 60 to 90 percent; floors at least 15 to 35 percent. Matte finishes (flat or low-gloss surfaces) on walls and ceilings diffuse light and reduce reflections of light sources. Glossy, highly polished or glazed surfaces produce reflected glare.

REFLECTANCE TABLE

Color	*Approximate percent reflection*
Whites:	
Dull or flat white	75–90
Light tints:	
Cream or eggshell	79
Ivory	75
Pale pink and pale yellow	75–80
Light green, light blue, light orchid	70–75
Soft pink and light peach	69
Light beige or pale gray	70
Medium tones:	
Apricot	56–62
Pink	64
Tan, yellow-gold	55
Light grays	35–50
Medium turquoise	44
Medium light blue	42
Yellow-green	45
Old gold and pumpkin	34
Rose	29
Deep tones:	
Cocoa brown and mauve	24
Medium green and medium blue	21
Medium gray	20
Unsuitably dark colors:	
Dark brown and dark gray	10–15
Olive green	12
Dark blue, blue-green	5–10
Forest green	7
Natural wood tones:	
Birch and beech	35–50
Light maple	25–35
Light oak	25–35
Dark oak and cherry	10–15
Black walnut and mahogany	5–15

New furnace filters put in now should carry through the summer in the northern states.

April 15

Prepare Your Car for Summer

Don't delay any longer removing winter tires from your car. Their thicker tread causes more heat buildup (and faster wear) than you get with standard tires. In hot summer driving, the increased heat can even cause blowouts.

If your winter tires are studded, your state laws may *require* their removal about now. When studded tires are demounted from the wheels, make sure each one is marked so it can be replaced on the same wheel at the same position on the car. Also chalk arrows on the tire to show direction of rotation. Because studs wear at a slant, they would wear in the opposite direction if mounted backwards. This could cause the studs to be thrown out of the casing.

The time of switching from winter tires is also an appropriate time for periodic rotation, following your chosen rotation pattern. Or see November 2 for a plan you may want to adopt.

Store the off-season tires where the rubber will not be subject to deterioration caused by ozone generated by operating electric motors. Wrap or cover them for protection against dust and dirt.

A lube job, changing oil, and a thorough washing to clean off remaining winter road salts can also be timed with removal of snow tires.

Your Own Reminders

Week of April 9–15

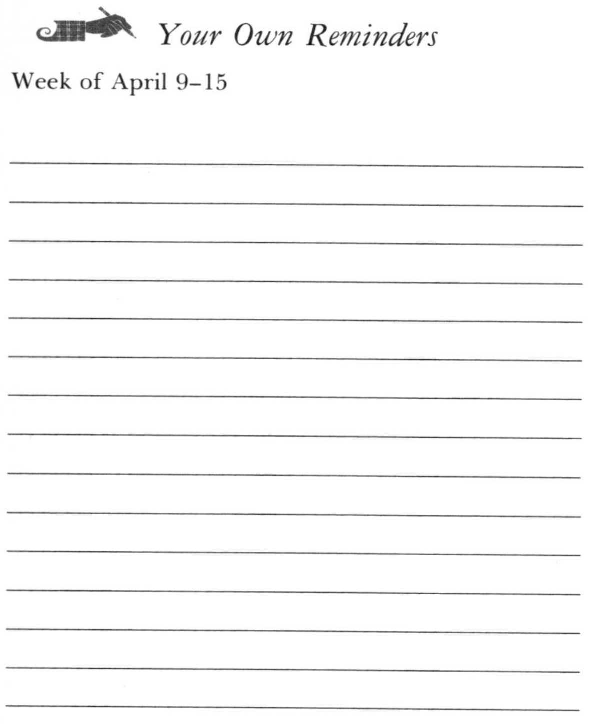

Plant early vegetables in Spring Region III. Better get the soil prepared for the entire plot. See Appendix E at the back of the Almanac.

Set out plants and sow seed of flowers in those southern regions where frost-free dates are April 15 or earlier.

When tulips are about three inches tall begin a weekly spraying for the disease known as "fire."

Remove winter mulch from peonies before new growth gets too far along. Spread a summer mulch of straw or peat moss an inch or two thick around the plants.

April 16

Watch for Tent Caterpillar Webs

Egg masses of the tent caterpillar hatch just as new leaves begin to unfold. Their white nesting webs appear in the notches of limbs and twigs of the host trees, small at first but expanding rapidly as the days go by. You find the caterpillars mostly on wild cherries, but they also attack apples and other home fruit trees. Host trees usually are stripped of leaves.

If possible, prune out webs while they are still small and burn them. Do this in the evening, even after dark, when most of the pests have returned to the web for the night. Webs in larger notches, where pruning is impossible, or high in a tree beyond easy reach can be controlled by spraying with an approved insecticide or by burning with a wad of oil-soaked rags on a long pole. Burning is successful if you envelope the entire web in flame at once, especially from directly underneath. Brief application of the flame usually will not injure the tree.

Take control measures as soon as you discover the webs and you are most likely to destroy the entire community of caterpillars. Caterpillars mature in about six weeks and wander off individually to pupate in dry protected places. Fuzzy brown moths appear three weeks later and lay their eggs within a few days. The following spring, different egg masses in any given locality may hatch over a two- or three-week period. The farther south you live, the earlier they appear, of course.

April 17

Unusual Vacations in the U.S.

Are you stumped about where to go and what to do for a sightseeing vacation this season? Various publications that you can buy from the Government Printing Office offer a variety of unusual suggestions. Would you like to hike and camp in wilderness regions? The Forest Service has the areas all listed and described in "Search for Solitude." Are history and historical sites of interest to the members of your family? The National Park Service has many publications covering the subject. Would you like to visit an Indian reservation and attend a powwow or other scheduled event? The Bureau of Indian Affairs offers the "American Indian Calendar," a booklet listing interesting events all through the year throughout the country. For how to order, see June 23.

April 18

Today in History: On April 18, 1906, the city of San Francisco was rocked by a major earthquake. The fire that followed burned over more than four square miles.

Will a 'Quake Shake Your Home?

Wherever you live in the United States and Canada, you may personally experience an earthquake right at home. Records compiled by the Coast and Geodetic Survey show that earthquakes have either centered or been felt in every state of the union. In the matter of earthquakes at least, history definitely tends to repeat itself.

The Survey has compiled a record of 'quakes dating back to the early 1600's. Hundreds are listed by date and apparent or actual intensity. More than 20 are rated as major.

Of the major earthquakes, seven were centered east of the Mississippi River. One on August 31, 1886, caused extensive damage and loss of life in Charleston, S.C.

April 19

Today in History: In the year 1775, British troops fired upon American rebels on April 19 at Lexington and Concord, Mass., beginning the Revolution. Of this battle, Ralph Waldo Emerson later wrote:

By the rude bridge that arched the flood,
Their flag to April's breeze unfurled,
Here once the embattled farmers stood,
And fired the shot heard round the world.

Time to Prune Your Lilacs?

Keep track of your blossoming lilacs. When the blossoms fade, remove them promptly. This also is the best time of the year to prune the shrub. The time is very limited. A lilac stops growth very soon after blossoming.

Do you remove flowers during the blossoming period for decorative use in the house? Then prune as you cut. Don't cut only the green flower stem. Cut back to a side bud, removing a good piece of woody stem along with the flower stem. New shoots then will develop for another year below the point where the cut was made. Follow this same pruning procedure if you wait to prune until the flowers have faded.

You can cut off and discard the woody part if necessary for better arrangement of your bouquets.

It is not advisable to attempt lilac pruning during the winter dormant period. Flower buds for the next year already have formed at the ends of twigs when winter comes.

The doors are all wide open: at the gate
The blossomed lilacs counterfeit a blaze,
And seem to warm the air.
Henry W. Longfellow, *Three Friends of Mine*

April 20

Have You Started a Compost Pit?

Begin a compost pit this spring—and a year from now the composted material will be ready for use in your flower and vegetable gardens, or around your shrubs. If you are not quite ready to make use of all of the compost at the end of the first year, start a second pit during the spring, and you never will lack for compost to enrich your soil.

Compost provides one of the easiest and cheapest ways to increase fertility. Too, a compost pit is a handy place to get rid of garden waste—dead foliage, vegetable tops and peelings, grass clippings, and any other plant material that will rot quickly.

Dig your pit three to four feet deep and as wide and long as your needs (and waste supply) dictate. Line the sides with boards.

Put in a six-inch layer of plant material. Sprinkle this layer with lime and 5-10-5 fertilizer—one cup of each to a square yard of litter.

Add a thin layer of soil to keep the litter in place. Wet down thoroughly.

Make the center lower than the sides, to allow rainfall to drain into the litter. Cover with plastic so the compost will not dry out. Water as often as necessary to keep the compost moist.

Turn the pit contents top to bottom after three or four months.

Rather than go to the trouble of digging a pit, some gardeners heap up compost with a wire or board enclosure around it.

April 21

Get a Willow Tree Free

Are there willow trees in your neighborhood? Pussy willows? Weeping willows? Others? If you can get a small branch, you can start a tree of your own at no cost. Choose a branch not larger in diameter than your finger. Thrust it a foot or so into moist soil, allowing about as much to project from the ground.

After the new tree is well started, say about the middle of the summer, you can move it to any spot where you'd like it.

April 22

Plant a Tree for Arbor Day

Today is Arbor Day in Nebraska, the first state to set a day each year for planting trees. Today also is the birthday of J. Sterling Morton, who proposed the first Arbor Day in that state—on April 10, 1872. Through Morton's efforts, the Nebraska State Legislature offered prizes to the groups and individuals who would plant the most trees. As a result, more than a million trees were planted on that first day. After Morton died, the Nebraska Legislature switched the date to his birthday and made it a legal holiday. Dates vary, but almost all other states now have Arbor Days.

This is an appropriate time to plant a tree in practically all parts of the U.S.

For a bare-root tree dig a planting hole wide enough to receive the roots spread in a natural position. For balled trees, dig the hole two feet wider than the ball. Set the tree at the same level it previously grew. If soil removed from the hole is poor, try to replace it with good soil brought from another site. Leave a saucer-like basin around the trunk for watering.

If the site has poor drainage, you might dig a deep hole several feet away, fill it with rocks and lay drain tile to it from the tree site. In heavy clay, it helps to set the tree on the high side and fill in around it with good soil.

In all situations stake or guy the tree. For a

tree with a trunk diameter three inches or less, set two heavy stakes beside the rootball before filling the hole. For larger trees run out three guy wires equally spaced around the tree.

Settle the soil by thorough watering. Then, starting at the top, wrap the trunk with strips of burlap or creped paper to prevent sunscald. Remove the wrapping after two years.

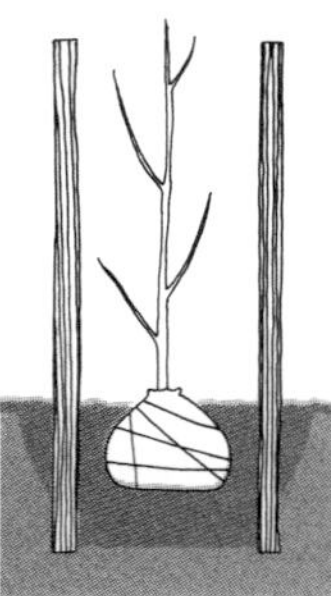

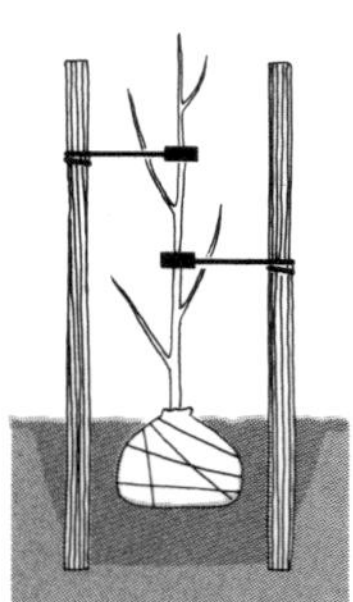

Three steps in planting a tree.

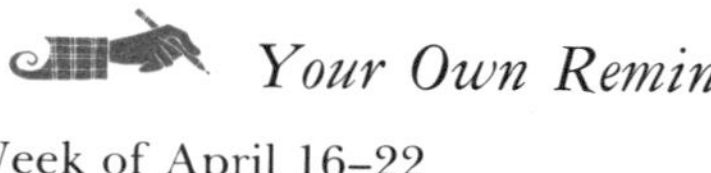

Your Own Reminders

Week of April 16–22

April 23

Repairs to a Brick Walk

A brick walk is an architectural asset to the home grounds. But eventually, its surface may become uneven and require relaying. This is a good chore to undertake at this time of the year before the weather becomes hot.

Brick walks normally are floated on sand; that is, they are placed on a tamped bed of sand about four inches thick, with regular spacing (about 3/8 inch) between the bricks. Sand also fills these spaces.

Today in History: This is St. George's Day. St. George has been venerated as the patron saint of England since the Crusaders brought home his fame from the Holy Land. Legend says he slew a dragon in Libya early in the Christian era. His cross, which is red, is represented on Britain's flag on a white background.

If only a few bricks are higher or lower than their neighbors, you may find it necessary only to pry out and re-lay these at the correct level. Scrape the sand from the cracks surrounding each brick and lever it up with a pry bar or piece of strap metal. If the brick has been too high, trowel out some of the sand, level it off, and try the brick in the opening. If the brick has been too low, tamp enough sand into the depression to level it. Finally, tamp sand into the cracks around the brick.

If the entire walk has taken on a wavy surface, you may want to take it all up. See if you can find a reason why the walk became uneven, tree roots, perhaps. Eliminate any such problem first. In doing this, you may have to remove most or all of the original bed of sand. Level off the soil surface below the walk area at a suitable depth to allow for a four-inch bed of sand, plus the approximate thickness of the bricks, so as to bring the level of the finished walk even with the ground surface on either side.

Bricks are laid in various patterns as seen in the accompanying drawings. In building a new walk or replacing an old one, you can choose the one you like most. For a small area repair, of course, you would use the existing pattern.

After the bricks are in place with the desired spacing, sweep sand over the entire surface. Do this several times—until all cracks are filled. Then sprinkle the walk area to settle the sand between the bricks. After a rain or two, you may want to sweep additional sand into the cracks.

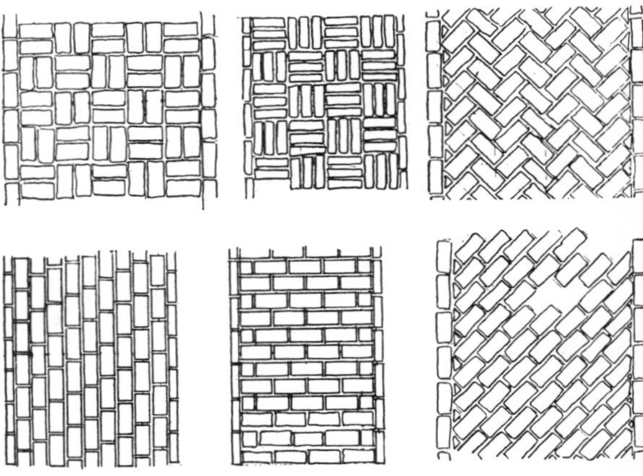

Patterns for laying brick in a wall.

If you have fig bushes only a year or two old, apply a third of a pound of 8-8-8 fertilizer each month from now until the end of August.

April 24

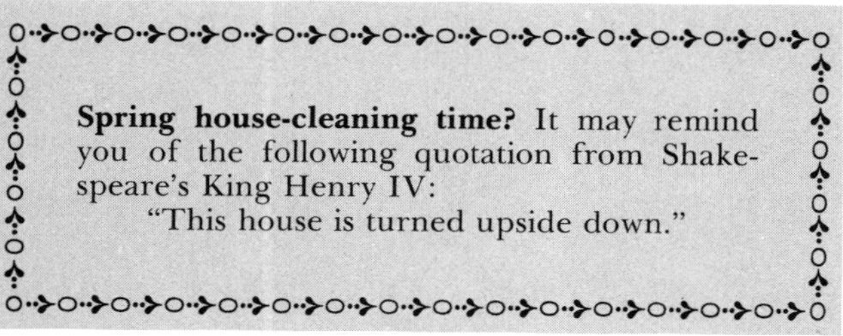

Spring house-cleaning time? It may remind you of the following quotation from Shakespeare's King Henry IV:

"This house is turned upside down."

Daylight Saving Time Arrives Soon

Daylight Saving Time normally begins on the last Sunday of April in those states which observe it. Turn your clocks ahead one hour on the date your newspaper will announce for the current year.

Shown here is the U.S. map of official time zones issued by the Department of Transportation. U.S. time is fixed at the U.S. Naval Observatory in Washington, D.C. When it's noon there, it's 11 a.m. in the Central Zone, 10 a.m. in the Mountain Zone, and 9 a.m. in the Pacific Zone. Note that the time zone boundary divides some states. Hawaii uses Alaska Standard Time, two hours earlier than Pacific. Puerto Rico lies in the Eastern Standard Zone.

The same zones apply to Canada. Atlantic Standard Zone (one hour later than Washington, D.C.) begins there on a line eastward from

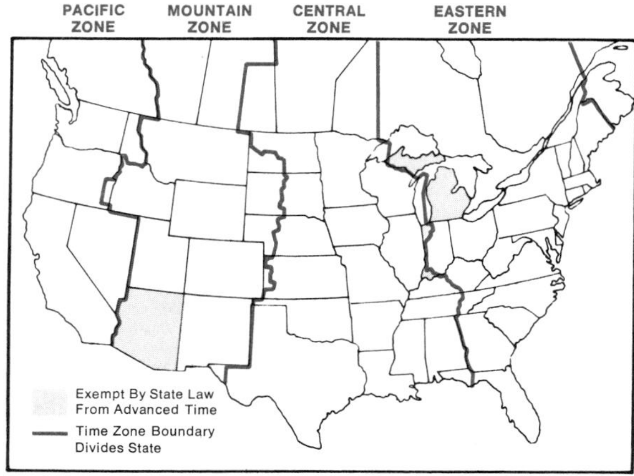

the northeastern border of Maine. There's also Newfoundland Standard Time, one and one-half hours later than Washington, D.C. To the northwest, Canada also has a Yukon Standard Time Zone, one hour earlier than that of the Pacific Zone.

Put up stakes or other guards to protect young trees or shrubs from being bumped or scraped by mowers.

Check azaleas for leaf miner. If they are present, repeat the spray described two weeks ago.

Water any newly-planted evergreens if there has been little rainfall. Soak the soil slowly to a depth of 8 to 12 inches. This should last about 10 days. Water newly-planted plants regularly during the first year.

Plan to spray flowering crabapples for rust and scab weekly from budbreak until two weeks after petal fall.

April 25

Symbols of Electronic Components

In our everyday lives we constantly make use of electrical and electronic conveniences and necessities. When trouble occurs with one of them, you may want to refer to its wiring diagram. The accompanying chart will help you understand the diagram.

Today in History: Born April 25, 1874, in Bologna, Italy, Guglielmo Marconi won fame for inventing wireless telegraphy, forerunner of modern radio and the world of electronics.

Wait ten days or two weeks after azaleas have bloomed to spray the plants for leaf miner or leaf roller. Use an emulsion containing 20 percent lindane diluted 1 ounce to 4 gallons of water. Spray the foliage completely.

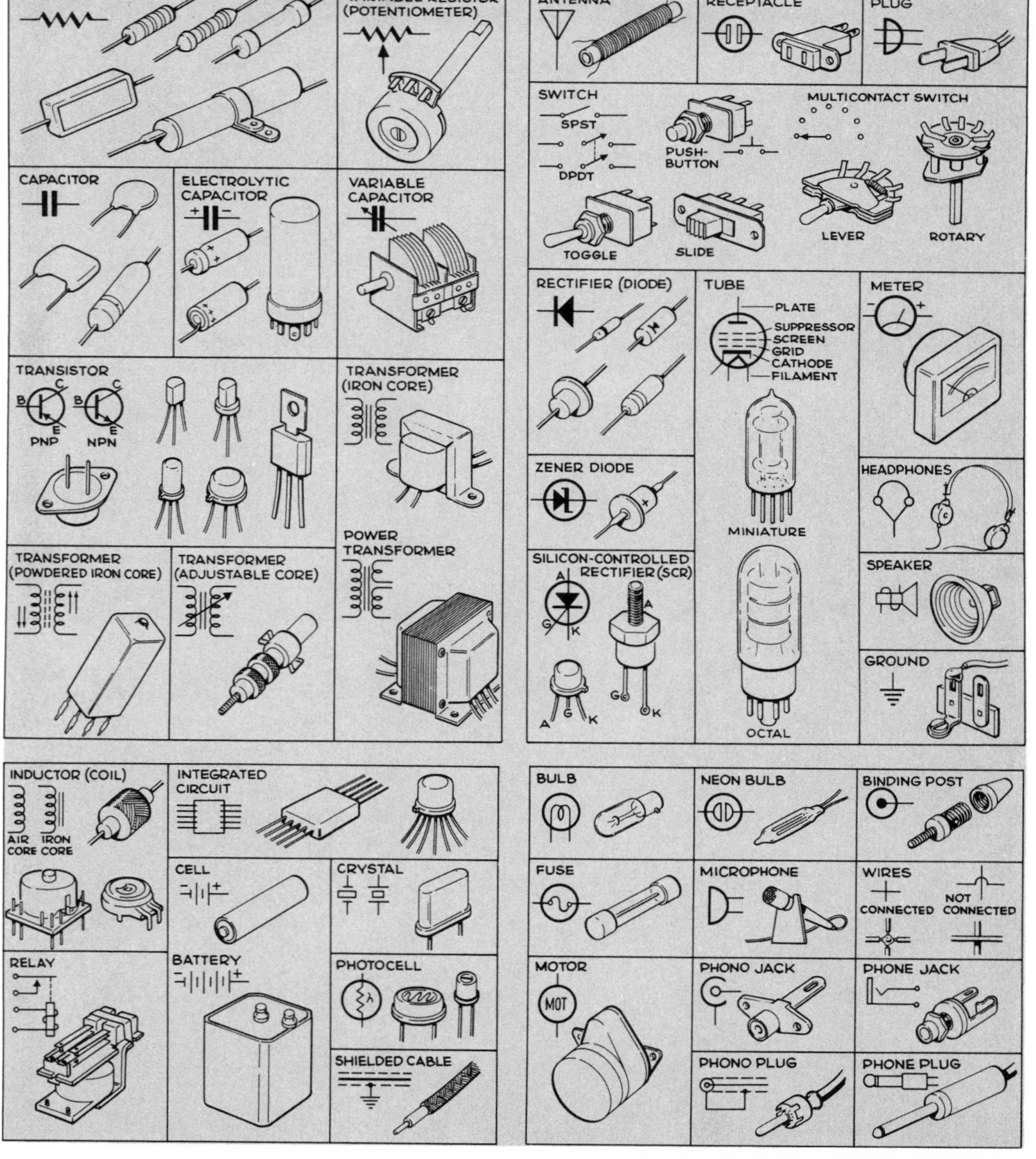

April 26

Slide-Out Kitchen Racks

These racks bring order out of the chaos that always develops when the housewife stores pots on shelves in a kitchen base cabinet. You hang each pot on its allotted hook. You pull out the rack for easy access to the utensil that's needed at the moment.

Almost all modern kitchens have a base cabinet where such racks can be installed. Why not check out yours today?

Existing shelves must be removed, of course. The drawing shows a simple installation—grooved strips of wood screwed inside the cabinet, top and bottom, to receive sliding racks of perforated hardboard. Install blocks up under the countertop to drop the upper grooved member below the door frame. Size the rack panels to suit the space available after the grooved strips are in place.

Install stops to keep each panel from being pulled out of the grooves and spilling the pots. These stops can consist of a small wood block cemented to each outer edge of the upper grooved strip—and a pin through the hardboard in a position to strike the block when the rack is pulled most of the way out. Spray a coating of lubricant into the grooves and on the edges of the hardboard.

Instead of making the grooved slides, you might substitute commercial drawer slides. These are available in various forms, some of them with roller bearings.

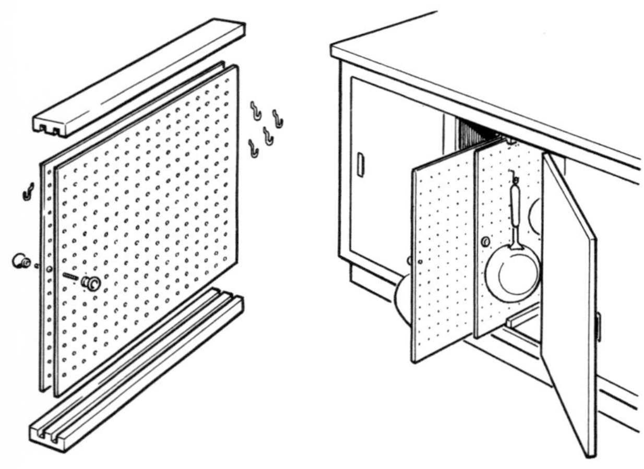

Slide-out kitchen rack of perforated hardboard.

Should you remove sod from around young fruit trees? Now is a good time to consider that question. Apples and pears will grow satisfactorily surrounded by sod if you remember to fertilize well each year. Peach, sour cherry, and plum will do much better if they don't have to compete with sod for moisture and nutrients.

You can also apply mulch around the trees, whether sodded or not—straw, hay, lawn clippings. A mulch both conserves moisture and improves soil fertility.

Some modern lawns are cut vertically instead of horizontally. A machine called a verticutter," or vertical mower, is used on lawns of Bermudagrasses. These put out stems along the ground. An ordinary horizontal mower would not touch the stems.

April 27

Time to Lay up Snowthrowers

Wherever you live, it's now unlikely that you'll have more snow this season, at least very little if any. So the time has come to put a snowthrower away, unless it's convertible to summer use.

First, wash the exterior with detergent and hot water. Then hose it down.

Second, apply oil and grease to all points indicated in your instructions.

Third, let the engine idle a few minutes until the crankcase is warm. Drain the oil while hot and refill.

Fourth, while the engine is warming and/or the oil is draining, check all nuts, cotters, and clevis pins for tightness.

Fifth, drain the fuel tank if this is readily done before starting the engine again and letting the tank and carburetor run dry. Because snowthrower engines are shrouded for winter warmth, confine engine running to a few minutes—or pick a cool day for it. Running the system dry is perhaps the most important lay-up step. This keeps fuel from gumming up the system during storage, a situation that usually makes it impossible to start up the engine.

Finally, remove the spark plug, shoot a few drops of oil into the cylinder, crank the engine momentarily to distribute the oil, and replace the plug. Plan to install a new properly gapped plug next fall.

After moving the machine to its storage area, throw a sheet of polyethylene over it and weight down the edges.

Noise apparently slows plant growth. Researchers grew twelve tobacco plants in water baths in a sterile chamber for two weeks in virtual silence. They then repeated the experiment, but added a loudspeaker that poured out constant noise equal to a jet plane overhead. Plant growth dropped 40 per cent.

April 28

Feed Nitrogen to Shade Trees Now

For growth and health, trees on your lawn need an annual feeding of nitrogen. April or May is usually considered the best time for this annual feeding. However, applications in October or November will still be available to stimulate growth the following spring.

Surface application of nitrogenous fertilizer is easy and effective. Rain and supplemental watering will carry the fertilizer down to the root zone. Using a spreader, make an even distribution to a little beyond the limb spread of the tree. Do this while the grass is dry. Then wash the fertilizer into the soil with a lawn sprinkler or spray hose before it has a chance to burn the grass.

Apply at the rate of 6 pounds of actual nitro-

gen per 1,000 square feet. This amount can be obtained from 13 pounds of urea (45-0-0), 18 pounds of ammonium nitrate (33.5-0-0), or 29 pounds of ammonium sulfate (21-0-0).

Trees also may need applications of phosphorous or potassium. These may already be available in some soils. If so, adding more will have little or no effect on the trees. But it is usually desirable to add these nutrients at intervals of three to five years. Apply phosphorous at 3.6 pounds of phosphoric acid per 1,000 square feet, potassium at the rate of 6 pounds of potash.

Phosphorous and potassium fertilizer must be put down into the root zone if they are to do any good. You can accomplish this by punching or drilling holes 15 to 24 inches deep at 2-foot intervals on parallel lines over the area embraced by the limb spread. (Make no holes within 2½ feet of the tree trunk.) For phosphorous, place 2 level tablespoons of superphosphate (0-20-0) into each hole or one of double superphosphate (0-40-0). For potassium, place 1 level tablespoon of muriate of potash (0-0-60) in each hole. If you are applying a balanced fertilizer, say a 10-10-10, pour a half cup into each hole. Water the area after the fertilizer application and fill the holes with good soil, humus, or peat moss.

A sharp "needle" attachment for a garden hose can also be used to carry water soluble fertilizer to the root zone.

If you plant a floral tree on arbor day, consider a late blooming tree to lengthen your season of blossoms. Examples are Chinese dogwood, crape myrtle, or goldenrain tree.

Crawling or flying insects are apt to be appearing in your home now. A safe spray for these pests is pyrethrum.

Grass muffles noise and helps you find peace in in a small yard. Architects sometimes forget this and specify paving for most or all of an enclosed city yard. The more grass the better—even if you do have to fertilize it heavily and mow it.

April 29

Control Gypsy Moths Now if You Have Them

The gypsy moth times things just right. As trees begin to leaf out in late April and early May in the Northeast, masses of overwintering eggs hatch into wriggling caterpillars, each one with an appetite that keeps it feeding

for 12 weeks or more. Feeding shows up first as small holes in the new leaves. Before long the leaf has completely disappeared. In regions of severe infestation, entire trees are stripped.

The caterpillars feed on more than 500 varieties of trees and shrubs. If hard pressed, older caterpillars will even strip the needles from pine, spruce, white cedar, and hemlock.

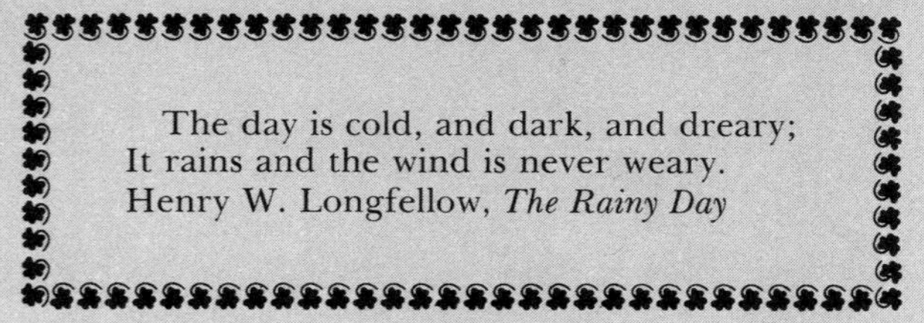

The day is cold, and dark, and dreary;
It rains and the wind is never weary.
Henry W. Longfellow, *The Rainy Day*

Defoliations in two successive years may kill hardwood trees. A single defoliation may kill evergreens such as white pines and hemlocks.

The caterpillars keep on the move throughout the feeding period. You see them hanging from silken threads as they advance from tree to tree. This gives you an opportunity to attack them—even though somewhat futilely.

If nothing else, you can hand pick them as they move up the trunks of trees. Garden-supply houses in your area also may have a sticky substance, like old-fashioned flypaper, that can be applied in a broad ring around the tree trunks. The crawling larvae become trapped in this. Replenish the substance daily during the period of caterpillar activity.

Carbaryl (Sevin) is an insecticide that will control the caterpillars. But follow directions carefully. You may want to call in a professional spraying firm if your trees are large. Don't apply this insecticide to a tree in blossom; it is toxic to bees.

When fully grown—usually in July—the caterpillars pupate by spinning a loose cocoon on trees and rocks. You can successfully hand pick the cocoons at this time. Look for them in clusters on the branches and trunks of your trees—or even on rocks in the vicinity.

You can take still another crack at the insects when the adult moths appear in July and August. Bug traps of various types, including those with black light, can be placed in your yard with good hopes of success.

When buying perennial flower plants, avoid any that have pale yellow stems and leaves. They have been held in a warm area too long. Choose plants that are compact and dark green.

Set out sweet potato plants in the South.

Spray apples and pears with oil for scale insects, red mite, and red bugs when the fruit buds show green at the tip and before they show any pink color. See February 10.

Would you like a black walnut tree? Spring is the time to plant seedlings. See October 19.

Ring perennial flower plants with 5-10-5 and soak it into the ground.

Your Own Reminders

Week of April 23–29

April 30

Planting Perennial Flower Seeds Outdoors

Delay sowing seeds of most perennial flowers outdoors until after the last frost. Most seeds will not germinate until the soil warms to about 60 degrees. Sow the seed in vermiculite-filled furrows. Otherwise, the seeds may fail to germinate because the surface of the soil cakes and prevents the entry of water. For the best timing for specific flowers, see Appendix G in the back of this book.

First, make furrows in the well-prepared soil about one-half inch deep. Fill these furrows with fine vermiculite and sprinkle the entire surface with water. Then make a fine furrow in the vermiculite and sow the seed in it at the rate recommended on the packet. Cover the seed with a layer of vermiculite sifted on. Finally, using a nozzle adjusted for a fine mist, water the entire bed thoroughly.

To retard water evaporation, cover the seeded area with sheets of newspaper or polyethylene film (plastic garment bags from the dry cleaner are excellent). Support the newspaper or plastic on blocks or sticks one or two inches above the surface of the bed. Remove the paper or plastic when seedlings appear.

When most outdoor-grown perennials develop two true leaves, they should be thinned to the recommended spacing. This allows the plants to have enough light, water, nutrients, and space for them to develop fully. If they have been seeded in vermiculite-filled furrows, the excess seedlings can be transplanted to another spot without injury.

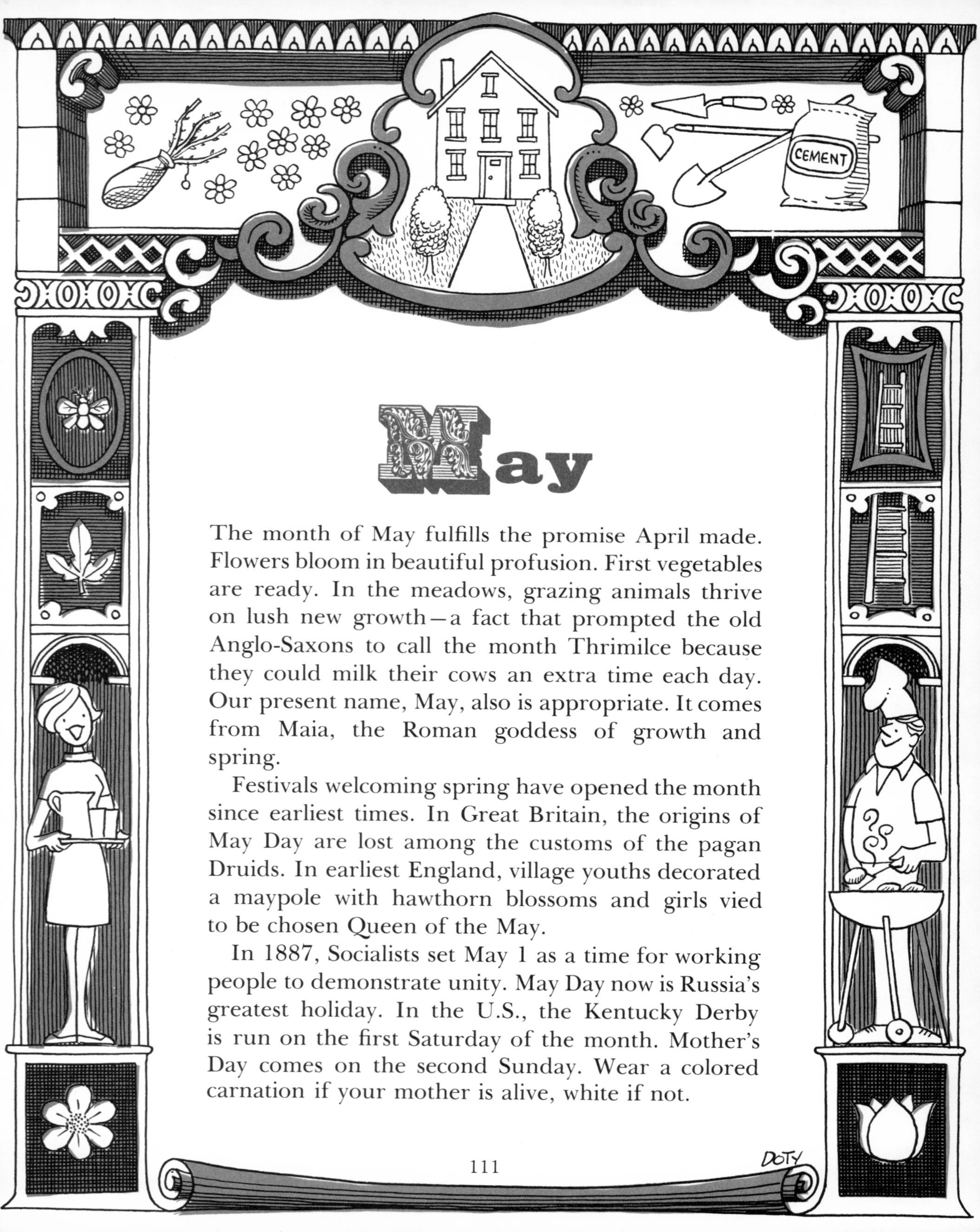

May

The month of May fulfills the promise April made. Flowers bloom in beautiful profusion. First vegetables are ready. In the meadows, grazing animals thrive on lush new growth—a fact that prompted the old Anglo-Saxons to call the month Thrimilce because they could milk their cows an extra time each day. Our present name, May, also is appropriate. It comes from Maia, the Roman goddess of growth and spring.

Festivals welcoming spring have opened the month since earliest times. In Great Britain, the origins of May Day are lost among the customs of the pagan Druids. In earliest England, village youths decorated a maypole with hawthorn blossoms and girls vied to be chosen Queen of the May.

In 1887, Socialists set May 1 as a time for working people to demonstrate unity. May Day now is Russia's greatest holiday. In the U.S., the Kentucky Derby is run on the first Saturday of the month. Mother's Day comes on the second Sunday. Wear a colored carnation if your mother is alive, white if not.

May 1

May Day

Today in History: "Nation's Christmas Tree." The General Grant Tree in California was so designated May 1, 1926 in a dedication by the mayor of Sanger, Calif. The tree is a sequoia with a base diameter of 40 feet and a height of 200 feet.

The Joys of Sassafras Tea

Sassafras was probably America's first export. Roots of this widespread small tree were shipped from Spanish America for medicinal purposes soon after Columbus' voyages, and its fame spread through Europe. English explorers knew of it—and found it. The first ships to Jamestown carried back a cargo of sassafras to England.

For years now, country people have brewed sassafras tea as a spring tonic. It may or may not provide health benefits. But those who have tried sassafras tea will tell you that it's a delightful hot drink.

Now's the time for it. You can gather the tea makings—the sassafras roots—from the wild almost anywhere in the eastern U.S. and southern Ontario. The small tree or shrub is common along roadsides, fencerows, and railroad rights-of-way. It has leaves of three different shapes, one of them resembling a mitten. In winter and early spring the twigs have green bark.

Pull up small shoots, digging down to get as many of the roots as possible. Take home only the roots if you're just going to make tea. Take home several small plants with lots of roots if you wish to start your own clump of sassafras. Keep the roots moist en route home and set the plants into a spot in the yard or lawn where they can expand into a clump. This will happen in only a few years. New shoots keep coming up as roots spread outward. If you live outside the normal range of sassafras, why not consider buying plants from a nursery?

To make tea, scrub all soil from a handful of roots. Older roots have a rough outside bark which should be scraped off. Cut the roots into short pieces, cover them with several cups of water in a pan, and boil until the liquid turns a red tea color. Sweeten to taste—and enjoy.

Use grass clippings as a mulch around annual flowers. This will keep the soil from crusting, prevent weeds, add organic matter.

A canvas soaker hose is the ideal way to water flower beds. The slow moving water does not disturb the soil or reduce its capacity to absorb water. Water from sprinklers wets the foliage and makes it susceptible to disease. Allow the soil to dry moderately before watering again.

After annual flower plants are set out or thinned, cultivate only to break the surface crust. Stop cultivating when the plants begin to grow. Pull weeds by hand. Feeder roots spread out—and cultivation may injure these. Cultivation also may uncover other weed seeds and cause them to germinate.

Check stems of prized lilacs for indications of borers. Kill them by digging from the stems or probing with a fine wire. If burrowing is extensive, cut and destroy the infested stems.

May 2

How to Prepare for Tornadoes

Tornadoes cause a heavy loss in lives and property damage each year in North America. More of these violent storms occur at the present season than at any other time of the year. The greatest number hit the central states of the U.S., but no region is entirely immune. The chart and maps in Appendix L support these statements.

A tornado usually develops during a severe thunderstorm. You recognize it as a funnel-shaped cloud extending from a thundercloud toward the earth. It spins rapidly and roars loudly.

Home owners can prepare for these potential disasters and lessen their damage. Operating under the U.S. Department of Commerce, the Environmental Science Services Administration and the Weather Bureau have set up a warning system that enables tornado-prone communities to send everyone to safe shelters. You can order publications describing the warning system from the U.S. Government Printing Office, Washington, D.C. 20402—"Tornado Preparedness Planning." If your region does not now have a warning system, you and your neighbors ought to promote one. Regional Weather Bureau offices in Kansas City, Mo.; Salt Lake City, Utah; Garden City, N.Y.; Fort Worth, Tex.; Anchorage, Alaska; and Honolulu are ready to help you, even to the extent of sending a representative to address a community meeting.

Individual home owners in areas of frequent tornadoes should give thought to construction of storm cellars. Or the safest portion of the basement should be selected and the family drilled to use it.

During periods of heavy storms, keep your radio on, tuned to a local station for any advance warnings that may be broadcast.

May 3

Tornado Safety Rules

When a tornado hits, or is about to, seek inside shelter if possible. If you are in the open, move away from the tornado's path at a right angle. In the center of the U.S., tornadoes most frequently approach from the southwest. In the southeastern states, where tornadoes are sometimes associated with hurricanes, they may advance from the east. If there is no time to get out of the tornado's path, lie flat in the nearest depression, such as a ditch or ravine.

Otherwise, seek safety in designated public or private shelters or as follows:

In office buildings, the basement or an interior hallway on a lower floor is safest. Upper stories are unsafe. If there is no time to descend, a closet or small room with stout walls, or an inside hallway will give some protection against flying debris. Otherwise, under heavy furniture must do.

In homes with basements, seek refuge near the basement wall in the most sheltered and deepest below-ground part of the basement. Additional protection is afforded by taking cover under heavy furniture or a workbench. Other basement possibilities are the smallest room with stout walls, or under a stairway.

In homes without basements, take cover in the smallest room with stout walls, or under heavy furniture, or a tipped-over upholstered couch or chair in the center part of the house. The first floor is safer than the second (or third). If there is time, open windows partly on the side away from the direction of the storm's approach —*but stay away from windows when the storm strikes.*

Mobile homes are particularly vulnerable to overturning and destruction during strong winds, and should be abandoned in favor of a preselected shelter, or even a ditch in the open.

Factories, auditoriums, and other large buildings with wide, free-span roofs, should have preselected, marked shelter areas in their basements, smaller rooms, or nearby.

Parked cars are unsafe as shelter during a tornado or severe windstorm; however, as a last resort, if no ravine or ditch is nearby they may provide some shelter from flying debris to those who crawl under them.

Did you plant citrus trees this season? Be sure you have wrapped the trunks in several thicknesses of newspaper for protection from the sun during the first season. Tie the papers loosely.

Use flue tiles as planters. Building supply dealers have them (or can get them) in many sizes—in square, rectangular, or oval cross section. The tiles will never rot out as wood boxes do. You can vary the heights by sinking them part way into the ground.

May 4

How to Plant New Roses

Roses are one flower that you can grow in any part of the United States, even in those high northern and Rocky Mountain regions where the growing season is short. In regions where winter temperatures regularly go under 10 degrees below zero, spring is the only recommended time for putting new plants into the ground.

Planting roses should not be a spur-of-the-moment spring happening, however. Prepare

the soil during the previous autumn. See October 2. Then rework the soil again in the spring about a month before the time you plan to plant. That way you'll be ready to set new plants as soon as you receive them.

If you cannot plant them as soon as received, moisten the packing material and repack the plants. You can keep them safely this way for two to three days. If you must wait longer, heel them in. Place them in a trench in the garden and cover the roots with moist soil. If the canes are dry, cover them with soil, too.

Cut off all damaged roots before you plant, as well as any broken or dead canes. Cut the canes back to 12 inches—no less—if the nursery failed to do so. Move the plants to the garden with their roots in a bucket of water. Never expose the roots to the sun or drying winds.

Before bringing out the plants, you already should have placed a small, cone-shaped mound of fine soil in the center of each planting hole. Spread the roots down over this mound.

Adjust the depth of the plant to your local temperatures. If temperatures are regularly lower than ten degrees below zero, set the bud union (see arrow) so it will be two inches below ground level when the hole is filled. If winter temperatures range from ten below to ten above, locate the bud union one inch below ground level. In warmer regions, place it at ground level.

Work fine soil around all the roots as you fill the hole. When the roots are covered, spray water into the hole to settle the soil well around the roots. Fill the hole—and the job is finished if you live in the deep South. If there still is danger of frost, mound the soil about ten inches high around the canes of bush and climbing roses, three or four inches around miniature roses. Remember to remove the soil mound when frost danger has passed.

Drive a stake into the soil near tree roses and tie the trunk to the stake to keep the trunk from whipping in the wind and loosening the roots.

Recommended spacing for rose plants varies with winter temperatures. You can place them closest together—about two feet—where the temperature regularly goes below minus ten. This applies for hybrid teas, grandifloras, polyanthas, and floribundas. Raise the spacing to two and one-half feet where lowest winter temperatures range between ten below and ten above. Put them at least three feet apart where winters are mild. In all areas, space hybrid perpetuals three to five feet apart, climbers from eight to ten.

"Did not the boundless blue sea fill you with emotion?"

"Yes," replied the traveler, "at first it did. But after a while it sorter emptied me."

May 5

Check Out That Air Conditioner

Hot weather will arrive soon, if it hasn't already, and you'll be wanting to use your air conditioner—if you have one.

The service manager for the York Division of Borg-Warner Corporation makes these suggestions:

If a window unit has been stored for the winter, place it upright on a level surface for 24 hours to allow oil in the sealed system to drain back into the compressor.

Dust all exposed surfaces, paying special attention to air inlets and outlets; wipe down plastic surfaces with soap and water, and oil according to manufacturer's instructions. Clean and paint any rusted parts.

Test-run the unit on the floor before installation. Choose a day when room temperature is in the 70's and the outside temperature is in the mid-60's. Let the air conditioner run for five to ten minutes. Note the cooling effectiveness and listen for unusual noises that may indicate that the unit requires more extensive checking. If it does not cool, it may have lost its charge of refrigerant.

If the conditioner was left in the window over the winter, a change of filter and oiling may be all the maintenance required.

If you have central air conditioning with common ductwork for heating and cooling, follow through these steps:

Reset dampers for air conditioning. (Damper adjustment is required only when there are separate ducts for the cool air.)

See that air inlets and outlets, both indoors and out, are free from obstruction.

Clean or replace filters.

Lubricate where called for. (This is generally limited to fan motors and bearings.)

Turn on the power for at least one day before you start the compressor. Run the fan only, with the cooling thermostat set high. In the compressors of many makes of air conditioners, power is required to prewarm and improve the lubricating qualities of the compressor oil. Even when this is not a necessity a 24-hour warm-up can do no possible harm.

If there is an auxiliary drain pan under the unit, as is the case in many attic installations, be sure this pan is cleaned out and that the drain is open. Flush with a pitcher of water to check run-off because insects sometimes block drains.

Pick a day when outside temperatures are in the mid-60's for a test run. Shift the thermostat from "Heat" to "Cool" and run equipment for five or ten minutes by dropping the thermostat to below room temperature. Listen well for any unusual noises, either indoors or out. If any unusual noises persist, call in your dealer.

If yours is a "split system," that is with a compressor-condenser section outdoors and a cooling evaporator in the house, it will require all the checks just listed as well as a few others:

When piping leads outside, check the condition of the insulation and exposed metal surfaces (for rust). Make sure concrete foundations have not been broken or tilted by frost.

You should also look at air intake and discharge vents, making sure that both are open and free of leaves and other garden debris.

May 6

Seasonal Tips About Flowers

Watch the newspapers for plant sales conducted by garden clubs or other local groups. You can sometimes get quality plants at bargain prices—and support a worthy cause, too.

In the North, don't be too hasty about setting out frost-tender plants.

Do your perennials all have an adequate mulch?

Annual flowering vines look great growing over a fence or other support. Plant the seeds as soon as frost is out of the ground.

When peony buds are pea size, spray the plants for blight.

Rose pruning time has arrived in most of Region III. First, of course, remove any winter covering materials. See January 5.

Staking of perennial flowers is due in southern latitudes. Pull developing weeds.

Danger of spring frost has just about passed for those who live in Region III. See the February 8 map. You can plant all flowers (and vegetables) now in Region III and many in Region IV.

When tulips bloom, fertilize them lightly with 5-10-5. Keep the fertilizer off the leaves and away from roots. A little bone meal is also a good source of nitrogen for promoting growth for next year.

Are you proud of your home and garden? Would others enjoy visiting you? Then let a garden club know that you're willing to open your home for a local tour.

If you have an in-ground swimming pool, consider giving it a floral setting. A bed of marigolds at one side is a possibility.

Wildlife on home grounds is sometimes attractive—but deer, rabbits, raccoons, and the like can be destructive. If you have the problem, consider the use of chemical repellants available from garden centers.

Beware of Jimson weed! This plant has an interesting history. Its name comes from the colonial settlement of Jamestown, Virginia. Also known as thorn apple (from its fruit), it grows almost everywhere in backyards, wastelands, and barnyards. Its white, trumpet-shaped flowers resemble morning glories. All parts are poisonous, the leaves and seeds especially so.

Your Own Reminders

Week of April 30–May 6

May 7

Garden-Hose Repairs

Either plastic or rubber, a garden hose costs considerable money—and it pays to keep it in repair.

Small leaks in either kind can usually be repaired. If the hose is rubber and the leak very small, you may be able to stop it by working liquid rubber (available in squeeze tubes) into the opening and letting it dry. When the break is larger, use an auto tube-patching kit and apply the type of patch that's suitable for either natural or synthetic rubber.

When the hole develops in a plastic hose, heat a soldering gun. Then carefully and briefly touch the hot tip to the edge of the hole, pushing the melted plastic into the hole. A cement suitable for use on plastic can also sometimes be used to cement on a patch. Cut the patch from the end of a damaged hose if nothing else is available.

If a large break occurs in the hose, cut out the damaged section and connect the parts with a metal hose mender available at hardware stores and from mail-order catalogs. Some menders are suitable only for rubber hose, some for plastic. If a mender is not available, look for a clincher coupling—a male part for one piece of hose, a female part for the other. These are installed by cutting the end of the hose square and then hammering the clincher prongs into the hose.

Installing a new rubber washer in the sill-cock end of the hose at the beginning of each summer season is a good precaution against leaks at that point.

Your own wildflower garden? Many home owners have them now—and the number is increasing each year. As you might expect, you must grow wildflowers under conditions similar to their natural habitats—usually a shady, wooded area for springtime bloomers. Rather than attempting to transplant wildlings, buy your stock from nurseries that offer plants and seeds.

May 8

Today in History: A U.S. patent for a rubber tire was granted on May 8, 1847, to Robert Thomson of England. His tires were for carriage wheels.

Do You Know Your County Agents?

Today is the anniversary of a service that every home owner should know about—the Cooperative Extension Service, established by the Smith Lever Act passed by Congress on May 8, 1914. The Service operates under the U.S. Department of Agriculture.

As representatives of these agencies, your county agricultural agent and county home agent have a number of publications on lawns, gardening, shrubs, trees, flowers, and on food for the family, clothing, money management, and home furnishings. Or you can write the U.S. Department of Agriculture, Washington, D.C. 20250 for a list of popular publications on any of these and other subjects. Single copies of most of the publications are free.

Extension Service agents also give out a great deal of helpful information in your local newspapers and on radio and television. They conduct a number of meetings and demonstrations in your community. Many of them also prepare messages on home and garden subjects which you can hear by dialing a telephone number.

Your county agents do not have time to come to your home and help you with individual problems, but they can help you with some of them by telephone or mail. In the telephone directory, they may be listed under your county's name or the name of your state university, or as Extension office or agent. See Appendix M in the back of the book for your state address.

Are birds likely to take your berries or fruit? Garden centers now carry large mesh covers.

May 9

Facts About Clothes Moths

Temperatures are high enough through most of the northern states now so that woolens and other warm wearables—and blankets—can be stored away until fall. And that, of course, brings up each year the question of how to provide protection from clothes moths.

It's the larva, not the moth, that causes damage. The larvae feed on articles that contain wool, mohair, feathers, down, fur, or hair. Good housekeeping practices will remove waste material and lint upon which they feed. These practices should include a semiannual vacuuming of the storage-closet interior to remove

accumulations of food material from cracks or crevices.

Two species of clothes moths are commonly found—the webbing and casemaking. With wings folded, adult moths are about one-fourth inch long. The webbing moth is golden buff-colored and has a satiny sheen. The hairs on its head are upright and reddish. The casemaking moth is drab with indistinct dark spots on the wings and lighter-colored hairs on its head.

Larvae have pearly-white naked bodies, dark

heads, and are about three-eighths of an inch long fully grown. Their fecal matter often is the same color as the material they consume. A casemaking larva makes a silken parchment-like case into which it withdraws when disturbed. The silken case is always dragged behind as it looks for new sources of food. Larvae of the webbing moth live within silken burrows which they spin. These burrows often include parts of the fabric on which the larva is living. Larvae are most destructive to articles left undisturbed for long periods of time. The moths prefer darkness. When infested garments are disturbed, the moths rapidly conceal themselves. A new generation of moths can develop in a month under favorable conditions (sufficient food and warmth) but may take over a year under less favorable circumstances.

Woolen scraps or garments stored for long periods on shelves or in corners, boxes, or drawers are often a source of infestation. Stored articles should be shaken and aired periodically if they are to be saved.

See tomorrow's report on other procedures for avoiding moth damage.

Spray oaks and maples for cankerworm. Malathion can be used. The same spray may take care of leaf rollers on oaks.

May 10

How to Foil Clothes Moths

Many dry-cleaning establishments provide summer storage of winter garments at no charge above what you pay for cleaning alone. The garments are stored in refrigerated atmospheres and usually are insured. Seasonal garments should be cleaned anyway before storage. So how can you beat such an offer? Dry cleaning kills the insects—moths and any others—in all stages of development.

To rid woolens of insects, their eggs and larvae, brush the articles thoroughly, especially in seams, folds, and pockets, and hang them in the sun. Larvae missed in brushing will fall from the clothing if they cannot find protection from the light.

Insecticide oil solutions are a time-proven method for protecting clothing and blankets. This insecticide is sold as a liquid oil solution to be applied by a sprayer. It also comes in spray containers. Heed all directions and cautions on the label.

Woolens may be hung on a clothesline and sprayed lightly and uniformly until the surface is moist. Do not soak or saturate woolens. Too

much spray may result in a white deposit after the fabric dries. A slight excess of deposit may be removed by brushing lightly—a heavier deposit may require dry-cleaning, but the protection is lost.

Infants' apparel such as sweaters, blankets, or other woolen articles may be sprayed with an insecticide *only if they are to be stored. Launder or dry-clean before using again.* Allow treated woolens to dry before storing them.

May 11

Today in History: B. F. Goodrich announced tubeless tires on May 11, 1947.

Repairing Brick Walls or Chimneys

Once a year check brick walls or chimneys for loose or missing bricks and loose or cracked mortar in the joints. Cracks in the mortar can permit water to enter and damage the interior of the wall or chimney.

Buying a prepared mortar mix is a convenient first step toward either repointing or resetting bricks. Mix a batch of mortar according to directions on the bag, noting especially that its entire contents should be carefully intermixed before water is added.

Using a cold chisel or old screwdriver, clean all loose mortar you can from the joint. Then swab out the joint with a stiff brush and a liberal amount of water, leaving the joint area damp.

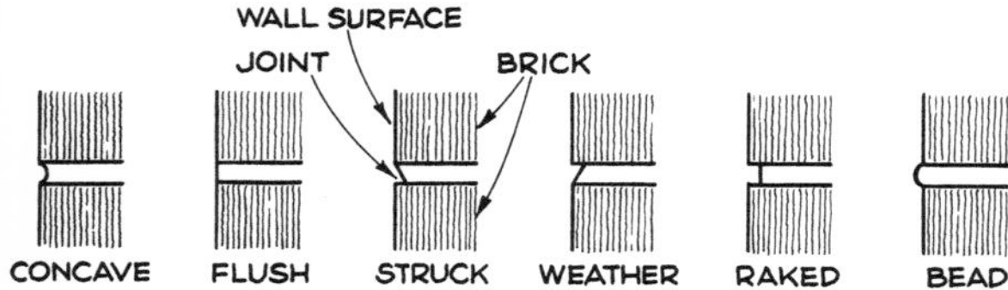

Immediately, fill the joint with mortar. This can be done neatly and without mess by using a jointing tool to slide mortar off the upper surface of a trowel held level with the joint. Press in the mortar to fill all cavities. Scrape off excess. Finish the joint to match the one used in the wall, using a trowel or jointing tool. See the accompanying sketches of typical masonry joints. Brush across the joint after a few minutes to clean any mortar from the bricks. Finish the joint again if necessary.

Use generally the same procedures if you must reset a few bricks. Chip all the old mortar from the bricks and the joints. Then dampen the bricks and joint area thoroughly. Level off a three-quarter inch bed of mortar mix on the upper surface of the wall being repaired. Butter one end of each brick before you lay it. Press the buttered end sideways against the adjoining brick until a three-eighths inch vertical joint results. Tap down the brick to leave the same joint horizontally. Clean excess mortar from your joint with the trowel. Finish the joint with the trowel or jointing tool as the mortar begins to set. Butter both ends and top and bottom of the brick if you are inserting it into a space from which one has been removed.

Buy muriatic acid and scrub the repaired area about a week later to remove mortar splatters that you have not been able to brush off.

May 12

Look Out for Lace Bugs on Evergreens

It's time now to be on the lookout for the work of lace bugs on rhododendron, azalea, laurel, and andromeda—a grayish mottled appearance on the upper surfaces of leaves where chlorophyll has been destroyed. Turn the leaf over and you'll find brown to black spots of excrement and perhaps skins of the feeding nymphs.

Different races of lace bugs feed on the three plants named, but control measures are the same. These pests pass the winter as eggs on the undersides of the leaves. Spraying should be delayed until the eggs hatch. This may occur from early May until deep into June. Apply a summer-type foliage contact spray as recommended on the container, being sure to cover the undersides of the leaves. Make a second application about two weeks after the first.

May 13

Leaflets Three? Let It Be

An old folk rhyme has common sense advice for all of us. The "leaflets three" are almost certain to be poison ivy or oak, now growing abundantly in almost every part of the U.S. and southern Canada. In early spring, the young leaves begin life as an attractive red be-

fore changing to green. All parts of the plant can produce a skin rash on contact. If you pull up and burn the plant, avoid the smoke.

Attack poison ivy with a herbicide. A campaign against all of it you can find on your grounds every three or four years will keep it under control. Formulations containing 2,4-D, amitrole, silvex, or ammonium sulfamate are all effective. Read the directions—and heed them. Spray the herbicide where the ivy grows in masses. Choose a time when there is little or no air movement, preferably in early morning or just before dusk when the air is cool and moist. The plants may take two weeks or more to die. Further applications may be needed.

If the ivy is growing among valuable flowers or other plants, mix some of the weed killer in a coffee can and apply it selectively with an old paint brush, using gloves. Discard can and brush.

Common poison ivy in some form grows over southern Canada and all parts of the U.S. except California and Nevada. Leaves may vary in shape—but they are always three in number. This rule of three applies also to eastern oakleaf poison ivy, which some people call poison oak. Western poison oak occurs in all Pacific Coast states. It also has three leaflets and is related to poison ivy, not oaks.

The rule of three falls down, however, when you come to poison sumac, a large shrub commonly found on the edges of swamps in all states east of the Mississippi. Leaves of poison sumac consist of 7 to 13 leaflets, arranged in pairs with a single leaflet at the end of the midrib. Poison sumac has slender hanging clusters of white fruit, never red. Red fruits are borne only by harmless varieties of sumac.

Your Own Reminders

Week of May 7–13

May 14

Today in History: A property tax law was approved on May 14, 1634 in the Massachusetts Colony.

Blast-Furnace Barbecue Starter

Mild weather has now brought another outdoor barbecue season to most of the country. Before the season gets any older, ask yourself this question: Do I really like to use those smelly liquids to set fire to the charcoal or briquettes? If the answer is no, do this:

Buy one length of four-inch black stovepipe from your hardware store. This comes flat—or almost so, its edge crimped to clip together when you form it into a tube. Don't do this yet. With a pair of tin snips, cut the sheet in half crosswise, keeping the cut edge as smooth as possible. File off any jagged edges or turn them under and hammer them flat. Lay the cut edge of one of your pipe pieces on solid wood, say a length of two-by-four. Clamp it to the wood. Then with an electric drill, space a series of holes about an inch from the edge. Use a quarter-inch bit or larger. Lacking the drill, you can punch the holes through the metal, using a hammer and large nail, a punch, or other sharp instrument. Smooth off any projections around the holes on the inner surface of the metal.

Finally, force the mating edges of the stovepipe together and hook them as they are meant to be. Now form a bail handle from a wire coat hanger and wood package handle. Attach it to the tube by punching holes at the uncut end. Bend the ends of the wire so the bail handle pivots easily.

You now have made a small blast furnace for starting the barbecue fire.

To start the fire, first place a bed of charcoal or briquettes on the cooker. Then stuff newspaper loosely into the bottom of your blast furnace and put a layer of charcoal or half a dozen briquettes on top of the paper. Set fire to the paper from the bottom and set the furnace on the grille, pivoting the long handle to one side so it won't get hot. When the charcoal or briquettes are glowing, lift off the little furnace and hang it where no one will touch its hot metal.

Do you still have a cherished elm? If so, better attend to spraying it now. Ask your county agent for the spray recommended.

In the North, begin a weekly spray program for roses. Spray apples again for scale.

Clean out garden pools—and buy any needed aquatic plants.

Have you moved house plants outdoors? It's safe now almost anywhere. You might sink some of them, pot and all, into beds or borders.

Lawns of Bermudagrass should be cut only a half-inch high from now on. Cutting higher may cause the lawn to look untidy.

May 15

Repairing Concrete Sidewalks

Frost heaving and growing tree roots often buckle the slabs of concrete sidewalks, causing them to crack. Make it a practice of checking yours once a year.

When you find cracks, buy a bag of prepared concrete sand mix and plan to make repairs when you have the time. Using a mallet and cold chisel, widen and deepen the crack all along its length, undercutting the edges when possible.

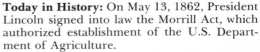

Today in History: On May 13, 1862, President Lincoln signed into law the Morrill Act, which authorized establishment of the U.S. Department of Agriculture.

Reminder: A representative of the Department has help for you in maintaining your home. See the entry for May 8.

Wash out the loose material with a hose. Make a stiff mortar of the sand mix and trowel it into the crack, tamping down well. Trowel it off flush and smooth after an hour.

If the cracks are so bad that you must replace an entire section of sidewalk, break out the concrete in chunks, using a sledge, chisel, and other tools. Dig out the soil below if the original slab was laid directly on the ground. If you find that a tree root had caused the breaks, remove all of it you can. If there is no root, the trouble probably came from frost heaving.

For the new slab, provide a base of two or three inches of coarse gravel, or break up the original slab into small pieces and use the chunks along with or in place of the gravel. Leave space for a slab four inches thick.

Make a wood form along the two outer edges of the walk, putting stakes outside to hold the two-by-four form boards in place. Level the top of the form boards between the old slabs. Coat the inside surface of the form with a light oil.

Using prepared concrete mix in bags, mix according to directions and pour into the form. Level the surface with a strikeboard—any straight-edged board that will span and be guided by your two form boards. Work a wood float over the surface in a half-arc motion to smooth it. Buy, borrow, or rent an edging tool to round off the edges. You can remove the wood form in a couple of days.

Spray programs should be underway now for a number of ornamental shrubs, flowers, and fruits. Be guided by the literature available from your county agent or state agricultural experiment station.

Automatic sprinkling of lawn or garden is usually better than doing it by hand. The latter seldom gets moisture deep enough.

Watch out for crabgrass seedlings in flower beds. Pull them out.

Fertilize citrus trees at this time and water in the fertilizer thoroughly.

May 16

Paint on a Vapor Barrier?

In any redecorating you do in your home, it would be well to consider the use of paint with vapor-barrier qualities. Approved house-building practices now call for a vapor barrier on all inner surfaces (the warm side) of outside walls to help control damaging condensation during the winter.

What can you do if your home was built before the importance of vapor barriers was recognized? In Alaska, a state where extreme cold makes condensation a serious home problem, an Extension Service bulletin says:

"Existing homes with no internal vapor barrier may be protected by painting the inside surface of all exterior walls and ceilings with a good grade of paint having accredited vapor barrier qualities. If wallpaper is to be used, walls should first be given two coats of a good vapor barrier paint before the paper is applied. Coated fabric-type wall coverings are generally good vapor barriers. Wall linoleum and ceramic, metal or plastic tile are equally effective as vapor barriers."

You might also redecorate and install a vapor barrier at the same time by placing foil-backed gypsum board over the inner surfaces of your walls. Still another possibility: A sheet plastic vapor barrier under new wall paneling.

Today in History: Minting of nickels (five-cent pieces) was authorized on May 16, 1866.

What paint should you choose? Many modern interior latex paints are resistant to vapor penetration. The label may tell you. If not, ask your paint dealer or write to several manufacturers.

In areas where temperatures regularly drop to ten degrees below zero or lower, some builders now recommend use of a second vapor barrier—still on the warm side of the wall, of course. In such cases, the second barrier can be painted on.

May 17

Wallpapering Tricks and Tips

In applying wallpaper, tyros can compete quite successfully with the pros—and they have been doing so for years.

You do need a few special tools for the job. You can find these already assembled as a kit in local stores or in mail order catalogs, perhaps with instructions. For conventional wallpapering, you need a paste brush, a smoothing brush, a seam roller, and a sharp-edged trimmer disk. When you come to do the job, you'll also want a plumb bob (for plumbing the first strip), a sharp pair of scissors, a straightedge such as a yardstick, and a cleanup sponge (for removing paste slopped on the front of the paper). Be sure to

insist that the wallpaper shop do necessary edge trimming before you bring the paper home. If you are hanging prepasted paper, your equipment should include a plastic water tray for wetting the paper.

Prepare the wall first by removing old paper. Soaking and steaming will make it possible to scrape off most papers. Special stripping tools are sold to help you with this.

Abrade plastic-coated paper lightly with sandpaper so the water and steam can penetrate. When all paper is off, apply a cold-water size to the wall surface. This will give better adhesion.

In the case of a sheetrock wall, you may not be able to get old wallpaper off without seriously damaging the coating paper on the panels. To make removal possible from a sheetrock wall in the future, first apply a coat of water paint or other coating recommended for the purpose.

A large sheet of hardboard clamped to a table top makes a convenient work surface for preparing and pasting the wallpaper. In cutting each strip to length be sure to allow for matching the pattern. After applying paste evenly to the back of the strip, fold the strip back on itself with the pasted sides touching to make a bundle short enough to handle. Place one end in position at the ceiling line and work the strip down the wall, unfolding it and matching the edge as you descend. Use the smoothing brush to slap the ends into close contact at the ceiling end and at the baseboard. Run the disk trimmer across the strip along the ceiling and baseboard lines to cut it to length. If the trimmer does not cut through the paper, pull enough of each end away from the wall so you can follow along the partly-cut line with your scissors. Then slap the paper back to the wall with the smoothing brush. Sponge any excess paste from the front of the paper—and from your work table.

Professionals have special equipment for cutting strips to proper width vertically when they come to a window or door. You can do it by putting the strip into position (before or after pasting), marking it with a pencil and your straightedge and then cutting carefully with your scissors.

As you work around the walls, don't be afraid to use your smoothing brush vigorously on the edges. Then run the roller along the seams.

What about leftover paper when you paper a room? If you have attic space that's used only for storage, unroll the paper and let it hang from the highest point in the storage area. It then will change color gradually, the same as the paper on the wall. If a patching job becomes necessary, the attic paper will match that on the wall.

May 18

Prune Ramblers After Blooming

Most horticultural experts will tell you that hardy rambler roses may be pruned right after they bloom—unless you need the foliage for shade or screening. This means that the time for this chore will be coming along soon in your area—if it hasn't already.

After the ramblers have bloomed, new canes will have started at the base. You can cut away all of the old ones. Train the new ones as they grow during the summer. You'll get plenty of blooms from the new canes next spring. If you feel you really need the old foliage during the summer, you *can* delay pruning it out until early winter, but interference of the new canes will make it more difficult to cut out the old ones.

Pillar roses also should be pruned as soon as blooming is over. Cut off all old canes close to the ground—or close to new canes if these develop low on the trunks. Stake up the new canes.

May 19

Today in History: Nathaniel Hawthorne, author of "The House of Seven Gables," died May 19, 1864, at the age of 60.

Mail Order Catalogs as Reference Manuals

Seasonal catalogs of the large mail order firms offer shopping convenience for thousands of home owners, either by mail or telephone. But did you ever think that such a catalog—even one that is out-of-date—can also be a handy general reference manual?

For a home owner, the sections devoted to tools, hardware, appliances, furnishings, auto supplies, and hobby supplies can be a gold mine of information. Suppose you're doing preliminary sketching for kitchen remodeling and want to know whether a dishwasher will fit into a certain niche. The catalog will give you typical dimensions. Suppose you need to know some facts about hardware cloth. The catalog has them. Suppose a neighbor in casual conversation mentions a molding-head guard for a radial-arm saw—and you wonder what he's talking about. The catalog will have a picture. The accurate illustrations of items offered, in fact, can become your very own pictorial encyclopedia. Encourage the youngsters to use the catalog for this purpose, too.

So even though you may not buy from it, add a mail order catalog to your home reference library. Perhaps a neighbor who *does* buy will let you have one that's several seasons old. Find out, too, what special catalogs the firm offers—on tools, photographic equipment, garden supplies, etc.—and lay in those that coincide with your own interests.

Perennial flowers may need staking now.

May 20

Pointers About Wood Porches and Steps

You can't expect to prevent all wood decay in parts of porches and steps exposed to rain, but proper construction in the first place and regular painting and maintenance thereafter will go a long way toward delaying it. Check yours with this questionnaire:

Is there plenty of ventilation under the porch? If not, moisture from the ground may condense on the wood and eventually bring about decay. If a closure is desired, latticework is better than a solid door.

Are the lower ends of stair stringers based on masonry above the level of the ground?

Does the porch floor have a slight outward slope so water will drain off?

Do railings and the step handrail extend over the top of posts and balusters with a minimum number of joints? When a joint must be made, caulk it annually and douse with thick paint to keep moisture out of the joint.

Do frames for screens around the porch have enough openings at the bottom so water can drain outward at times of heavy, driving rain?

A federal government consumer service bulletin suggests that when building a new porch or repairing or replacing an old one, you use only preservative-treated wood. Brush preservative on cut ends and edges before putting the pieces into place.

Does your state university offer a summer short course in landscaping for home owners? Some do. This would be a pleasant and profitable way to spend a vacation week.

Better get window boxes planted now. Put a drainage layer in the bottom and be sure there are holes for water runoff.

Have webworms formed unsightly webs on the branches of flowering crabapples? See your county agent for control measures.

Do not cut tulip leaves after flowering if you want to leave the bulbs in the ground for another season. Green leaves produce food for plant growth the next year. When you cut blooms for indoor displays, leave as much green on the stalks as you possibly can.

Evergreens may drop some leaves at this time of year. Don't be disturbed by it. It's natural.

Let the foliage of daffodils and similar plants brown naturally. Don't be too hasty about cutting it.

Your Own Reminders

Week of May 14–20

May 21

Remove Stains from Concrete Driveway

Take a look at your driveway. If it's concrete, chances are you'll find stains left by oil dripping from your car or others.

Lubrication oil penetrates some concrete readily. It should be mopped off immediately and the spot covered with Fuller's earth or other dry powdered material such as hydrated lime, whiting, or dry portland cement. If treated soon enough, there will be no stain. However, when the oil has remained for some time, other methods will be necessary.

Hardware stores carry brand-name concrete floor and driveway cleaners. Buy and use one of these as directed. Or, if such a product is not available, ask the hardware store for trisodium phosphate (TSP) instead. Buy a pound or two, depending on the extent of the staining. Pour

Today in History: Connecticut enacted a law on May 21, 1901 regulating the speed of automobiles. Top legal speed on country roads was set at 15 m.p.h., in cities at 12 m.p.h. Furthermore, the law stipulated that if a horse drawing a horse-drawn vehicle "appears to be frightened the person in charge of said motor vehicle shall stop."

scalding water on the oily area, sprinkle it with TSP granules, and scrub vigorously with a stiff brush. Go over the entire driveway quickly.

While the concrete is still wet, dust straight portland cement over a section of it, not exceeding 50 square feet at a time. Starting at the high point of the driveway, use a sweeping brush to spread the slurry evenly. The cement will sink into the driveway pores, helping to hide any stains left after the scouring. Rewet the driveway as you need to. Push surplus slurry off the low end of the drive. Let the cement set for about six hours and then hose off.

The same procedure can be used to freshen concrete walks or floors.

May 22

Remove Faded Blossoms to Strengthen Leafy Evergreens

Should you remove faded blossoms from rhododendron and mountain laurel? (Blossoming time ranges from late May into July, depending on variety and latitude.) Horticulturists say that whether you remove the dead blossoms from a well-developed mature plant is mostly a matter of taste. Under ideal conditions, these plants can both bear flowers annually and produce seed pods without weakening the plant. But do remove flower stems when growing conditions are not the best. Snip off the stems with your fingers, being careful not to damage the leaf buds just below the stems.

May 23

First Japanese Beetles Due Soon

Japanese beetles are a serious plant pest in the northeastern U.S., and they have been gradually enlarging their territory to the south and west. The first beetles of the season appear at about this time in the latitude of North Carolina, about a month later in the middle of New Jersey, and around July 1 in southern Vermont, New Hampshire, and Maine.

The beetles are not choosy about their diet. They eat the leaves, flowers, and other succulent parts of a great range of plants, shrubs, and trees. The peak of the beetle population in an area is usually reached four or five weeks after the first ones appear. But some beetles emerge later than others. Consequently, you may have a scourge of beetles until frost.

When numbers are limited, you can attempt control by hand. Put about a half inch of kerosene or gasoline in the bottom of a wide-mouth can or jar. Hold the container directly under a mass of the beetles, jar their support, and most of them will drop into the liquid and die. You can soon collect a large mass of beetles in this way. But if the year's infestation is especially heavy, you will probably prefer to see what advice your state Extension Service can offer about spraying the beetles.

An offensive against the beetle grubs, however, may yield best results in the long run. The female beetles thrust their way into moist earth and lay eggs there. The grubs that hatch feed on the roots of your lawn grass. At this stage, the pest is subject to a natural control called Milky Disease. The grub ingests the spores of this dis-

Today in History: Captain William Kidd was hanged as a pirate in London on May 23, 1701. Treasure hunters still are on the lookout for the gold and other treasure he is reputed to have buried at various points along the Atlantic Coast of the U.S.

ease and eventually dies. The disease has no known adverse effect on other insects, earthworms, plants, or animals.

You can now introduce the spores that cause this disease into your lawn. Your garden shop may have packages of this material—a powder containing the spores. If not, you can get information by writing Fairfax Biological Laboratory, Clinton Corners, N. Y. 12514.

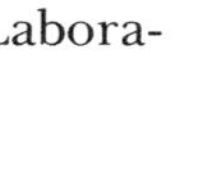

May 24

What's Your Ladder Situation?

Every home owner needs a few ladders. So let's consider today whether you have what you should for the repair, maintenance, and painting jobs you will undertake in the years to come.

Properly cared for, ladders will last you a lifetime. Therefore, why not buy the best you can afford if you decide to supplement what you have now?

The house you live in obviously will affect your decisions about ladders. Most important in your list of ladders must be the one that enables you to reach every part of the house—safely. A single straight ladder will often be just right for this if yours is a ranch house.

However, the ladder should extend at least two feet above the eaves line if you are to climb up and down with confidence and safety for work on the roof.

But suppose you move to a two-story house in the future? You will then need an extension ladder with enough span to take you up to the highest gable. Therefore, you might be smart to buy the extension ladder in the first place. Take the sections apart, and each becomes an individual ladder so two people can work simultaneously at painting a house. Two ladders also are sometimes used to rig a scaffold. Such multiple use actually may justify purchase of both an extension and a straight ladder, shorter than either of the extension sections.

The straight ladder will then become your choice when you need to climb only to medium height—say to the top of a first-floor window, a level that most stepladders won't safely reach. The straight ladder also should fit under the usual wide roof overhang of a one-story house.

You'll want a stepladder mostly for work inside the house. Two variables should be considered in making your choice—your own height (or reach) and the height of your ceilings. As a safety measure, don't use the two top steps either for climbing or standing. Try out several stepladders to find which one, used this way, enables you to work at ceiling height comfortably.

Today in History: May 24, anniversary of the birth of Queen Victoria, is observed as British Empire Day.

A stepstool is a third type of ladder that you'll probably want to buy. You can sometimes combine this with kitchen use, perhaps even keeping it there. Use the stepstool only for those jobs that are just above tiptoe reach.

Instead of any of the ladders already mentioned, you might find that a combination ladder will suit your needs. The two parts of this can be set up as a tall stepladder or as an extension ladder. Check out a couple and see what you think.

Aluminum or magnesium ladders are much lighter and easier to handle than wooden ones, but some of the lower-priced metal ladders are pretty flimsy. Mistreatment can bend them out of shape. Remember, too, how dangerous they are near power lines. Beware of bargain ladders offered at sale prices. Perhaps they really are bargains. But check them first against the non-bargains. Note such things as ladder width and rail sizes. Rungs can also vary considerably in thickness.

If you buy a wooden ladder, plan to store it indoors to avoid rot.

May 25

Watch Out for Narcissus Bulb Fly

Next time you see what looks like a small bumblebee among your flowers at this time of year, take a closer, second look. Does it fly in a zigzag fashion along rows of plants or among leaves eight or ten inches above the ground, producing a high-pitched hum? Do you find it feeding on pollen and nectar of such flowers as strawberry or apple blossoms, morning glory, and dandelion? Is it about one-half inch long with a black body covered in bands of colored hairs—black, yellow, orange and buff?

These are characteristics of the adult narcissus bulb fly, which feeds for about a week in late spring and early summer before laying 50 to 75 eggs singly on narcissus leaves at the ground level. This insect probably occurs wherever narcissus bulbs are grown. It is believed to infest at least half of all narcissus plantings in home gardens.

The larvae hatch from the small white eggs in about ten days, wiggle down through the soil and enter the bulb through or near the roots. There they develop during the summer and fall. The larva leaves the bulb the next spring and changes into a pupa from which the adult fly finally emerges.

Dust new bulbs with chlordane before planting to prevent damage from this insect. Dig up established plantings and destroy damaged bulbs. Treat others with chlordane before replanting. In the spring apply chlordane dust to foliage, especially between the leaves. Use chlordane with extreme caution. Read the directions—and heed them.

May 26

Get Swimming Pool Ready

Temperatures normally already favor outdoor swimming in the warm climates at this time of year—and it won't be long in the northern states either.

Getting a swimming pool ready for the season varies considerably. Usually the first step is clearing the cover of accumulated leaves and water. While doing this, you can probably be adding water to the pool itself if the level was lowered for the winter. When the cover has been taken off and spread out to dry before folding for storage, you will be able to start up the filter and add chlorine and other chemicals as needed. Many filters should be started and run following specific steps that you should have received from the company that installed the pool or filter.

May 27

Today in History: This is the birthday of the late Rachel Carson, author of "Silent Spring," the classic exposé on the dangers of pesticides to our environment. She was born May 27, 1907.

Conservation Pledge

In 1946, the magazine *Outdoor Life* and a board of outstanding conservationists, scientists, and educators sponsored a contest for a personal statement that would help conserve America's natural resources. The winning pledge was written by L. L. Foreman, of Sante Fe, New Mexico. *Outdoor Life* then presented the pledge to the nation at a ceremony

in Washington. Since then, the Conservation Pledge has been read and recited by untold millions.

It follows:

> "I give my pledge as an American to save and defend from waste the natural resources of my country—its air, soil and minerals, its forests, waters, and wildlife."

In the national contest, Rachel Carson won second prize. Her entry:

"I pledge myself to preserve and protect America's fertile soils, her mighty forests and rivers, her wildlife and minerals, for on these her greatness was established and her strength depends."

Your Own Reminders
Week of May 21–27

May 28

Have Your Trees Set Too Much Fruit?

All types of fruits except cherries set too much fruit in most seasons. Consequently, quality is impaired. An overloaded tree does its own thinning in late May and June by dropping developing fruits that have not received enough water and plant food. However, it's often a good idea to remove some of the fruit by hand. This is no problem on dwarf trees.

Thin apples and pears to single fruits when they occur as doubles and triples. If the set is heavy, do further thinning to space remaining fruits six to eight inches apart. Peaches and nectarines also do best the same distance apart. Thin plums to three or four inches apart.

May 29

You Should Be Pruning Privet Now

Periodic pruning of a privet hedge should be underway now. If you want a dense hedge, covered with foliage to the base, clipping every two weeks is not too often.

To establish a good privet hedge, set hardy plants close together. Cut them back at once almost to the ground—to six inches or so. In the following winter, while the plants are dormant, cut back the entire hedge to about 12 inches—or even to six inches to develop density at the base.

During the second season of growth, cut back the top halfway several times during the period of rapid summer growth.

May 30

Today in History: The first state legislation regulating installation of plumbing was enacted on May 30, 1881 in Illinois.

Facts About Plastic Plumbing

When you need to extend the plumbing system in your home or change it in any way, consider whether you may not be ahead by using PVC (polyvinyl chloride) plastic pipe. It's easy to install, non-corrosive, and no scale builds up inside the pipe. There are two drawbacks, however: Some local building codes do not accept it (so check yours), and it is not recommended for water above 180 degrees.

You can tie in plastic plumbing lines to existing copper tubing or iron pipe systems. You can interrupt a copper tubing line almost anywhere. Cut a section of the tubing out and install a plastic takeoff tee of the correct diameter with copper-tubing adapters. In iron pipe, locate the takeoff point close to a union.

Plastic plumbing is easily cut to length with a fine-toothed saw. Make the cut square by using a miter box. Scrape burrs from the cut end with a dull knife. Lightly buff an inch or so of the pipe at the end that is to slide into the plastic tee, elbow, or other connection. You buy a special cement to make watertight connections. Some connections also are threaded.

May 31

Fertilize Your Fruit Trees?

Did you plant young fruit trees during the spring? Then you may find it desirable, on poor soils, to apply a supplementary fertilizer in late May or early June. Use one-fourth pound of sodium nitrate or other nitrogenous fertilizer for each year of tree age. For example, if you planted two-year trees, apply a half pound of fertilizer. Spread it in a circle around the tree, but away from the immediate trunk.

June

In June, as the poet says, come "perfect days"—perfect either for outdoor work or play, usually not yet too hot and not too cool. Anglo-Saxons called June "joy time." How could you find a better word for it? More flowers bloom now than in any other month, roses being supreme among them, and bees are busy all day long. An old rhyme says "a swarm of bees in June is worth a silver spoon."

When the month is two-thirds gone, spring ends and summer comes. On June 21 or 22, the sun reaches the peak of its northward swing from the equator and we have the Summer Solstice—a word of Latin origin meaning "the sun stops." On that day we enjoy our longest day of the year.

Learned men fail to agree on how June got its name, but many of us like to feel it came from Juno, Roman goddess of women and marriage. June has always been popular for weddings.

Flag Day, June 14, is the month's outstanding holiday. Many Southern states observe the birthday on June 3 of Jefferson Davis, president of the Confederacy. Many Protestant churches conduct Children Day exercises on the second Sunday of the month. Father's Day also comes in June.

June 1

Today in History: An electric voting machine was patented on June 1, 1869, by Thomas A. Edison. Turning a switch to the right or left registered a yes or no vote.

What About an Attic Fan?

Some home owners equate an attic fan with an air conditioner. They reason that if they have one, they do not need the other. Nothing could be further from the truth. An attic fan can help promote summer comfort indoors, even if you have an air conditioner. By keeping the attic cooler, the fan should take some of the load off the air conditioner.

The accompanying sketches show temperature conditions that might prevail in a modern home before and after installation of a cupola-type fan. Such a fan can be automatically controlled in two ways—by a thermostat to keep attic temperatures from rising above a set limit, say 100 degrees; or by a humidistat to keep attic relative humidity from rising beyond a certain point, say 90 percent. The latter feature helps control winter moisture condensation and roof ice dams. (See February 20.)

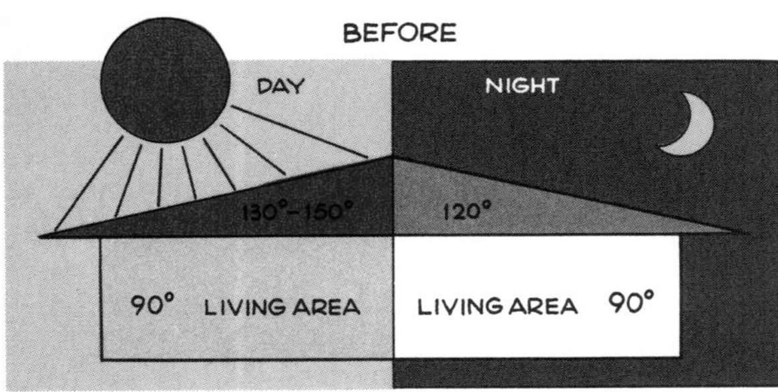

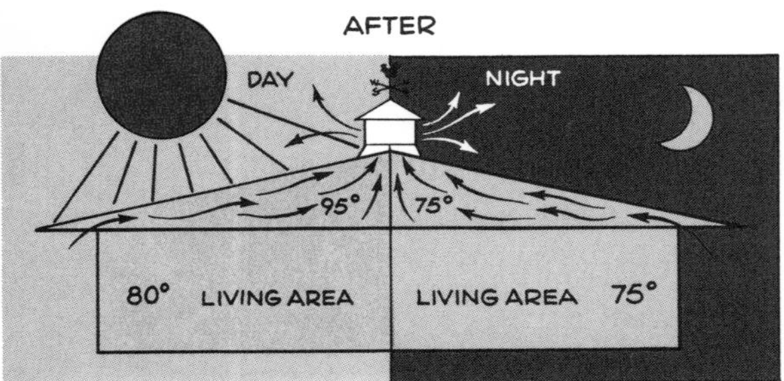

An automatic fan should be combined with enough louvers, or other openings, to move air through the entire attic space.

In northern areas, a large attic fan alone will promote your comfort considerably by driving hot air from the attic and drawing cool air into the living areas at night. A fan won't equal an air conditioner in the daytime, though, and it will not lower humidity, an important factor in summer discomfort.

Begin spraying the undersides of chrysanthemum leaves to control leaf spot. Use zineb or ferbam at the rate of two tablespoons in a gallon of water. Repeat at 10-day intervals until August.

It's time now in the North to put in dahlia tubers. Work rotted manure, peat moss, or other organic material into the soil. Plant tubers about six inches deep at least three feet apart. Drive stakes four to five feet high in the holes as you plant.

In semitropical areas, prune bougainvillea, lantana, hibiscus, and cape honeysuckle. Cut out dead wood at the same time you remove excess growth.

Watch out for crabgrass and Bermudagrass seedlings in flower and shrub areas. Get rid of them at once.

Do you have mulches in place around all garden plants and shrubs that benefit from them?

Spray pachysandra for scale sometime during June.

Visitors to Philadelphia at this time of year can attend open house on Elfreth's Alley, one of the first residential streets in America. The event usually is scheduled for one day in the first week of June.

June 2

Will You Dig and Store Spring Bulbs This Year?

Most spring bulbs should be dug up and divided after some years. Best tip-off—although a year late in being heeded—is the growth of nothing but small flowers in crowded clumps. This happens to tulips after about three years. Tulip bulbs that you dig and replant often fail to bloom. Consequently, many gardeners prefer to buy and plant new bulbs yearly. Narcissi usually require dividing in three or four years. Many smaller bulbs can go for many years.

In warm areas, you should dig and discard bulbs each year after the blooms have faded. Bulbs seldom flower well in hot climates after the first year.

Make sure your bulbs have matured before you dig them for replanting in the fall. When the leaves on the plants turn yellow, uncover a few bulbs without disturbing them. If the bulb coats are tan to brown, the bulbs are ready to be dug. The coat of an immature bulb is white.

Use a spading fork to lift the bulbs from the ground. Very little soil will cling to them. Wash off any soil that remains on the bulbs and remove any old, dry scales.

Today in History: The first practical sewing machine to produce a single-thread chain stitch was patented on June 2, 1857 by James E. Gibbs of Mill Point, Virginia.

Inspect your bulbs for signs of disease. Keep only large, healthy bulbs that are firm and free of spots. Discard undersized bulbs, which require one or two years growth before they bloom; many never bloom.

Spread the bulbs you keep in a shaded place to dry. When the outer scales have dried, store the bulbs away from sunlight in a cool, dry basement, cellar, garage, or shed at 60° to 65°F. Avoid temperatures below 50° or above 70°F.

If you have only a few bulbs, you can keep them in paper bags hung by strings from the ceiling or wall. You should store large numbers of bulbs on trays with screen bottoms. Separate your bulbs by species or variety when you store them.

Be sure that air can circulate around your stored bulbs. Never store bulbs more than two or three layers deep. Deep piles of bulbs generate heat and decay the bulbs.

Inspect bulbs in storage several times during the summer. Remove any that are decaying as soon as possible. A musty odor may indicate that your bulbs are decaying.

When you dig and store bulbs, replant them in the fall at the times recommended elsewhere.

Destroy ragweed growing on or near your property. Within a few weeks it will begin casting off the pollen that causes so much of the allergy called hay fever. Old timers can identify the plant for you—if you don't know it.

In canyons and hillsides of California where forest fires are a threat, this is probably a good time to clear underbrush away from homes—as required by law in some areas. The Los Angeles Fire Department recommends that all native brush be removed within 100 feet of a structure. Use a brush cutter or chainsaw equipped with a spark arrester.

June 3

Choose Peonies Now for Planting Later

Peonies should be displaying their finest blooms now—or very soon—in many parts of the country. If you have none of these fine flowers, check a grower, or gardens in your neighborhood, for colors that you prefer. You can then buy and plant the tubers in the fall.

Check for leaf spots on laurel and rhododendron.

Winter protection can be removed from roses in the warmer parts of Region IV. At the same time, prune them as described in the January 5 entry.

Your Own Reminders

Week of May 28–June 3

June 4

Attack Those Mosquitoes

Keeping down the number of mosquitoes is a community affair: Do your share by removing all breeding places on your property. The insects lay eggs in stagnant water—and hatching occurs very soon. So get rid of it, wherever it may occur. Clean out gutters. If water stands in a gutter, improve the incline so that it is self-draining. Drain and clean out bird baths at least once a week during the season that mosquitoes are most in evidence.

If you note areas of stagnant water in your community, insist that your local government drain or treat them.

June 5

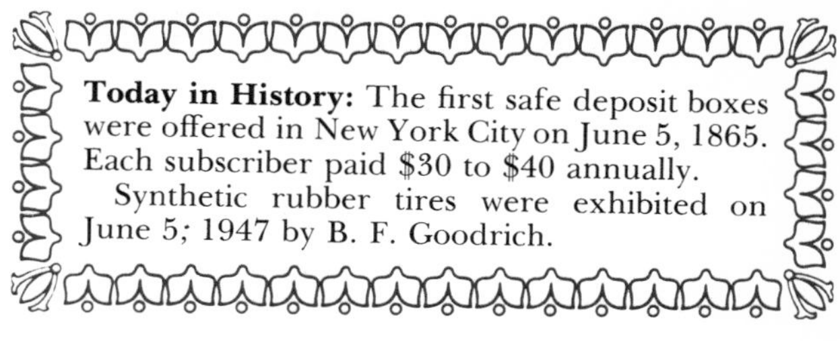

Today in History: The first safe deposit boxes were offered in New York City on June 5, 1865. Each subscriber paid $30 to $40 annually.

Synthetic rubber tires were exhibited on June 5; 1947 by B. F. Goodrich.

Is It Time to Plant a Fall Garden?

For a successful crop, vegetables must be planted early enough so they can mature before the first killing autumn frost. By that rule, then, the time has now arrived for final planting of some vegetables in high-altitude regions of the Rockies—those regions where the average date of the first frost comes about August 30.

Check out these early-frost regions on the autumn frost map that you will find accompanying the entry for September 20. Then check the August 30 column in Appendix F at the back of this book. In this column, note that you would now have to make plantings very soon for quite a list of hardy vegetables. At the same time, check out these same vegetables in Appendix E—the chart for spring planting—and you will find that in high-altitude and other regions with a short growing season you have a very brief period during which you can make plantings and hope for success.

While you are considering the question, why not determine the latest recommended planting dates for your area? Refer first to the September 20 map and find when you can expect the first killing autumn frost where you live. Then refer to this date heading the columns in Appendix F. Look down this column to find the final dates on which you can plant various vegetables—and still have a reasonable expectation that the vegetables will mature before winter sets in.

Remember to Do These Garden Chores in Early June

Do you find discolored and shriveled areas on the bark of apple trees? This is a sign of the presence of flathead apple tree borers. Ask the county agent about it.

Conserve moisture for newly-planted shrubs or trees by putting down a mulch. Use an inch or two of peat moss or two to three inches of compost.

Renovate strawberry beds in the middle states after fruit has been picked. Hoe out old plants. Cut off the tops of others.

Spray apples and pears for scab, mites, and codling moth two weeks after petal fall.

Watch broadleaved evergreens for needlelike holes in the leaves caused by lace bugs. Spray with Malathion.

Indoor tropical plants can now be safely moved outdoors almost everywhere.

St. Augustine grass can be planted now in southern areas. Buy it in flats, or get it from a friend whose lawn needs edging.

Palms are beginning their most active growing period. Increase their watering schedule.

Spray arborvitae for bagworms, andromeda for lace bugs, azalea for spider mites, shade trees for cankerworms.

Fertilize spring-planted roses now. In the North begin a weekly spray or dusting program with a combination insecticide-fungicide material.

June 6

Today in History: The first federal gasoline tax was enacted on June 6, 1932. It imposed a levy of one cent a gallon.

Vacation Home Exchange

This is a great idea. You find a family in Paris that wants to visit New York. You, living in New York, would like to visit Paris. So you exchange homes for two weeks or whatever period you agree upon. Wherever you live, wherever you want to go (within reason), chances are good that you'll be able to effect a vacation home swap.

If you wish, you might try to locate another interested family by advertising in the area of your choice. Or you can watch the classifieds in the metropolitan newspapers in your own region for advertisements placed by out-of-towners who want to come to your region. But there's a surer way.

You can join a club—the Vacation Exchange Club, 663 Fifth Avenue, New York, N. Y. 10022. For an annual membership fee of $8.50 the club will supply a directory listing thousands of U.S. and foreign families who are interested in swapping their homes or apartments at vacation time—in summer or winter, for weeks or months. When you receive the directory, the rest is up to you. You do all of the correspondence and make your own arrangements.

The Vacation Exchange Club was founded in the early '60's by schoolteacher David Ostroff. Its listings and membership soared in 1971 when Pan American World Airways began promoting the club as a customer service.

The airline naturally hopes that you'll fly to your vacation home. But no need to if you're heading for a destination on this continent. Just get in your car and go—with all the kids, cats, dogs, and canaries. But *do* make your arrangements first.

And leave behind for your visitors, notes about things *you'd* want to know—the name, hours, and telephone number of your doctor; the name of a plumber, electrician, and the like; and perhaps the name of a neighbor who might help solve unexpected problems.

The last spring frosts should have occurred now and you can safely set out seedlings of flowers and plant seeds. See the April 2 map.

Frozen-fruit juice cans can be used to mark plants in your garden. Stuff the empty seed packet in can and place upside down on a stake.

June 7

Keeping Your Home Safe While You Vacation

Newspapers, packages, and throw-aways piling up at the door while you are on vacation are an open invitation to burglars. As the first step towards protecting your home, arrange with a neighbor or relative to check the premises each day. If you have an outside delivery box, ask the neighbor to remove the mail as it arrives. Discontinue newspaper and milk deliveries. If laundry is outstanding, ask the neighbor to accept it on arrival. Give the neighbor a door key.

Make a tour of the yard and put away any maintenance equipment, toys, and bikes. Arrange for lawn mowing if you will be away for an extended period. In the winter, arrange for someone to remove snow from the walks, steps, and driveway.

Unless you are taking household pets along, deliver them to a kennel—or arrange for the neighbor to care for them. If the latter, store an adequate supply of food.

At the same time you visit your bank for vacation money and travellers checks, take along any valuables that you normally keep at home—jewelry, coin collections, and the like—and store them in a safety deposit box. Send furs to storage.

Unless the neighbor will water your house plants as needed, water them well the day you leave and move them out of direct sunlight. Then encase each plant in a large plastic bag. Tie the bag around the pot.

Paragon Electric Company, Two Rivers, Wisconsin 54241, which offers a free pamphlet "25 Home Protection Tips," suggests that you make your home look lived in at night while you are away. Do this by hooking up a timer to turn on a lamp or two automatically.

Notify your local police that you will be away and for how long. Let them know if a timer will be operating.

If you are making a winter trip, adjust the furnace thermostat to a minimum setting to prevent freezing of water pipes. Arrange for automatic fuel delivery if you don't already have it. Ask the neighbor to check the furnace daily.

The day you are leaving, after you have packed and the kids are in the car, make a tour of the house and do these things:

Turn the refrigerator to vacation setting. (Or, perhaps you'll want to empty it the day before and turn it off.)

Turn the water heater to vacation setting.

See that the range, washer, dryer, and all other appliances except those noted above are turned off.

Turn all water faucets to the off position. (If you have your own water supply, you may want to turn off the pump.)

Turn off lights, radio, television, and hi-fi sets.

See that you haven't discarded rags and papers that might cause spontaneous combustion. Put all such trash in a metal garbage can outdoors.

Close screens or storm windows and lock the windows. (Do not draw draperies, curtains, or shades except for protection against the sun's rays.)

See that none of the kids has forgotten his toothbrush, and pat yourself to be sure you have your wallet. Then leave the house, locking the door behind you.

Lock the garage, too; get in the driver's seat, and—believe it or not—you're off.

At last!

Ring perennial flowers with 5-10-5 fertilizer and water it into the ground.

Cultivate flower beds lightly. If plants are well developed, pull the weeds by hand.

June 8

How to Cut Roses for Bouquets

What's in a name? That which
  we call a rose
By any other name would
  smell as sweet.

—*Romeo and Juliet*

Cutting roses for display in our homes is a pleasant chore that ought to be timed for late afternoon. Roses cut then seem to keep best.

Roses cut just before the petals start to unfold will continue to open normally and remain in good condition longer than those cut when fully open.

Use sharp tools and make a clean cut. Never break or twist off flowers. Improper cutting can decrease the plant's vigor. Cut stems only as long as needed. At least two leaves should remain between the cut and the main stem.

Removal of foliage with long stems robs the plant of its food-manufacturing capacity and cuts down on its growth. During the plant's first season, cut flowers with very short stems. Or better yet, cut no flowers at all during the first season and let the plant develop fully.

If you do not cut the flowers, remove them when their petals begin to fall. Cut them with a sharp tool just above the topmost leaf. A withered individual flower in a cluster should be removed to give others in the cluster room to develop. After all flowers in a cluster have withered, cut off the entire cluster just above the top leaf.

Cut roses that begin to wilt can often be revived by making a slanting cut an inch or so from the end of the stems and immersing the stems in very hot water for a few minutes.

Boiling water removed from the heat for a few minutes is satisfactory. Then plunge the stems into cold water. The hot water drives off any air bubbles that have formed in the stems. The cold water can then rise and revive the blooms. The treatment will not revive very old flowers or those which have been wilted for several hours.

You cannot pluck roses
  Without fear of thorns,
Nor enjoy a fair wife
  Without danger of horns.

—Poor Richard

7 Rules for Beautiful Roses

1. Set new plants in well-prepared ground (see October 2), located where they will get at least six hours of sunshine daily. If you have a choice, locate the roses where they will receive the morning sun. Leaves that remain wet with morning dew are apt to develop diseases.

2. Water them frequently, soaking the soil with a mist or slow-moving stream to a depth of at least eight inches. Mulching helps conserve moisture.

3. Fertilize them as required.

4. Cut flowers from the plant without damaging remaining parts of the plant.

5. Prune the plants every year. See January 5. If roses are not pruned, they soon grow into a bramble patch and the blooms are small and of poor quality. Shoots that come from the understock should be removed as soon as they appear or they may dominate the plant.

6. Spray or dust them weekly during the growing season with a combination insecticide-fungicide.

7. Protect the plants from winter injury. See September 18.

June 9

Today in History: John Howard Payne, a playwright who wrote the words of the famous song, "Home Sweet Home," was born June 9, 1791 in New York City. The song was sung publicly for the first time May 8, 1823.

Home Sweet Home

'Mid pleasures and palaces
'Tho we may roam
Be it ever so humble,
There's no place like home.
A charm from the skies
Seems to hallow us there,
Which seek through the world
Is not met with elsewhere.
An exile from home
Splendor dazzles in vain;
Oh, give me my lowly
Thatched cottage again.
The birds singing gaily
That come at my call,
Give me them with that peace
Of mind dearer than all

(Refrain)

Home! Home! Sweet, sweet home!
There's no place like home!
Oh, there's no place like home!

June 10

Spray for Scale Crawlers

The young of various kinds of scale insects are likely to be active about now on a number of trees, shrubs, vines, and plants in a good part of the U.S. and southern Canada. They are small, but a hand lens should show them up if present.

Summer oil sprays will get rid of the crawlers, but the oil may cause harm to the leaves and other parts of the plants. Malathion usually is considered a good spray for the purpose. One recommendation: Dilute an emulsion containing 50 percent malathion at the rate of two tablespoons to three gallons of water. Be sure to cover the plant completely.

Plants which may be treated for scale at this season include rhododendrons, azaleas, hemlock, arborvitae, pines, ivy, pachysandra, juniper. See February 10 for more information.

A malathion spray at about this time may also control lacebugs on azalea and bagworm on arborvitae.

Your Own Reminders

Week of June 4–10

June 11

Check Broadleaved Evergreens for Fungi

Have you found various leaf spots on rhododendron, azalea, or mountain laurel? Caused by a variety of fungi, these may show as yellow, purplish, brown, or black spots scattered haphazardly over the leaf surface. The time to control these fungi is just as the blossoms of the affected plant begin to fade. This may range from May to July, depending on variety and your latitude. For control, spray the leaves with one of the ferbam fungicides at the rate of two tablespoons to a gallon of water. Add a small amount of spreading agent or detergent to the water. Spray at ten-day intervals from the first spray date, continuing as long as the plant is actively growing or humid conditions prevail.

Check late this month also for signs of borers in rhododendron—a fine, sawdust-like material on the ground or mulch. This material is pushed out by larva feeding in the cambium layer of the bark.

When you know or suspect that borers are present, apply a residual spray to the entire plant some time during the last week of June or first week in July.

Biennials such as foxgloves, Canterbury bells, sweet william, and hollyhocks will blossom next year if seed is sown now. See Appendix G.

Fertilize new 'mums started from cuttings this year. Apply 5-10-5 fertilizer at the rate of one to one and one-half pounds per 100 square feet. Water it in well.

When tulip leaves turn yellow, cut and destroy the stems and foliage. Do the same for other spring-flowering bulbs. The dead material may carry disease over to the next year.

Fertilize mature fig trees and bushes. Apply about one-third pound of 8-8-8 for each foot of height.

Water pecan trees thoroughly every two or three weeks during the summer.

June 12

Clean Out Those Plumbing Traps

Why wait until your household drains clog up entirely before doing something about them? Clogging usually occurs gradually—and a few minutes devoted periodically to cleaning out the traps may forestall an expensive plumber's bill. You'd be smart to clean them at least once a year.

Begin with the traps under the kitchen sink and bathroom lavatories. Place a pail or other container below and screw out the plug in the bottom of the U-trap if there is one. Otherwise, take off the entire trap, first placing adhesive tape around the nut or wrapping the wrench jaws with cloth to prevent marring the metal surfaces. Use a piece of wire to claw out any material inside the trap and pipe. When you remove the trap, new rubber gaskets usually will be required when you replace it.

A plumber's friend, a large rubber suction cup on a handle, ought to be part of the equipment in every home. Use it whenever drainage in any fixture becomes slow or stops entirely. Remove any strainer or plate on the drain entrance, pour a kettle of boiling water into the drain, place the suction cup over the opening, and work it up and down vigorously. It may help to add a little household ammonia to the hot water poured into the system.

Kitchen-sink stoppages are most often caused by liquid fats carried into the pipes by dishwater. One film of fat builds on another in the cold pipes, along with coffee grounds and other waste, until the pipes become clogged. Pour excess grease into a can and dispose of it with the garbage. Running several gallons of hot water down the sink each day will help keep the drain clear.

You may want to have an auger, or "snake," on hand for actual drain stoppages. But use it very carefully in a toilet trap. Too much vigor can crack the toilet bowl. Use only a thin and very flexible snake in bathtubs or sinks.

Devote some time to floor drains, too, during your periodic cleaning. Remove the cover, dig out whatever waste matter you can see, and then use a heavy wire or snake to clean out the trap below. Pour several pails of very hot water through the drain to wash away material you have loosened. Check and clean the strainer itself before returning it to the opening.

If a floor drain is used infrequently, water may evaporate from the trap, allowing sewer gases to enter the room. Make a practice of pouring water into the drain twice a year.

The large waste pipes of plumbing systems usually have one or more clean-out plugs for use in solving major stoppages. Know the location of these, and keep them accessible.

Be wary of chemical drain cleaners. If used at all, handle them with care. They can cause severe burns. Incorrectly used, chemical cleaners can damage the plumbing system. Never use one in case of an actual drain stoppage.

Arrival of hot weather may increase fruit drop on citrus. Keep the trees well supplied with moisture and fertilizer.

June 13

Have You Fertilized Your Roses?

The recommended time for fertilizing roses is when new spring growth is well established and danger of severe freezing has passed. A second application can be made later in the season if the plants show evidence of mineral deficiencies—yellowing of leaves from lack of nitrogen, leaves turning grayish green from lack of phosphorous, or browning of leaf margins from lack of potassium. Be careful about applying fertilizer late in the season, however. Fresh growth may not have time to harden enough to withstand winter killing. In the North, do not fertilize after July 15, in mild climates not after August 15.

Apply a complete fertilizer—for example 5-10-5—at a rate of about three pounds per 100 square feet or one heaping tablespoon for each plant. Scratch the fertilizer into the soil around the plants and then water. A complete fertilizer supplies nitrogen, phosphorous, and potassium.

Roses grow best in soil that is medium to slightly acid (pH 5.5 to 6.5). Ask your county agent or write to your state agricultural experiment station for information about testing your soil.

When you find the soil pH below 5.5, apply agricultural lime at the rate of three or four pounds per square foot. If the pH is over 6.5, apply sulfur. Use a pound of sulfur per 100 square feet if the pH is between 7 and 7.5, two pounds if it is 8, and three pounds if it is 8.5.

Retest the soil at monthly intervals thereafter. The pH can change quickly. Apply further lime or sulfur as indicated.

Calcium deficiency in the soil causes leaflets to die and drop off, and the blooms may show brown spots on the petals. Have your soil tested when these symptoms appear. Add lime if the pH is below 5.

Iron may be lacking in some soils—for example in the Great Plains. Rose foliage then will turn yellowish white. Spray with ferrous sulfate mixed at the rate of one ounce to two gallons of water, or with iron chelates mixed according to directions on the package. If you find the pH above 7, apply sulfur to lower it.

In dry, hot periods, keep shaded grass well watered.

Palms can be transplanted at this season. Keep the depression around the roots thoroughly wet for several weeks after transplanting.

For next year's bloom in semitropical areas, plant seeds now of such flowers as columbine, coral bell, gaillardia, Iceland poppy, and scabiosa.

Be careful about the moisture needs of roses in all areas where there's little summer rain. Use a mulch two to four inches thick over the root areas.

Azaleas, camellias, and gardenias are in their active growing stage now. Fertilize them regularly.

June 14

Flag Day

Today in History: The Continental Congress adopted our flag on June 14, 1777. Flag Day was first officially observed in 1877 on the 100th anniversary of the flag's adoption. The Rev. Francis Bellamy wrote the pledge of allegiance to our flag.

The Pledge of Allegiance

I pledge allegiance to the flag of the United States of America and to the Republic for which it stands, one Nation under God, indivisible, with liberty and justice for all.

June 15

Today in History: Lucky, lucky Ben Franklin! It was on June 15, 1752 that he flew a kite to show that lightning is electricity. That was NOT a good idea. Two years earlier he had invented lightning rods and installed them on his Philadelphia home. That WAS a good idea.

Why Lightning Rods Are a Good Thing

Years ago while certain con men were selling non-existent shares in the Brooklyn Bridge, others were roaming through the countryside selling "lightning rods." Here today but gone tomorrow, the rod salesmen usually were beyond the reach of local law when their victims discovered the rods were made of wood and the apparent metal cables actually were rope dipped in metallic paint.

Lightning-rod salesmen still must work to overcome the bad reputation their product received during that period. That is a shame. Properly installed, lightning rods are nearly 100 percent effective in preventing lightning damage.

Actually, more lightning rods are in use than you might believe. Pencil-thin and perhaps only 10 inches high, they are not easy to spot atop a home, and the conductor cables, real metal, are usually concealed within the structure.

You definitely need lightning rods if your home sits alone on an elevation. In a built-up area, the chances of your home being hit usually are slim. There usually are higher targets in the vicinity on which lightning can spend itself. But many rural and suburban homes are sitting ducks. Lightning causes more than a third of rural fire losses.

An effective lightning protection system consists of three parts—the air terminal (or rod) varying from 10 to 24 inches in length, conductor cables made of copper or aluminum (galvanized steel is no longer recommended), and an effective ground. The ground should not be simply a metal stake driven a short distance into the ground. The conductor cable usually should extend to a depth of ten feet into the ground—and there be connected to a copper grounding plate (about 3′ x 3½″) or the strands of the cable should be untwisted and spread through charcoal in the bed of a deep trench.

These facts are given for your information only. It's possible for you to buy the necessary parts and attempt a do-it-yourself installation. But you will not get the UL approval that you should expect to receive if the installation is made by an approved commercial concern.

Spray locusts to combat the developing mimosa webworms. Spray dogwood and lilacs for borers.

When you have decided that you want lightning-rod protection (and you may, just for peace of mind) check the business-listing section of your telephone book for a company that provides UL label installations. If a salesman appears at your door, check his identification, demand the names of three customers for whom his company has made installations and telephone all three to be sure the work and materials have been satisfactory. Refuse to permit work to begin until you have found the UL label on all parts and you have signed an application blank for a UL Master Label plate. This is a brass plate that the manufacturer of the equipment will mail to you.

Don't be hurried into making an installation—but don't delay it either, if you need one. Perhaps you would like more information on the subject than it's possible to give in the space available here. The Government Printing Office has several informative publications. One is called "Thunderstorms." Another is entitled "Lightning Protection for the Farm," a U.S. Department of Agriculture bulletin. Ask for particulars (including prices) from the Superintendent of Documents, U.S. Government Printing Office, Washington, D.C. 20402.

Towards the southern limit of their range, all canes of dewberries should be removed after the fruit is picked. In the middle states, however, leave the new canes alone.

Spray apples and pears for scab, codling moth, and aphids about a month after petal fall. Continue spraying every two weeks.

Japanese beetles are due now in the middle Atlantic states. See May 23.

Are caterpillars stripping your trees? You may have an infestation of the gypsy moth. See control measures under date of April 29.

A weekly dusting or spraying of roses is now in order in all except the late-spring regions of the U.S. Use a combination insecticide-fungicide material.

June 16

Today in History: American consumers were given two helping hands by the federal government on June 16, 1933. The Agricultural Adjustment Act authorized appointment of an attorney to safeguard the interests of consumers. The National Industrial Recovery Act provided for establishment of a consumers' advisory board.

How to Rent Money—and Save

Buying on credit is an essential part of the American way of life. But you don't have to take the first deal that's offered you. Shopping around for a loan can save you money. It's like pulling dollars right out of the sky.

Here's how you do it: Get the cash price for an item from several dealers. Find out if there would be a discount for paying cash. Get the cost of loans from several sources. It might

cost less to borrow money from a bank or credit union so you can buy for cash and escape the installment sales charges. Get all the costs involved to pay on the installment sales plan.

The dealer is required to put all information regarding costs on the installment sales contract, but don't wait until the contract is made out—get the facts before you commit yourself. The size of the monthly payment can be almost any amount you want to pay. Remember that small payments and long contracts increase the finance charge.

Compare final costs from the sources you have contacted. When you know the facts you can see which is the best deal.

The cost of consumer credit can be measured in two ways—dollar cost or interest rate.

The dollar cost of credit is the difference between the amount received on loan, or the cash price of an item, and the total amount you pay to the lender or to the dealer. The total amount you pay is the down payment plus all other payments, including the carrying charge and any other fees.

The interest rate is the dollar cost of credit expressed as a percentage of the money used or borrowed. This may be expressed as interest per month or interest per year. Interest also may be charged on the original amount for the entire period or on the unpaid balance owed each month.

To compare the interest rate between different sources of credit, you should convert all stated interest rates to the common denominator of the "true annual interest rate." This is the annual rate charged on the unpaid balance or money actually used during the loan or payment period.

If the contract specifies a monthly interest rate on the unpaid balance owed each month, the true annual interest rate would be 12 a month is 12 percent a year. This method of (months) times the stated rate. Thus 1 percent a month is 12 percent a year. This method of reporting interest rate is used by credit unions and finance companies. It is also used to figure the charges on revolving charge accounts.

What is corn? You may think you know, but possibly you do not. The dictionary defines corn as the important cereal crop of a particular region. Thus, in England corn is wheat, in Ireland oats, and in North America it's Indian maize.

If the contract states an annual rate on the original debt and repayment is made in 12 equal monthly installments, the true annual interest rate is approximately double the stated rate. That's because the average amount owed for the year is about half the original debt, yet you pay interest each month on the entire amount. Thus 8 percent a year turns out to be a true annual rate of 14.7 percent. This method is used to figure the charges on installment sales and on some bank loans. The interest may be discounted on certain bank loans.

If the contract states an annual interest rate on the original debt, and you pay the whole amount plus interest at the end of the year, the true annual rate is the same as the stated rate. A stated rate of 8 percent becomes a true annual rate of 8 percent.

Annual and perennial flower plants should be large enough about this time for spreading a mulch about two inches deep over the bed to conserve moisture. Use buckwheat hulls, peat moss, salt hay, or other organic material that will decompose slowly. Water the mulch into place.

Are the scales on your trees dead? These insects often remain in place after spraying. Crush one and examine under a hand lens. If the insect is still moist when crushed, it has not been killed. Dead insects dry up.

If you ride, use horse sense about common safety rules. Avoid mounting near a fence, trees, overhead projections, or in a small barn. In a group, do not crowd other riders. Stay a horse length away.

June 17

Could You Use an Evaporative Cooler?

In dry areas of the southwestern U. S., homes are commonly cooled by evaporating water. The method is inexpensive and satisfactory there because summer humidity is low.

Water is sprayed or dripped on excelsior or other water-absorptive material. The cooling unit often is placed in a window. A fan draws air through the wet excelsior into the house. The water evaporates cooling the air, and the cool air in turn cools the house.

Maximum cooling is provided by an air velocity of 150 feet per minute through the water-carrying material. From five to ten gallons of water per hour are needed to cool the average house.

Today in History: A 15-cent U.S. stamp mourning the death of Abraham Lincoln was issued on June 17, 1866. It had a portrait of the martyred President on a black background. Lincoln was assassinated April 14, 1865.

Your Own Reminders

Week of June 11–17

June 18

Today in History: On June 18, 1878, Congress adopted "an act to organize the Life Saving Service"—forerunner of the U.S. Coast Guard.

Rules for Swimming-Pool Safety

If you drink, don't dive!

That's not a typographical error. It's a bit of advice that applies to hosts and guests alike at poolside parties.

"Alcohol and water don't mix—at least not at a swimming party," says the National Safety Council. "Although children are most often involved in drownings or near-drownings, adults need supervising, too. Swimming and roughhousing should be taboo after a drink or two. A drink, then a dip or push into the pool could mean a tragic ending to an evening of summer fun."

Whether the patio-pool area is the site of a swimming party for eight-year-olds, a shindig for teenagers, or a Saturday night barbecue for adults, all party-goers and givers should heed safety rules.

Rotisseries, portable record players, radios and other electric devices should be kept well away from the pool; electricity and water (even a wet patio surface) is a dangerous combination.

During the party, the host and hostess should check the immediate pool area to be sure that glasses, bottles, and other potential accident-causers such as silverware and sharp barbecue utensils have not been left near the pool.

When planning a swimming party, make certain that rescue devices are handy. (Should an emergency arise, a shepherd's crook—a long pole with body-size hook—is usually the easiest and quickest way to reach a floundering swimmer and pull him to the poolside.) If swimming is scheduled for after dark, the pool area should be well lighted.

Designate a responsible person—a good swimmer, well-trained in rescue techniques and first aid—as "lifeguard," to enforce such pool rules as no ducking, no swimming alone, and only one person on the diving board at a time.

If someone kids you about being a party-pooper, remind him that drownings in home swim pools have tripled since 1963.

Have you tied up tomato plants? Prune so that only two main stems develop.

Application of acid-type fertilizer to rhododendrons and similar evergreens is now in order.

Peat and bone meal applied now will improve the soil around established iris plants. It's time also to divide and reset iris.

Is once-a-week too often to mow your lawn? Mowing by the calendar is not always best for the health of the turf. Let the growth between mowings determine the frequency.

Wash bonzai foliage occasionally with a fine spray of water.

June 19

Spare Tire as Life Saver

Remember this, if you should see a swimmer in distress this summer: an inflated spare tire from an automobile can serve as an effective life ring. A tire from a standard American car will provide buoyant support for as many as three adults.

If you can't swim, move the tire towards the swimmer with a stick, pole, or oar. If you pitch the tire from an elevated position, be careful to keep it away from the person in the water. The heavy tire and wheel could severely injure the person in distress.

If you do swim, but doubt your ability to handle a drowning person, tow the floating tire along with you as you make the rescue.

Today in History: Automatic doors in public places date back to June 19, 1931. On that day, the Stanley Works installed a "magic eye," or photoelectric cell, to operate swinging doors between the kitchen and dining room of a restaurant in West Haven, Conn.

June 20

Poison Plants You Should Know About

Since the beginning of time, humans have lived close to plants that can cause skin irritations, illness, or even death. Among them are a number of our prized ornamental shrubs and flowers—even some of our vegetables.

Not everyone reacts the same way to all plants. What is safe for one person may produce a severe allergic reaction in his neighbor. Consequently, when you include all plants that have ever produced an undesirable reaction in humans, the list becomes very long indeed.

Victims of poison plants most often are children who eat attractive fruits or leaves. Castor bean seeds will kill even an adult. The foliage of castor bean seedlings also is poisonous. All parts of the oleander are poisonous, even dried leaves.

In the yard and garden, the leaves and flower of tree of heaven, the young stems of asparagus, the leaves of rhubarb, the leaves and stems of parsnips and primroses, the leaves of buttercup, and iris rhizomes have all caused dermatitis in some people.

The green skin sometimes seen on an Irish potato contains a poison. Get rid of it.

The accompanying chart tells you what is likely to happen if certain parts of poison plants are eaten. The chart was produced as a public service by Geigy Agricultural Chemicals.

IN THE HOUSE AND GARDEN

Plant	Toxic Part	Symptoms
Hyacinth, Narcissus, Daffodil	Bulbs	Nausea, vomiting, diarrhea. May be fatal.
Oleander	Leaves, branches	Extremely poisonous. Affects the heart, produces severe digestive upset and has caused death.
Dieffenbachia (Dumb cane) Elephant ear	All parts	Intense burning and irritation of the mouth and tongue. Death can occur if base of the tongue swells enough to block the air passage of the throat.
Rosary pea, Castor bean	Seeds	Fatal. A single rosary pea seed has caused death. One or two castor bean seeds are near the lethal dose for adults.
Mistletoe	Berries	Fatal. Both children and adults have died from eating the berries.
Larkspur	Young plant, seeds	Digestive upset, nervous excitement, depression. May be fatal.
Monkshood	Fleshy roots	Digestive upset and nervous excitement.
Autumn crocus, Star-of-Bethlem	Bulbs	Vomiting and nervous excitement.
Lily-of-the-valley	Leaves, flowers	Irregular heart beat and pulse, usually accompanied by digestive upset and mental confusion.
Iris	Underground stems	Severe, but not usually serious, digestive upset.
Foxglove	Leaves	One of the sources of the drug digitalis, used to stimulate the heart. In large amounts, the active principles cause dangerously irregular heart beat and pulse, usually digestive upset and mental confusion. May be fatal.
Bleeding heart (Dutchman's breeches)	Foliage, roots	May be poisonous in large amounts. Has proved fatal to cattle.
Rhubarb	Leaf blade	Fatal. Large amounts of raw or cooked leaves can cause convulsions, coma, followed rapidly by death.

VINES, SHRUBS, AND TREES ON LAWNS

Daphne	Berries	Fatal. A few berries can kill a child.
Wisteria	Seeds, pods	Mild to severe digestive upset. Many children are poisoned by this plant.
Golden chain	Bean-like capsules in which the seeds are suspended	Severe poisoning. Excitement, staggering, convulsions and coma. May be fatal.
Laurels, Rhododendron, Azaleas	All parts	Fatal. Produces nausea and vomiting, depression, difficult breathing, prostration and coma.
Jessamine	Berries	Fatal. Digestive disturbance and nervous symptoms.
Lantana camara (red sage)	Green berries	Fatal. Affects lungs, kidneys, heart and nervous system. Grows in the southern U.S. and in moderate climates.
Yew	Berries, foliage	Fatal. Foliage more toxic than berries. Death is usually sudden without warning symptoms.
Cherries, wild or cultivated	Twigs, foliage	Fatal. Contains a compound that releases cyanide when eaten. Gasping, excitement, and prostration are common symptoms that often appear within minutes.
Oaks	Foliage, acorns	Affects kidneys gradually. Symptoms appear only after several days or weeks. Takes a large amount for poisoning. Children should not be allowed to chew on acorns.
Elderberry	Shoots, leaves, bark	Children have been poisoned by using pieces of the pithy stems for blowguns. Nausea and digestive upset.
Black locust	Bark, sprouts, foliage	Children have suffered nausea, weakness and depression after chewing the bark and seeds.

PLANTS IN THE WILD

Jack-in-the-pulpit	All parts, especially roots	Like dumb cane, contains small needle-like crystals of calcium oxalate that cause intense irritation and burning of the mouth and tongue.
Moonseed	Berries	Blue, purple color, resembling wild grapes. Contains a single seed. (True wild grapes contain several small seeds.) May be fatal.
Mayapple	Apple, foliage, roots	Contains at least 16 active toxic principles, primarily in the roots. Children often eat the apple with no ill effects, but several apples may cause diarrhea.
Water hemlock	All parts	Fatal. Violent and painful convulsions. A number of people have died from hemlock.
Buttercups	All parts	Irritant juices may severely injure the digestive system.
Nightshade	All parts, especially the unripe berry	Fatal. Intense digestive disturbances and nervous symptoms.
Poison hemlock	All parts	Fatal. Resembles a large wild carrot. Used in ancient Greece to kill condemned prisoners.
Jimson weed (thorn apple)	All parts	Abnormal thirst, distorted sight, delirium, incoherence and coma. Common cause of poisoning. Has proved fatal.

June 21

Today in History: Long-playing records running at $33\frac{1}{3}$ revolutions per minute were introduced by Columbia Records on June 21, 1948.

Use Treated Lumber for Repairs

When it becomes necessary to replace wood parts of a house, perhaps because of wood decay or termites, you will be well advised to use only preservative-treated lumber. At the same time, of course, you should try to remove the cause of the problem.

To be fully protected, wood must be deeply impregnated with the preservative. This can be done best by treatment under pressure, using, when necessary, preservatives that permit painting. Less effective protection is given by soaking or dipping the wood.

Sills or plates, sleepers, joists, beams, and girders in or on concrete, and exposed porches and steps are the parts of a house for which the extra cost of thorough preservative treatment can be most easily justified.

Where moisture cannot be controlled, use only preservatively treated wood or wood that is naturally durable, if available. Heartwoods of Douglas fir, southern pine, and white oak are classed as moderately resistant. Most cedars, tidewater red cypress, and redwood are highly resistant to decay. Heartwood of these can even be used in contact with soil. But be sure no sapwood is included.

The summer solstice occurs about this date. The earth is now tilted $23\frac{1}{2}$ degrees on its axis and the northern half is nearest the sun. Days are long because the sun passes through its greatest arc from horizon to horizon.

June 22

Avoiding Wood Decay in Crawlspaces

You know how vapor from the air condenses on cold water pipes or a glass of ice water. Moisture coming from the ground into the air in a crawlspace can collect as water droplets in the same way on wooden parts of the seldom-seen underbelly of your house in cold weather. Most water usually condenses on the sills and beam ends at the outer edges of the house. The open grain of the beam ends absorbs the condensation as fast as it forms. Before long the moisture content of the adjacent wood will have risen to the minimum of 20 percent required to support the fungi that cause wood decay.

Unless your home was built on a concrete slab, you should have a crawlspace with a minimum clearance of 18 inches between the soil and bottoms of the beams under all parts of the house except where you have a full cellar. This much clearance is standard to give air ventilation, provide access for wiring or plumbing located there, and for periodic inspection of the area.

Moisture condensation in a crawlspace can be minimized, or eliminated, by one of two methods—and you may want to use both. If you don't already know, today is an appropriate time to check up on the situation now prevailing in any crawlspace in your home. Space under an open porch should be considered in the same way.

Adequate ventilation is the first thing you should look for. Measure the total length of the wall space surrounding the crawlspace. Then measure all openings through which air can enter. Determine the total square footage of these openings. If the vents have grilles in them, count only the actual openings. Do you have at least one square foot of ventilating space for each 25 linear feet of wall? This formula provides sufficient ventilation for most crawlspaces.

But if the vents have louvers, the vents should be twice as large—and three times as large if there are both louvers and insect screening. Because insect screening becomes clogged with dirt and cobwebs, it is better to use quarter-inch wire mesh to keep out rodents. The vents should remain open during the winter. Depend on insulation to protect pipes and floors from cold.

If the openings into your crawlspace fail to satisfy the formula, you can solve the problem by stopping the moisture at its source. Do this by placing a vapor-resistant cover over the ground in the crawlspace. Smooth-surfaced roll roofing weighing 55 pounds or more per roll of 108 square feet has been used successfully for this purpose for many years. Roll out the roofing with a two-inch lap at the edges. No cementing is needed. Or use polyethylene film instead of the roofing. With this vapor barrier in place, you can have smaller vents, or even close them completely in winter, without danger of producing wood decay.

June 23

Today in History: An Act of Congress on June 23, 1860 established the Government Printing Office. Another Act, on January 12, 1895, authorized the Superintendent of Documents to distribute and sell government publications.

Information from Your Government

Publications on a wide range of subjects are printed by the Government Printing Office and distributed by the Superintendent of Documents. Many are of interest to home owners. Reference is made to some of them at various points throughout your Almanac.

To help you order, the Superintendent's office assembles lists of related publications on various subjects. Write and ask for what's available on the subject that interests you. Address the Superintendent of Documents, Government Printing Office, Washington, D.C. 20402.

In addition to mail-order service, the Government Printing Office operates a number of regional bookstores throughout the U.S. Each store has in stock about 1,000 of the most

popular titles. You are invited to stop in at any time. Five stores are located within Washington, D.C. Others are:

Atlanta, Ga.—Room 100, Federal Building, 275 Peachtree Street NE.

Birmingham, Ala.—2121 Eighth Avenue North.

Boston, Mass.—Room G25, John F. Kennedy Federal Building, Sudbury Street.

Canton, Ohio—201 Cleveland Avenue SW.

Chicago, Ill.—Room 1463—14th floor, Everett McKinley Dirksen Building, 219 South Dearborn Street.

Dallas, Tex.—Room 1C46, Federal Building—U.S. Courthouse, 1100 Commerce Street.

Denver, Colo.—Room 1421, Federal Building—U.S. Courthouse, 1961 Stout Street.

Kansas City, Mo.—Room 135, Federal Office Building, 601 East 12th Street.

Los Angeles, Calif.—Room 1015, Federal Office Building, 300 North Los Angeles Street.

New York, N.Y.—Room 110, 26 Federal Plaza.

Pueblo, Colo.—Public Documents Distribution Center, Pueblo Industrial Park.

San Francisco, Calif.—Room 1023, Federal Office Building, 450 Golden Gate Avenue.

Spider mites may be damaging Italian cypress at this point in the warm regions where it grows. Apply a recommended spray once or twice a month. Keep the trees well watered.

Colchium leaves may be yellowing now, but don't rush to remove them. Leave them alone until they are completely brown.

If you have peach and nectarine trees, find out the proper time to spray in your area for the Oriental fruit moth. Exact timing is important—and the time will come soon.

Keep old flowers trimmed off rosebushes now in bloom. Apply fertilizer during the bloom period and you'll enjoy a longer bloom period.

Water roses twice a week in California and the southern states. Water as much as three times a week in desert areas.

June 24

Where's That Septic Tank—Or Well?

If you have a septic tank, could you locate it exactly—possibly under snow and a foot or so of frozen earth? Suppose you need to have it pumped out. Could you open it up without a lot of labor and expense? Until you have the experience, you wouldn't believe how difficult it is to pick the right spot in an open lawn to dig down to it.

So why not prepare for trouble now, while you can dig with comparative ease? A metal probe may be helpful in finding the tank cover.

Remove soil from the cover—or from enough of it to learn whether it has a small pump-out opening (and cap). An opening no larger than six inches across will permit your local septic maintenance man to thrust in a pump-out hose without removing the entire cover. Most modern building codes require that septic tanks be made of concrete. Covers for these sometimes are cast with a pump-out opening. If yours doesn't have one, you may want to cast a new cover with such an opening. If the cover for your tank is metal, you can cut a small opening with a drill and hacksaw. A flat stone or flat piece of cast concrete will serve to close the opening.

This time don't throw dirt over the cleanout opening. Use bricks (no mortar) to build a walled enclosure around it, up to the level of the ground. An enclosure about 12 inches square is large enough. Fill in soil around the outside of the brick wall. Cast a concrete slab large enough to cover the opening—or buy a single large flagstone. Locate a sundial or a birdbath on a pedestal atop the slab. Then, when the tank needs pumping out, you simply lift away the birdbath or sundial, pry up the slab, and uncover the pump-out opening.

It's smart to make similar access arrangements for a drilled well that's now covered with soil. Dig out the soil over the casing. You may find that the elbow leading from the casing to the house is as deep as three feet—to put it below frost line. Enlarge your hole to a diameter of three feet or more. Use concrete blocks to lay up an enclosure large enough to permit uncapping the well if necessary. Cover the enclosure with a cast slab. You'll then have ready access to the well, even when the ground is frozen hard. And that's exactly the time when submersible pumps most often seem to demand repairs.

Set out flower seedlings now in the mountain regions of the West. See the April 2 map.

Most perennial flowers are top-heavy and need staking. The proper time has arrived in much of the country.

Your Own Reminders

Week of June 18–24

June 25

Digging a Dry Well

Pick-and-shovel work for a few hours, plus a supply of small stones or rocks, make up the recipe for a dry well—a hole dug into the ground for drainage of excess water. You may need a dry well to handle water draining from the house roof (the most common use), to drain water from a swimming pool, to receive water from an outdoor shower, or simply to drain a wet area on your property.

The flow of water a well is likely to receive can determine its size. A hole about four feet across and four or five feet deep should handle the drainoff from a single house downspout if the ground normally soaks up water fairly rapidly. If percolation is slow, you may need a larger well. In any case fill the hole up to about a foot from the ground level with gravel or small stones.

If the well is for house-roof drainage, locate it either 15 or 23 feet from the downspout and you'll be able to use either two or three eight-foot sections of black drainpipe to make the underground connection. Buy an elbow to connect downspout and drainpipe. Dig a trench and incline the pipe sharply to the well, letting it project at least a foot inside the well. Cover the top of the gravel with several pieces of roll roofing or heavy plastic to keep soil from working down through the gravel. Cover the roofing with at least a foot of good soil and sod it over.

Keep a record somewhere of the well location.

Cultivated blackberries are due to ripen soon at the lower limits of their range in the middle states. After the fruit has been picked, remove all canes, both old and new, and strong new ones will develop for next season. In the mountains of the South and in the North, however, where seasons are shorter it is best to remove only the old canes.

June 26

Today in History: On June 26, 1848, Congress approved "an act to prevent the importation of adulterated and spurious drugs and medicines." It was superseded by the Pure Food and Drug Act, adopted June 30, 1906.

Should You Clip Shoots from Lilac Roots?

The answer depends on what you want and the type of plant. Hybrid varieties sometimes are grafted on the roots of the common lilac. In that case, suckers arising from the roots may grow so vigorously that the main plant may eventually weaken and die out if the suckers are not checked. On such lilacs, remove the suckers as soon as they show above ground. Dig down to the root where the sucker originates and cut it off there. Cutting off any sucker at the ground level will cause it to branch like a limb on the tree itself.

When you know that a French lilac is on its own roots, suckers are an excellent way of propagating new plants or restoring the old top. Dig down and remove some of the original root along with the shoot. Transplant the shoot to a new location, keep it well watered, and you'll soon develop a hardy new plant.

Removal of suckers from lilacs can be carried on at any time during the growing season. Spring or early summer is best, however, for development of new plants.

Another spray for scale crawlers is in order now if you didn't get them the first time. See June 10. Pay special attention now to pines, hemlock, ivy, rhododendron, and azaleas.

June 27

A Pond on Your Property?

Your own pond isn't as improbable as it may seem at first. Admittedly, most urban and suburban lots have no space for a pond. But the chances improve steadily as you pass through outer suburbia into the rural areas.

So let's do some realistic dreaming about the situation—today.

How large a plot do you need before a pond becomes practicable? That probably depends on two major factors—whether you have a constant source of water (a brook, for instance) and whether your property is served by a sewer line. If you have a septic tank, you must have enough land so the effluent from the distribution field won't seep into the pond. If you have a sewer and a brook or spring, you might have a fine half-acre pond on a one-acre plot—and still live well on the other half-acre. If you have a septic tank, a four-acre plot may be better.

So, if you *can* have a pond, why should you want it? Swimming and fire protection are two logical uses. You might also stock it with fish, skate on it, or use it for nature study. Moreover, ponds conserve water—and that's a big point in your favor in these days of ecological considerations.

The local office of the Soil Conservation Service can tell you whether your site is suitable for a pond. A representative may even design the pond and help supervise its construction. If there are local restrictions about pond-building, he will help you comply with them.

Spray pines with Malathion for tip worms.

June 28

Any House Wood Contacting Soil?

Good building practice aims to keep any wood parts of a house from contacting the soil around or under it. There are two sound reasons for this: the soil-wood contact is a ready-made route for termites to spread into the house wood without being seen; it also is sure to provide entrance for moisture that eventually will cause wood decay. Decay organisms can work through a surprisingly large amount of wood from one small soil-wood contact.

Therefore, a thorough checkup of your home is in order. After a visual inspection around the exterior foundation or slab edge, go into the basement and any crawl spaces. Remove any surplus wood that you find—grade stakes, or concrete forms, even if not in contact with permanent wood of the house. Look closely at any open porches. Do you have a dirt-filled porch or stoop? The sketch shows what may have happened in that case if the builder was careless. There's usually little you can do about such a hidden soil-wood contact except to watch for the trouble that may develop.

Piles of firewood against a house may remain long enough to generate decay. Place them elsewhere.

When wood basement windows face below-grade window wells, be sure to keep the wells clear of leaves and other debris that may raise the bottom of the well into contact with the wood. Painted metal windows and frames are better for such situations.

Elderberry blossoms are appearing about now in the North—and it's the right time to use them for making wine.

Those insect hordes. Entomologists estimate that not less than 700,000 different kinds of insects have been described and named throughout the world.

June 29

Blueprints of Your House?

If you plan any additions to your home in the future, you would find it helpful to have on hand a set of blueprints of the existing house. Blueprints also may help you understand construction features that now are hidden.

Possible sources are previous owners, the builder, or perhaps a municipal office that is charged with inspecting and approving local construction. If you buy a brand new house, insist that the builder supply a copy of the prints, with notations about any changes made.

Store the blueprints with other important papers pertaining to your home. See January 3 and January 11.

Want to build a log cabin? The Extension Service at the University of Alaska publishes an excellent booklet on the subject. For information, write to the Extension Service, University of Alaska, College, Alaska 99701.

Do you like to dry herbs for future use? Do so before they blossom.

June 30

Just for Fun: Wit from Old Almanacs

On some days, you should relax, not work. So today we present for your idle pleasure a collection of jokes, conundrums, and other wit (so-called) culled from old almanacs that bemused and instructed our parents, grandparents, and great-grandparents. But we *must* warn you: You'll find some dreadful stuff here.

Advice to the cook: To prevent cakes, pies, and other goodies from spoiling, give the pantry key to the children.

Edison has invented a machine for condensing the noise of the elevated railways in New York City, running it down a pipe to the Battery, loading it there on the Long Island Sound steamboats and dumping it near Brattleboro, Vt. Great man, that Edison! The People of Brattleboro expect to can the noise and sell it for Fourth of July celebrations.

(In our modern world, you might call this "noise recycling." *Editor*).

Only a ring is necessary to engage a wife, but nothing short of cash will secure a hired girl.

A barefoot boy went to his father crying the other day and told him he had kicked a fly that had a splinter in its tail.

Says the policeman to Pat
"Come, I'll have none of that!"
As Paddy of whisky was drinking his fill.
With a satisfied sigh,
As he finished the rye,
Says Paddy
"Be jabbers. I don't think you will."

"Beware!" said the potter to the clay, and it was ware.

A good meat for tramps: cold shoulder.

"How is Jim Bullard getting along?" asked a stranger at a western railroad station.

"Jim committed suicide 'bout er month ago," replied a native.

"Committed suicide? How so?"

"He called me a liar, stranger."

Today in History: A patent for furniture casters was granted on June 30, 1838 to Philos, Eli, and John Blake, of New Haven, Conn.

Transistors were demonstrated on June 30, 1948, by the Bell Laboratory scientists who invented them.

July

How do you pronounce July? Those who lived before the beginning of the nineteenth century apparently sometimes placed the accent on the first syllable instead of the second, recalling the word's origin from Julius. In 1798, Wordsworth rhymed it with "truly" and another poet, writing in 1646, rhymed it with "newly."

But however you pronounce it, July is a time for serious thoughts about such things as keeping the house cool, the advisability of having a backyard pool, and making final plans for your vacation. Outdoors, your problems tend to multiply, for the month often brings drought that browns lawns and other vegetation and garden insects may be at their worst.

Called Quintilis when it was the fifth month of the old Roman calendar, the month was renamed for Julius Caesar in 44 B.C., the same year that he died at the hands of Brutus. The Anglo-Saxons called it several things but Maed Monath was a favorite. Mead is an alcoholic drink made by fermenting honey.

July 1

Today in History: This is Dominion Day in Canada, also sometimes called Canada Day. Under the British North American Act, the provinces of Canada were united into one government on July 1, 1867.

It's Hot. Remember the Need for Watering Plants

The hottest period of the year is beginning all over the continent. Wherever you live—and especially in the South—remember to keep all your shrubs and flowers well supplied with water.

In citrus-growing regions, keep the trees supplied with a balanced fertilizer as well as water as hot weather begins. This guards against excessive fruit drop.

If you have a timer to control lawn and other watering (and buying one is a good investment), choose early morning before 6 A.M. as the time for watering. For plants susceptible to mildew, early morning watering lets leaves dry off before nightfall.

Chlorosis may develop in gardenias, azaleas, citrus, pyracantha, and warm-climate plants unless well supplied with plant food that includes chelates.

Watch growth of espalier plants and thin where too much is developing.

When pyracantha becomes matted with white bloom, spray for fireblight.

July 2

Let Nature Help Control Plant Pests

When nature is in balance, the plant pests that now trouble us have an important place as all or part of the food of other creatures. Consequently, the pests are kept under control. We can help restore that situation.

Lady beetles and praying mantises are two important insect controls that we can introduce to our gardens and lawns. Lady beetles dine on aphids, the praying mantises on a variety of nuisance insects. Where do you get them? Check local garden supply stores for advice—or the garden pages in newspapers and magazines often have mail-order advertisements.

Hand picking of pests often makes it unnecessary to use pesticides. In grandfather's day, children were sometimes sent into the fields to pick off potato bugs and bean beetles. You can still attack various insects that way—tomato hornworms, Japanese beetles, and assorted caterpillars. Wear gloves to pick them. Cut off and burn branches containing nests of webworms and tent caterpillars. Do the same with the spruce-gall aphid that disfigures spruce trees and weevils in the leaders of white pine.

You might also like to try companionate planting. This phenomonon is not well understood, but observers will tell you that certain plants repel insects not only from themselves but also from other plants in the neighborhood.

Marigolds have proven toxic to soil worms. Garlic growing among roses is said to guard against mildew, aphids, and blackspot. Parsley among roses is said to drive away rose beetles while geraniums will repel Japanese beetles from grapes or roses.

Why not experiment in your own garden with plant associations? There's still much to be learned.

Shiny aluminum foil repels aphids when used as a ground cover under plants of the melon family. As a result, crop yields are increased. Research at an agricultural experiment station has proved this. It's believed that ultraviolet rays reflected from the foil confuse the flying aphids and cause them to go elsewhere.

Your Own Reminders

Week of June 24–July 2

July 3

Facts You Never Knew About Air Conditioning

Many of the same practices that you use in winter to conserve heat and make your home comfortable will also work during the summer to conserve power and make central air conditioners more efficient.

Keep storm windows in place during the air-conditioning season on all windows except those used for ventilating. Storm windows—and

insulating-glass windows as well—may not stop the penetration of solar radiation but they form significant barriers to the transfer of outdoor air heat to the indoors.

Keep windows and doors closed. Also keep storm doors in place. Screens are for use primarily in homes without central air conditioning.

Weatherstrip windows and doors at movable joints and caulk cracks and openings at their frames. Seal all cracks and openings in exterior walls.

Close and seal all passages or openings between the air-conditioned space and the attic, including cracks around attic doors.

Close the fireplace damper tightly.

Operate kitchen or exhaust fans only as long as needed to remove water vapor and cooking heat. Don't let them send your cooled air outdoors.

Cut away old canes of raspberries after the fruit has been picked. Pinch or cut off new shoots of black varieties to 12 to 18 inches in height.

Should you head back new shoots of red raspberries? Opinion is divided. Follow the local practice.

Berries that ripen on the vines are usually sweeter. Don't pick too soon.

Make the season's second shearing of evergreen hedges and foundations now. Shear away about half of what has grown since the early shearing.

July 4

Today in History: The Declaration of Independence was adopted July 4, 1776. Other important anniversaries on this date:

Work began on the Erie Canal in 1817.

Songwriter Stephen Foster was born in 1826.

The song "America" was first sung publicly in 1832 in Boston.

The cornerstone of the Washington Monument was laid in 1848.

France presented the Statue of Liberty to the U.S. in 1884.

Preamble to the Declaration of Independence

When in the course of human events, it becomes necessary for one people to dissolve the political bands which have connected them with another, and to assume among the powers of the earth, the separate and equal station to which the Laws of Nature and of Nature's God entitle them, a decent respect to the opinions of mankind requires that they should declare the causes which impel them to the separation.—

We hold these truths to be self-evident, that all men are created equal, that they are endowed by their Creator with certain unalienable Rights, that among these are Life, Liberty and the pursuit of Happiness.—

That to secure these rights, Governments are instituted among Men, deriving their just powers from the consent of the governed,

That whenever any Form of Government becomes destructive of these ends, it is the Right of the People to alter or to abolish it, and to institute new Government, laying its foundation on such principles and organizing its powers in such form, as to them shall seem most likely to effect their Safety and Happiness. Prudence, indeed, will dictate that Governments long established should not be changed for light and transient causes; and accordingly all experience hath shown, that mankind are more disposed to suffer, while evils are sufferable, than to right themselves by abolishing the forms to which they are accustomed. But when a long train of abuses and usurpations, pursuing invariably the same Object evinces a design to reduce them under absolute Despotism, it is their right, it is their duty, to throw off such Government, and to provide new Guards for their future security.

July 5

Avoid Those Bee Stings

Garden with care if you know you are allergic to bee and other insect stings. Deaths occur every season from the stings of bees, wasps, yellow jackets, hornets, and fire ants. Have a doctor-approved first aid kit on hand if you are allergic.

Prune hardy rambler roses after they have flowered.

Check magnolias now for Florida wax scales. These have thick white and waxy covering on reddish-brown bodies.

In the southern states, start transplants of such garden vegetables as tomatoes, broccoli, cauliflower, cabbage, and peppers.

July 6

Lightning Safety Rules

W**hen you are indoors** during a severe electrical storm:

Don't venture out unless absolutely necessary.

Stay away from open doors or windows, fireplaces, radiators, stoves, metal pipes, sinks, and plug-in electrical equipment.

Don't use the telephone—lightning may strike the lines outside.

When you are outdoors, heed the following rules:

Don't fly a kite. Ben Franklin was a darned fool in that respect.

Don't work on fences, telephone or power

lines, pipelines, or structural steel fabrication.

Don't use metal objects such as fishing rods and golf clubs.

Don't handle flammable material in open containers.

Stop tractor work, especially when the tractor is pulling metal equipment. Dismount and move away. Tractors in open fields are often struck.

Get out of the water and off small boats. Stay inside large boats.

Automobiles offer excellent lightning protection, but they are unsafe places when a tornado or severe thunderstorm approaches.

Seek shelter in a building; otherwise, in a cave, ditch, ravine, or under headhigh (at least) clumps of growth in open forest glades.

When there is no shelter, avoid the highest object in the area (and avoid *being* the highest object). If only isolated trees are nearby, your best protection is to crouch or lie in the open, keeping at least as far away from isolated trees as they are high.

If you have metal on your costume, such as golf spikes, get rid of it. You may be grounded and attract lightning strongly.

Avoid hilltops, wire fences, metal clotheslines, exposed sheds, and any electrically conductive elevated objects.

When you feel the electrical charge—if your hair stands on end or your skin tingles—lightning may be about to strike you. Drop to the ground immediately.

July 7

Fertilize Lawns in the South

Lawn-fertilizing time has arrived in the southern areas where Bermudagrass, zoysia, St. Augustinegrass, and other warm-season grasses make their maximum growth in hot weather. These grasses are variable in their nitrogen requirements. So you may want to check your county agent about it.

July 8

Revealing Rhymes for High Altitude Cooking

Cooks who have lived for awhile at high altitudes already know that favorite sea-level recipes usually need adjusting. But newcomers and vacationists may not. So for them, we present the following rhymes:

The "three minute" egg is easy to fix,
If you increase the minutes to five or six.

To cope with high altitude, use a pressure
saucepan,
It tenderizes faster than boiling can.

For candies and frosting, the cold water test
Is as good at high altitude as at the wave's
crest.

If you move up a mountain and bake a cake,
A new recipe you may want to take.

Potatoes and doughnuts, all foods that you fry,

Take a lower temperature when done "sky high."

The rhymes come from "A Cook's Almanac for Altitude Problems," a useful pamphlet available from the Cooperative Extension Service in several high altitude Rocky Mountain states. Because water boils at a lower temperature as altitude increases, cooking by boiling takes longer. For baking, more flour is required but less leavening.

July 9

Prune Some Shrubs in the Summer

Although most shrubs should be pruned during their dormant season, some can be pruned for best effect during the summer. One that demands it, in fact, is spiraea thunbergi. Fine twigs and leaves on this small shrub become so dense that new shoots have little chance to develop at the base. So watch for the end of the shrub's blooming period. Then thin out the top as necessary to admit light into the lower part of the plant.

Summer pruning also will often induce a second period of blooming, late in the season, on such summer flowering spireas as waterer, froebeli, japonica, and others. As soon as petals fade from the first blooming, remove the flower clusters and cut back the stems, almost to the ground. New shoots will grow and produce blossoms before frost comes.

A limited form of summer pruning is beneficial for such varieties of forsythia as viridissima and intermedia. These may develop new shoots with nodes so widely spaced that flowers the next spring will be very sparse. When these canes have grown to about six feet in midsummer, the top few inches should be removed. This will cause development of side shoots that will bear more flowers.

Today in History: On July 9, 1878, Henry Tibbs, of Washington, Me., received a patent for a corncob pipe.

Japanese bettles are due now at the northern limit of their range. See May 23.

Check Appendix B to see what vegetables can still be planted in your region—and have time to mature before frost comes.

Your Own Reminders

Week of July 3–9

July 10

How to Buy Cement

When you must undertake a masonry repair job, you can buy your supplies in three ways:

For convenience in getting a small job done fast, you can't beat the prepared mixes that come in bags. Sakrete is the brand most widely known. It offers three types—a concrete mix, a sand mix, and a mortar mix. Be sure to buy the one best suited for the job you plan. Read the bag label. Whichever you buy, empty out the full contents of the bag on a smooth surface and spend the time needed to make sure the ingredients are evenly spread through the mixture. This is important. In transport, the ingredients tend to separate.

The second way to produce concrete is to buy cement, sand, and aggregate separately and mix the parts yourself, either by hand or with a power mixer that you own or rent.

The accompanying table gives approximate amounts needed for batches of various size. In the U.S., the standard bag of cement weighs 94 pounds; Canadians should remember that theirs weighs only 80 pounds—and estimate accordingly. Mix a trial batch using amounts shown in the table. If this does not give good workability, vary the amounts of aggregate, either up or down. Never vary the amounts of cement and water.

Materials Needed for Concrete

A 1:2¼:3 mix = 1 part cement to 2¼ parts sand to 3 parts 1-in. max. aggregate.

Concrete Required cu. ft.	Cement lb.	Max. Amount of Water to Use gal. U.S.	Imperial	Sand lb.	Coarse Aggregate lb.
1	24	1¼	1	52	78
3	71	3¾	3⅛	156	233
5	118	6¼	5¼	260	389
6¾ (¼ cu. yd.)	165	8	6¾	350	525
13½ (½ cu. yd.)	294	16	13½	700	1,050
27 (1 cu. yd.)	588	32	27	1,400	2,100

To find how much concrete you should mix for a particular job, multiply the width, length, and thickness of the desired slab in feet, divide by 27, and you will get the cubic yardage needed. Note that if you want a slab 4″ thick, you would convert this to ⅓ foot for the formula.

Large concrete jobs these days practically always use ready-mixed concrete delivered by truck. See tomorrow's report for information about ordering and using this.

Spray locust trees again for mimosa webworm and pines again for tipworm.

Have you ordered new iris rhizomes for planting next month? Better do so now.

In Florida, July is considered the best time to apply oil sprays to citrus. Treatments made now give good control of scale insects and avoid unfavorable results.

July 11

The Tools You Need for Concrete Work

Let's consider today what tools you may want to have on hand for repair jobs involving the use of portland cement. You do need certain special tools for such work—a pointed trowel, jointing tool, steel trowel (or float), edger, and a wooden hand float. For large jobs, you might also want a steel-body wheelbarrow and a shovel.

You might rent some of this equipment when you need it, especially the wheelbarrow, but maintaining a home requires masonry repair fairly frequently. So you may want to buy some of the tools. You will want the pointed trowel and jointing tool especially for working with bricks. You use the edger for rounding off the edges of concrete-walk slabs.

July 12

How to Order Ready-Mix Concrete

For small repair jobs, you may never have any interest in ready-mix concrete delivered by truck. But for major improvements—a new driveway, a sidewalk, a patio, or a slab for a garage or other building—ready-mix is a wise choice since it eliminates the work of mixing and proportioning the ingredients.

Air-entrained portland cement is usually the best choice for the uses outlined above. It contains an agent that is formed of billions of microscopic air bubbles in concrete. When hardened, air-entrained concrete virtually eliminates scaling from freezing and thawing. It also resists de-icing salts.

To order ready-mix, first figure how much you need—in cubic yards—by using the formula given yesterday. When ordering, remember the numbers 6-6-6. These stand for 6 bags of cement per cubic yard, 6 gallons of water per bag of cement, and 6 per cent entrained air.

Before the load arrives, be sure you are prepared for it—your forms in place, coated with light form oil; your tools at hand, lots of strong-back help, and the know-how to do the job.

Today in History: Josiah Wedgewood, famous English potter, was born on July 12, 1730. His beautiful china is still much sought after.

July 13

Today in History: The U.S. patent numbering system was begun on July 13, 1834. Before that, 9,957 unnumbered patents had been issued.

It's Lube Time Again

Many points of friction need lubricating in your home twice a year. Better take care of them soon—for the second time this year.

See February 1 for a guide about what to do at this time.

New muscadine grape vines can be developed by starting layers now. Place a young cane in the ground. Cover with four or five inches of soil after stripping leaves from the part to be underground. Leaves should be kept on the uncovered tip. Plan to cut the cane from the parent plant during the following winter. See February 15.

July 14

Understanding a Home-Gas System

A large percentage of homes make use of gas (city or bottled) for some essential services—cooking, heating water, drying clothes, or heating the entire home. It is unwise and unsafe for do-it-yourselfers ever to attempt repairs to any part of a gas system. But you should make sure all adults in the home understand how to operate each gas appliance, expecially how to turn it on and off. Everyone should know the location of the main shut-off valve, too, for use in an emergency.

As your good household deed for today, check it and make sure it works easily.

Today in History: A tape measure enclosed in a circular case with a spring lock was patented July 14, 1868, by Alvin J. Fellows, of New Haven, Conn.

July 15

Today in History: This is St. Swithin's Day. The Bishop of Winchester was buried in the cathedral July 15, 971. Remember the old rhyme:

St. Swithin's Day, if thou dost rain,
For forty days it will remain;
St. Swithin's Day, if thou be fair,
For forty days it will rain nae mair.

Start Up Your Snowthrower

The neighbors may think you're crazy, but it is a good idea to take the wraps off your snowthrower now, if you have one, put a very little gas in the tank, and let it run dry. This slight use will overcome oxide buildup on ignition points, fuel-system gumming, and any tendency toward corrosion inside the engine.

July 16

Today in History: A patent for ready-mixed paint was granted on July 16, 1867 to D. R. Averill, of Newburg, Ohio.

Does Your House Need Painting?

This is a good time of the year for an annual check—and to make your preparations if the time has really come for repainting. Take a close look especially at the south side of the house. Exposed to the most sunlight, the south side usually takes the worst beating. Cracking, blistering, or peeling are all indicators that a repaint job is probably due. But be sure about it. Don't paint more often than needed. Perhaps the paint is simply dirty, and all that's needed is good scrubbing with a stiff brush, household detergent, and water. In your checkup, take a good look at horizontal surfaces like window sills. Paint there will give you the first danger signals.

If you do decide that repainting is needed, a period of warm weather during September is an ideal time to do it or have it done. Spend your spare time until then making your preparations—removing old paint, estimating and buying the paint you'll need, reputtying the windows, doing any necessary caulking, and assembling the ladders, brushes, and other equipment you'll need.

Check for and destroy any cocoons of the gypsy moth in the trunks of your trees and shrubs.

Your Own Reminders

Week of July 10–16

July 17

Check Outdoor Power Cords Now

Extension cords for use outdoors are an exception to the rule that fixed wiring should replace extension cords. You can carry power underground to outlets at fixed points throughout your lawn and garden, but flexible cords still are necessary for the use of such electrical conveniences as hedge shears, lawn trimmers and edgers, and lawn mowers.

Be careful to keep such outdoor cords in top condition. Now, at the middle of the outdoor season, is a good time to inspect them, as well as make your second annual safety checkup of the power cords that feed all of your electrical conveniences indoors and out.

Proceed generally as suggested in the entry for February 18. Check over the entire length of your outdoor cords and see that everything is shipshape with the plug and receptacle at the ends. Check also the short cord usually found on outdoor electrical tools.

When you find it necessary to buy a new outdoor cord, you may be well advised to choose one with a third grounding wire in preference to a less expensive two-wire cord. Double-insulated power tools are now fully accepted, and the two-wire cord will serve them well. But you may want to use your outdoor cord at some time with a tool that relies on a third wire for grounding.

If you find any cord in need of a new plug, or an appliance in need of a new cord, either make the repair now, or take the cord or appliance out of service, affixing a label: NOT TO BE USED UNTIL REPAIRED.

Do not fertilize roses in the north any later than this week. Any new growth would not withstand killing winter temperatures.

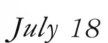

July 18

Put Labels on Your Plants

Have trouble remembering the correct names of some of your favorite plants? Many people do.

You can make your own weatherproof labels in various ways. Scratch them into soft aluminum with an awl or sharp nail. Rectangles cut from flashing aluminum should be good. Mark names on wood with crayons or waterproof pencils and spray with a clear waterproofing material. Burn the names into wood.

You probably will find name tags most rewarding on new and unusual flowers that you introduce to your garden. But they might go, too, on shrubs and trees that visitors to your home frequently ask you to name for them.

Remove all faded blooms to maintain vigorous growth of flower plants. Check the entire garden once a week from now on.

July 19

What to Do About Moles in the Lawn

Moles have been troublesome to man so long that they are now a part of folklore. Ask any countryman and he'll probably offer you what he calls a foolproof control method. None of the many ideas is truly satisfactory—and that is probably just as well for all of us. Actually, the little furry creature with the pointed snout may do us more good than harm. Moles feed on grubs and harmful insects, and their tunnels help aerate the soil. But the tunnels just under the sod make them a nuisance in lawns.

Removing the food supply by dosing the ground with chlordane is the surest way of eradicating moles. But this poison may poison everything else around, too—birds, beneficial insects, snakes, etc.

For a few moles on a suburban lawn, one or two harpoon traps offer safer control. Most hardware stores stock the traps. Locate a runway that is in active use and gently press down an inch or two of it. Set the trap by pulling up the spring-loaded prongs and place it astride the runway, with the trigger pan nestling against the soil you have tamped down. The idea is that the mole will push up the soil and the trigger, freeing the deadly prongs, thus impaling itself.

One home owner with a sporting bent stalks moles with a bow and arrow. Standing silently over an area of mole activity with drawn bow, he looses the arrow into the heaving soil. A sharp shovel poised in the same watchful attitude will slice the unsuspecting creature in half. A vacuum-cleaner hose with one end clamped to the exhaust pipe of a power mower and the other thrust into the mole run may have asphyxiated a few moles. But maybe not. There's too much chance for escape of the carbon monoxide to make this a reliable means of killing off moles.

England is plagued by moles, too, and it's from there that our final notion comes. It goes like this:

Bury an empty bottle, perhaps a beer bottle, in a mole run. Let only the neck protrude from the ground—and don't stopper it.

Before long, our informant tells us, the moles will vanish. Why? No one's quite sure. But there's a theory: The wind whistling across the open neck sets up vibrations that moles apparently can't bear, and they hightail out of there.

That, at least, is what the Englishman says.

July 20

Marble Chips for Your Lawn?

Landscape architects sometimes specify marble chips for certain areas of the home grounds. You may want to consider them, too.

Marble chips are used for appearance, to improve drainage, as a mulch to keep down weeds, and to substitute for lawn grass or ground covers in problem areas. Their white color makes a beautiful contrast with a green lawn and the colors in a flower bed.

Garden centers can usually supply marble chips in bags. You usually have a choice of chips in two or more sizes.

July 21

Have You Cleaned the Kitchen Fan?

A kitchen ventilating fan is designed to carry off odors and air heavy with cooking grease. It is natural, then, that some of the grease should adhere to the fan and the interior

of the discharge chute leading to the outdoors. Cleaning away this grease is a chore that ought to be done at least twice a year, even oftener if the fan is used daily. Neglect may lead to two major hazards—a fire in the chute and complete stoppage of the fan by grease.

Some ventilators are equipped with a mesh

filter (like a furnace filter) over the opening of the discharge chute—and all of them should be. If yours has a filter, remove it and wash it in a sinkful of detergent water once a month. But everything beyond the filter should still be cleaned periodically. A hot day at this time of year is a good time for it. The grease then will come off most easily.

Remove the entire motor and fan assembly from the ventilator housing. You may want to turn off power to the unit, although you'll probably find that the motor simply plugs in. The cleaning instructions that came with the ventilator should be helpful at this point. If you don't have such instructions, write to the manufacturer.

If the cleaning has been long delayed, you'll face a really messy task. Prepare for it by blanketing a work surface with a disposable covering.

Using hot water and detergent, moisten a cloth and wipe off all surfaces that are accessible on the motor and blower unit. When the surfaces are clean, wipe them dry. If any parts are removable, immerse them in a detergent washing solution. But don't immerse the motor. That would short it out. Oil the motor with a light oil.

While the chute is clear, use hot dampened cloths to wipe its interior surfaces clean. Depending on its length and conformation, you may be able to thrust through a wad of cleaning cloths on the end of a wire. Alternately, you might be able to draw through a wad of cleaning cloths by working from the outdoor end. At least check the discharge opening to be sure that it is clear.

In Alaska, the period from July 15 to August 1 is the preferred time to seed lawns in areas where water is not readily available. Summer rains begin then.

Fertilize mature fig trees. Apply about one-third pound of 8-8-8 fertilizer for each foot of height.

July 22

What to Do About Sticking Windows

Most windows are supposed to open. If yours don't all open easily, better devote an hour or two to setting things right. Common causes of sticking are accumulated paint, humid-weather expansion, and distortion from house settling. In a comparatively new house, the latter cause is the most likely one.

Try lubrication as the first cure. One of the new spray lubricants containing a fluorocarbon compound often works wonders in improving the action of adjoining wood surfaces. Melted paraffin mixed with a little turpentine also does a good lubricating job.

If you are unable to move the sash at all, you may be able to break it loose by driving a piece of thin metal into the groove. Or pry off the stop beads around the sash, scrape off any paint that has accumulated on the edge adjoining the sash, and replace the beads with greater edge clearance.

If the sash still moves with difficulty when the bead is out, remove the sash and sand or plane down its edges. The parting strip will have to be pulled out to free the upper sash. Sand the surfaces of the parting strip too. Brush all unpainted surfaces with linseed oil and let it soak in. Wipe off the excess.

Sticking metal casements can sometimes be cured by a little careful prying. Be sure all rubbing surfaces are kept well lubricated.

July 23

Maintaining Casement Windows

A steel casement window will outlast the house if it is periodically maintained. If you must force the crank to open or close it, take this as a sign the window needs attention.

For easy cranking, clean and lubricate the gear box once a year. Remove the screws holding the gear box to the frame and slide the swing-arm out of the window groove. Remove the shouldered screw that holds the gears in mesh and wash the parts in kerosene. Lubricate with heavy motor oil or light grease and reassemble. Oil the hinge pivots and swing the window in and out to free them.

Adjust the strike plate to make the latch pull the window snug against the frame when closed. Oversize screw holes usually make adjustment simple. If this doesn't produce a tight closure, or if the screws are rusted in and can't be loosened, bend the lip of the strike plate inward so the latch cam will bring the window in closer.

A casement window's worst enemy is rust. At the first sign of it, sand and wirebrush the entire frame. Protect it with red lead or rust-resisting paint, and finish with a good exterior paint.

Add ties from time to time as vines and some other plants grow during the summer season. Plastic clothesline or pliable insulated electric wire can be used.

Oil sprays are commonly applied to citrus (except lemons) in California from late July through September. A time is selected when the younger, more susceptible stages of the scale insects are most evident.

Strange tales about insects, most of them untrue, were told by Pliny the Elder, writing his natural history about the time of Christ. Among them: that locusts in the Orient grew to such size that their hind legs were dried and used as saws.

Your Own Reminders

Week of July 17–23

July 24

Check All Window Putty

Using a ladder, inspect all windows on the outside once a year to see the condition of the window putty. A considerable amount sometimes crumbles away, especially in older houses where linseed-oil putty was used and not modern glazing compound. Carry along a small can of the latter and a putty knife so you can replace missing sections.

There's a real knack to laying down a smooth triangular-section of putty against the glass and the wood frame. Instructions like this can never substitute for watching how an expert does it. But until you have that opportunity, you can get by, especially in patching, by rolling a wad of compound into a rope-like form between your palms, pressing it into place, and smoothing it off with the tip of the putty knife.

July 25

Seal and Patch Roofs Now

A warm day at this time of year is the ideal time for repairing roofs with various liquid coatings and cements. The coatings usually are more easily applied when temperatures are high.

Consider your need for black roof cement first. You can use this on practically all roofs to seal cracks and provide waterproofing around vent pipes, chimneys, and sky lights, as well as to cement down loose or torn shingles. Apply it in patches about 1/4″ thick, using a putty knife.

Today in History: A detachable paper collar was patented on July 25, 1854, by Walter Hunt, of New York City.

You will find several different types of general roof coatings in mailorder catalogs and at building-supply dealers. Check the labels to see which type you can use to best advantage. Roof and gutter paints and asphalt fiber coatings usually are the least expensive. They'll lengthen the life of asphalt composition, metal and roll roofing. These black coatings may or may not be approved for application on shingles.

Where under-roof heat is a problem during the summer, take a look at the available aluminum coatings. They're especially good for flat roofs. The aluminum reflects the sun's rays and the space below the roof remains cooler.

To apply most of these coatings, you'll need a long-handled brush made especially for the purpose.

Remove any galls you see on spruce trees.

Remove mature flowers and seed pods from annual flowers if you want to maintain vigorous growth. This is particularly desirable with ageratum, calendula, cosmos, marigold, pansy, rudbeckia, scabiosa, and zinnia.

July 26

Check Shingle Roofs for Needed Repairs

This is also a good time to examine a shingle roof, whatever it's made of, for any needed repairs.

If a shingle is missing, you can replace it by gently lifting one or several above it just enough to slip the new one under. Slide a hacksaw blade under the upper shingle and cut off any nails that keep you from sliding the new shingle in place. Then fasten both shingles in place by applying roof cement underneath. This procedure works for both wood and composition shingles.

You sometimes find the lower edges of composition shingles raised or curled up, permitting wind-driven rain to go under them. This raising may be caused by nails that backed out. Remove or cut off the nails and seal the holes with caulking. Lift each shingle, squeeze a dab of roofing cement under it, and press the shingle down.

Nails that have loosened are sometimes a source of leaks, especially along the ridges. Drive new ones in an adjacent spot and fill the old holes with caulking. Apply cement over rusted nails.

A small piece of flashing metal or polyethylene film can also be used to stop a leak that occurs between shingles. Coat the metal on part of its upper surface with roofing cement, lift the adjoining shingles, and slide it under until it covers the hole.

An unusual candlestick for the patio can be created by turning a small clay flowerpot upside down. Paint it for permanent use. Taper the bottom of the candle for a snug fit in the drainhole.

Wing beats of insects may be as rapid as 350 strokes a second.

July 27

Shower Head Clogged?

Did you get an uneven spray the last time you took a shower? That's a sign the shower head needs cleaning. The newest shower heads are self cleaning, but many old ones are not. So why not give yours a checkout now—today? You might be surprised at the improvement.

You'll probably need a wrench to unscrew the head. Pad the jaws with cloth or tape to avoid marring the metal.

Clean the back surface of the head with a stiff brush and use a coarse needle to clear mineral deposits out of all of the holes.

A water softener prevents formation of such deposits.

July 28

Chop Up Fallen Limbs for Mulch?

Now that open-air burning is forbidden in more and more communities, how can you dispose of the branches that break or are pruned from trees on your property?

If you have a fireplace, you can make good use of all free firewood from such sources. But otherwise, what do you do? Just let the local refuse collector haul everything away?

As a conservation measure, why not plan to chop up such material into chips that you can use as a garden mulch. A heavy-duty mulcher is required for such work, the size now used by some road departments and tree surgeons. It wouldn't pay a home owner to buy this machine, but you might want to rent one for half a day and chop up all the debris you've collected in the past year. Perhaps several of your neighbors could be induced to make it a joint project for a summertime Saturday morning.

Or a conservation group could rent a mulcher and offer free mulch-making service at an advertised time and place. One group recently disposed of Christmas trees in this manner at a well-attended mid-January chopping of the greens.

July 29

Watch Out for Plant Mildews

In the middle of summer in the northern states, the foliage of flowers and shrubs often becomes spotted with a whitish mildew. This is of two kinds—downy mildew and powdery mildew. These are found in different environments and are controlled in different ways.

Downy mildew shows up in a moist situation. Rain helps it spread. It shows up on such vegetables as lettuce, spinach, and cucumbers, on small flowers like pansies, and on nut trees—pecan and walnut. Control the fungus by thinning plants to increase air circulation and reduce humidity. Avoid watering in late evening, leaving the leaves damp all night. For chemical control, spray with Bordeaux mixture or the fungicide zineb.

Powdery mildews damage a wide assortment of shrubs, trees, and vines—lilac, azalea, blueberry, dogwood, and grape among them. Zinnias and phlox are among the flowers, and tomatoes, peppers, and squash among the vegetables. A sulfur spray early in the season will kill over-wintering spores on trees, but avoid using this on flowers. Check garden books for control measures later in the season.

To clean sticky fingers on the road, fill an empty squeeze-type plastic bottle with water and keep it in the glove compartment.

July 30

"Rainbow In Morning, Sailor Take Warning"

There just may be some truth to those old weather proverbs that Grandpa used to recite—proverbs that have somehow miraculously survived our scientific age of meteorological know-how.

In fact, even the U. S. Weather Bureau acknowledges that weather folklore has a way of proving to be more fact than fable. Take one of the best-known weather proverbs:

> "Rainbow in morning, sailor take warning
> Rainbow at night, sailor's delight."

"This old proverb makes sense, particularly from a scientific point of view," says Ivan Brunk, meteorologist for the U.S. Weather Bureau.

"A rainbow appearing in the morning in the western sky indicates that rain is falling at some nearby point in the west. Since weather normally moves from west to east, rain may be expected soon," Brunk added.

"A rainbow appearing in the eastern sky at night indicates that rain is falling to the east, meaning that bad weather has already passed."

Other proverbs with a scientific explanation:

"Clear moon, frost soon."

Weathermen explain that when the moon is clear, the atmosphere is clear and cloud-free. The earth cools rapidly by radiation. If no wind exists and temperatures are low, frost may form.

"Red sun at night, sailor's delight.
Red sun in the morning, sailors take warning."

Atmospheric conditions determine the sun's appearance. A red or pink sky in the west often results from dust rather than vapor and is usually a sign of fair weather. A dark red, menacing morning sky is caused by excessive vapor which comes before a storm.

"When leaves show their undersides,
Be very sure that rain betides."

Plant scientists teaming up with meteorologists explain that the leaf stalk absorbs moisture, causing the leaf's underside to show. They explain that all noticeable plant changes on which weather predictions can be based are due to changes in humidity, temperature and sunshine.

"A year of snow, a year of plenty."

The old-timers reasoned that when the weather was cold and the earth was covered with snow in early spring, the likelihood of fruit trees blossoming prematurely and being nipped later by a freeze was lessened. Too, a snow blanket and a cool spring reduced the chances of alternative thawing and freezing, decreasing the chances of wheat and other winter grains being damaged by a late frost.

"When the grass is dry at morning light
Look for rain before the night."

"When the dew is on the grass
Rain will never come to pass."

When the sky is clear and the air dry and still, the temperature of the grass falls many degrees, chilling moisture below the current saturation temperature. As a result, dew forms.

But if the sky is clouded or the air humid, there will be a relatively large amount of return radiation to the clouds. So, the grass is not as likely to be cool enough for dew to form.

Old-timers even linked human behavior with the weather. As one old English proverb puts it:

"Do business with men when the wind is in the northwest."

The logic stands to reason—when weather is most likely to be fair, a person's mood tends to be buoyant, cheerful and optimistic.

NOTE: The foregoing is reprinted by permission from *IH FARM,* a magazine published by International Harvester Company. It was written by Steve Rhea, the editor.

"One touch of nature makes the whole world kin."

—Shakespeare

Pull out severed rose canes from the top in pruning. The reason: Rose thorns curve downward. If canes are pulled downward or through the side, the thorns will hook on remaining canes.

You can attract colorful butterflies to your garden at this time of year in the warm-climate states by growing a butterfly bush—common name for a half dozen varieties of buddleia that can be grown in the U.S. from the middle latitudes southward.

Your Own Reminders

Week of July 24–30

Is there a growth that looks like an English walnut on any of the main stems of your rose plants? This is a sign of crown gall disease. There is no cure. Pull up the plant and burn it.

The sting of the imported fire ant is very painful. You may encounter their mounds in Alabama, Florida, Mississippi, Louisiana, Arkansas, Georgia, Tennessee, Texas, and South Carolina.

July 31

Time Now to Plant "Autumn Crocus"

More home plantings should include colchicums, sometimes known as autumn crocus or meadow saffron. They are easy to grow. They last practically forever. They are beautiful in any garden. They blossom from early September to late October in the northern latitudes. Colchicums belong to the lily family.

If all of this induces you to action, now is the time to act. Colchicum corms are dormant from late July until early August—and that is the time to plant them. It may be, however, that your garden supplier will not have the corms until September. Whatever the time, plant them as soon as you can.

The corms are sometimes quite large—as much as two inches across and four inches long. Plant the corms upright in a hole dug about ten inches deep but filled at the bottom with enough compost or peat moss to locate the tip three inches or so below ground level.

Some gardeners like to locate colchicums in the midst of a ground cover. The latter then serves as a green background for the leafless and stemless colchicum blossoms. Leaves appear on colchicums only in the spring.

August

Summer reaches its height in August—and begins to wane. Hot sultry days come. High humidity sometimes causes sticking problems. Lawns almost always need watering. Gardeners may note that the Anglo-Saxons had an apt name for this month, too: Weod Monath, the time when weeds flourish. Nevertheless, harvests go on in earnest and wild asters and goldenrods brighten fields and roadsides.

Towards the end of the month, crickets, katydids, and other insects each night offer a noisy prelude to approaching autumn. On hearing the first katydid, country people have long had a saying: "It's six weeks to frost." In the northernmost latitudes, nights grow cool and the first frosts come (ahead of the saying) as the earliest bird migrants turn southward.

In the original Roman calendar, August—then the sixth month—was called Sextilis. Its modern name came from the Emperor Augustus. Never a shrinking violet, Augustus named the month for himself because that was the time his greatest triumphs had occurred. Jesus was born during his reign.

August 1

The Hurricane Season Is at Hand

The hurricane season has begun. If you live along the Atlantic seaboard, make sure you have stocked supplies to carry you through an emergency and that you know what to do if it comes. Hurricanes also form along the west coast of Mexico and Central America, but their effects are seldom felt as far north as California.

Hurricane winds do much damage, but drowning is the greatest cause of deaths. As the storm moves across the coastline, it brings huge waves, raising tides some 15 feet or more above normal. The rise may come rapidly and produce floods in coastal lowlands or may come in the form of giant waves.

Hurricanes that strike the Eastern United States are born in the tropical and subtropical North Atlantic Ocean, the Caribbean Sea, and the Gulf of Mexico. Most occur in August, September, and October.

On the average, six Atlantic hurricanes occur per year. However, there are significant deviations from this average. In 1916 and 1950, 11 hurricanes were observed, and no hurricanes were observed in 1907 and 1914. During 1893, 1950, and 1961 seasons, four hurricanes were observed in progress at the same time.

Hurricane winds rotate clockwise in the Northern Hemisphere because of the coriolis force, the apparent force imparted by the earth's rotation. Wind rotation is counter-clockwise in the Southern Hemisphere.

August 2

Hurricane Safety Rules

Enter each hurricane season prepared. Recheck your supply of boards, tools, batteries, nonperishable foods, and the other equipment you will need if a hurricane strikes.

When you hear the first tropical cyclone advisory, listen for future messages. If your area receives a hurricane warning, leave low-lying areas that may be swept by high tides or storm waves.

Moor your boat securely before the storm arrives, or evacuate it to a designated safe area. When your boat is moored, leave it, and don't return once the wind and waves are up.

Board up windows or protect them with storm shutters or tape. Danger to small windows is mainly from wind-driven debris. Larger windows may be broken by wind pressure.

Secure outdoor objects that might be blown away or uprooted. Garbage cans, garden tools, toys, signs, porch furniture, and a number of other harmless items become missiles of destruction in hurricane winds. Anchor them or store them inside.

Store drinking water in clean bathtubs, jugs,

Today in History: The first street letter boxes for the deposit of mail were set up on Aug. 2, 1858 in Boston and New York City.

bottles, and cooking utensils; your town's water supply may be contaminated by flooding.

Check your battery-powered equipment. Your radio may be your only link with the world outside the hurricane, and emergency cooking facilities, lights, and flashlights will be essential if utilities are interrupted.

Keep your car fueled. Service stations may be inoperable for several days after the storm strikes, due to flooding or interrupted electrical power.

Stay at home, if it is sturdy and on high ground; if it is not, move to a designated shelter and stay there until the storm is over.

When the hurricane has passed, drive carefully along debris-filled streets. Avoid loose or dangling wires, and report them immediately to your power company or the nearest law enforcement officer. Report broken sewer or water mains to the water department. Check refrigerated food for spoilage if power has been off during the storm.

Remember that hurricanes moving inland can cause severe flooding. Stay away from river banks and streams.

To lessen the chance of winter damage to new growth, do not fertilize grapes any later than this in the North.

Established colchiums that have been in place for some years should be dug up promptly now, during their dormant period, and replanted, say about eight inches apart. Dig holes deeper than the corms are long, fill the bottom with compost, and set the corms upright with the tips three inches or more below the surface.

Green manure crops planted last spring as a prelude to fall lawn seeding should be turned under about now. Wait four to six weeks before planting grass seed.

August 3

Who's That Lady? She's a Hurricane!

The Weather Bureau has set up four sets of feminine names to designate hurricanes in the Atlantic and Pacific. The names available for use each year are arranged in alphabetical order. Names beginning with Q, U, X, Y, and Z were not included because of their scarcity. A separate set of names is used each year, beginning with the first name in each set. Although each set is used again every four years, names used for major hurricanes—like 1965's Betsy—are retired for at least ten years and another name substituted.

Names for hurricanes in the Eastern North Pacific:

1973: Ava, Bernice, Claudia, Doreen, Emily, Florence, Glenda, Heather, Irah, Jennifer, Katherine, Lilian, Mona, Natalie, Odessa, Prudence, Roslyn, Sylvia, Tillie, Victoria, Wallie

1974: Adele, Blanca, Connie, Dolores, Eileen, Francesca, Gretchen, Helga, Ione, Joyce, Kirsten, Lorraine, Maggie, Norma, Orlene, Patricia, Rosalie, Selma, Toni, Vivian, Winona

1975: Agatha, Bridget, Carlotta, Denise, Eleanor, Francene, Georgette, Hilary, Ilsa, Jewel, Katrina, Lily, Monica, Nanette, Olivia, Priscilla, Ramona, Sharon, Terry, Veronica, Winifred

1976: Annette, Bonny, Celeste, Diana, Estelle, Fernanda, Gwen, Hyacinth, Iva, Joanne, Kathleen, Liza, Madeline, Naomi, Orla, Pauline, Rebecca, Simone, Tara, Valerie, Willa

Names that will be given to hurricanes that originate in the Atlantic, Caribbean, and Gulf of Mexico:

1973: Anna, Blanche, Camille, Debbie, Eve, Francelia, Gerda, Holly, Inga, Jenny, Kara, Laurie, Martha, Netty, Orva, Peggy, Thoda, Sadie, Tanya, Virgy, Wanda

1974: Alma, Becky, Celia, Dorothy, Ella, Felice, Greta, Hallie, Isabel, Judith, Kendra, Lois, Marsha, Noreen, Orpha, Patty, Rena, Sherry, Thora, Vicky, Wilna

1975: Arlene, Beth, Chloe, Doria, Edith, Fern, Ginger, Heidi, Irene, Janice, Kristy, Laura, Margo, Nona, Orchid, Portia, Rachel, Sandra, Terese, Verna, Wallis

1976: Abby, Brenda, Candy, Dolly, Evelyn, Frances, Gladys, Hannah, Ingrid, Janet, Katy, Lila, Molly, Nita, Odette, Paula, Roxie, Stella, Trudy, Vesta, Wesley

August 4

Time for Maintenance of Air Conditioners

A mid-season maintenance for air conditioners is now probably overdue. The first thing to do is check the air filter. Filters are universally used on central cooling systems to keep dust and lint from depositing on the air blower and the cooling surfaces, as well as to deliver cleaner air to living spaces. Look at the filter now. If it looks dirty, change or clean it. Your system is designed to operate efficiently with relatively clean filters. For the average household a filter check is necessary every 30 to 60 days.

Window air-conditioners also contain filters that can easily be inspected by removing the room-side cover. It is especially important to check those units that are made with the air filter in immediate contact with the cooling coil.

If the filter is dirty, a buildup of frost and ice can occur that will impede the flow of air. Operating a window unit when the weather is mild can also cause frosting of the cooling coil, and when the frost melts it can cause water damage to window frames, walls, or furnishings beneath the air-conditioning unit. To prevent frosting and save energy, the best procedure is to keep the filter clean and avoid using your air conditioner in mild weather.

Keep the condenser clean. The condenser in an air-conditioning system is located outdoors (both in window units and central systems). The finned surfaces of the condenser should always be kept clean and free of leaves, mud, etc. Also, the air flow through the condenser should not be impeded by shrubbery or placing it too close to walls.

Lubricate bearings and tension the fan belt. The bearings on the blower and electric motor unit should be lubricated to maintain maximum efficiency. Lubrication instructions can usually be found on the nameplates or in the manufacturer's manual for the equipment. These should be followed at least once a year, preferably at the start of the cooling season.

Pulleys on a motor and blower are usually connected by a belt to transmit the rotative power of the motor to the blower. Power is transmitted at maximum efficiency when this belt is at the proper tension. A simple check of belt tension is to shut off the electric power to the motor and press down on the belt midway between the pulleys. The distance the belt depresses with a few pounds of force applied to it. should be between 1/4 and 1/2 inch. The tension of the belt usually can be controlled by adjusting screws on the mounting frame.

Is the gypsy moth rampant in your area? Now is a good time to trap and destroy adult moths.

The most popular drink: "the same."
—*Old Almanac*

Why is the busy bee like human contentment? Because it's a humbug.—*Old Almanac*

August 5

Today in History: Electric traffic signals got their start on Aug. 5, 1914. The place: Cleveland, Ohio.

Switch Your Tires Now?

It's probably time now for periodic switching of the tires on your car or cars. Follow your own rotation plan—or see November 2 for a plan you may want to adopt. Perhaps you can time the switch with a periodic lube and oil change.

August 6

Wet Basement? Condensation or Seepage?

Either condensation or seepage may cause dampness in a basement. Seepage usually is apparent, but it's sometimes a question about whether condensation or seepage is causing a damp area on a masonry wall or floor. A simple test will tell.

Mount a thin flat sheet of bright tin against the damp area, using adhesive to keep it in place. Examine the tin after an hour or so. If the outside surface of the tin remains dry, the dampness comes from seepage. If moisture collects on the surface, condensation is causing at least part of the probelm although seepage may also be occurring.

Dampness from condensation may be prevented or minimized by either heating the basement air, dehumidifying the air, or by ventilation. Ventilation is particularly effective in carrying off excessive amounts of water vapor from washing and drying clothes, shower baths, etc. However, if dampness persists, the problem may be largely one of seepage.

In that case, you may want to seek the remedy as described in the entry for April 11.

If correcting the outside drainage and filling cracks inside fails to solve the problem, a trench can be dug outside the basement wall to the depth of the footing. The exterior surface of the wall should then be coated with cement and tar in the manner recommended for all new homes.

Be sure your lawn has water during the hot season. Sandy soils require frequent watering in small amounts. Clay soils need it infrequently —in large amounts. Apply water when the grass shows signs of wilt.

Your Own Reminders

Week of July 31–Aug. 6

August 7

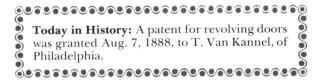

Today in History: A patent for revolving doors was granted Aug. 7, 1888, to T. Van Kannel, of Philadelphia.

Repairs for Sticking Doors

Sticking doors or doors that won't stay closed result from many things: loose or poorly set hinges, screws loose in the wood, house settling and forcing the jamb out of square, wood swollen from moisture or shrunk from dry heat.

Before tightening loose hinges, prop up the bottom of the door with a wedge to take the strain off the screws. Otherwise, the weight of the door may cause the screws to strip the holes when tightened.

If screws can't be tightened, try longer ones of the same diameter, or use sheetmetal screws, threaded along the entire shank. If thicker screws are used, enlarge the hinge holes for their heads.

Where the screw holes are hopelessly stripped, remove the screws and tamp in steel wool or wood putty, or force in fiber screw anchors or glue-coated wood plugs. Wait until the glue or wood putty sets before driving in the screws.

If resetting the screws won't work, your best bet is to shift the hinges to give the screws a fresh start in new wood. Most hinge pins can be tapped out with a hammer to separate the two halves. Shift the hinge leaf enough to clear the old screw holes and scribe in the area to be chiseled away. After enlarging the hinge gain to the new position, fill in the gap below the hinge with a thin sliver of wood. Glue it in place and sand flush.

Sometimes a bit of paper folded in half may be the answer to a door problem. Remove the hinge screws and cut the paper to fit the gain. Use two or more sheets if necessary to make a shim of the required thickness.

Remember that a shim placed under the lower hinge will lift the door upward; placed in the top hinge it will move the door outward and down. Shims under both hinges may help a latch to reach the strike plate.

Light sanding may free a door that catches only on small high spots. Sandpaper tacked to a wood block will cut down high spots on the jamb without removing wood or paint from inside edges of stop strips.

If the door rubs the threshold when closed, or if it scrapes the floor when fully opened, place a sheet of coarse sandpaper on the threshold, hold it with one foot and work the door over it until it no longer makes contact.

Budding of fruit trees can be done at any time during August or early September. Budding is better than grafting for peaches.

New black raspberry shoots can be pinched off to induce lateral branching.

If you must conserve water during a drought, put it first on trees and shrubs. Let the grass go. It will come back with the first rain.

August 8

Today in History: On Aug. 8, 1899, A. T. Marshall, of Brockton, Mass., received a patent for a household refrigerating machine.

Fighting Insect Pests During August

Spray the trunks of peach trees early in the month to provide protection from moths of peach tree borer. Also drench the soil around each tree.

A Malathion spray at this time of year has been found effective against bagworm larvae. Mix 57 percent emulsion concentrate at the rate of two teaspoons per gallon of water.

Spray locust trees again for the damaging and unsightly mimosa webworm. When webs have formed, consider pruning off the limbs and burning them.

Check off-color foliage on conifers for red spider mites. Spray if necessary.

Plan to spray the trunk and foliage of willows for borers in late August.

If mildew appears on lilac leaves in August or September, it can be controlled by spraying with Bordeaux mixture, wettable sulphur, or dusting sulphur.

August 9

Destroy Those Toadstools

Mushrooms and toadstools may appear in lawns in northern and middle latitudes about now—or even up until about a month from now. If there are children around who may be tempted to taste them, better pick and discard the mushrooms as they appear.

August 10

Facts About Cockroaches

You may encounter cockroaches in your home at any time of the year. They hide during the day in sheltered, dark places. They come out and forage at night. If you suspect their presence in any part of the house, enter the room cautiously late at night and switch on the light. If any are present, you will see them scatter for shelter.

If you seldom or never see a cockroach, it may be a credit to your good housekeeping. Thorough and regular cleaning reduces the chances that they will stay, even if they do enter the house. To keep them out—and this would be a

Today in History: Production of the sound-absorbing insulation board known as Celotex was begun on Aug. 10, 1921.

worthwhile chore for this time of year—go over the house and fill all cracks passing through floors or walls with putty, caulking compound, or a woodcrack filler. Pay special attention to water and steam pipes entering rooms as well as cracks leading to spaces behind baseboards and doorframes.

When you bring baskets, bags, or boxes of food or laundry into the house, be aware that cockroaches may be hiding in them. They may also ride firewood into the house.

Various insecticides are available to combat cockroaches. Use them carefully—only as directed. Be careful not to contaminate food or leave the insecticide where children may encounter it. Apply the insecticides to places where the cockroaches hide. To find the hiding places, enter a dark room quietly, turn on the lights, and watch where the cockroaches run.

August 11

Avoiding Water-Pipe Condensation

In areas where the air gets hot and humid, condensation (sweating) is very likely to occur on pipes carrying cold water. This can be prevented by insulating the pipes. The insulation will also help to keep the water cool. To prevent condensation from collecting in the insulation, it should be covered with a vapor barrier. Vapor barriers are ordinarily available from the same sources as the insulation.

When cold water enters a water closet tank, it may chill the tank enough to cause "sweating" (condensation of atmospheric moisture on the outer surface of the tank). This can be prevented either by warming the water before it enters the tank or by insulating the tank to keep the temperature of the outer surface above the dewpoint temperature of the surrounding air. A tempering device that will mix a little hot water with the cold may be installed on the water-supply line to the tank to warm the water. Insulating jackets or liners that fit inside water closet tanks and serve to keep the outer surface warm are available from plumbing-supply dealers.

Today in History: Sprinkler heads for fire protection were patented on Aug. 11, 1874 by Henry S. Parmelee, of New Haven, Conn.

An electric-light socket with pull-chain switch was patented on Aug. 11, 1876 by Harvey Hubbell, of Bridgeport, Conn.

August 12

Plumbing On the Patio?

Outdoor living has become a favorite summer pastime. It's only natural, therefore, that some of the home's plumbing conveniences should be extended to the patio or elsewhere in the yard.

An outdoor drinking fountain is a big worksaver for the mother in a household with small children. It saves countless trips into and out of the kitchen. Drinking-fountain attachments for outdoor sill faucets are available. These are ready for use as soon as you screw them on an existing faucet. Not all are good buys, however. Shop carefully to be sure the attachment is well made.

A protected sink on the patio with hot and cold water makes it possible to wash sticky young fingers in a jiffy. Dishes and cooking utensils can be washed on the spot when the family eats outdoors or entertains friends there. The bartender will also appreciate having cold water handy.

Still a third outdoor plumbing facility to consider is a shower. Its use on returning from the beach or community pool will take the load off the indoor shower.

In cold-weather areas, make provision for cutting off water to the outside facilities when autumn comes.

Bush and pole beans can be planted now in Louisiana and other southern states for harvest about November 1.

After geraniums have flowered, cut them back to prevent legginess. You can increase your stock by putting cuttings four to five inches long in water or soil to root—and provide indoor plants for the winter.

Your Own Reminders

Week of Aug. 7–12

August 13

Add Color to Concrete?

Concrete surfaces don't have to be drab. They can sport attractive colors. Think about the information given today—next time you plan an improvement involving the use of portland cement.

Colored concrete is usually made in one of four ways: (1) mixing a mineral oxide pigment in the concrete, (2) working a mineral oxide pigment into the surface of the concrete after it is placed but while still workable, (3) using colored aggregate but leaving it exposed, or (4) by applying commercial acid stains as a special surface finish. See the accompanying table.

Colors will be best if white portland cement is used, as well as white or light-colored aggregates.

Do not use more than 9 pounds of pigment for each bag of cement. Follow the directions of the pigment manufacturer. Ask your local building-supply dealer where to buy it.

You can also apply portland cement paints in a variety of colors to the surface of concrete. For information about this, see tomorrow's entry.

CONCRETE COLOR GUIDE

Color desired	Materials to use
White	White portland cement, white sand
Brown	Burnt umber, or brown oxide or iron (Yellow oxide or iron will modify color)
Buff	Yellow ocher, yellow oxide of iron
Grey	Normal portland cement
Green	Chromium oxide (yellow oxide of iron will shade)
Pink	Red oxide of iron (small amount)
Rose	Red oxide of iron
Cream	Yellow oxide of iron

August 14

Want to Paint Concrete?

Various paints are available for painting concrete surfaces—latex paints, rubber-based paints, and portland cement paints among them. Any of these will give satisfaction if used according to label directions over properly-prepared surfaces. For an interior surface requiring frequent cleaning, better choose a latex, but a portland cement paint is especially recommended where there's a need to repel water—as on the exterior surface of concrete block masonry. Two to three heavy coats are sometimes used successfully to combat dampness on an interior basement wall.

Portland cement paint consists largely of portland cement, ground with other materials. White portland cement is ordinarily used. Limeproof and sunproof mineral pigments are ground with the other materials to produce the colored product. A wide range of colors can be obtained, especially if standard available colors are blended. It is sold in dry powder form to be mixed with water before applying.

Portland cement paint should be distinguished from other cold water paints. Many of the latter are referred to as cement paints although they contain little or no portland cement and are made up largely of hydrated lime, casein glue, or other materials. Some of these materials offer little resistance to weather or other adverse conditions and serve only as temporary color coatings when exposed to these conditions. For outdoor use and locations subject to moisture, only paints which the manufacturer can definitely show to have satisfactory service records should be used.

Portland cement paint is easily applied and bonds with any properly prepared concrete surface, concrete masonry or portland cement stucco, common brick, soft tile, limestone, or any other type of cement work or masonry with a clean surface and some absorption.

Portland cement paint can be applied successfully to masonry surfaces that are damp. In fact, all surfaces must be damp when the paint is applied. Portland cement paint can be applied to concrete immediately after the forms have been removed, or to portland cement plaster or stucco as soon as it has hardened, but there are advantages in permitting the surface to season before applying paint.

One advantage of delaying painting is to allow time for oil from forms to weather off. Another advantage is that most efflorescence which is likely to occur will come to the surface during the early age of the concrete and can then be removed before painting. This is especially important in the case of dark-colored paints, since the efflorescence will show more on a dark than on a white or very light paint.

Concrete cast against plywood, fiberboard, or steel forms is sometimes so smooth as to make good adhesion of paint difficult to obtain. Such surfaces should be acid-washed, sand-blasted lightly, or rubbed with abrasive stones to provide a slightly roughened surface.

Today in History: The U.S. Social Security Act was approved on Aug. 14, 1935.

August 15

Watch That Crabgrass

If crabgrass is showing up in your lawn, rake to raise the seed heads within reach of the mower. Then mow the lawn with a grass catcher —and destroy the cuttings. Preventing seed production for a few years will usually reduce the weed to the point where it no longer is a problem. When there are only a few plants, pull them by hand.

August 16

Need A De-Humidifier?

Periods of high humidity sometimes occur in late summer in the northern latitudes. This can promote development of mold on house furnishings. Condensation also may occur at any time of the year in several parts of the house.

This excess moisture suggests the need for a de-humidifier.

Two types of dehumidifiers are available—chemical and mechanical refrigeration. Chemical types use silica-gel or other chemicals to absorb moisture from the air. The chemicals must be replaced or dried out periodically. Mechanical-refrigeration types draw the air over a refrigerated coil (called a condenser), where the moisture condenses and drains off into a drain or a collection pan.

An air conditioner will cool the house and remove moisture at the same time. Even better is a type of air conditioner designed to dehumidify as well as to cool. It will cool to a predetermined temperature and then automatically switch over to dehumidifying until the desired setting on a humidistat is reached.

August 17

You Can Plant Evergreens Now

The period during the next month is one of the two best times of the year to plant evergreens. The other is spring. (See March 11). But by planting soon, the plant will have time to develop a vigorous root system before the ground freezes and makes it difficult for the roots to take up the water the plant needs all through the year.

Today in History: Charles F. Kettering, of Detroit, Mich., patented the electric self-starter for cars on Aug. 17, 1915.

Running the furnace briefly at this time of year will help dry out a humid house. It will also remove rust-producing moisture from the furnace and the stack pipes.

August 18

Today in History: Plant patent No. 1 was granted Aug. 18, 1931 to Henry F. Bosenberg, of New Brunswick, N.J., for his rose "New Dawn" which blooms successively through the season instead of just once, in June, like its parent, "Dr. Van Fleet."

Your Own Free Nursery

Homeowners with a few square feet of open land are missing a bet if they don't establish their own nursery for trees and shrubs. Commercial nurseries often offer bargains in trees too small to set out at their final sites. A few companies specialize in making such offerings. For example, how about 15 Scotch pines, three to six inches tall, for a total outlay of $3? Or 25 baby hemlocks for $7?

You could easily set out and tend such bargain purchases in a plot of ground only six feet by six feet. Spade up the ground a foot or more deep well in advance of the date the trees or plants will be delivered. Enrich the soil with humus well mixed in. Work the soil to a fine.

Your tiny bargain trees need little room at first. A spacing of 12 inches in rows 12 inches apart will do for the trees mentioned above. Apply a thick straw mulch between the trees to conserve moisture and keep down weeds. Keep the trees well watered in periods of drought. Enclose the plot with small-mesh fencing to keep off youngsters and animals.

In two or three years, the trees will have grown so much that you can move them to permanent sites, if you wish, and give them the spacing they will need when mature. In any case, dig up and reset the trees after two years, putting them back in the nursery if you wish. But allow them more room this time.

What are the advantages of such a program? You eventually get trees for your home at a much lower cost than you might otherwise. Or maybe you will want to sell several to your envious neighbors—still at a bargain price for both the neighbor and you. Or, if you are growing evergreens, you could supply yourself a Christmas-tree bargain for years to come.

Where do you buy such bargain trees? Two possible sources: Western Maine Forestry Co., Fryeburg, Maine 04037; and Musser, Box 531, Indiana, Pa. 15701. Write for their catalogs.

August 19

Legal Lore About Fences

Fewer fences exist around home plots nowadays because they no longer are needed in most cases to keep stray animals out. But there is another important reason, too. Fences frequently lead to neighborhood squabbles. So, if no fences are built, good neighbors are more likely to remain so.

Should you plan to build a fence, make sure you know the exact location of the property line. Check out local restrictions as to fences, too. Some communities limit fence height; some even forbid them. And don't forget to discuss the matter with your neighbors before you begin. The mere existence of a fence says: Keep out! Some neighbors may be so touchy about this aspect of the situation that they'll chop you off their calling list.

Check your lawyer or your town ordinance about where the fence can go. In some areas, laws require that a fence must be set directly on the boundary line. In others, boundary-line fences are forbidden because of the legal squabbles that so frequently occur.

If you and a neighbor decide to locate a fence on the boundary line and share construction and maintenance costs, make the agreement a part of the respective deeds. Otherwise, a new owner may refuse to honor the agreement. If you do locate the fence on the boundary, remember that you'll have to step on the neighbor's property to paint or repair his side of it. That's called trespass.

A fence set back on your side of the line may seem to be the solution. But maybe not. If the neighbor mows the grass on the other side, and otherwise uses the strip of land, he may gain title to the strip under an old legal process known as adverse possession.

Never use barbed wire for a town fence. If a youngster rips an arm on it, you may be held legally responsible. A fence topped with barbed wire is sometimes legal, however, when used around a pool. Sharp pickets could lead to an injury—and a damage suit. Electrically-charged fences have been outlawed in most built-up communities.

At the front of your house, know the street and sidewalk requirements before erecting a fence or planting a hedge (which most communities view as a fence). Most communities forbid fences on public rights-of-way.

August 20

A Painting of House Makes a Welcome Gift

Have you been stumped to find an appropriate gift for a friend? Or perhaps you have been seeking a large picture for one of your own walls.

A painting of the house, in oils or watercolors,

could be the solution in each case. This time of year usually puts a home in its most colorful setting, ideal for a painting that you or your friend would cherish for years.

Where do you find an artist willing and capable of undertaking such a commission? You might advertise in your local paper. Or ask the art teacher in your local high school for leads—or a local art shop.

If getting a painting turns out to be impossible, or too expensive, old photos of the house, assembled and tastefully arranged in one large frame, may be a good substitute.

Your Own Reminders

Week of Aug. 14–20

August 21

Today in History: A patent on a "manner of retaining in any desired position the slats of venetian blinds" was granted to John Hampson, of New Orleans, on Aug. 21, 1841.

Repairing Venetian Blinds

Checked over your venetian blinds lately? Chances are, unless they're almost brand-new, that they need minor fixes that you can take care of. If you uncover the need for major replacements, parts can be obtained at your convenience from department stores and mail-order houses.

Wood and metal blinds differ in minor ways. At the top of metal blinds, the tilting assembly and cord locks are located within the head box that substitutes for the wood head rail of the other type. The ladder tape is thumbtacked under the bottom rail of wood blinds; a clip holds it in metal ones.

Remove the blind from the window and suspend it from the top of an open door for easy access while you make repairs, using two hooks bent from wire coat hangers. Blinds usually are easily removed from the window by hinging down the facing of the head box and pulling out the assembly that rests there.

Cords tend to wear out faster on metal blinds because the sharp slat edges scrape them. The cords will last longer if you rub a piece of beeswax along them. One end of the tilt cord often creeps up to the wheel. Prevent this by making the ends of the cord even and then crimping a piece of thin sheet metal around the cord just ahead of the wheel. Or you might run a length of heavy thread through the cord at this point and wrap thread around it until you have a mass that won't pass through the wheel.

Cross straps that support the slats between the parallel ladder tapes may work loose from the tapes. Repair with any good household cement that will hold fabric to fabric, keeping the strap end in place with a paper clip for 24 hours until the cement has set. Or staple it to the ladder tape with a stapling gun.

Shortening the blind is another easy fix you can make if you find that it originally was installed overlong. After freeing the ends of the

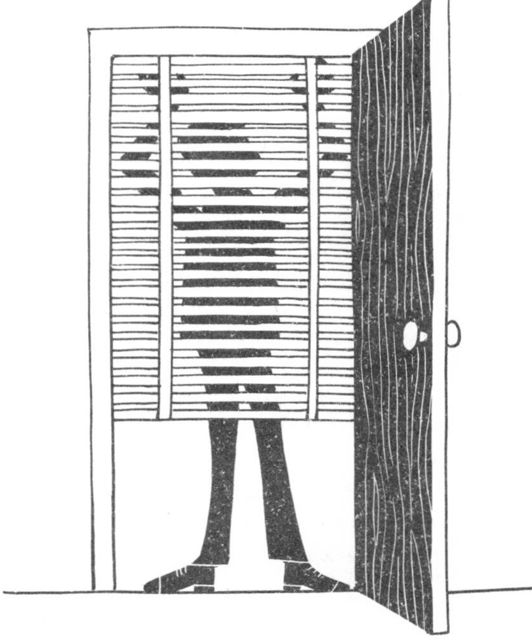

lift cord and ladder tape, discard slats and cut off enough tape to produce a blind length that just clears the window sill. When a blind hangs free, wind can cause an annoying rattle when the window is open. Secure the blind to the sill with a cuphook in one and a screweye in the other—or attach rubber bumpers made for toilet seats.

When the lift cord has become frayed or breaks, it is easily replaced. Attach broken ends to each other with a needle and thread. Then free both bottom ends of the old cord. Butt one end of the new cord against the end of the old one and secure them with needle and thread. Or use a stapler for an easy and secure joint. Then, with the blind hanging free over a door, pull on the other end of the old cord, threading the new cord through the blind without it coming apart. When you do this, remember that the lift cord is one unbroken length. To make the replacement you will of course have to remove any equalizer from the pull loop. To find out how much new cord you need, multiply the length of the blind by two, add the blind width, and add six feet more for the pull loop.

Replacement kits also include new ladder tapes, and you usually have a choice of colors. To substitute a new tape for the old, support your blinds over a door, remove the bottom slat, and pull the ends of the lift cord up through the slats but don't remove it from the pulleys. You then can remove all the slats from the tapes.

Cut your new tape exactly the length of the old one—with the same number of cross supports in the same positions as the old ones. Install the new tapes in place of the old, attaching at the top as the old were. Then slip the slats into the new tapes. Finally thread the ends of the lift cord down through the holes in the slats, locating it on the opposite side of each successive ladder strap. Replace the bottom rail and you're finished.

If tape replacement seems too difficult, you may want to settle for covering the old ones with adhesive-backed tape, available in a choice of colors for just this purpose.

August 22

Today in History: A phonograph with a horn enclosed in the cabinet—the Victrola—was introduced in Camden, N.J., Aug. 22, 1906.

Aerate Your Lawn Soil?

Has the soil under your lawn turf become compacted so that water needs a long time to sink in? Some soils tend more toward this than others.

Aerating the soil at this time of the year should permit better penetration of both water and fertilizer. A roller with prongs is available for doing the job. The prongs leave holes in the ground.

Check Kentucky bluegrass lawns for signs of rust infection. Ask your county agent about treatment if you find or suspect its presence.

August 23

Repairing Asphalt Drives and Walks

Blacktop drives and walkways should receive two kinds of maintenance to prolong their life and improve appearance. Patch any holes that appear and seal the surface. Hardware stores have packaged material for both jobs.

Today in History: Auto tire chains were patented on Aug. 23, 1904 by Harry D. Weed, of Canastota, N.Y.

Repair broken surfaces as soon as they appear to avoid further breakup. Hack out all broken blacktop back to solid material and brush out the loose stuff. Then pour in packaged repair material until it is about a half inch higher than the surrounding surface. Pack it down level with the back of a shovel or a wood tamper.

If you have blacktop in good condition, now's the appropriate time to apply a thin coating of a sealer made for the purpose. Choose a time when the temperature is above 65 degrees. Sweep all dust and loose material from the surface. Spread the coating thinly and evenly with a stiff pushbroom or paint roller according to directions. Allow the sealer to dry overnight before walking or driving on the surface.

August 24

Dig the Soil for New Iris Beds

Irises are hardy, live for many years, make a spectacular display each spring and summer in a garden, and require a minimum of care. Varieties are available for every section of the United States.

Buying rhizomes is the simplest way to establish your own beds. These should be planted in the late summer or early fall so the plants will be well established before winter. Prepare the bed a week or two before making the actual plantings.

Dig and loosen the soil at least 18 inches deep. Break up all lumps. Spade organic matter into the soil to improve its structure. For poor soil, thoroughly mix a half pound of 5-10-5 fertilizer into each 50 square feet of area—or about a half cup for every six or seven rhizomes you plan to put in.

Mix the fertilizer evenly through the soil and rake the soil level. Then wait for a week or two to let the soil settle before you put in the rhizomes—either new ones that you have bought or some that you have divided from already-established beds in your garden.

Plant lily-of-the-valley pips now in lightly shaded areas. If you have an established bed that has become crowded, this also is the time to divide the pips.

Do not fertilize roses any later than this date in most parts of the middle latitude and southern states.

August 25

Removing Stains from Masonry Homes

Copper and bronze stains are nearly always green, but in some cases may be brown.

Mix dry 1 part ammonium chloride (sal ammoniac) and 4 parts powdered talc. Stir in ammonia water to make a paste. Place this over stain and leave until dry. A stain of this kind that has been collecting for some years may require several treatments to remove it. Aluminum chloride may be used instead of sal ammoniac.

Aluminum stains appear as a white deposit which can be removed by scrubbing with a 10 to 20 per cent muriatic acid solution. Flush off with water after two minutes. Then neutralize with ammonia solution (1 tablespoon per cup of water). Rinse with water again. On colored concrete a weaker solution (1 part muriatic acid added slowly to 5 parts water) should be used.

Wire brushing may be all that's needed to remove efflorescence from bricks. For stubborn cases, scrub on commercial muriatic acid, diluted with two parts water. Neutralize as for aluminum stains.

Make a bleach for rust stains by dissolving

two tablespoons of oxalic acid crystals in a pint of water. Mop on the rust area with a cloth. Rub down with water after two hours. Remember that oxalic acid is poisonous. Mix it in glass or earthenware containers.

When smoke discolors a chimney around the top, the appearance may sometimes be restored by the following process: scour with powdered pumice or grit scrubbing powder to remove surface deposit. Then make a solution of trisodium phosphate and chlorinated lime. Fold a white flannel cloth to form three or four layers and saturate with the liquid. Paste this over stain, and cover with slab of concrete or glass, making sure the cloth is pressed firmly against the surface. Devise a method to hold the flannel and its covering snug against the stain. Resaturate the cloth as often as necessary. Deep pitch stains may require several treatments.

August 26

Store Extra Produce in Cellars

Those who till large garden plots should keep in mind that surplus cabbage, onions, and potatoes can be kept in good condition through the winter if stored in pits and cellars. Some types of apples also keep until spring. Other fruits and vegetables can be stored successfully but for lesser periods. Preservation by storage can supplement canning and freezing.

Strangely enough, however, winter storage is successful only in the cooler latitudes. Outdoor temperatures must average 30 degrees or lower. Otherwise, you will not be able to keep the fruits or vegetables cool enough. They should not be subjected to freezing temperatures, however.

A well-ventilated basement under a house with central heating may be used for ripening late tomatoes and for short-term storage of potatoes, sweet potatoes, and onions. But to store vegetables and fruits over winter in a basement that has a furnace you must partition off a room and insulate it. No heating ducts or pipes should pass through it. The room should have at least one window for cooling and ventilating the produce.

Cone-shaped outdoor pits are often used for storing potatoes, carrots, beets, turnips, salsify, parsnips, and cabbage. They are sometimes used for storing winter apples and pears. The pit may be built on the ground, or in a hole 6 to 8 inches deep in a well-drained location. Build the pit as follows:

Spread a layer of straw, leaves, or other bedding material on the ground.

Stack the vegetables or fruits on the bedding in a cone-shaped pile. Do not store vegetables and fruits in the same pit.

Cover the vegetables or fruits with more bedding.

Cover the pile with 3 or 4 inches of soil.

Firm the soil with the back of a shovel to make the pit water-proof.

Dig a shallow drainage ditch around the pit.

Small pits containing only a few bushels of vegetables or fruits will get sufficient ventilation if you let the bedding material over the vegetables extend through the soil at the top of the pile. Cover the top of the pile with a board or piece of sheet metal to protect the stored products from rain; a stone will hold the cover in place.

To ventilate large pits, place two or three boards or stakes up through the center of the pile of vegetables or fruits to form a flue. Cap the flue with two pieces of board nailed together at right angles.

It is difficult to remove vegetables and fruits from cone-shaped pits in cold weather. And once a pit is opened its entire contents should be removed. For these reasons it is better to construct several small pits rather than one large one. Put a small quantity of different vegetables in each pit. This makes it necessary to open only one pit to get a variety of vegetables. When several vegetables are stored in the same pit, separate them with straw or leaves.

You can learn more about such storage from a government pamphlet—"Storing Vegetables and Fruits in basements, cellars, outbuildings, and pits," available from your county agent or from the Superintendent of Documents, U.S. Government Printing Office, Washington, D.C. 20402.

August 27

Today in History: Petroleum began to flow on Aug. 27, 1859 from the Drake oil well, the first one near Titusville, Pa.

It's Time for Your Annual Heating-Plant Checkup

Accumulations of soot and dust should be cleaned from your heater, stack pipe, and chimney at least once a year if the system is to operate efficiently. You can, of course, do this yourself, but many prefer to make it a part of an annual servicing contract with their fuel supplier or heating serviceman.

At the same time that the cleaning is done, all operating parts of the system should be checked over and put into top condition—the oil burner and all of the controls, automatic and manual. Like all mechanisms, oil and gas burners have a limited life. It may be more economical to replace the entire burner than to attempt repairs.

Annual servicing should also include oiling the motors and checking and/or replacing the blower belt. But don't overoil.

In a hot-air system, annual maintenance should include vacuuming out the ducts, both delivery and return ducts. The pro has special equipment for this. The household vacuum cleaner should be applied to heat registers and return-air openings occasionally during the heating season as part of housecleaning routine.

Also clean steam and hot-water radiators and convectors of dust and lint at the beginning of the heating season and several times during it. Use a thin brush and the vacuum cleaner.

Make sure that all radiators are venting properly. Bleed off accumulated air that stops circulation. Waterlogging sometimes occurs in the pressure tank in closed hot-water systems. Drain the tank.

Your Own Reminders

Week of Aug. 21–27

August 28

Faucet Washers on Hand?

Installing a new washer to stop a faucet leak still is a common need in many homes, even though some of the newest faucets work without washers. If you don't know which type you have, why not pay your plumber for a call when a drip develops? Washerless faucets have a limited life, and replacement may be necessary. Ask the plumber for his recommendation about the size and type of washers if your fixtures use them. Some washers are suitable for cold water taps but not for hot. Soft neoprene washers usually serve well in both. Lay in a supply when you know what you need.

Shut off the water to the faucet as the first step in replacing a washer.

How you open up a faucet varies somewhat depending on the brand. If yours stumps you temporarily, examine it closely until you discover its secret. Be sure to wrap the wrench jaws with cloth or thick tape to avoid scratching the finish on the fixture as you loosen the main nut—the packing nut. After the stem has been removed, you'll find a screw holding the washer on the lower end. Soaking with kerosene or penetrating oil may help loosen the screw if rust has locked it in. When the screw is out, clean out the old washer and install your new one. It should fit snugly, without forcing. Use a piece of cloth to clean the valve seat inside the faucet. In replacing the stem, tighten the nut just enough to stop seepage.

Some faucets may require repacking inside the packing nut to stop leaks around the stem when the faucet is opened, and it may be necessary to regrind the seat from time to time. A faucet-seat dressing tool is inexpensive and may be a worthwhile investment although many will prefer to leave such repairs to a plumber.

Do not let perennial flowers set seed. This will promote the growth of side shoots.

August 29

Will You Plant A New Lawn This Fall?

In the extreme northern parts of the U.S. and in the high altitudes of the western mountains, new lawns should be planted now to give the grass time to establish itself before the ground freezes. As in the spring (see March 15), new lawns can be established in the fall with seed or with vegetative grasses.

The U.S. Department of Agriculture recommends that the following types of grasses be established by fall seeding: Chewings fescue, sown at the rate of 3 to 5 pounds of seed per 1000 square feet; colonial bentgrass (Highland Astoria), 1 to 2; creeping bentgrass (Seaside), 1 to 2; crested wheatgrass, 1 to 2; Kentucky bluegrass, common, 2 to 3; Kentucky bluegrass, Merion, 1 to 2; red fescue, 3 to 5; redtop, 1 to 2; rough bluegrass, 3 to 5; ryegrass (domestic and perennial), 4 to 6; tall fescue (Alta, Ky. 31), 4 to 6; and velvet bentgrass, 1 to 2.

For sunny areas, the Department recommends a mixture of 75 percent bluegrass and 25 percent red fescue; for shady areas, a mixture of 25 percent bluegrass and 75 percent red fescue, both mixtures seeded at the rate of 2 to 4 pounds per 1000 square feet.

Creeping bentgrass and velvet bentgrass are the only varieties listed for vegative planting in the fall.

Refer to Appendix A to see which of the fall-planted grasses are recommended for your region. Your county agent can provide helpful information about the job. You might also write to your State Experiment Station.

Established lawns of cool-weather grasses should get the first of two fertilizer applications now.

Find a lot of fleas in your home on returning from vacation? Fleas practically always come from a pet—a dog or cat. One favorite breeding place: the animal's bedding.

August 30

Have You Cleaned the Fireplace Chimney?

Every few years you may want to call in a professional cleaner (located through the telephone book Yellow Pages) to perform this chore, but you can also do a creditable job yourself.

First, open the ash pit cover in the base of the fireplace and open the damper. Then apply a sheet of plastic over the entire fireplace opening, making sure all edges of the plastic are sealed. Put a ladder to the top of the chimney or climb up on the roof, and drag a tire chain at the end of a rope up and down the fireplace flue for a few minutes to dislodge the soot. While you're at it, you may want to give the same treatment to the flue that serves your heating plant.

Now return to the fireplace, open it up, and brush the dislodged soot down the ash pit. With your brush, also clean off all interior chimney surfaces that you can reach, including the smoke shelf up beyond the damper. If you own one, you might use a shop vacuum cleaner for this chore. After cleaning, make sure the damper is working smoothly. A little oil may help.

As the final step, open the clean-out doors at the base of the chimney and remove the soot and ash accumulations. This is valuable fertilizer. So apply it to the ground around some of your favorite perennial flowers or to your vegetable garden.

A fireplace may smoke because a kitchen ventilating fan is drawing air down the chimney. Turn the fan off. In a modern, well-insulated home, a fireplace also may smoke because it can't get enough air to produce a good draft. Open a window or door slightly.

August 31

Back to Adult School for You?

Among the adult education courses now offered throughout the U.S. you can often find several of value in maintaining a home. The practice you get and the repair procedures you observe in these courses will remain of practical value to you for the remainder of your life.

Check the course lists, especially for woodworking, appliance repair, electrical work, plumbing problems, and general handyman know-how. If you note a scarcity of such courses, check your neighbors and friends to see if they might be interested. If so, telephone or call on the director of the adult education program, and ask if a particular course can't be arranged for next year.

The morrow was a bright September morn;
The earth was beautiful as if new-born;
There was that nameless splendor everywhere,
The wild exhilaration in the air,
Which makes the passers in the city street
Congratulate each other as they meet.

—Henry W. Longfellow

September

Early names for September in northern lands reflect the fact that harvests reached their peak in this ninth month of the year. Charlemagne's calendar forthrightly dubbed it harvest month. The Swiss still call it that. Anglo-Saxons named it barley month because this important grain usually is harvested then.

The full moon nearest the Autumnal equinox—between September 21 and 23—is named Harvest Moon. In early times its brightness gave extra hours after dusk for completing the year's harvest.

All ancient peoples celebrated harvest's end with feasts and festivals of thanksgiving. Our present harvest home suppers and agricultural fairs grew out of these early festivals. Sukkot or Feast of the Tabernacles—one of five Jewish holidays in September—originally was a harvest festival. During the month, Jews also celebrate Rosh Hashanah, or New Year; Tzom Gedaliah, a fast day; Yom Kippur, the Day of Atonement; and Simhat Torah, a day of rejoicing that winds up Sukkot.

Canada and the United States celebrate Labor Day the first Monday of the month. It has been a national holiday since 1894.

September 1

Degree Days Are Important Now

For most of the country, this date is considered as beginning the new heating season. Therefore, the daily recording of "degree days" becomes important to you. You'll find newspaper and radio weather reports including this figure along with temperature, humidity, and wind readings.

The degree-day figure was devised half a century ago. The heating industry has been making use of it since the 1930's. Here's how it's arrived at for each day:

Take the maximum and minimum temperature for the day. From these determine the mean, or average, temperature. Subtract the mean temperature from 65 and the result is the degree-day figure for the day.

Normally, heating is not required in a building when the outdoor average temperature is 65°. A day with an average temperature of 50° has 15 heating degree days (65 minus 50 equals 15). One with an average temperature of 65° or higher has none.

Several characteristics make the degree-day figures useful. They are cumulative. Therefore, the degree-day sum for a period of days represents the total heating load for the period. The relationship between degree days and fuel consumption is linear, i.e., doubling the degree days usually doubles the fuel consumption. Comparing normal seasonal degree days in different locations gives a rough estimate of seasonal fuel consumption. For example, it would require roughly 4½ times as much fuel to heat a building in Chicago, Ill., where the mean annual total heating degree days are about 6,200 than to heat a similar building in New Orleans, La., where the annual total heating degree days are around 1,400.

Adoption of the degree-day system paralleled the spread of automatic fuel systems in the 1930s. Since oil and gas are more costly to store than solid fuels, this places a premium on the scheduling of deliveries and the precise evaluation of use rates and peak demands. The system enables your fuel company to determine when to deliver fuel to you if you work it on an automatic-delivery contract.

A quote for Labor Day: "Labor in this country is independent and proud. It has not to ask the patronage of capital, but capital solicits the aid of labor."—Daniel Webster, speech April 2, 1824.

Autumn vegetable gardens can still be planted in the middle latitudes of the U.S. See Appendix F.

Apply a ring of 5-10-5 fertilizer around late-blooming perennial flowers and water it in.

September 2

Are Your Storm Doors Safe?

Youngsters have suffered many bad cuts by thrusting their arms accidentally through glass in a storm door. This is such a frequent mishap that some communities now are recommending a non-glass glazing in hazardous locations.

If your doors have glass, why not substitute an unbreakable or other safe plastic? Check your building-supply dealer to see what he has available. It's impossible to break some types. Others may break, but the fragments lack the sharp cutting edges of shattered glass. The materials cost considerably more than glass, but remember what you gain in safety. Install the plastic just as you would glass.

Basement windows and windows in garage doors are also good candidates for plastic glazing.

September 3

How to Get Rid of Stinging Insects

What do you do about hornets, wasps, and yellow jackets when they become an outdoor problem at this time of year? Leave them alone, if possible. Many of these insects benefit humans by preying on flies and caterpillars.

However, yellow jackets often choose to nest in the ground where they are a menace to anyone passing. If you suspect the presence of a nest, watch the direction the insects are flying. Sharp eyes will soon lead you to the spot. A well-established yellow jacket nest in the ground has a very obvious entrance—as much as an inch in diameter.

Mark the entrance well and wait until dark. At that time all members of the colony will have returned home and the darkness will protect you from stings.

Local stores will sell you a powder or spray recommended for exterminating the insect. Shoot dust into the hole with a garden duster. Then plaster the hole shut with wet soil. You may prefer the old country treatment, however. Pour a pint or so of gasoline into the entrance (if it's in the open yard away from buildings). Then ignite the gasoline with a flaming oil-soaked rag at the end of a pole.

A spray bomb is the best means for disposing of a large hornet or wasp nest in a tree or under the eaves of a building. Again, apply the treatment at night.

Sit out in your yard at this time of year and keep tab on the movements of butterflies. Chances are you'll find them progressing generally southward. Like many birds, some butterflies migrate to warmer climates.

Your Own Reminders

Week of Aug. 28–Sept. 3

September 4

> **Today in History:** The first Kodak was patented on Sept. 4, 1888 by George Eastman. A fixed focus box, it used roll film with 100 exposures and took a round picture $2^1/_2$ inches diameter.

Plant New Irises—or Divide Old Ones

Established iris clumps should be divided periodically—anywhere from each two to five years. You can then plant the divisions exactly as you would new rhizomes. If you have prepared the soil as explained under date of August 24, you can now make the actual plantings.

Before dividing, cut the iris leaves back to a third of their full length. Do this each fall—even if you do not plan to divide the clumps.

Drive a spade under the clump and lift it all at once. Wash away soil with a garden hose. Cut the rhizomes apart with a sharp knife. Each division must have at least one growing point (or fan of leaves), a few inches of healthy rhizome, and a number of well-developed roots. Make small divisions if you do not want to redivide iris for at least three to five years. Make large divisions if you prefer to have many flowers the year after planting—and want to make divisions oftener, say each two to three years.

There is a special trick to planting rhizomes. Scoop out a shallow hole in the prepared soil, large enough to receive a rhizome or clump of rhizomes. Then form a cone of soil in the center of the hole as a planting base. In medium soil, make the cone high enough so that the planted rhizome, with its roots spread down the slopes of the cone, will be just under the soil surface. In light, or well-drained soil, make a low cone so the rhizome will be two inches below ground level. In heavy soil, let the rhizome be slightly above the level of the surrounding ground.

After carefully arranging the roots around the cone, fill the hole with soil and press it firmly around the rhizome. Finally, thoroughly soak the surrounding soil.

Consider sowing seed of pansy and viola for blooms next spring.

Order nursery stock now for fall planting—shrubs, fruit trees, shade trees, tulip bulbs, etc.

Suspend summer trimming of privet. If clipped now, tender new growth probably will winter-kill.

Keep tab on magnolias for the next few weeks for the appearance of tulip tree scales. They are oval and dark brown. They often crowd together.

Remove old canes from cultivated blackberries after they have fruited in the northern states.

Be sure pecan trees have water while they are producing their nuts. Water thoroughly now and again about three weeks hence.

September 5

Get Out a Caulking Gun

A caulking gun defends a home against cold. This is a good season to use one to go over the entire house outside and seal up cracks that let drafts enter during the winter.

Drive a bead into any poorly-butted wood siding midway in a course. But pay particular attention to the frames around windows and doors. Very few homes are well sealed there. Fill any openings where siding butts against window, door, or corner trim. If the trim strip overlaps siding, take the time to fully caulk all openings.

Check over the entire house, from foundation to roof peak, before you call the sealing job complete. A good caulking job should last for some years. But better check annually.

Check ornamental and fruit trees for discolored leaves. If the undersides look as if they had been dusted with fine white powder, you have found spider mites. Destroy the affected leaves.

September 6

Hood for a Fireplace Chimney

Does rain or snow sometimes come down a fireplace flue and seep out on the hearth? Does a downdraft occasionally blow smoke back into the room because the chimney top is lower than adjoining trees and buildings?

A chimney hood is the solution to all such problems. A hood also adds an attractive finishing touch to the silhouette of any house.

For the cap, you might use a cast concrete slab about two inches thick or a flagstone cut to proper size. Let the cap project an inch or so beyond its supports on all sides.

Chimney hoods must have at least two sides open and the open area must be greater than the flue cross section. The slab or flagstone can rest on corner or end pillars formed of two or three courses of bricks.

September 7

Prepare to Plant Spring-Flowering Bulbs

Now is the time to make sure you will have a grand display of spring-flowering bulbs next year. You should order new bulbs without delay so you will have them on hand for the proper planting time in September, October, and November (in areas north of South Carolina and Southern California). You should also prepare the ground now. For guidance in digging a new flower bed, turn to the entry for September 29.

Most bulb plants need sunshine. Try to select a site that has five or six hours of direct sunlight each day. If you plant bulbs in a southern exposure near a building or wall, they will bloom earlier than bulbs in a northern exposure.

Plant bulbs in groups, never in rows. Buy enough bulbs of one color for a good display of that color. Many gardeners leave enough space between clumps for planting annual flowers.

If your bulbs arrive before planting time, store them in a cool, dry place. A temperature not above 60 or 65 degrees will keep them healthy until you plant them. Temperatures higher than 70 degrees will damage the flower buds inside the bulbs.

Plant bulbs upright and press the soil firmly over them to prevent air pockets underneath. Water the planted beds thoroughly to help settle the bulbs in the soil. In loose sandy soil, plant bulbs three or four inches deeper than the depths shown in Appendix H. Plant all bulbs at recommended distances apart so they will have space to develop new offshoots.

September 8

Weatherstrip to Stop Drafts

Almost all doors and windows need weatherstripping to reduce or stop the flow of cold air inward through the closure crack. Many new doors and windows have the weatherstripping built in. Normally this will remain permanently effective. But chances are that in an older house the weatherstripping will require replacement every few years, perhaps every year, depending on the type used.

Strips of springy or interlocking metal are the most effective form of weatherstripping. This is available for do-it-yourself installation on both doors and windows. You can also get door thresholds with built-in closures to stop drafts under the door.

You simply press some weatherstripping into place—caulking strips, tape, and adhesive-backed foam, for instance. These types are all fully effective only so long as the window remains closed. Opening usually will deform the material and ruin the seal. You screw or nail in place other types—felt, vinyl, and combinations of metal and felt or vinyl. The flexible part is installed to press against the movable sash or door. This type may remain effective for several years, but it would be best to replace it periodically.

September 9

Dirt Shield for Garage Door

To keep dirt and leaves from blowing under an overhead garage door while it's closed, tack or cement a strip of old carpeting along the bottom edge of the door's inner face. As the door comes down, the strip will fill the gap. Keep the strip narrow and it won't be noticeable from the outside.

The first automobile fatality was Henry W. Bliss, 68, knocked down and run over in New York City, on Sept. 13, 1899.

September 10

Plant Sweetpeas in the South

In Southern California and other warm areas, seed sweetpeas and snapdragons now for blossoms around New Year's Day. But don't delay. Plants should reach the bud stage before night temperatures drop to 50 degrees.

Today in History: The first paved highway from coast to coast was proclaimed open on Sept. 10, 1913. It was the Lincoln Highway, running from New York City to San Francisco.

 *Your Own Reminders*

Week of Sept. 4–10

September 11

Prepare Ground for New Peonies

Peonies are one of the most satisfactory of perennial flowers. Once established, they bloom each year, in May and June, with little attention for many years. You can grow them in all states north of Texas and South Carolina. Some varieties will grow farther south, but they seldom bloom. Winters must be cold for the buds to develop properly.

Plant them in clumps, in masses, or among other perennials such as iris, daylily, chrysanthemum as a background border for smaller plants.

Two general types are available—garden varieties, on bushy stems two to four feet tall; and tree peonies, which grow to eye-level height on woody stems with few branches. Colors of garden peonies are white, yellow, cream, pink, rose, and deep red. Tree peonies are yellow, pink, white, rose, crimson, scarlet, black, and purple. Tree peonies are less common than garden types. They have one serious fault: stems are weak at the top.

Although fully grown plants are available in the spring, these may die during a hot, dry summer. It is better to buy tubers in the late summer or fall and plant them in September or early October—in time for them to become established before winter comes. Prepare the soil now so it will have two to four weeks to settle before you actually plant the tubers.

Choose a sunny site. Peonies will grow where they have shade two or three hours a day, but sun is better. Avoid placing them near or under trees or shrubs that could rob them of nutriment and moisture. Locate them to have shelter from strong winds.

Peonies thrive in deep, fertile clay loam that is well drained. Roots quickly rot in soil that holds water.

Spade organic matter—compost, well-rotted manure, or peat moss—into the entire area where you want to locate the peonies. Dig a hole

18 inches across and 18 inches deep for each tuber. Space the holes at least three feet apart.

Fill the hole about half full of fine soil with which you have mixed a handful of 10-6-4 fertilizer. Leave the rest of the soil until planting time—two weeks or a month from now.

Order tubers with from three to five eyes.

September 12

Troubleshooting a Kitchen Sink Spray

If water doesn't divert satisfactorily in an automatic faucet spray, you have four possible sources of trouble—the aerator (if any) on the swing spout, the spray head, hose, and diverter valve. With some faucets it's normal for a little water to drip from the spout as the spray is used.

Clogged screens in an aerator nozzle attached to a swing spout may create an imbalance of water pressure that prevents a diverter valve from working. Remove the aerator and clean the openings with a toothpick, pin, or brush. Then flush thoroughly with clean water and reassemble the unit.

Next, clean the spray nozzle. Remove the nozzle of a single-hole-type spray and make sure the hole is open. Depress the thumb control and run water through the head to flush out sediment. With multiple-hole sprays, remove the nozzle or rubber head, depending on the type, clean openings, flush, and reassemble.

A kink or leak in the hose is sure to knock out a faucet spray. So when trouble occurs, check the hose under the sink to be sure it is hanging as free as possible of all pipes. If a new hose must be installed, see whether your fixture has 1/8″ female, 1/8″ male, or 1/4″ male threads for the hose connection. Replacement hoses have a 1/8″ male connection at the faucet end. Each comes with a universal coupling.

To troubleshoot the diverter valve, wrap the coupling at the base of the swing spout with tape or cloth and back it off with a wrench to release the spout. Lift out the diverter valve with tweezers (in some faucets a bushing must be removed first). Clean the valve with a toothpick or brush. Before reseating the valve (with stem up), put the spout back on temporarily and flush hot and cold water through the pipes. If you find the valve damaged, get a replacement from a plumber.

September 13

Time to Plant Some Spring-Flowering Bulbs

New beds dug this fall for spring-flowering bulbs (see September 7) should be settled enough now for planting of those bulbs that can go into the ground at this time.

They include allium, chionodoxa, eranthis, fritillaria, galanthus, leucojum, narcissus, and ornithogalum. Refer to Appendix.

September 14

Today in History: As the mists cleared away from Chesapeake Bay about 7 A.M. on Wednesday, Sept. 14, 1814, an American prisoner aboard a British warship saw an inspiring sight—the American flag still flying over Fort McHenry. The warship had bombarded the fort steadily during the previous day and during most of the night. The waving flag so thrilled the prisoner, Francis Scott Key, that he pulled out an old envelope and wrote most of the words of a new song—"The Star Spangled Banner."

The Star-Spangled Banner

Oh! say, can you see, by the dawn's early
light,
What so proudly we hailed at the twilight's
last gleaming?
Whose broad stripes and bright stars,
thro' the perilous fight,
O'er the ramparts we watched were so
gallantly streaming?
And the rockets' red glare, the bombs
bursting in air,
Gave proof thro' the night that our flag
was still there.
Oh! say, does the star-spangled banner
yet wave
O'er the land of the free and the home
of the brave?

On the shore, dimly seen thro' the mist
of the deep,
Where the foe's haughty host in dread silence
reposes,
What is that which the breeze, o'er the
towering steep,
As it fitfully blows, half conceals, half
discloses?
Now it catches the gleam of the morning's
first beam,
In full glory reflected, now shines on the
stream.
'Tis the star-spangled banner. Oh! long may
it wave
O'er the land of the free and the home of
the brave!

And where is that band who so vauntingly
swore
That the havoc of war and the battle's con-
fusion
A home and a country should leave us no
more?
Their blood has washed out their foul foot-
step's pollution.
No refuge could save the hireling and slave
From the terror of flight or the gloom of
the grave,
And the star-spangled banner in triumph
doth wave
O'er the land of the free and the home of the
brave.

Oh! thus be it ever when freemen shall stand
Between their loved home and the war's deso-
lation,
Blest with vict'ry and peace, may the Heav'n-
rescued land
Praise the Pow'r that hath made and preserved
us a nation.
Then conquer we must, when our cause it is
just,
And this be our motto, "In God is our trust."
And the star-spangled banner in triumph
shall wave
O'er the land of the free and the home of
the brave.

Check the flashing on roof and around windows.

Autumn is a season of red berries in the wilds. Why not take a hike into the woods or fields and see how many you can find and identify?

In northern latitudes, better move in any house plants that remain outdoors.

Check the humidifier to see that it's ready for the new season. Turn on the water if you turned it off for the summer.

September 15

Facts About Frost

Understanding the nature of frost may help you extend the life of a garden deeper into autumn. The first killing frost often is followed by several weeks of mild weather. If you can tide the plants over a single night, you still may be harvesting vegetables and enjoying flowers as much as a month later.

Meteorologists define frost as the condition that exists when the air temperature falls to 32 degrees F. or below, cooling off plants and soil surfaces.

White frost, or hoar frost, occurs when atmospheric water vapor is deposited as feathery ice crystals. Black frost is one with little or no ice crystals deposited because the air at ground level is too dry to form them.

Frost is most likely to occur on a clear night with no wind. A layer of clouds helps keep ground-level temperatures higher. A layer of cold air forms just above the surface on still nights. Winds will mix warmer air from above with the ground-level cold air.

Gardens in low areas will suffer from frost first in the autumn. On still nights, cold air, being heavy, flows down hillsides and collects in the lowest spots it can find.

Gardens on a hillside usually will remain unaffected by frost later in the autumn—and such gardens can be planted earlier in the spring. Hillside orchards always do best.

If your garden plot is on sloping ground, remember that a building or stone wall on the downhill side may dam down-flowing cold air and form a frost pocket.

When the thermometer dips toward 32 degrees and a killing frost seems likely, what can you do?

Covering the plants that you most want to preserve is the first obvious step. Drape plastic or a similar covering over them. Remove the covering first thing in the morning.

Running the sprinkler over all or part of the garden also may protect it. The water will give up heat, raising the air temperature to the point where no frost may occur.

Get rid of weeds and spent plants in a vegetable garden. These shade the ground during the day, preventing the sun from warming the ground. At night, weeds hold in a blanket of still cold air.

September 16

Furnace Filters on Hand?

How's your supply of furnace filters? They're used to remove dust from air circulated through forced-draft warm-air furnaces and air conditioner systems. If you have such a system, right now is a good time to make sure you have enough replacement filters to carry you through the coming heating season. Tests have shown that fiberglass throwaway filters become clogged with dust and demand replacement not less than three times a year—or even once a month during the height of the heating season. So why not lay in half a dozen? Pulling out one from the furnace will show the size—the thickness and other dimensions. Mail-order catalogs list filters if you don't have a local source. If your furnace takes a hammock-style filter instead of a framed one, you will want to have a roll of the fiberglass filtering material on hand. This comes in rolls, and you cut off what you need to make a replacement.

You can also buy cleanable filters. One of these costs less than what you pay for a season's supply of throwaways. If you go that route, remember to clean the filter once a month according to the instructions that come with it.

Your Own Reminders

Week of Sept. 11–17

September 17

Support Young Trees Against Winter Winds

Are all new young trees and shrubs well supported by guy wires? If not, winter winds may whip the roots loose from the soil. Wires around the trunks should be covered with rubber hose.

It's cleanup time in the South for many trees. Remove dead fronds from feather and fan-shaped palms. Cut suckers away from around evergreen pear, citrus, and olive trees.

September 18

Protect Roses From Winter Injury

The first killing frost is due by this time in the northern parts of the country. Immediately afterwards, while the ground can still be worked easily, pile soil eight to ten inches high around the canes of bush roses. Bring the soil from another part of your grounds. Digging in the rose beds may injure the roots. After mounding the soil, tie all the canes together to keep them from being blown about and loosening the roots. In areas where the temperature seldom goes much below zero, this is all the winter protection required. In most of the country, you should pile hay, straw, or strawy manure over the mounded canes and leave the covering in place until all danger of severe frost has passed in the spring. Hold the protective material in place by throwing on a few shovels of soil.

Climbing roses also need protection. Lay the canes on the ground, hold them down with wire pins or notched stakes, and cover with several inches of soil. Pile straw on the soil.

Where the temperature goes to 10 or 15 degrees below zero, tree roses should be protected too. Dig carefully under the roots on one side of the plant, lay the plant over on the ground without breaking its root connections, and cover the entire plant with several inches of soil. Set the plant upright in the spring after there is no further danger of frost.

It is important to remember that you are providing protection both from low and fluctuating temperatures. Roses that are hardy in the North where temperatures always are low sometimes are injured farther south where winter temperatures fluctuate considerably.

September 19

Renovate Lawn in the North

In the North, this is a good period to renovate a poor lawn. A lawn that consists of at least 50 percent desirable grasses can usually be renovated without digging it up. Remove all weeds, leaves, and undesirable grasses, rake the lawn vigorously to loosen the soil surface, lime and fertilize, apply new seed, and rake it in.

September 20

Autumn Is On Its Way

The first killing frosts have blackened vegetation in some spots along the Canadian border of the U.S. by this date, if the season has been average, and from now on we can expect an increasing number of cold nights. In the Northeast leaves of native trees and shrubs will begin to turn soon in their brilliant autumn spectacle, and some may already have turned.

There's a question about when autumn begins in some parts of the U.S.—if we time it from the first killing frost. Check the dates of the first 32 degree temperatures for the high altitudes of the western states, including the mountains of Northern California. On the accompanying map, you will note that these frosts occur, on the average, before July 30. Now check the dates for these same regions on the spring-frost map given with the February 8 entry. These regions have a very brief summer. It is possible for spring to blend right into autumn.

But in September, autumn begins to roll down the map in earnest. By this date, according to

When Autumn Comes to the Eastern United States

When Autumn Comes to the Western United States

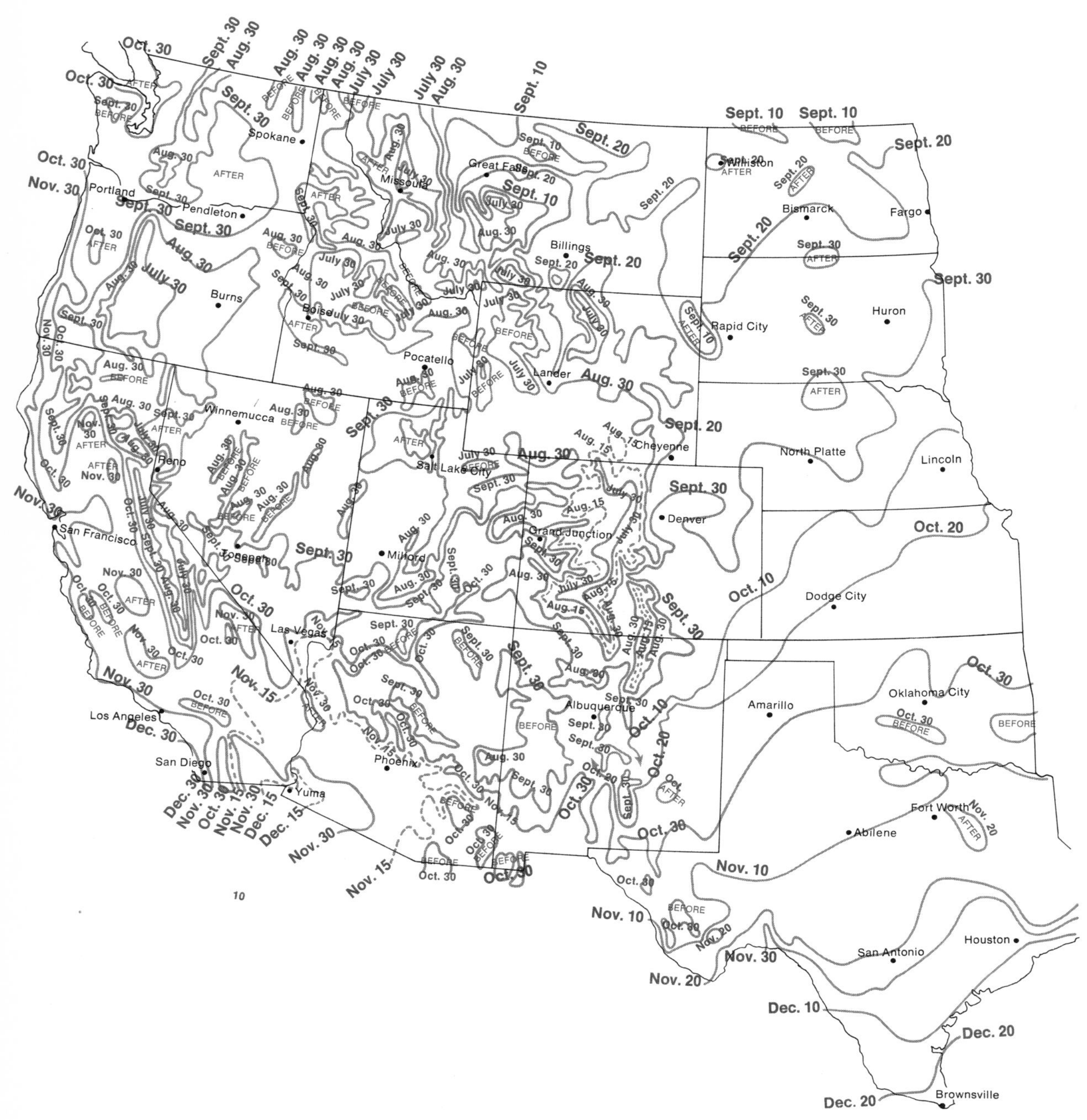

the map, it has come to most of the Rocky Mountains and dipped deep into the northern Great Plains states—even into the high altitudes of the Northeast. From now on, each week will carry the line of average 32-degree temperatures steadily southward, with islands of still earlier autumn temperatures preceding the general advance. Islands of milder temperatures also remain behind the general line.

You must remember, of course, that all dates given are mean dates of the first 32-degree temperatures in the autumn period. They are based on 2565 Weather Bureau station records compiled over a period of more than a quarter of a century. Some years the first killing frost came earlier than the date given. Some years it occurred later. The government workers who prepared the map urge, therefore, that you be cautious about using it, adding:

"Sharp changes in the mean date may occur in short distances due to differences in altitude, slope of land, type of soil, vegetative cover, bodies of water, air drainage, urban heat effects, etc."

These are the influences that cause the circled temperature variations that you find on the map—the islands of early or later frosts that accompany the mean temperature lines as they move southward with the advancing calendar dates.

As a supplement to the spring map for February 8, our autumn map shows the median dates for the first killing frosts. In the inland valleys of Alaska, which is not shown on the map, where the final spring frost occurs about June 15, the first autumn freeze may come about August 15. Around Sitka and in the Aleutian chain of islands, the first autumn frosts may not come until September 30 or later.

Have you removed crop plants from some parts of your vegetable garden? Sow ryegrass in the bare spots now and plan to turn it under next spring.

September 21

Cover Up That Old Resilient Tile Floor

Replacement of worn or outdated resilient flooring isn't the messy, time-consuming process it used to be. Nearly every type of resilient flooring can be installed directly over an existing floor provided the original surface is reasonably smooth and level. Not having to remove the old floor means lower costs, faster installation, and less disruption of household activities.

It's possible, for example, to install sheet vinyl over linoleum, linoleum over tile—even some heavy gauge vinyl-asbestos tiles directly on top of tile. Some new flooring is designed for do-it-yourself installation, but some should be put down by a contractor. A good floor-covering store can give you the details.

You can plant broccoli, carrots, escarole, lettuce, mustard, parsley, radishes, and turnips now in many southern states for fall or winter harvest.

September 22

Note: The accompanying statement, the High Holy Day message of the Jewish Theological Seminary of America, was first published on Sept. 22, 1971 in the New York Times. Because its thoughtful words have so much meaning for all people, it is presented here once again as appropriate to the current season, whatever the year. It is reprinted with permission.

. . . יגעתי ומצאתי תאמן*

Of course

The Good is harder

. . . it's worth more

The good is more, not less.

And we know it.

For who does not want
to find joy in life
to fulfill his talents
to love and to be loved
to be respected
to have a good family?

You have every right to want all of these— and the powers to seek and enjoy them all.

What, then, interferes with your achieving what you want most?

Aren't you reasonable . . .
sensitive . . . responsible . . .
hardworking . . . loving?

Of course you are.

Yet aren't you . . . sometimes . . . also impulsive or inconsiderate or lax or harsh?

It is in the conflicts we all experience . . .
being reasonable, yet sometimes impulsive;
sensitive, yet sometimes inconsiderate;
responsible, yet sometimes lax;
loving, yet sometimes harsh . . .
that you will always have the chance
to choose what will enlarge you or
make you smaller;
what will build your life or
take away from what you want most.

In Your Family

Of course you want and need love, understanding and attention from your husband or your wife.

Yet you diminish your own marriage when you cannot be reasonable and sensitive enough to continue the effort to give what you also want most to receive . . .

Each recognizing the other as a person, not as a possession.

And we as parents know it is often easier to spoil a child than to educate him; or to be harsh than to be loving.

You can be sure that, if all you ask of your child is obedience . . . and you do not have the patience to honestly listen to him . . . you are undermining your own influence on his growth.

Each of you, parent and child, must learn to respect the other's individuality.

It is not always easy to do this.

Yet isn't it worth it?

In Your Career

Certainly, you want and need recognition for your work.

A deeper satisfaction, however, is to feel a sense of achievement in what you are doing.

When you cannot get as much fulfillment from your responsibilities as from your earnings, you cannot truly enjoy your work.

In becoming rich,
you can easily become impoverished.
In achieving status, you can often be scorned.

You must not win "success" in *any* career by cutting yourself off from the rest of life.

If you pour almost all your energies into only this one part of your life,
you can easily become a failure as a person.

Is it worth it?

In Yourself

Do not make the mistake of thinking of yourself as less important than you really are.

In your concern for others, you are not asked to neglect yourself. It is only through achieving your own development that you can best live in harmony with someone else.
For you cannot relate well to anyone if you feel incomplete within yourself.

You have been endowed with a mind and with five senses. These open you to the wonders of the world without, and the world within— whose challenges and beauties can expand and refresh you; strengthen and delight you.

Despite all the strains and outer pressures on you—
and the inner controls you must exert on yourself—
you can find ways to give fuller expression to your own interests and talents,
to your God-given individuality.

To be a complete person, you must cultivate this diversity within yourself.

Isn't it worth it?

The Good is Whole

To get more, we must do more.

And to achieve the good, we must do far more than concentrate on any fraction of it.

Important and difficult as it may be to seek any part of the good: whether this be a good family *or* a truly meaningful career *or* a more complete self, we must understand that no one of these alone is enough to create a good life.

While we can discuss parts of the good, as we did, the good itself is not divisible. In our private lives, as in our efforts to build a better community and a greater nation, we must struggle continuously to be involved with all the dimensions of the good—
in proper balance, at the same time.

To think that any one of these can be the way to a good life is a modern idolatry: worshipping a part of the good as the whole of it.

We must not think of the good as simpler than it really is. Or as less than it really is.

אם יאמר לך אדם . . .
לא יגעתי ומצאתי אל תאמן
יגעתי ומצאתי תאמן

'If anyone tells you:
"I achieved something
without struggling at it,"
do not believe him. But if he tells you:
**"I struggled and achieved something,"*
you then may believe him.'

Talmud Megillah 6b

September 23

Fall begins each year at the time of the autumnal equinox—about September 23. The equinox, a time of equal day and night, occurs when the sun is directly overhead as it moves south in relation to the earth.

Violent equinoctial storms occur at this season—and there's a reason. Because the sun is moving fastest at this point in its southward travel, warm air masses also tend to shift, sometimes rapidly, and the storms result.

How To Plant New Peonies

You should not delay longer planting new peonies. Otherwise, they will not be well established before cold weather arrives. The ground should already have been prepared as described under date of September 11.

At least eight inches of open space should remain in each hole—from the level of the ground to the level of the fertilizer-enriched soil. Place the tuber above the latter soil, not in it. Plant garden tubers so the uppermost eye will be not more than two inches below the final level of the soil. Put a little soil around the tuber and water thoroughly. Then fill the hole with the remaining soil, press it down firmly, and water again.

Plant tree peonies with four or five inches of soil covering the graft. You can recognize the graft by the ridging on the stem and the different texture of the bark.

Harvest Moon is the name given to the full moon that occurs nearest to the date of the autumnal equinox, about Sept. 23. For several nights in a row, the bright harvest moon almost turns night into day. In the early days, farmers could see to complete some of their final harvesting chores.

It's time to plant currants and gooseberries in those regions where the climate is suitable for them.

September 24

How to Check for Termites

Every home should have a termite check at least once a year. This is suggested for this period because outdoor duties should be less at this time of year and temperatures shouldn't be so low that crawling into cold crawl spaces will be unpleasant. Using a good flashlight, check over all interior surfaces of the foundation—in basement or crawl space—as well as the adjoining wood members of the house understructure. Look especially for the mud-walled tubes through which subterranean termites travel back and forth to a source of moisture. Carry with you an ice pick, awl, or other sharp instrument. At intervals jab this into the framing wood. Infestations sometimes are not visible on the outside surface. In coastal areas of the South and West, your home may be invaded by drywood termites. These require no water source. They may strike any part of the house—even the attic.

At any time during the warm months, you may find swarms of what appear to be flying ants somewhere on your property. These may indeed be ants. They may also be termites in the winged phase. Flying termites are thick-waisted; ants have a very narrow waist. If you are not certain of the identification, collect several of the flying insects in a small bottle or jar and take them to your county agent.

Call an exterminator whenever you find the least sign of an infestation.

Your Own Reminders

Week of Sept. 18–24

September 25

Day-by-Day Practices for Reducing Heating Costs

A new heating season is at hand. How much you will have to spend to keep warm during the coming winter depends partly on the family's daily living habits. Ask all family members to cooperate in the following:

Close outside doors promptly. Make sure storm doors are fully closed.

Close bedroom doors at night if windows are opened for sleeping. Close off heat to the room.

When a room is not to be used for an extended period, shut the door and turn off the heat.

Keep the attic door closed.

Keep the damper closed while a fireplace is not in use. Lots of heat can be lost up the chimney.

Keep storm windows in place. If one is opened for sleeping, close it in the morning.

On warm days during the winter, reduce the thermostat setting so windows or doors will not have to be opened to get rid of excess heat.

Operate exhaust fans just long enough to carry off cooking odors and excess humidity. Overuse will carry off heat too.

Keep radiators or registers clear of heat obstructions—rugs, furniture, clothing, etc.

Draw shades and draperies at night to help insulate the windows. Open them during the day to let sunshine help warm the house.

How old is the thermostat (or thermostats) that control your heating system? Even the best of these instruments eventually operates less efficiently—and may need replacement after 12 to 20 years. Each season pull off the cover and vacuum dust from the mechanism.

September 26

Repair A Basement Leak

Your building-supply dealer can sell you a product to fill wall cracks that allow water to seep into a basement. It is hydraulic cement. A can costs around two dollars.

Today in History: Hydraulic cement was patented on Sept. 26, 1871 by David O. Saylor, Allentown, Pa.

Tunnel builders have used hydraulic cement for years to control running water. It sets fast. As it cures, it expands, plugging the space into which you have placed it. You may want to try it on visible cracks if you already have done all you can about draining water away outside.

If possible delay the repair job until the entering water is no more than a trickle. Using a cold chisel and hammer, enlarge the crack to a minimum width and depth of 3/4″. Slightly undercut both sides of the chiseled groove.

Flush away chips and dirt. When the surface is clean, mix a small amount of the cement and force it into the crack, starting at the top and working downward. If water is only trickling in, pack the crack full of cement and hold the trowel over it for several minutes while it sets. If water is flowing vigorously, hold a ball of cement in your hand until you can feel it getting warm or becoming dry. Then pack it firmly into the crack and exert full pressure with the palm of your hand or the trowel for several minutes. Do not release pressure too soon.

Continue mixing small batches of fresh cement, and work your way down the crack six or eight inches at a time. Wet the area occasionally as you work, and keep the patch damp for at least 15 minutes after completing the job to prevent it from drying out too quickly.

September 27

Today in History: A patent for "book matches" was granted on Sept. 27, 1892 to Joshua Pusey, of Lima, Ohio. The Diamond Match Company made the first ones in 1896.

Seal That Hearthstone

Have a fireplace? You may want to build a cheering fire some cool evening soon. Before that time comes, how about applying an approved sealer to the hearthstone? Home-supply stores have such sealers. They protect the surface of the stone and make it easier to clean.

Better check your kindling supply, too, and replenish it if necessary.

September 28

Southerners: Buy Tulip Bulbs

If you live in the South or in the warm parts of the Southwestern States, it's time now to buy your tulip bulbs if you want blooms next spring. By buying now you can make sure they are properly stored until planting time. To simulate the winter rest that the bulbs need, store them in a refrigerator or other cool place for four to six weeks. They will then be ready for planting in November.

September 29

It's Time To Dig New Flower Beds

When you want to grow flowers where you never have had them before, it's usually advisable to do the preliminary digging the autumn before you plan to plant the seed

or set out plants. This is especially true for perennials.

As a preliminary, have your soil tested. Your county agent can advise you about this. When you send in the soil sample, let the Experiment Station know you are planning to grow flowers.

Before digging the soil, also check its water-holding capacity. Instructions for this come from "Growing Flowering Perennials," Home and Garden Bulletin No. 114, available from the U.S. Government Printing Office, Washington, D.C. 20402:

"Dig a hole about 10 inches deep and fill with water. The next day, fill the hole with water again and see how long the water remains in the hole. If the water drains away in 8 to 10 hours, the permeability of the soil is sufficient for good growth.

"If an appreciable amount of water remains in the hole after 10 hours, it will be necessary to improve the drainage of the planting site; otherwise, water will collect in your prepared flower bed and prevent development of roots.

"To improve drainage, bed up the soil. Dig furrows along the sides of the bed and add the soil from the furrows to the bed. This raises the level of the bed above the general level of the soil. Excess water can seep from the bed into the furrows.

"You may find gullies in raised beds after heavy rains. You can prevent gullying by surrounding the beds with wooden or masonry walls, making, in effect, raised planters.

"Also, raised beds dry out more quickly than flat beds; little moisture moves up into the bed from the soil below. Be sure to water beds frequently during the summer.

"After forming the beds, or determining that drainage is satisfactory without bedding, spade the soil to a depth of 8 to 10 inches. Turn the soil over completely. In this spading remove boards, large stones, and building trash, but turn under all leaves, grass, stems, roots, and anything else that will decay easily.

"Respade three or four times at weekly intervals. If the soil tends to dry between spadings, water it. Pull weeds before they set seed.

"In spring, just before planting, spade again. At this spading, work peat moss, sand, fertilizer, and lime into the soil."

September 30

Drain Rust from Your Hot-Water Heater?

Rusty sediment accumulates in the bottom of many, perhaps all, hot-water heaters, and its removal should be a once-a-year job. You'll find a petcock at the base of the tank for the purpose. This often is equipped with a hose thread so that you can connect the garden hose and carry the water to the basement drain without mess. Turn off the heater several hours before doing the job and use up the existing hot water. Draw off water until it comes out clear. Then start up the heater again.

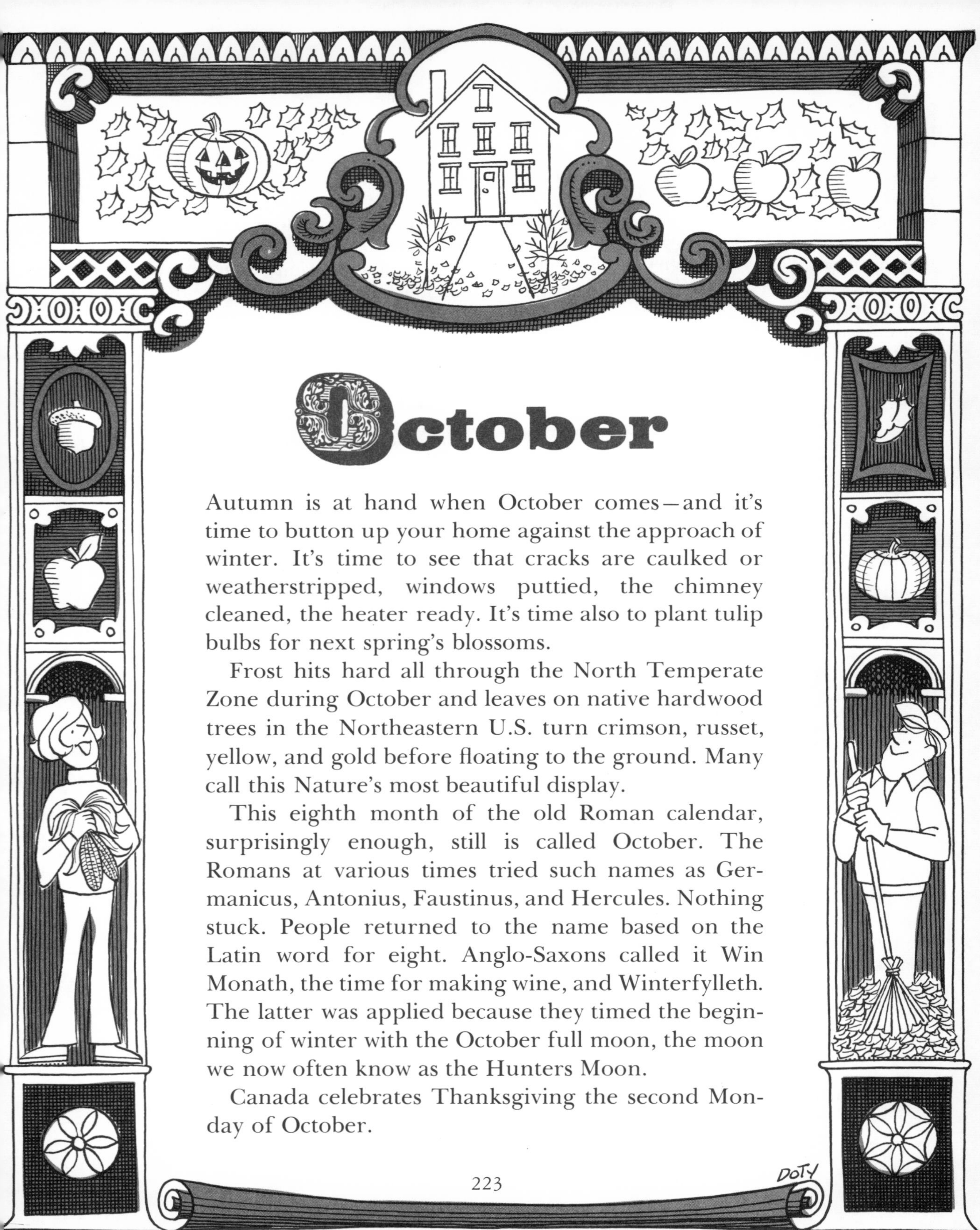

October

Autumn is at hand when October comes—and it's time to button up your home against the approach of winter. It's time to see that cracks are caulked or weatherstripped, windows puttied, the chimney cleaned, the heater ready. It's time also to plant tulip bulbs for next spring's blossoms.

Frost hits hard all through the North Temperate Zone during October and leaves on native hardwood trees in the Northeastern U.S. turn crimson, russet, yellow, and gold before floating to the ground. Many call this Nature's most beautiful display.

This eighth month of the old Roman calendar, surprisingly enough, still is called October. The Romans at various times tried such names as Germanicus, Antonius, Faustinus, and Hercules. Nothing stuck. People returned to the name based on the Latin word for eight. Anglo-Saxons called it Win Monath, the time for making wine, and Winterfylleth. The latter was applied because they timed the beginning of winter with the October full moon, the moon we now often know as the Hunters Moon.

Canada celebrates Thanksgiving the second Monday of October.

October 1

A Bit About the Birds

Brisk winds bring down the first leaves from some trees at this time of the year in the northern latitudes—a sure sign that real autumn is not far away—and from high in the skies overhead, both night and day, come the lonesome calls of wild geese migrating southward in great V-shaped formations.

Goose music is a good reminder that the time has come again to be sure backyard bird feeders are stocked with sunflower seeds, suet, and the small grains that winter birds like. An early supply of feed outside your window will be a constant invitation to migrants to stop in—birds that you might not otherwise see as they pass through your area.

We all owe a lot to the birds, more than most of us are aware of. One city that recalls its debt constantly is Salt Lake City. A monument to gulls was erected in that Utah city on October 1, 1913. The monument commemorates the timely arrival in May 1848 of flocks of gulls that saved the settlers' grain fields from hordes of devouring insects.

Today is also an important anniversary in the development of a man-made "bird"—the jet plane. The first jet designed and built in the U.S. was flown on October 1, 1942.

Today in History: Henry Ford built his first Model T car on Oct. 1, 1908.

"Don't give up the ship!" These words, for years a watchword of the U.S. Navy, were the dying statement of James Lawrence, captain of the U.S.S. Chesapeake in a battle with the British ship Shannon in the War of 1812. Lawrence was born Oct. 1, 1781, in Burlington, N.J.

Your Own Reminders

Week of Sept. 25–Oct. 1

October 2

Prepare The Ground for New Roses

Now is a logical time to prepare the ground for new roses, whether you still plan to plant them this fall—or wait until spring.

Dig individual holes at least 18 inches wide and 12 inches deep if you are planting only a few roses. Prepare a bed by spading 12 inches deep, then working the soil, and making separate planting holes within the bed.

Improve your soil by adding organic matter if the soil is very heavy, if it is light and lacking in fertility, or if the house builder used subsoil to level the lot. Peat moss, leaf mold, or manure will serve as organic matter. Add about one-half pound of superphosphate to each bushel of manure.

Spread a layer of organic matter two to four inches deep over a freshly-dug bed. Then work this into the soil to spade depth. If you dig single holes, mix organic matter with the soil removed from the holes. Use one part of peat or leaf mold to four parts of soil, or one part of manure to six parts of soil. Mix all of this thoroughly before using.

After the planting holes are dug, 12 inches deep, either individually or in the beds, loosen the soil in the bottom of the hole and work in about a spadeful of well-rotted (never fresh) manure.

Finally, mound up fine soil in the middle of the planting hole to receive the plant. See May 4.

Onions for harvesting next spring can be planted now in many southern states.

When you buy (or sell) firewood, know your cords. Properly, a cord is the amount of wood that can be neatly stacked in 128 cubic feet of space—four feet high, four feet wide, and eight feet long. But watch that four-foot width. Some dealers sell by the face cord—the width dimension of the stacked pile being only the length of one log (18 or 24 inches).

October 3

Act Now to Control Mice

A surprisingly large and active mouse population exists in any community, urban or rural. As the season becomes cooler, they try to enter homes, seeking warm places to hole up for the winter. It is possible in a modern house to close up all openings by which they might enter. And you should try. They can pass

through such narrow crevices, however, that you need not be surprised if a few do get in. For these, you need a second line of defense—a few inexpensive spring-type mouse traps set and baited today at points where they are most likely to enter—in cellarways, crawl spaces, garages, atop foundation walls. If children or pets are likely to disturb the baited traps, shove each one into a short piece of drain pipe, kept for the purpose, or lean a wide board from floor to wall and place the trap in the passageway. Cheese, bread, and raisins are all suitable bait.

In your outbuildings, check to be sure that you have not stored various materials in a way that will give the rodents winter protection. Such shelters are apt to attract rats as well as mice, especially if located in the vicinity of a stream. If you do discover the presence of a rat at any time, buy a poison recommended for the purpose and use it carefully, exactly as directed.

Protect tulip bulbs from moles, field mice, or chipmunks by planting them inside small cages shaped from wire mesh. Use mesh with about 1/4-inch squares.

The season's final application of fertilizer to cool-weather grasses about now will help keep the lawn green until winter sets in in earnest.

October 4

Choose Plantings Now for Fall Coloring

Would you like to have more trees and shrubs with good autumn leaf coloring? Now is the time to choose them at a local nursery, and in most cases you can still plant them this fall. Young trees or shrubs that show good color in the nursery can be expected to continue this trait as long as they live, if well cared for.

Today in History: The automatic player piano was patented in the U.S. on Oct. 4, 1881, by Edward H. Leveaux of England.

Boasting of her industry, an applicant for a housemaid's job said she always arose at five, and made all the beds in the house before any-one else was up.

October 5

Today in History: The Gregorian calendar, our present one, was introduced on Oct. 5, 1582.

Protect Concrete From Spalling

Now is the time to protect outdoor concrete surfaces from the possible ravages of winter. Alternate freezing and thawing and chemical action induced by ice-melting salts can cause surfaces of driveways, sidewalks, and patios to flake and chip away. This action is called spalling. To lessen the chances it will happen, you can use an anti-spalling compound sold by hardware and department stores.

Whatever the brand name, the compound creates a tough membrane over the concrete surfaces. The membrane keeps salt solutions and water from penetrating the pores in concrete. The compound also tends to harden the outer layer of concrete and checks any spalling that already has begun.

You buy the stuff in one-gallon cans or larger, and brush, roll, or spray it on the dry concrete. You may have to avoid use of the treated areas for a certain time until the solution has dried. The instructions on the container should give you the details. A second application may be recommended. One treatment may last for as long as four years.

October 6

Today in History: Le Corbusier was born on Oct. 6, 1887. This famous Swiss architect designed houses as "machines for living."

Button Up the House For Winter

In all areas where winters turn sharply cold, home owners may want to set aside a single day at this time of year to take care of all the little chores needed to prepare their homes and yards for the change in seasons.

They will make sure, for instance, that all outdoor furniture has been moved indoors or stored where it will not be damaged by the elements. They will also see that gardening tools and all items of grass cutting equipment have been put away. They will put up storm windows, if they make a seasonal switch from screens. They will install storm doors, or switch from screen to glass inserts in combination doors. They will cut off water to outdoor sill cocks and make sure that no water remains in the lines to freeze. They will do the same for fountains and pools.

Those whose windows are filled with combination storm/screen inserts will also want to make the switch soon to the all-glass storm window. The time of the switch is also a good time to wash the windows well, both inside and out, for a clear view outward during the winter.

These chores are just a beginning in most cases. Check around and you'll probably find more.

Are your outdoor sill cocks self-draining? If not, you may want to switch. The self-draining type automatically shuts off water inside the house wall where it is unlikely to freeze. During the winter, you can safely drain water from it even when the temperature is well below freezing.

October 7

Today in History: James Whitcomb Riley, "The Hoosier Poet," was born on Oct. 7, 1849, in Greenfield, Ind. The poem below was first published in a collection entitled "The Old Swimmin'-Hole and 'Leven More Poems" printed at the author's own expense in 1883.

When the Frost Is On the Punkin

When the frost is on the punkin and the
  fodder's in the shock
And you hear the kyouck and gobble of the
  struttin' turkey-cock,
And the clackin' of the guineys, and the
  cluckin' of the hens,
And the rooster's hallylooyer as he tiptoes on
  the fence;
O, it's then's the times a feller is a-feelin' at
  his best,

With the risin' sun to greet him from a night
  of peaceful rest,
As he leaves the house, bare-headed, and goes
  out to feed the stock,
When the frost is on the punkin and the
  fodder's in the shock.

They's something kindo' harty-like about the
  atmusfere
When the heat of summer's over and the
  coolin' fall is here—
Of course we miss the flowers, and the
  blossums on the trees,
And the mumble of the hummin'-birds and
  buzzin' of the bees;
But the air's so appetizin'; and the landscape
  through the haze
Of a crisp and sunny morning of the airly
  autumn days
Is a pictur' that no painter has the colorin'
  to mock—
When the frost is on the punkin and the
  fodder's in the shock.

The husky, rusty russel of the tossels of the
  corn
And the raspin' of the tangled leaves, as golden
  as the morn;
The stubble in the furries—kindo' lonesome-
  like, but still
A-preachin' sermons to us to the barns they
  growed to fill;
The strawstack in the medder, and the reaper
  in the shed;
The hosses in theyr stalls below—the clover
  overhead!—
O, it sets my hart a-clickin' like the tickin' of a
  clock,
When the frost is on the punkin and the
  fodder's in the shock!

Then your apples all is gethered, and the ones
  a feller keeps
Is poured around the celler-floor in red and
  yeller heaps;
And your cider-makin' 's over, and your
  wimmern-folks is through
With their mince and apple-butter, and theyr
  souse and saussage too! . . .
I don't know how to tell it—but ef sich a thing
  could be
As the Angels wantin' boardin', and they'd call
  around on *me*—
I'd want to 'commodate 'em—all the whole-
  indurin' flock—
When the frost is on the punkin and the
  fodder's in the shock!

In the southern states, it's time to divide clumps of some perennial flowers. See April 12 for how to do it.

Destroy any pokeweed, Jerusalem oak, Jimson weed, wild blackberry stalks, and wild geranium on your property. Spider mites overwinter in such hosts, waiting to attack trees in the spring.

Your Own Reminders

Week of Oct. 1–7

October 8

Today in History: The great Chicago fire began Oct. 8, 1871. Did a cow kick over a lamp while Mrs. O'Leary was milking? Probably not. More likely the fire started when one of two young women dropped a lamp into the straw of the barn. The pair were milking the cow by stealth to get milk needed for a neighborhood party celebrating the arrival that day of a young man from Ireland.

Is Your Home Safe From Fire?

Do you have at least two dry-powder, carbon dioxide, or all-purpose fire extinguishers handy—in kitchen and/or garage or home shop areas?

Do you have a screen in front of your fireplace?

Are all waste-paper, tin-can, and refuse containers made of metal or plastic?

Do you have sufficient wall outlets—so you can avoid octopus connections?

Do you remember to clean an outside-venting exhaust hood and duct as often as required?

Are all flammable liquids kept in safety cans?

Do you store oily rags in air-tight containers—if you must keep them on hand?

Do you keep your basement, garage, attic, and utility room free of combustible materials?

Do you keep matches out of the reach of children?

Do you have two ways of getting out of each room in the house? A window large enough to escape through is usually the best second method. Store a rope ladder in each room high from the ground.

Do you clean and service the heating plant and chimneys each year?

Do you discard or repair frayed electrical cords and those otherwise unsafe?

Is your home equipped with fire-retardant curtains, bedding, and other fabrics?

If you have a fire or smoke detector system in your home, does it include only approved components and was it installed according to UL specs? A warning system that fails to work is worse than none at all.

Do you use fuses of the proper amperage for the circuits they protect?

Have weeds, brush, old lumber, and other fire hazards been eliminated from around the house?

Do you have a box of sand stored in the garage or basement to help in fighting possible oil or gasoline fires?

Does everyone in the family (and the babysitter) know the location of the nearest firealarm box? Does everyone know how to telephone the fire department?

Has everyone in the family been instructed in a plan of action in case of fire at night?

Is there a dead or dying tree on your street? If you live in a city, let the authorities know so it can be replaced next spring.

Check your local nursery or garden center for possible bargains in shrubs and trees that may have arrived too late for a fast sale.

October 9

Today in History: An electric blanket was made on Oct. 9, 1946 by the Simmons Company, in Petersburg, Va. An "electronic" thermostatic control regulated the temperature.

Winterizing An Outdoor Grille

With cold weather approaching, it is unlikely in northern latitudes that you will have further need of an outdoor grille this season. You can insure it longer life by cleaning it up before storage for the winter.

First of all, clean out all ashes or unburned charcoal, using a brush or whisk broom. If left in, the ashes might promote rusting of metal surfaces.

Then scrape away all burned-on grease from the cooking surfaces, wire-brush them, and rub with heavy steel-wool pads. Finally, mix a strong detergent solution in one of the large plastic bags in which drycleaned garments are delivered. Immerse the removable grille in this and let it soak for several hours to clean away the final traces of grease.

Soak a cloth in a household cleaning solvent, meanwhile, and wipe all metal parts of the cooker, especially the chrome. This cleaning may uncover some areas that are beginning to rust. If so, wire-brush this bright and use a heat-resistant spray paint to coat all metal surfaces except the cooking grille. Ask your hardware or paint store for paint for use on hot surfaces.

Wipe cooking oil on the cooking surfaces.

October 10

Protecting Water Pipes From Freezing

You may lose in three ways if water pipes freeze during the winter. You are inconvenienced while the water flow is closed off. The expanding ice will weaken the pipe, perhaps even rupture it. You will have to shell out for a plumber's call unless you want to thaw the pipes yourself. So why don't you check out your pipes now to see if they're properly protected for the approaching winter?

Are any of the pipes located in or near exterior walls? If so, you'd be well advised to move them if at all possible. If pipes must remain where they'll be subject to freezing temperatures, you can wrap them with insulation. Plumbing supply houses can supply this. It comes in half sections to enclose the pipe. Place a moisture-resistant covering around the insulation and hold everything in place with metal bands supplied for the purpose.

So long as water flows steadily, such insulation

Today in History: Griswold Lorillard appeared at the Tuxedo Club in Tuxedo Park, N.Y., on Oct. 10, 1886, wearing a tailless dress coat and a scarlet waistcoat. This is said to have been the first appearance in America of the tuxedo coat, a fashion that originated in England.

will usually keep it from freezing. But water will freeze if it stands in a pipe, even an insulated one, for any length of time in cold weather.

Pipes laid in the ground are usually difficult to insulate effectively because of moisture. Insulation must stay dry to be effective. But a pipe below frostline is not likely to freeze even if not insulated.

Pipes sensitive to freezing can also be protected by wrapping the exposed area with heating tape. Let the tape completely spiral the pipe about every 24 inches. An ordinary light bulb gives off considerable heat. If the cold-sensitive area is limited, say about two feet, a lighted bulb strapped to the pipe there will give protection.

In today's inspection, make sure to close windows or other openings that might allow freezing temperatures to reach the pipes.

October 11

Today in History: Four patents were granted on Oct. 11, 1938, to Games Slayter and John H. Thomas, of Newark, O., for glass wool and machinery for making it. Owens-Corning Fiberglas Corporation was founded Nov. 1, 1938, to market the new building insulation.

Tips About Installing Insulation

Insulation is normally put into place while a home is being built. Even so, you may find it missing in some parts of a home—for instance, the wall between living space and an unheated garage or storage room, ceilings with unfinished attics above, or in floors above vented crawl spaces. All of these are possible places where you may want to add insulation during a remodeling project. You might also want to install it if you undertake the job of finishing off an attic or a basement.

In doing the job, keep in mind the following guide lines:

Always plan to wind up with a vapor barrier on the inner face of the wall.

Some insulation blankets have a vapor barrier on one surface. Be sure to keep this to the inside of the house.

Stuff small pieces of insulation between rough framing and door and window heads, jambs, and sills. Staple the vapor barrier over these small spaces.

Push the blankets into stud spaces so they touch the sheathing or siding. Working from the top down, space staples every 8 inches, pulling down the flanges to fit snugly against the studs. Cut the blanket ends to fit snugly against the top and bottom plates. You might

also cut the batts slightly overlength and staple through the vapor barrier to the plates. Tape a piece of polyethylene vapor barrier over any rips and tears in the barrier.

When pressure-fit blankets without a vapor barrier are used, wedge them into place. Cover the inside face of the wall with a polyethylene vapor barrier 2 mil thick. Staple it to the top and bottom plates and around windows and doors. Avoid cuts or breaks in the vapor barrier.

Foil-backed gypsum board enables you to install vapor barrier and finish wall in a single step. Use it instead of polyethylene.

Push insulation behind (the cold side in winter) pipes, ducts, and electrical boxes.

When finishing off masonry walls (for example, in a basement) first attach two-by-two or one-by-two furring strips vertically to the wall on 16″ or 24″ centers. Buy insulation to suit these dimensions—insulation normally 1-inch thick to go between one-by-twos, or R-7 insulation for two-by-twos.

There are three ways of installing blanket insulation in ceilings. If the ceiling is unfinished, the blankets can be stapled, or pressure-fit blankets can be shoved into place from below. When the ceiling has been finished, it can be placed from above.

When finishing off an attic, locate insulation in the knee walls. Also place it between the collar beams, leaving open space above for ventilation.

In an older house, you also may want to consider installing insulation between the joists of a floor above a crawl space. In that case, remember to locate the vapor barrier side up (adjoining the subfloor).

In contrast, when blankets are laid between the floor beams in an attic, place the vapor barrier surface down (against the ceiling). If the attic is later finished, this insulation should be removed from the floor space if possible.

Plant roses in those areas where winter temperatures do not go below -10°. That includes a good part of the U.S.

Do you have new young trees still struggling to get a good start? The bark probably is still tender. To lessen the danger of frost cracks from exposure to the sun and winter wind, wrap the trunk now from the bottom limb to the ground. Use tree-wrap paper or strips of burlap or white cloth. Remove the wrap in the spring.

October 12

Today in History: Columbus first sighted land in the New World on Oct. 12, 1492.

Columbus

Behind him lay the gray Azores,
Behind the Gates of Hercules;
Before him not the ghost of shores;
Before him only shoreless seas.
The good mate said: "Now must we pray,
For lo! the very stars are gone.
Brave Adm'r'l, speak; what shall I say?"
"Why, say: 'Sail on! sail on! and on'!"

They sailed. They sailed. Then spake the mate:
"This mad sea shows his teeth tonight.
He curls his lip, he lies in wait,
With lifted teeth, as if to bite!
Brave Adm'r'l, say but one good word:
What shall we do when hope is gone?"
The words leapt like a leaping sword:
"Sail on! sail on! and on!"

Then, pale and worn, he paced his deck,
And peered through darkness. Ah, that night
Of all dark nights! And then a speck—
A light! A light! At last a light!
It grew, a starlit flag unfurled!
It grew to be Time's burst of dawn.
He gained a world; he gave that world
Its grandest lesson: "On! sail on!"

—Joaquin Miller

October 13

Today in History: The cornerstone for the Executive Mansion in Washington, D.C., was laid on Oct. 13, 1792, the proposed building being modeled after the palace of the Duke of Leinster, in Ireland. The walls remained standing after the British burned the structure in 1814. When the building was restored, it was painted white to hide the smoke stains. Hence, the name: White House.

Set Up a Shoeshine Center

Every modern home needs shoeshine facilities. There are two good reasons why—for convenience and to avoid the present high prices charged for commercial shines.

The shine center shown here has at least two advantages over the usual shoeshine box. It provides self-storage, in a convenient location; it provides support for the shoe-clad foot at a convenient working height.

Make it of any wood you have handy—3/4″ pine or 1/2″ or 5/8″ plywood. Locate it in a spot where the person giving himself a shine will not interfere with other household activities or traffic. This might be in a corner of the kitchen, in a utility room, or in a basement, finished or unfinished.

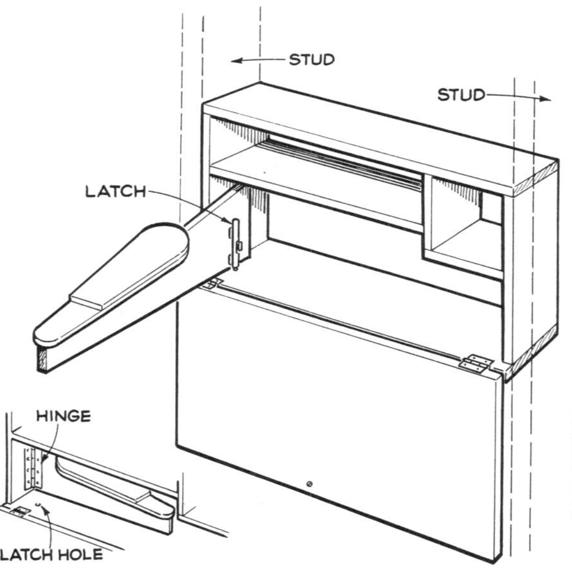

Size it to fit within the wall between two studs. For ordinary two-by-four studs on 16″ centers, this will give you a box 3 5/8″ deep (front to back) and about 14 1/2″ long (between the studs). Make the vertical dimension about 10″ and you'll have plenty of space for the shine supplies and the hinged arm on which you rest your foot. Use a door-locking bolt to keep this arm in place while you shine the shoes. Drill a hole in the bottom of the box to receive the sliding bolt. Shape the shoe holder to the sole of a man's shoe, but keep it narrow enough to fit into the wall box.

Let the cover for the box be outside the wall surface. Finish or paint it to suit its surroundings. A cabinet catch, perhaps magnetic, will keep it closed.

October 14

Today in History: Dwight D. Eisenhower was born on Oct. 14, 1890, in Denison, Texas. The future Supreme Commander in World War II and President of the United States spent his boyhood in Abilene, Kansas.

Winterize a Swimming Pool

In all except the warmest southern regions, dropping temperatures indicate that you might as well forget about using an outdoor swimming pool until another year.

Follow these steps to prepare a pool for the winter, whether it's an in-ground or above-ground pool:

Lower the level enough so that water can drain from the lines that circulate it through the filter.

Drain all water from the filter itself, opening

the plugs provided for this purpose. Cover the plugs and the threaded openings with grease to prevent rust.

Wrap the filter motor snugly with a sheet of plastic. Cover the filter if it is not protected.

Cut off power to the filter at or near the fuse box.

Remove and store equipment such as diving board and ladders.

Put a heavy charge of chlorine into the water.

Draw a protective plastic cover over the entire pool, letting it either rest on the surface of the water or on floats that you buy to hold the cover up. Covers with water-filled sleeves at the edges are ideal for in-ground pools.

If you have a pool heater, now is a good time to check out its heat exchanger for lime build-up, and to de-lime it if necessary. Better call in a pool service man for this.

Keep protective mulches an inch or so away from the trunks of newly planted shrubs and trees to avoid rodent damage during the winter.

Week of Oct. 8–14

October 15

A Good Time to Plant Lilacs

Best time to plant lilacs usually is autumn after the leaves fall and before the ground freezes. That way new roots can start growth before the buds become active. Where winters are especially severe, spring planting before the buds start to unfold may be preferred. But the period is very brief since lilacs start so early.

Buy nursery-grown stock or dig up young well-rooted shoots around your own bushes. Lilacs on their own roots are better than grafted ones. Disease often affects the latter. You may want to grow your own shoots in a nursery or your garden for a couple of years before planting them in a permanent location.

Select a well-drained site in a sunny location. Lilacs need room if they are to produce flowers on all sides. They will grow in shade but become undesirably tall and flower poorly. Set the plant two or three inches deeper than it grew before. Make the hole large enough to accept all roots without crowding. Fertilize young plants each spring until they begin to flower.

October 16

Store Small Engines for the Winter

Most small engines are in storage many more months than the number of months they are in use. This applies to the outboard engine, the lawn mower, the garden tractor, and also the chain saw. The proper preparation of these engines for storage will insure longer life and will have a real bearing on how easily they start when needed.

Recommendations for storage differ somewhat depending on the type of engine but some apply to both the two and the four stroke cycle engine. Two-stroke engines are most commonly found on the outboard engine and chain saw while the four stroke is used on the lawn mower, garden tractor, snowblower, and small electric plant.

The major deterioration in storage comes from rusting of the cylinder and piston rings. This is more critical in four stroke cycle engines where the oil is not mixed with the fuel.

First, let's consider the proper preparation of an outboard engine for storage. If the engine has been used in salt water, its cooling system should be flushed out with fresh water, or, even better, it should be operated for a few minutes in fresh water. This can be accomplished in a water barrel. The engine cylinder and crankcase parts can be effectively rust-proofed at the same time by operating the engine on a quart or less of normal mixture of gasoline with a high detergent oil. The best high detergent oils contain a rust preventive additive.

The next step is to completely drain the engine, fuel lines and carburetor of remaining fuel. This will be accomplished if the engine is permitted to run until the tank is dry and the engine stalls.

Next, drain the lower gear case of water and lubricant and force out any remaining water by refilling with new lubricant. Finally, wipe off exposed metal parts with a rag and a few drops of that detergent motor oil, and store the engine in its normal vertical position indoors.

The steps to follow in preparing other two-stroke engines and the four-cycle engine for storage are similar:

Remove fuel from tank.

Start engine to use all fuel in carburetor and line. This is not necessary on engines with a suction type carburetor.

Remove carburetor bowl, clean thoroughly and replace.

Today in History: A patent was granted on Oct. 16, 1928, to Marvin Pipkin for an electric lamp bulb frosted inside.

Remove spark plug and insert one teaspoon of a highly detergent oil in cylinder. Crank engine several times to distribute oil. Stop engine with piston at top of stroke.

Replace spark plug.

Clean outside of engine, including cooling fins on cylinder and head.

Service the air cleaner.

Store inside a building. If not possible, cover for protection from rain and snow.

In the spring, follow generally the same rules to store a snowblower for the summer. See April 27.

(Note: The foregoing instructions were prepared by the Extension Service in Alaska, a state where they really know about winter problems.)

Do you own a camping vehicle? Did you visit or camp this summer in the northeastern states where the gypsy moth is a serious threat to our trees? Then check the undersurfaces of your vehicle now for egg masses that you may unwittingly have transported into your home area. See the entry for February 4.

October 17

Have You Cleaned Those Gutters?

Before real winter sets in, better not neglect the annual chore of cleaning leaves and other debris from all the gutters on your home. Leaves that impede water drainage could lead to damage during the winter.

A ladder and a whisk broom is one of the simplest approaches to the cleaning job. The broom sweeps out the granules that wash down from a composition-shingle roof. A garden trowel also is helpful in digging out debris packed into the curved bottom of a gutter. As a final step, you might flush out each gutter with a garden hose.

Before calling the job complete, remove the elbows leading to the downspouts and see that everything is clear. Also give a thought to the gutter hangers to make sure all are doing a proper job of supporting each gutter at an incline to carry off the rush of rainwater.

There's a tool you could make to avoid climbing a ladder when the gutters need cleaning. Get a length of pipe or tubing (3/4″ or 1/2″) long enough to reach above all gutters. Bend a hook into that end—like a cane handle. Thread the other end and turn on it a garden hose-to-pipe thread adapter available at hardware stores. Get the right size to suit the pipe and hose you are using.

When a gutter needs cleaning, you can then open the downspout at the lower end, hook up the cleaning tool to the garden hose, turn on the water, and do a fine job of flushing out all debris—while standing on the ground.

October 18

Plan Now for Live Christmas Tree

Planting a live Christmas tree offers several advantages if you want additional evergreen plantings on your property. It's a case of "having your cake and eating it, too." For very little more (sometimes less) than you pay for a cut—and doomed—tree, you buy a balled or potted evergreen that will bring you joy during the coming Yuletide—and then again, out in your yard, for years thereafter. As the tree grows, adding beauty and value to your grounds, it will remain something very special in the memories of members of your family.

You can buy live any type of evergreen that you might buy as a cut tree. But now is the time to make your decision, not at Christmastime. Place your order so your local nursery-man will have on hand a balled or potted plant of the kind and size that you want. For ease of handling specify a tree that is not too large, perhaps no more than five feet tall. A wet root ball can be surprisingly heavy. A potted tree, when you can find one, usually will be small enough for easy handling.

Today, or on some subsequent balmy day during the fall, dig a hole for your tree—before the ground freezes. Dig it perhaps thirty inches across and fifteen deep to receive the typical balled evergreen. As you remove the soil, place it in small cardboard cartons on your wheelbarrow. Keep the best topsoil separate and label the carton. As you fill the cartons, trundle them to your garage or basement—somewhere that the soil will not freeze as winter comes. Pile straw or dry leaves into the hole until you have a mound a foot or more high. Cover the mound with a sheet of polyethylene or other plastic film, and weight down the edges, to keep out rain water and prevent freezing of the ground until you are ready to plant the new tree soon after Christmas.

Prepare for the wet season in California and elsewhere by spreading a mulch of peat moss under camellias. This should help reduce the blight problems that occur during the wet season. Also keep the soil moist around azaleas and gardenias.

October 19

Time to Gather and Plant Black Walnuts

Over a good part of the country black walnuts are available free for the gathering at this time of the year. Look for the trees at the edge of woodlands and along farm fencerows. Those who grew up in a rural area may already know the delights of hulling the nuts and letting them cure for cracking and eating on mid-winter days.

To break away the green hulls, spread the gathered nuts on firm ground in the backyard. Then crush away the hulls by tapping each nut sharply with a heavy hammer or the hammer edge of a single-bladed axe. Leave the nuts for a few weeks until the hulls have rotted and you can remove the nuts without staining your fingers. Use gloves if you want to do the job earlier.

Spread the hulled nuts out on an attic floor to dry for several weeks. They can then be stored in mesh bags. This way they will last for years.

The nuts must be cracked with a hammer. Place them on a flat stone or metal surface. A nut pick will help remove the meats. The process is a tedious one—but worth it for those who love the distinctive rich taste of the nuts.

You can use one of your gathered nuts to plant your own tree. This must be done at once, however, before the nuts dry out. A dry one will not germinate. Crack a couple of the green nuts to be sure the meats are fully developed. Not all are, especially from some trees. The squirrels are smart about such nuts. They do not waste time gathering imperfect ones.

Because of the squirrels, you must protect your planted nut. Choose a No. 2 tin can with one end already removed. Make an x-cut across the opposite end and bend out the four segments slightly—but not so far that a squirrel can get through. Burn off the tin from the can with a propane torch or other hot flame so the

can will rust rapidly in the ground and disintegrate.

With the open end up, place about two inches of soil in the can. Drop in a nut with the hull still on, fill the can with soil, turn the can with the open end down, and place it in a dug hole where you want the tree. Set the can deeply enough so you can cover the x-cut end with about an inch of soil.

Make two or three plantings like this within the same hole. If all seeds germinate, you can choose the best seedling and dig up and discard the others.

Locate your tree off by itself. Keep it away from sidewalks, garden areas, a clothes line, a swimming pool, or a pond. Both the nuts and leaves have a substance (juglone) which will stain you and your clothing. The juglone also poisons the ground under a walnut tree so that most garden vegetables will not grow there. In water, it will kill many fish.

If you prefer to buy and plant a seedling tree, spring planting usually is preferable in the North to avoid frost heaving.

In California, now's an ideal planting time for hardy shrubs, vines, and ground covers.

October 20

Today in History: Dr. Lee De Forest announced on Oct. 20, 1906 that he had invented the three-element vacuum tube, the amplifier that made possible long-distance radio.

Plant Fruit Trees Soon in Most of U.S.

Fruit trees require considerable open space. Yet you can usually find favorable sunny spots on even the smallest home grounds for a few dwarf or semidwarf trees, which at maturity stand from six to 12 feet tall.

All fruit trees should be planted while dormant. In most of the U.S. the preferred time is late fall or early winter as long as the ground can be worked. The exceptions are the coldest states, especially those in the northern Great Plains. See March 23 for a listing of those states where spring planting is preferred.

Plant the tree carefully. Don't skimp in digging the hole.

If you are planting a dwarf tree, adjust the depth so the graft union will be well above the ground. If the union were below ground, the graft might sprout and destroy the dwarf effect produced by the root.

In digging the hole, place all of the best topsoil in a pile on one side, the subsoil on the other. When the tree has been set in place, sift the best topsoil over the spread roots. If well-rotted compost is available, mix equal parts with the soil as you fill the hole. Leave a shallow depression around the tree. Soak the soil with a pail of water. Cover the surface with more soil, and pack it with your feet.

Prune the tree before you count the job complete. Cut back one-year apple and pear whips to about 36 inches. If you plant two-year trees, prune them severely, cutting away about half the growth. Remove branches from the trunk to a height of about 24 inches. Above that, remove branches that form a narrow angle with the trunk. Limbs that form angles of almost 90 degrees with the trunk will become the strongest. At the top of the tree, cut off one of any two branches that tend to divide the tree into a Y. Aim for one central trunk only.

Scatter a pound of 5-10-5 or 8-8-8 fertilizer over the ground in a circle, starting two feet from the tree (no closer) and continuing out to a little beyond the limb spread. This usually will be sufficient fertilizer for the first season.

Growers of lemons in California usually apply oil sprays in October and November to control scale insects. Other California citrus usually is treated in July. The delay for lemons avoids high temperatures which could result in fruit drop if they occurred immediately after oil is applied.

October 21

Today in History: Will Carlton, born on Oct. 21, 1845, near Hudson, Mich., wrote the famous ballad, "Over the Hill to the Poorhouse."

Patching Gypsum Board

Open holes through plaster board sometimes must be filled in. Such a hole may result from a sharp blow. Or perhaps an outlet or switch has been removed. Nails that hold a gypsum-board panel also frequently work loose and back out, and cracks may occur along the panel joints. To handle such problems, you ought to have patching materials on hand. Hardware and building-supply dealers usually can sell you this in one convenient repair kit—powdered joint cement (to be mixed with water), a roll of joint tape, a plaster broadknife for smoothing the plaster over joints, and an instruction sheet.

For large repair jobs, you also may need some scrap pieces of gypsum board of the same thickness used in your home. That's the route to take when a large hole confronts you. Locate the stud on either side of the hole. Then with a straightedge and pencil lay out a rectangle around the hole, locating the ends of the rectangle on the centerlines of the two studs. This means your patch usually must be exactly sixteen inches long since that is the normal spacing of wall studs. After chiseling out the edges of your rectangle, cut a new piece of gypsum board to fit. Secure it with nails driven into the studs. Then tape the joints, apply joint cement, work it smooth, and when fully dry, sand it to the desired smoothness.

A smaller hole can be patched with patching plaster by first securing a backing against the inner face of the wall. This backing can be a piece of metal window screening or a scrap of plasterboard. Hold it in place as shown by the

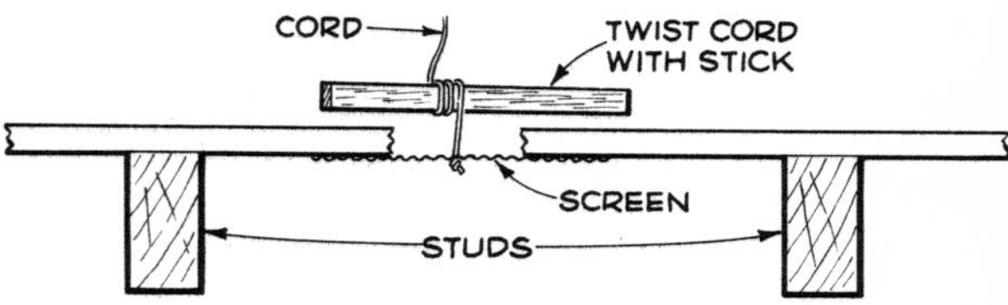

sketch. Then work in a layer of plaster, but don't fill the hole. When this layer has hardened, cut the string flush with the plaster, and apply a finishing layer of plaster.

Your Own Reminders

Week of Oct. 15–21

October 22

Plant Tulips and Other Spring Bulbs

The proper planting time for tulip bulbs is late October or early November in all except the deep South. Your ground already should be ready.

Besides tulips, plant the following bulbs at this time: crocus, hyacinth, iris (that grow from bulbs instead of rhizomes), muscare, and scilla. Refer to Appendix H for planting depths.

October 23

Test Garden Soil Now

Since the nutrient level of garden soil is at its lowest after the growing season, fall is an ideal time to get an accurate report on what lime and fertilizers you should add before planting time next spring.

Your county agent can tell you where to turn for a test if you do not already know. Or you may want to use a soil-testing kit.

October 24

Time to Lay Up Recreational Vehicles

Travel trailers, truck campers, motor homes, and camping and boating trailers are usually stored for more months than they are used. As much wear and tear can occur during storage as during use unless you lay up the vehicles carefully. So better get the job done soon—if you haven't already.

By all means store the vehicle under cover if possible. If not, try to locate it in the lee of a building. Attention to the tires is a second lay-up stipulation that applies to all RV vehicles except demountable truck campers.

Block up all wheels and deflate the tires to ten pounds. This prevents deformation of the tire during the storage period. If possible, remove the wheels (and tires) from the vehicle and store in a cool dry place away from the sun and electrical equipment. (Ozone produced by electrical equipment may cause rubber deterioration.)

If you live where the winter temperatures go below freezing, you will have to protect the water systems in the vehicle, if any—the engine cooling, toilet, and kitchen water supply. Drainage is best, of course. Use compressed air to clear all water from the kitchen supply and toilet lines after draining them. Be careful if you use a service station air base. Use the pressure only gently. Too much, or sudden spurts, may rupture the water lines. A paint compressor may be better. Put kerosene or other safe antifreeze in toilet bowls and sink

---

Winter-cover raspberries and tender grapes now in the northern Great Plain states and other areas of hard winters. Bend the plants to the ground, secure them with wire wickets or soil. Shove soil under the bend to prevent breakage. Mound soil over the entire plant. Locating the plants where snow drifts deeply also is a good idea. In some areas, the snow may be sufficient covering.

Today in History: Phosphorous friction matches were patented on Oct. 24, 1836. The patent was obtained by A. D. Phillips, of Springfield, Mass.

traps. Don't overlook draining a water heater.

If cooking gas is used in the camper, have the tank filled so that moisture will not form in it and condense. Turn off the main gas valve. Apply a film of grease over the inside of a trailer hitch socket, the hitch ball, and the bearing surfaces of hitch sockets and spring bars of an equalizing hitch.

A battery can freeze in extremely cold weather unless it's fully charged. So, better remove it from the vehicle and put it in a cool place. Every month or so recharge it.

Motorhome owners should follow manufacturers' instructions for layup.

October 25

What to do With Autumn Leaves

About this time of the year in a large part of the U.S. and southern Canada, the question comes up of what to do with autumn leaves—now that old-fashioned burning is usually forbidden.

The simplest way of getting rid of leaves is to rake them up, pack them into large plastic bags, and let your waste-service truck haul them away. But this may cost you extra fees and you lose the leaves as a mulch or compost.

You can handle a light fall of leaves by shredding them in place with a rotary mower. Start in the center of the lawn and work outwards in ever-widening circles, moving so that the mower chute blows the leaves in circles ahead of you. Rake up what's left, if any, when you reach the limits of your property. Use a rotary mower weekly in this way throughout the autumn as the leaves fall and you'll be able to recycle most of their nutrients directly into the natural food chain. Shredded leaves decompose quickly.

You might also compost them in place on a vegetable garden. First run a rotary mower over the garden to chop up the dead stalks. Rake the leaves from the lawn or use a lawn sweeper. Then spread them evenly to a depth of six inches or so over the entire garden plot. After the first rain, these leaves will usually stay in place. But you may want to place some branches on them temporarily.

In the spring, push the leaves aside while you

spade and plant the ground. After the seeds are planted, or plants set out, return the leaves to the ground as a mulch. This will conserve moisture and keep many weeds from growing. By fall, the leaves will have decomposed to just a thin layer—and you can start over again.

October 26

Ban Boxelder Bugs

Boxelder bugs may become household pests in the northern states when they seek warm hibernating quarters during the fall. Full-grown boxelder bugs are about one-half inch long and blackish with red markings on the front wings. During warm autumn days the elder bugs accumulate on sunny exposures of houses and crawl through cracks and crevices around windows, doors, or under the siding.

Seal all openings around windows and doors with caulking compound or a similar material to reduce the numbers which may migrate indoors.

The best time for full control of boxelder bugs is when they congregate in clusters on the bark of boxelder, maple, or ash trees in late summer before they migrate to nearby buildings.

October 27

Plant American Bunch Grapes in the Middle States

Now is a good time to plant grapes in the middle belt of the country. You can plant any time during October or November. In northern states it is better to wait until March or April. In areas normally frost-free, climate-suited varieties may be planted early in the year.

First-grade, one-year vines are first choice of experienced pomologists who say there is little advantage in using two-year plants. For the varieties suitable for your region, see Appendix J.

A location in full sun is best. Dig a hole wide enough so you can spread the roots. Prune injured roots to a clean cut. Set the plant about an inch lower than it grew in the nursery. Sift topsoil over the roots. You may mix rotted manure or compost with the soil but do not use fertilizer. Tamp the soil with your foot. Mound it around the plant so water will not collect.

It's usually best to prune one-year plants to a single cane of two buds although you may leave more buds on a vigorous plant. A two-year plant may be pruned to a single cane containing six to ten buds.

Today in History: The first radio station licensed was KDKA in Pittsburgh. The date: October 27, 1920.

October 28

Today in History: President Grover Cleveland dedicated the Statue of Liberty in New York harbor on Oct. 28, 1886. In 1903, a tablet was mounted on the pedestal of the monument. Inscribed on the tablet are the stirring words of a poem written by Emma Lazarus:

The New Colossus

Not like the brazen giant of Greek fame,
With conquering limbs astride from land to land;
Here at our sea-washed, sunset gates shall stand
A mighty woman with a torch, whose flame
Is the imprisoned lightning, and her name
Mother of Exiles. From her beacon-hand
Glows world-wide welcome; her mild eyes command
The air-bridged harbor that twin cities frame.
"Keep ancient lands, your storied pomp!" cries

she with silent lips. "Give me your tired, your poor,
Your huddled masses yearning to breathe free,
The wretched refuse of your teeming shore.
Send these, the homeless, tempest-toss'd to me,
I lift my lamp beside the golden door!"

October 29

Root a Rose Cutting? Here's How

In the North, where the ground still hasn't frozen, this is a good time to propagate prize roses. Choose a stem that has ripened well and cut off pieces eight or ten inches long. Remove all leaves. Plant the cuttings in a well-protected sunny spot with only the top bud above the ground.

The secret to having a well-rooted plant next spring is keeping the ground from freezing during the winter. Before the time for a hard freeze, cover the cuttings with up to a foot of loose mulch or straw. Or invert a glass canning jar over each plant. Remove the jars in the spring after frost danger has passed and you should have well-rooted plants.

Your Own Reminders

Week of Oct. 22–28

____

____

____

____

____

____

____

____

____

____

____

October 30

Hex Sign for Your Garage

At this time of year, as Hallowe'en approaches, witches are said to be abroad in great numbers. So you might want to borrow a trick from the good people in the Pennsylvania German country and put up a hex sign to ward off the galloping broom riders. Or perhaps you just might like to ornament an otherwise plain building.

You can buy colorful hex signs and simply mount them where you will—as many others do. But you can also create your own simple design, one incidentally that the Pennsylvania "Dutch" often swore by too.

The design may already be familiar to you, for it's often a practice exercise for beginning draftsmen. Lay out the design on a large sheet of hardboard or outdoor plywood and then cut out the circle for mounting. Or use a string and piece of chalk to outline it right on your building for later painting.

Choose any radius A1–A2 and outline Circle I. Then move your pivot point to A2—any point on the circumference of the circle and describe arc B–F, using the same radius. Continue on right around, using C, D, E, and F successively as pivot points. Finally lengthen your radius as desired and describe Circle II. Paint within the lines and arcs as indicated.

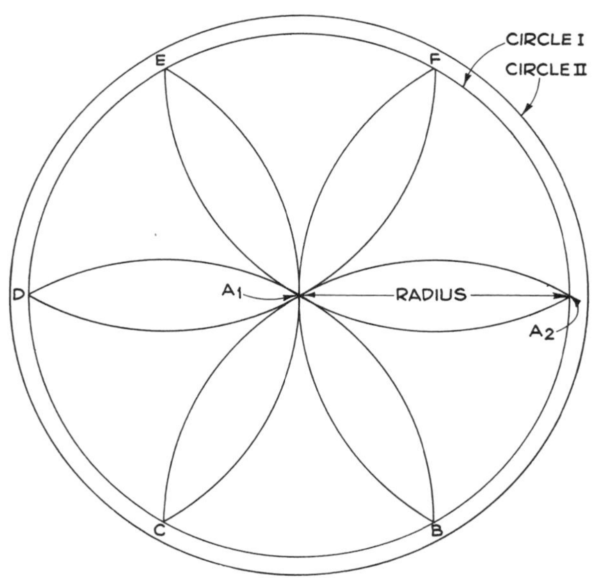

Dig, dry, and store dahlia tubers when frost has blackened their tops.

Move tender flowers indoors ahead of the frost line now moving rapidly southward.

October 31

Today in History: Tonight is Hallowe'en, the eve before All Hallows or All Saints Day on November 1. Young masqueraders will show up at your door tonight, many of them dressed as the goblins and witches that once were thought to prowl the earth on this date. Your visitor will say: "Trick or treat." So better be prepared.

Old-Time Apple Bobbing

Scotch and Irish immigrants brought a delightful Hallowe'en custom with them to the U.S.—apple bobbing, a happy custom that deserves to be kept alive at parties on or around this date.

In its simplest form, the game is played by suspending apples on strings or floating them on water in a large washtub. Players take turns trying to grab one of the apples in their teeth, with both hands behind them. Those who succeed should receive a suitable reward—as well as the apple.

Another version of the game requires a stick perhaps three feet long to be suspended and balanced on a cord tied to its center. An apple then is tied on a string from one end and (originally) a candle is suspended from the other. This time the object is to bite the apple

without being burned by the candle. A safer modern adaptation is simply to suspend an apple from each end of the stick and let two players compete—each trying to bite an apple.

Apples also are used for a race across the party-room floor. Each participant attempts to push the apple using only a toothpick held in his teeth.

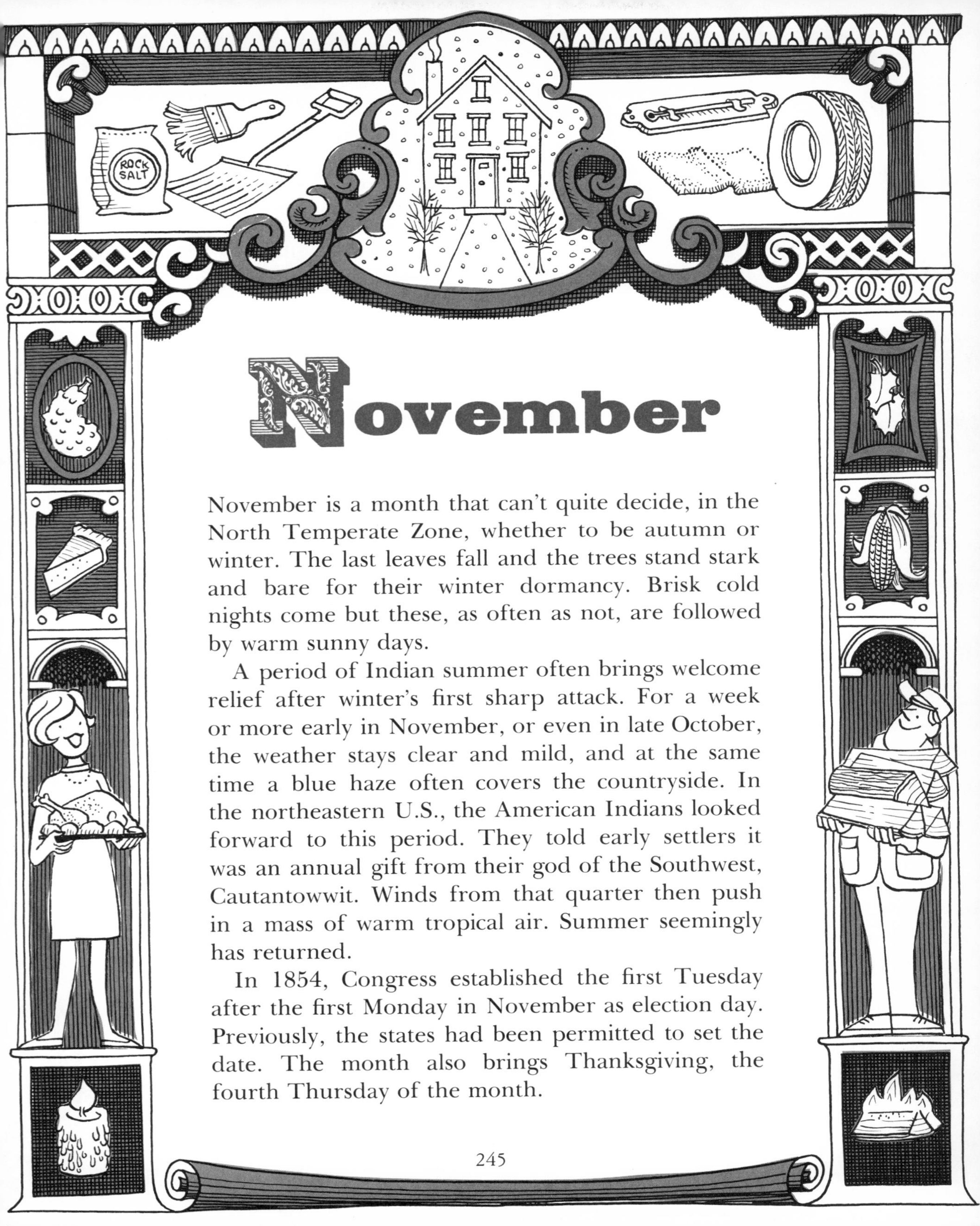

November

November is a month that can't quite decide, in the North Temperate Zone, whether to be autumn or winter. The last leaves fall and the trees stand stark and bare for their winter dormancy. Brisk cold nights come but these, as often as not, are followed by warm sunny days.

A period of Indian summer often brings welcome relief after winter's first sharp attack. For a week or more early in November, or even in late October, the weather stays clear and mild, and at the same time a blue haze often covers the countryside. In the northeastern U.S., the American Indians looked forward to this period. They told early settlers it was an annual gift from their god of the Southwest, Cautantowwit. Winds from that quarter then push in a mass of warm tropical air. Summer seemingly has returned.

In 1854, Congress established the first Tuesday after the first Monday in November as election day. Previously, the states had been permitted to set the date. The month also brings Thanksgiving, the fourth Thursday of the month.

November 1

Today in History: The U.S. Weather Bureau made its first forecasts on Nov. 1, 1870, basing them on telegraph reports from 24 sources. The Bureau had been set up by Congress on Feb. 9, 1870. The Act assigned meteorological duties to the Signal Corps.

How to Determine the Wind Chill Figure

Weather reports at this time of year usually include a cold-season detail—the wind chill figure. This refers to the fact that the chilling effect of wind makes the temperature seem actually colder than it is. You can compute this figure yourself.

First, determine the approximate wind speed by checking the accompanying Beaufort-scale table against the wind conditions that prevail in your vicinity. These conditions are used internationally to estimate wind force.

Second, read the temperature as shown by a thermometer.

Third, use the actual temperature and wind speed to find the wind chill figure on the accompanying table. Example: if the thermometer shows minus 5 degrees and you estimate wind at 11–16 miles per hour, the wind chill figure is minus 40 degrees—and that's far too cold for comfort.

Estimating Wind Speed on the Beaufort Scale

What You See	Weather Bureau Calls It:	Wind Speed (MPH)	Beaufort Number
Smoke rises vertically.	Calm	Less than 1	0
Smoke drift shows direction of wind. Wind vanes do not move.	Light Air	1–3	1
You feel wind on face; leaves rustle, wind moves vanes.	Light Breeze	4–7	2
Leaves and small twigs in constant motion; wind extends light flag.	Gentle Breeze	8–12	3
Wind raises dust and loose paper; small branches move.	Moderate	13–18	4
Small trees in leaf begin to sway; crested wavelets form on inland waters.	Fresh	19–24	5
Large branches in motion; whistling heard in telegraph wires; umbrellas used with difficulty.	Strong	25–31	6
Whole trees in motion; inconvenience felt walking against wind.	Near Gale	32–38	7
Breaks twigs off trees; impedes progress.	Gale	39–46	8
Slight structural damage occurs.	Strong Gale	47–54	9
Trees uprooted; considerable damage occurs.	Storm	55–63	10
Widespread damage.	Violent Storm	64–72	11
	Hurricane	73–82	12

When You Know Wind Speed Find the Chill Figure Here

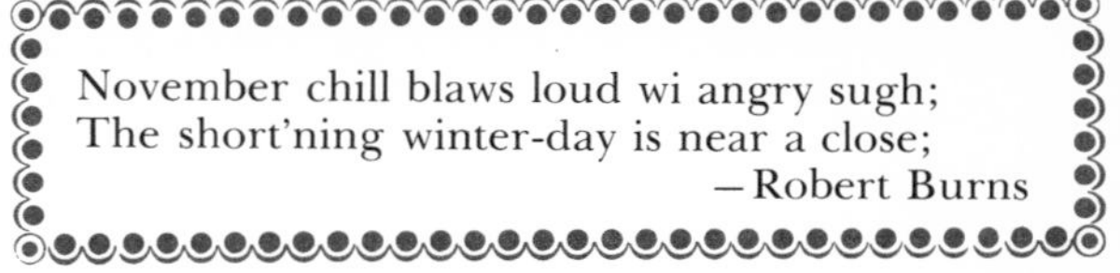

Equivalent Temperature (°F)

Windspeed (Miles per hour)																	
Calm	35	30	25	20	15	10	5	0	−5	−10	−15	−20	−25	−30	−35	−40	−45
5	33	27	21	16	12	7	1	−6	−11	−15	−20	−26	−31	−35	−41	−47	−54
10	21	16	9	2	−2	−9	−15	−22	−27	−31	−38	−45	−52	−58	−64	−70	−77
15	16	11	1	−6	−11	−18	−25	−33	−40	−45	−51	−60	−65	−70	−78	−85	−90
20	12	3	−4	−9	−17	−24	−32	−40	−46	−52	−60	−68	−76	−81	−88	−96	−103
25	7	0	−7	−15	−22	−29	−37	−45	−52	−58	−67	−75	−83	−89	−96	−104	−112
30	5	−2	−11	−18	−26	−33	−41	−49	−56	−63	−70	−78	−87	−94	−101	−109	−117
35	3	−4	−13	−20	−27	−35	−43	−52	−60	−67	−72	−83	−90	−98	−105	−113	−123
40	1	−4	−15	−22	−29	−36	−45	−54	−62	−69	−76	−87	−94	−101	−107	−116	−128
45	0	−6	−17	−24	−31	−38	−46	−54	−63	−70	−78	−87	−94	−101	−108	−118	−128
50	0	−7	−17	−24	−31	−38	−47	−56	−63	−70	−79	−88	−96	−103	−110	−120	−128

November 2

Mount Your Snow Tires Now

Snow tires make good sense during the winter in a large part of the U.S. and Canada. But why waste money, time, and effort each fall and spring mounting and demounting them? Buy an extra wheel when you buy a new car—or for your existing car now—and you can keep the two snow tires permanently mounted. Switching to and from snow tires then becomes as simple as changing a flat.

When you have a snow tire on a sixth wheel, you can make use of one of the snows as your spare during the summer and store the other. During the winter, one of the regular tires becomes the spare. You can also rotate your tires every three months as shown in the accompanying diagrams.

Never rotate studded snow tires, however. If you follow the sixth wheel plan, mark the snows "left" and "right" on removal in the spring—and remount them in the same position in the fall. If removed from the rim, mark each casing with arrows showing the direction of rotation so it can be returned to the same spot in the

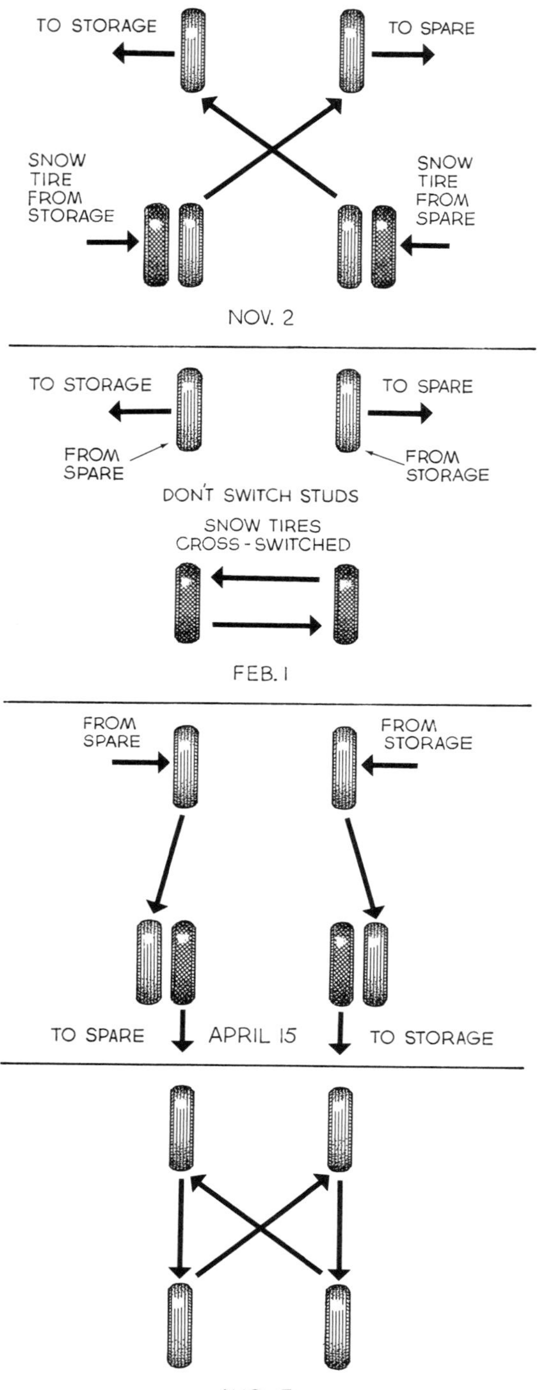

fall. Reversing the studs causes faster wear.

If you work into a sixth-wheel plan at the time you buy a new car, ask the dealer to supply a snow tire as the spare. He may do this at no extra cost—especially if you buy an extra wheel and second snow tire at the same time. The dealer can also paint the extra wheel to match.

Should your snows be studded? That depends on where you live. Some states forbid studded tires and quite a few limit the period they can be used. If you regularly drive across state lines during the winter, better find out the regulations for the neighboring states as well as your own.

In heavy snow states, you'd be wise to pack a set of tire chains and a short-handled shovel in your trunk at the same time you switch to snow treads. Make sure, wherever you live that you have at least one plastic scraper in the car for cleaning iced windshields and that the windshield washer is filled with an antifreeze cleaning solution. Some drivers store a bag or two of sand in the trunk at the onset of winter to add weight to improve traction. You can also shovel the sand under slipping tires to give them a grip.

Check out or add antifreeze to the cooling system of a water-cooled engine, and perhaps change the oil at the same time, and your vehicle is as winter-ready as it can be.

If you have a fig bush in a planter north of its usual range, better move the container indoors soon for protection from killing frosts. Farther south, protect young bushes or trees by piling loose soil around them to a height of of one or two feet.

Small plantings that you prize highly can be winter-protected from wind and snow by building a box of wooden slats. Paint it green.

Plant new roses in regions where temperatures range between ten below and ten above. See May 4.

Keep track of rainfall during the fall. Unless abundant, apply water to shrubs and young trees so they will winter well.

November 3

How To Store Off-Season Tires

Whether you mount and demount snow casings seasonally, or keep each one on its own wheel as suggested yesterday, you still must put one or more tires in storage during the off season.

You couldn't provide better storage than a trough-like rack such as those in which many service stations keep their supply of new tires. You might install this type of rack in the garage high overhead. Build the rack long enough to accommodate two tires for each car in the family, and you'll never lack for storage space.

You can also store a tire flat against the wall on two large dowels projecting from blocks nailed or screwed to the wall. Space the dowels so the tire can rest above them. Do not store a tire by hanging it on a single nail or dowel.

However you store the tires, it's a good idea to wrap them in sheet plastic or cover them to keep out dust and dirt. When the off-season tire remains on the wheel, deflate it to half pressure or less. Store the tires away from operating electric motors—heaters, freezers, and the like. Ozone produced by the motors checks and cracks rubber.

November 4

Ready for the Snow That's Coming?

If you live in the snow regions, better not delay any longer making sure you are prepared to plow or shovel it off your walks and drives.

Do you have a snow shovel, stored in a handy spot where you can locate it easily? Have you put off buying the new one you need? Wouldn't a long handle be easier on your back than a

short one? Most people think so, and there's no doubt that a Teflon-coated shovel slips through the snow and gets it up with less friction.

What about rock salt? Or a snow-melting chemical mix? Better check your shelves and get it on your shopping list if you find your supply low.

Will you depend on paying someone else to shovel or plow you out? Are the individuals who served you last year still in business? Better telephone and get on their work lists.

What's the condition of your removal equipment—if you plan to do it yourself? Do you attach a dozer blade or snowthrower to a garden tractor? Why not put on the equipment *before* it snows? If you have a self-contained snowthrower, now's the perfect time to install a new, properly-gapped sparkplug. The same for a garden tractor—if that's your motive power. Put just a little gas in the tank, start up the engine, and let the tank and carburetor run dry.

Refer to the entry for last April 27 and check through the suggestions you'll find there. Complete them now if you didn't then.

And finally, check the belt or belts on the snowthrower. If badly worn, or if they tend to slip, better get a new one on—perhaps by your dealer. Be sure to use factory part-number belts, not just any old thing that seems to fit.

Your Own Reminders

Week of Oct. 29–Nov. 4

November 5

Facts About Wood Decay

Let there be no doubt about it: wood decay is your house's worst enemy. Prevention is easy. Cure is sometimes expensive.

Wood is organic matter. When conditions are right, tiny plants can draw their food from it. The plants consist of microscopic threads called fungi. The threads are visible to the naked eye only when many of them occur together, but the fruiting body of the fungus grows on the surface of the wood in plain sight.

Fungi must have moisture to thrive and bring about wood decay. That fact is your clue to prevention. If your house was built of well-seasoned lumber, and if you keep it dry in all its parts, you need have no fear that decay will attack. But moisture can get into many different wooden parts of your house—and it will unless you are constantly on guard.

Some fungi merely discolor wood. Decay fungi destroy the wood fiber. Two species of fungi have the ability to spread from moist soil or wood into dry wood by conducting water through vinelike passageways. These can cause great damage to buildings. Fortunately most fungi cannot carry moisture in this way. The moisture must get there by itself before fungi can attack.

Fungi and termites sometimes work in the same wood. Decay fungi soften the wood. In the final stages, decaying wood shrinks, cracks, and crumbles. No fungus, however, produces the clear-cut tunnels or galleries characteristic of termite infestation.

Spores of decay fungi are carried through the air in wholesale fashion. You can't keep them away from wood. Air-dry wood remains safe, however. Wood must contain at least 20 percent moisture before fungi can grow.

But occasionally decay is found many feet from the nearest source of moisture. That is usually a sign of the presence of one of the damaging water-conducting fungi. These may produce thick and conspicuous strands between two layers of wood, for example between a floor and subfloor. The term "dry rot" often is applied to such conditions.

What do you do about it? A U.S. government home-service bulletin makes this recommendation:

"The treatment needed for these fungi is to trace the fungus back to its source of moisture, usually the ground, and cut off the connection. Often it comes up through a brace, frame, wooden concrete form, or grade stake that serves as a bridge to let the fungus grow from moist soil to a joist or sill. Sometimes a joist is in direct contact with a tree stump that has been left under the house. In other cases, the source from which the fungus is bringing its moisture may not be so easily located. These special fungi sometimes get their moisture from the soil, without direct wood contact, through strands of mycelium that grow a foot or two over the surface of foundation walls, or through cracks in loosely built masonry.

"Use sound dry wood to replace any that has been made useless by decay. If the sources of the moisture that enabled the decay to get started are entirely eliminated, replace only the wood that has been weakened. When there is any doubt as to the moistureproofing, however, especially if the original infection has spread rapidly, it is safest to remove also the apparently sound wood 2 feet in each direction from the part appreciably decayed and to make replacements with wood that has been thoroughly impregnated with a preservative. Before putting the new wood in place, give all adjacent old wood and masonry surfaces a heavy brush treatment with a preservative such as 5 percent pentachlorophenol, or copper naphthenate containing 2 percent copper."

Today in History: An automobile patent was granted on Nov. 5, 1870 to George B. Selden, Rochester, N.Y.

November 6

Southerners: Prepare for Lawn Seeding

Those in the warmer areas of the U.S. who want to seed a lawn next spring should consider planting a green manure crop now. Crimson clover, hairy vetch, winter rye, or ryegrass will make good organic matter if turned under next spring four to six weeks before lawn planting.

Magnolias seldom need fertilizing, but late fall is the time to do it if yours require it. Apply a lawn fertilizer around the tree.

Pecans should be maturing now. This is indicated by loss of the nut's bright green color and opening of the husks at tips or along the seams. The nuts may be left on the tree to cure naturally. Use them as they drop.

Have you stored gladiolus and dahlia corms and tubers for the winter? Keep separated in a cool dry place.

Winter mulch? It's still too early except in the extreme north. The proper time is after the ground has frozen hard.

November 7

Today in History: An elephant cartoon as the Republican emblem made its first public appearance on Nov. 7, 1874. Thomas Nast drew the cartoon for Harper's magazine.

Shield and Mulch Evergreens for the Winter

This is a good day to see that rhododendrons, laurel, and other evergreens have a good mulch and wind protection to carry them safely through the winter.

In the wild, rhododendrons and laurel are usually found in woodlands. The surrounding trees give them shelter. Leaves falling from the trees and the shrubs themselves form a natural mulch over the roots. The mulch supplies nutriments. It also prevents deep freezing of the soil.

If the ground is deeply frozen, the roots may not be able to take up water in sufficient quantity. If there is no surrounding protection for the shrubs, strong winds may increase the rate of transpiration. The green leaves may turn dry and brown and the wood may shrivel.

Where a winter mulch has not been provided naturally, you can apply a layer of pine wood chips or similar material. Do this for boxwood, holly, and azalea, as well as rhododendron and laurel.

It's also advisable to erect a windbreak for all of those plantings in areas where the temperature regularly goes below 20 degrees. Insert a series of stakes into the ground at least six inches beyond the shrub's outermost branches. Stretch burlap or other porous material around the stakes and tie or tack it in place. In the northernmost part of its range, boxwood should also have a shield over the top. This can be more burlap or a section of snow fence.

November 8

Keep Watering Your Evergreens

If the autumn has been dry, better make up for the lack of rainfall by watering your evergreens, both broad-leafed and narrow-leafed, before low temperatures freeze the ground. These trees and shrubs transpire moisture all through the year. Unless they have a regular supply of ground water, leaves and needles may turn brown in February, March, or early April—the injury that is often called "winter burn." Soak them all now to a depth of at least a foot. You might even do this once again before the fall freezeup that is now only a few weeks away.

The heating season is well under way in a good part of the country. Your furnace filters may need changing.

November 9

Ready To Thaw Frozen Pipes?

Despite all precautions, water pipes can sometimes freeze up during extremely cold periods. You can prepare for such emergencies by having on hand a heat lamp, a length of electrical heat tape, and/or a propane torch (with a full cylinder). You might also jot down the telephone number of a plumber you or another member of the household would call in such an emergency. It helps to have a good working relationship with such a plumber, for many others will be seeking his aid at the same time.

As the first step of your thawing procedure, open a faucet in the pipe that's affected so that steam can escape if your thawing methods cause it to form. Begin applying heat on the faucet side of the ice block and progress away from the open faucet. When the pipe is accessible, you can often locate the frozen area by feeling the pipe with your hand.

If there is combustible material near the pipe, better not take any chances with a torch. A heat lamp can be very effective in such cases. Or wrap the pipe with heating tape.

Lawn grass long and straggly? You may want to mow it once more before putting the mower away.

November 10

Restoring Old Paint Brushes

Paint rollers cover much more square footage these days than do brushes, but you still need a good brush or two. Somewhere around long-established homes you usually can find several hardened and paint-caked brushes that have survived from the days before water soluble paints made their welcome entry on the home upkeep scene. No matter how hopeless these may seem, you usually can soften and clean them up. Considering what you must pay for good brushes now, you may find this restora-

tion a worthwhile indoor activity at this time of the year.

Several effective brush cleaners are on the market. See what your hardware or paint dealer has and recommends. Use it as directed. Overnight soaking, or even soaking for several days, may be required for any brush. Aim especially to soften the hardened heel. But never try to break loose even part of a caked heel while the brush is dry for you will break valuable bristles in the attempt.

When the brush has become soft, knead it in water to work out the loosened paint. You may find it necessary to return the brush to the soaking bath several times—and knead it in water after each.

Next, spread the bristles with your fingers and sift fine, dry hardwood sawdust down into the heel of the brush. Then, under a stream of water in a sink, work it back and forth over a wooden rack made as shown in the drawing. Five to ten minutes of this, with the addition of sawdust as required, will clean most caked heels. The sawdust picks up particles of paint and carries them away in the water. Remaining flakes of dried paint can be removed by drawing the brush toward you across a stiff fiber scrubbing brush held bristles up in a vise.

When you are satisfied that you have removed all the paint you can, comb the wet bristles straight with a fine comb. Remove any loosened ones by grasping them between the thumb and the blade of a dull knife. Wrap the brush in heavy paper while it dries to give it a chisel edge. Dry it in the sun, turning every ten minutes or so for the hour or so needed for full drying. Then give the bristles a final trimming.

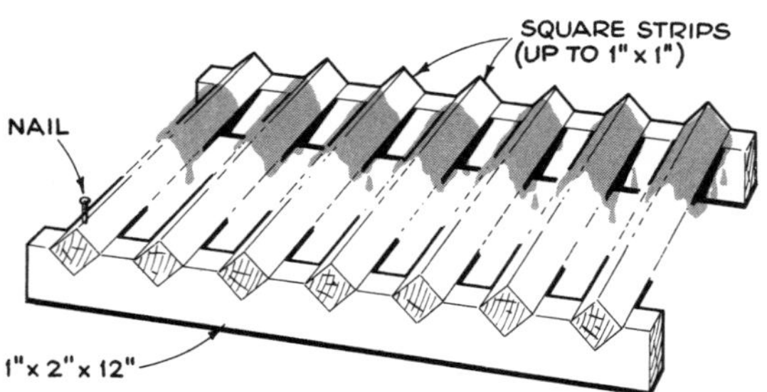

November 11

Today in History: At 11 a.m. on November 11, 1918, an armistice was signed ending World War I. For many years, the U.S. observed the date as a national holiday. It now has been superseded by Veterans Day, observed on a floating date. Canada has observed the date as Remembrance Day.

Time Now To Repair Any Split Trees

Because of the weight of leaves and fruit during the summer, trees with a crotch may end up the season with a new or worse split. Now is the time to inspect all your trees, locate these, and make repairs before winter comes,

bringing with it the chance of ice and snow that might cause part of the tree to collapse.

Most hardware stores have what you need to make the same repair that a trained tree man would make—threaded iron rods in various sizes about three feet long.

Drill holes through both members of the crotch, put the threaded rod through, hacksaw off any excess rod, place large washers and nuts on both ends. Turn up the nuts snugly against the tree. Keep turning until the break in the crotch is closed. Apply wound dressing to the break.

Now that the grass mowing season has passed, check all of your shrubs and trees for bark injury low on the trunk. Cut away any loose material, paint with shellac, and follow with regular tree dressing.

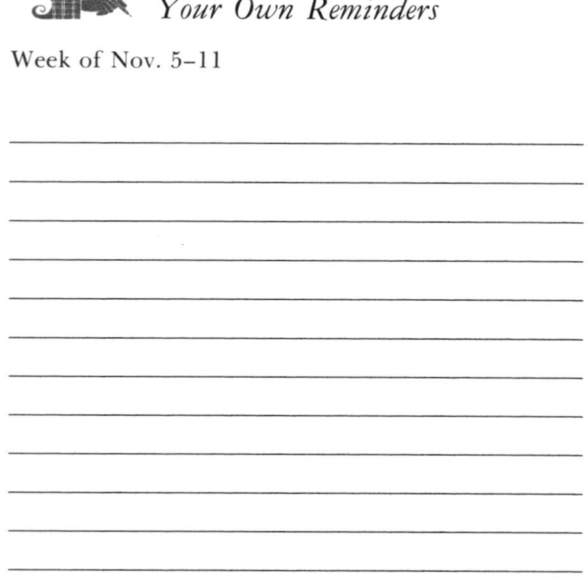

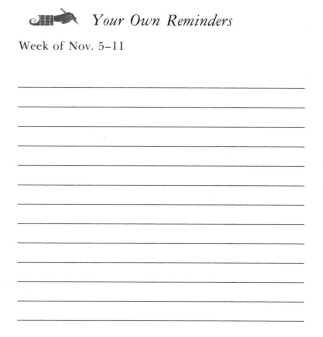

Your Own Reminders

Week of Nov. 5–11

November 12

Remove All Abandoned Nests

Remove abandoned nests of wasps and bees in or near the house. The more protected from the elements these are, the more likely they are to be infested with the larvae of insects that cause household damage—clothes moths and carpet beetles, for example. Apply this precaution also to abandoned nests of birds and rodents. Clean out any bird-nesting boxes you have on your property.

Use a putty knife to hack loose the mud homes of wasps plastered against any of your buildings.

Winter covering for roses is due now in most of the southern regions of the U.S. See September 21 for details.

November 13

Today in History: Artificial snow was produced on Nov. 13, 1946 from a natural cloud over Mount Greylock, Mass.

Prepare for Winter Storms

Strong winds during the winter can cause problems outside your house. Have you looked over the television antenna lately? Are its guy wires all snug? And what about the lead-in cable? If you have outside shutters, is each one securely attached to the house? There's no worse sleep disturber than a banging shutter on a snowy and blowy winter night.

What about tree limbs over and near the electrical and telephone cables leading to the house? If a tree or one of its larger limbs came down, would it knock out the power or telephone? If such a possibility exists, now's the time to prevent it.

November 14

Protect Young Shrubs and Trees from Rabbits

Are there cottontail rabbits in your neighborhood? If the answer is yes, you ought to provide protection now for any young and tender shrubs and trees that you have set out. Rabbits are especially fond of the bark on apple and pear trees, but they may damage any young plant. For example, their sharp teeth can slice off bittersweet shoots as cleanly as you could with a knife.

Guard young plants during the winter months by encircling them with wire netting. In areas of deep snows, you might want to use netting as much as two feet high, for rabbits are apt to seek out young trees when they can walk on the frozen crust of snow. Poultry netting will keep them off in such cases. But you may also want to protect the plants from mice damage. This requires ¼-inch mesh hardware cloth. Set one edge of the circular guard a few inches below the ground.

November 15

How Safe Is Your Home?

The National Safety Council has statistics to prove that more than 4,400,000 Americans are injured and 28,500 die in home accidents each year. The average home, therefore, is a hazardous place. But it doesn't have to be. You can easily eliminate all hazards.

Can you answer yes to all of the following questions? If not, better get busy making improvements or arrangements so that you can.

Do all stairways have sturdy handrails?

Are attic and basement stairs well lighted?

Do you avoid using stairways for storage?

Are stair treads, nosing, and carpeting in good repair—and secure?

Is there a sturdy grab bar for tub and shower?

Are all medicines and drugs stored out of reach of children?

Is there a textured surface on your tub or shower base? Or a nonskid mat?

Do you have a lamp within reach of your bed?

Do all small rugs have a nonskid backing? And do you avoid use at top of stairs?

Are stove and sink areas well lighted?

Do you have a kitchen rack or compartment tray for storage of sharp knives?

Do you keep and use all electric appliances away from sink, lavatory and tub areas? Does this include portable mixer and shaver? Are your hands always dry before using an appliance?

Do you hang at least two hot-dish holders near the stove?

Is there a sturdy stepstool available for reaching into high kitchen cabinets?

Do you have a list of emergency numbers near your telephone—police, fire, doctor, plumber, electrician, gas company, first-aid squad?

Do you keep your basement, garage, attic, and utility room free of clutter?

Are all power tools grounded before you use them— if they don't have double insulation?

Do you use safety glasses and power-tool guards where prescribed?

Do you keep tools generally out of the reach of children—or their switches locked?

Do you know the location of your main gas valve and how to close it? The same for the main electrical switch?

Are gas and water lines distinctly tagged?

Are your electric washer, dryer and dishwasher electrically grounded? Is your television antenna grounded?

Do you have a place of safe storage for each garden tool and return it there?

Are your ladders all in good shape?

Do you store internal and external medications in separate cabinets—or at least on separate shelves? Are all poisons locked up?

Do you hang one or two ring buoys near the swimming pool—if you have one?

Do you have a night light in hall and bathroom?

Do you have a first-aid kit and manual readily available? Does at least one member of the family know artificial respiration?

Can closet doors be opened from inside?

Are patio or other sliding-glass doors, and other extensive-glass areas in hazardous locations, all glazed with safety glass?

Do you always operate your power mower according to approved safety rules?

Even in the middle latitudes you should not delay longer putting up shields against winter winds around such evergreens as rhododendrons, laurel, boxwood, holly, and azalea.

November 16

Spray Lawn for Snow Mold

In all regions where snow falls during the winter, lawns may suffer from snow mold. This fungus tends to kill grass along the edges of drifts or piles of snow that you have removed from walks and driveways. You may also discover its effects on the lee side of a hedge or fence or on an abrupt rise where snow remains long after it has melted from the rest of the lawn.

Spraying these areas with a fungicide will control the disease. Do it now, again in late December, and in mid-February. Choose periods when there is little or no snow. Use the same stuff that golf-course greenskeepers use. A garden-supply store can probably recommend an effective brand.

November 17

Attic Access Panel Insulated?

In many homes, you gain access to an unfinished attic through a trapdoor. If that is the case in your home, is the upper surface of the trapdoor insulated? Chances are it may have been overlooked, even though there are insulation blankets (with the vapor-barrier side down) already in place over the ceiling.

Insulate the panel by stapling a piece of blanket insulation to its upper surface. To weatherstrip the opening, apply adhesive-backed foam tape around the edges of the trapdoor on its lower surface.

Vents should remain open in unheated attics through the winter for proper ventilation. See February 20.

November 18

When Wood Abuts Concrete

In many spots around a home wood must contact concrete or masonry structures. To avoid decay in the wood, the association of the wood and concrete must be contrived so that decay-producing moisture does not collect in or on the wood. Over the years, good building practices have been developed to prevent such decay potential. All wood-concrete contacts in your home may have been made in an accepted manner under these practices. But carelessness sometimes creeps in. Neglect and time also may have produced undesirable conditions. A checkup of all visible or accessible wood-concrete contacts around your house and grounds is your suggested chore for today.

Many modern homes rest on concrete slabs. Unless the construction was done properly in the first place, there's probably little correction you can make now. You will want to know, however, that good building practice calls for the use of preservative-impregnated or naturally durable wood for plates, sleepers, and other wood in contact with the concrete slab. The slab also should have a waterproofing membrane either in, under, or on top of it.

Spreading a waterproofing membrane over the sleepers when a wood floor is to go down on a slab is not good practice. The membrane keeps moisture in the sleepers, a condition that favors decay. Linoleum or other resilient flooring put down on such wood floors serves as a further vapor barrier, locking any moisture into the wood flooring itself. Remember that vapor barriers can be definitely harmful if placed where they may keep moisture from getting out of wood.

Treated or naturally durable wood is desirable for frames and doors of access openings in the foundation walls of houses built over a basement and/or crawl space. Even better in such locations near the ground and its moisture are steel frames kept coated with a protective paint. Any joists or girders framed into a masonry wall should have a one-half inch air space on each side, the top, and at the ends. For greatest insurance, the ends of the joists or girders should have been treated with a water-repellent preservative.

When a wood post must rest on a concrete floor, build a concrete pier three inches above the floor level and place the end of the post there. This will allow any moisture to drain away from the end of the post. Never embed a wood post in concrete, either indoors or out. Reason: when the wood shrinks, moisture can seep down around the post, producing a condition ideal for wood decay.

Today in History: Standard time was adopted at noon on Nov. 18, 1883 throughout the U.S. at the suggestion of the American Railway Association.

Your Own Reminders

Week of Nov. 12–18

November 19

Today in History: On the site where troops of the North and South had fought the bloody Battle of Gettysburg only a few months earlier, Abraham Lincoln delivered a memorable address on Nov. 19, 1863.

The Gettysburg Address

Four score and seven years ago our fathers brought forth, upon this continent, a new nation, conceived in Liberty, and dedicated to the proposition that all men are created equal.

Now we are engaged in a great civil war, testing whether that nation, or any nation, so conceived, and so dedicated, can long endure. We are met here on a great battle-field of that war. We have come to dedicate a portion of it as a final resting place for those who here gave their lives that the nation might live. It is altogether fitting and proper that we should do this.

But in a larger sense we can not dedicate—we can not consecrate—we can not hallow this ground. The brave men, living and dead, who struggled here, have consecrated it far above our poor power to add or detract. The world will little note, nor long remember, what we say here, but can never forget what they did here. It is for us, the living, rather to be dedicated here to the unfinished work which they have, thus far, so nobly carried on. It is rather for us to be here dedicated to the great task remaining before us—that from these honored dead we take increased devotion to that cause for which they here gave the last full measure of devotion—that we here highly resolve that these dead shall not have died in vain; that this nation shall have a new birth of freedom; that this government of the people, by the people, for the people, shall not perish from the earth.

The foregoing is taken from the second of five handwritten copies that Abraham Lincoln made of the address. It retains his own punctuation and capitalization. It is the version he delivered.

November 20

Aluminum Doors Freeze Up?

Complaints occur at this time of year that moisture is condensing on sliding aluminum doors and windows. Flowing downward, the water collects and sometimes freezes in the metal tracks, making it impossible to open or close the door or window.

Such condensation is at its worst in northern latitudes that have a big spread between outdoor and indoor temperatures. The aluminum frames carry the outside cold to their inner faces. The result: warm inside air in contact with the metal gives up its moisture.

What can you do about it? If you are building a new home or remodeling an old one, avoid such windows and doors unless you live where they will not cause condensation. If you already have the problem, you might string heating tape along the inner surfaces of the aluminum or focus a heat lamp on the area of greatest trouble to prevent freeze-ups.

November 21

Removing a Tree Stump

Burning has long been a favorite method of removing stumps, but all open-air burning is now forbidden in many regions. Digging out a stump is always possible but difficult. Many chemical preparations have been advocated, but tests have proven most of them of little value.

The easiest, cheapest, and safest method is to cut the tree trunk off as near the ground line as practicable, cover it with soil and/or sod and keep the area slightly moist. Grass sprigs or runners may be planted if sod is not used. Keeping the area moist helps wood-destroying organisms to speed up decomposition of the stump and also helps to keep the grass alive during dry periods.

To prevent sprouting, thoroughly paint the top surface of a freshly cut stump within a day of cutting, where the wood and bark join, with a herbicide such as 2,4,5-T or ammate.

Before covering the stump, bore several large holes, at least 1 inch in diameter, vertically into the stump, about 6 to 8 inches deep. This helps to hasten decaying. The decaying process is a slow one, requiring several years for nearly complete stump decomposition.

November 22

What To Do About Floor Creaks

You don't have to live with floors that creak every time you walk on them. The fixes are fairly easy, a good stormy-day job at this time of the year.

When you have access to the bridging (the crossed braces) between joists in a basement, check over each of these pieces and nail any that you find to be loose in the area of the squeak. The bridging pieces themselves are sometimes so close together that they rub and squeak when the floor deflects. Cure this by running the tip of a handsaw between the area of contact.

If you have trouble zeroing in on the location of the creak, have someone walk over the floor while you listen and watch below. If the subfloor rises and falls against the joists, drive shingle wedges between the floor and the tops of the joists until everything is secure. Finish flooring also may be moving on the sub-flooring. If you discover or suspect this, run several short wood screws up through the subfloor into the finish flooring.

When you must tackle the squeaks from above, first try a possible easy way out. Place heavy carpeting or several thicknesses of paper over the squeaky area to protect the finish and then hammer the entire area. This may seat any loose nails and solve your problem. If not, move a large magnet around over the area until it pulls downward. This will indicate the location of a nail in the joist. Then drive nails or run screws into this joist, countersinking the heads and filling the holes with putty or glued-in wood plugs. Use nails long enough to penetrate the subflooring and joist. This calls for threepenny nails for three-eighths inch matched hardwood flooring, eightpenny cut flooring nails for one-inch common flooring, and tenpenny cut flooring nails for 1¹⁄₁₆-inch flooring.

For squeaks under resilient flooring, take up part of the flooring when you must work from above. Re-lay it when the squeak has been corrected.

Cover peony clumps with an inch or two of straw or peat moss and a layer of evergreen boughs immediately after the ground first freezes—this week or sooner in the northernmost regions.

Established iris beds in northern regions probably should have a protective mulch. Apply it about now.

Reduce fertilizer applications to house plants about now. Days are shorter with less sunlight to promote growth.

November 23

Prune Grape Vines While Dormant

Vines of American bunch grapes should get an annual pruning during the dormant period. That means you can undertake the chore any time from now until March in the southern and temperate regions. (Where low winter temperatures injure the canes, wait until late winter or early spring.) Do the pruning while the temperature is above freezing. When frozen, canes are brittle and easily broken.

If the vine growth of bunch grapes is rather weak during the first growing season, it is advisable to cut the vine back at the end of the season to one or two buds and to train up a strong trunk during the second growing season. If the vine is to be trained to a two-wire system, tie it to a stake and let it grow upright until it reaches the top wire. At that point, pinch it off and lead out a lateral in each direction along the wire. During the second season, lateral canes will grow from all the buds along the trunk. Select two of these at the height of the first wire above the ground and tie them to that wire to develop fruiting wood. Rub off or pinch back the other branches along the trunk during the growing season. A vine can be trained to a fence in much the same manner.

As the fruit is borne on shoots from the canes of the previous season's growth, it is important that enough new wood be saved to provide for the next summer's crop. With healthy, vigorous vines, from 50 to 60 buds will produce as much fruit as the vine can mature properly. More wood may be left on vines for home production, provided sufficient space is available for the vine to develop. With vigorous vines, leaving more wood may result in a greater total quantity of fruit, but the individual bunches may be inferior in size and the fruit of poorer quality.

Vines of muscadine grapes are pruned somewhat differently. With these, the canes trained on the wires serve as permanent arms, and the new growth is pruned so as to leave fruiting spurs 6 to 8 inches long. Such spurs should be evenly distributed along the arm and so spaced as to allow free development of new shoots. Remove all excess wood.

November 24

Today in History: A patent for barbed wire was granted on Nov. 24, 1874 to Joseph F. Glidden, of DeKalb, Ill.

Mound Soil Around New Trees

Did you plant new shrubs, fruit trees, shade trees, during the current year? If so, you should have left a depression around them to improve moisture retention. At this point mound top soil slightly around the trunk to reduce winter heaving.

Also make sure the guy wires are secure. See September 17.

Californians who raise camellias might like to get an informative pamphlet from their Extension Service on control of diseases that affect this popular flowering shrub.

November 25

Apply Mulch to Perennials

It's probably time now to apply a winter-protective mulch to perennial flowers in northern latitudes. Choose your time well—not until after the ground has frozen. A thin layer of peat moss is a fine mulch. Keep it loose. Spring-flowering bulbs need the same type of winter protection.

Make use of that snow you must remove from your steps, your walks, and your driveway. If possible, pile it on areas where perennial flowers grow—or around shrubs and trees. Snow is a fine winter mulch, protecting roots from damage and watering the plants when it melts.

Today in History: A patent for machinery to produce evaporated milk was obtained on Nov. 25, 1884 by John B. Meyenberg, of St. Louis, Mo.

Your Own Reminders

Week of Nov. 19–25

November 26

Remove Debris from Boxwood

A mild day at this time of year is appropriate for an annual chore—removing dead leaves, twigs, and other debris collected in boxwoods. Shake the bush vigorously and much of the debris will come out. Pick out the rest. Debris in the crown may promote fungus.

Apply fertilizer around boxwood just before the ground freezes. Don't do it too soon or the fertilizer will promote new growth that will winterkill.

November 27

Spray Now to Kill Mosquitoes

Mosquitoes are no longer a problem as the northern and middle-belt areas of the country get set for the onslaught of winter. But oddly enough this is a fine time for residents of these regions to kill off some of the pests. The recommendation is a recent one from university entomologists.

What do you do? You spray with any of the insecticide formulations recommended for household use. The aerosol fly sprays available in grocery and hardware stores will also kill mosquitoes.

Where do you spray? The dark recesses of cellars and crawl spaces. Many mosquitoes spend the winter indoors in such secluded spots and come out again when it is warm. We may forget about them, but they are not really gone. One full spray coverage of your protected areas should be enough.

"If everyone in the neighborhood would do this," says Dr. Lyle E. Hagmann, Rutgers University entomologist, "it would delay mosquito buildup next summer by four to six weeks."

Organize some community action?

November 28

Have You Had a Household Fire Drill?

Experts agree that an emergency escape plan, well rehearsed, could save many lives lost in home fires. Base yours on the normal nighttime sleeping situation. Arrange for an alternate escape route for each member of the family if awakened by flames or the smell of smoke. Do this for each bedroom in the house.

When rooms are on the ground level, the second route can be through a window. But make sure the room's occupant can open the window easily—and remove any storm sash or screen. If the occupant is a child, give practice in going out the window. Make sure no furniture blocks the way to the window. Decide upon one window in each room as the escape window and check periodically that it can be opened easily.

If a bedroom is on an upper floor, store a knotted nylon rope or a rope ladder near the escape window. Tie one end of the rope to an anchor adjoining the window. Have a practice drill making use of the rope. A roof also sometimes offers an escape route from an upper floor.

In addition to making sure each family member has an alternate escape route from his sleeping quarters, drill into each one these points:

Use the escape route in case of fire. Opening a door into a hall or other part of the house may cause the fire to spread or the person to be overcome by smoke.

Crawl to the escape route when smoke is thick. Air is better at the floor level.

As soon as any member of the house is out of the house, hurry to the nearest fire alarm—or to a neighbor's telephone. Learn the location of the nearest alarm box. Post the fire department's number at your telephone.

Instruct baby-sitters in your household fire emergency procedures.

November 29

Plant Vegetables in South

Those of you who live in the southernmost part of the U.S. and in Southern California ought to be doing some planning about the vegetables you'll soon be able to seed or plant for the harvest early in the new year.

Dormant sprays can be applied now to trees and shrubs in the southern fringe of the U.S. (Zone I) and southern California. See the entries for January 26 and February 10.

November 30

Just for Fun: Old Proverbs in Big Words

EVERYTHING THAT CORUSCATES WITH EFFULGENCE IS NOT IPSO FACTO AUROUS

Why use little words when you can substitute big ones—and send your readers to the dictionary? The statements in the next column are perfect examples of saying something easy the hard way. All are familiar proverbs converted into 12-cylinder jawbreakers—genuine English words yanked right out of Webster. The statements appeared originally in a little booklet, "How's Your IQ on Epigrammatic Maxims?" published by Lasky Company, Millburn, N.J., and are used here by permission of Lasky's president, S. A. Barnhard.

Translate them into simple English? That's your fun task for today. You'll find the original proverbs listed on the next page.

1. A mass of concreted earthy material perennially rotating on its axis will not accumulate an accretion of byrophytic vegetation.

2. A superabundance of talent skilled in the preparation of gastronomic concoctions will impair the quality of a certain potable solution made by immersing a gallinaceous bird in ebullient Adam's ale.

3. Individuals who perforce are constrained to be domiciled in vitreous structures of patent frangibility should on no account employ petrous formations as projectiles.

4. That prudent avis which matutinally deserts the coziness of its abode will ensnare a vermiculate creature.

5. Everything that coruscates with effulgence is not *ipso facto* aurous.

6. Do not dissipate your competence by hebetudinous prodigality lest you subsequently lament an exiguous inadequacy.

7. An addle-pated beetlehead and his specie divaricate with startling prematurity.

8. It can be no other than a maleficent horizontally propelled current of gaseous matter whose portentous advent is not the harbinger of a modicum of beneficence.

9. One should hyperesthetically exercise macrography upon that situs which one will eventually tenant if one propels oneself into the troposphere.

10. Aberration is the hallmark of homo sapiens while longanimous placability and condonation are the indicia of supramundane omniscience.

Answers on Next Page

Today in History: A patent granted to A. J. Ehrrichson on Nov. 30, 1875, for "an improvement in oatmeal machines" helped establish the breakfast cereal business.

1. A rolling stone gathers no moss.
2. Too many cooks spoil the broth.
3. They who live in glass houses should not throw stones.
4. The early bird catches the worm.
5. All is not gold that glitters.
6. Waste not, want not.
7. A fool and his money are soon parted.
8. It's an ill wind that blows nobody good.
9. Look before you leap.
10. To err is human; to forgive divine.

December

For most of us the arrival of December brings an urgent warning: Get ready for real winter; don't delay. There's so much to do. How will we find time for everything on our schedule? To make matters seem even worse, the year's shortest day comes on or about December 21—at the Winter Solstice. But there's a solution for that: turn night into day.

On the calendar winter begins with the December Solstice. It begins in fact, too: The ground freezes hard in the North and the first heavy snows whiten the land. Freezing temperatures may occur during this month in just about any part of the continental U.S. The rainy season comes in tropical areas.

December's final days have long been a festive period. The old Romans exchanged gifts and visits at the windup of their week-long Saturnalia, their annual tribute to Saturn, god of harvests and sowing. The Druids of northern Europe, praising their sun god, hung up mistletoe as part of the decorations for their festival. They also burned a Juul (Yule) log. These and other ancient customs still survive in modern Christmas observances.

December 1

Sharpening a Screwdriver

You don't really "sharpen" a screwdriver. You grind off the tip so the edges are parallel and not bevelled. The tip then will fit snugly in the screw slot and not slip out and deform the slot as you exert twisting pressure. You can clean up a screwdriver tip, rather laboriously, by gripping the handle in a vise, and filing the tip crosswise. The better way is to hollow-grind the blade on the edge of a revolving grinding stone. Point the blade in the direction of wheel rotation, parallel to it, and tilted so about the first quarter inch touches the stone. If the tip has taken on a bevelled knife edge through use, as sometimes happens, place the tip flat against the revolving stone and grind it flat and blunt. The thickness of the edge should suit the thickness of the screw slot for which the driver is intended. This means you should have on hand three or four drivers with tips of varying thickness.

Time to root rose cuttings in the South. See October 29.

Have you filled feeders for the birds? Northern visitors are due.

December 2

Scale Insects on Your Trees and Shrubs?

Scale insects are one of the most widespread of plant pests. Wherever you live, a mild day at this time of the year can be chosen to check over the trees and shrubs on your property to see whether control measures should be planned within the next few months. Scales may not be present in sufficient numbers to justify spraying every year, but spraying should not be delayed until damage begins to show.

All scale insects are tiny. So look closely at the limbs and twigs, even using a hand lens if you have one. Most scales have a hard scale-like covering from which they get their name. At this time of year the armor probably will be guarding overwintering eggs.

See February 10 for control measures.

Has the gypsy moth appeared in your region? All possible help is needed in fighting it. Check your property now for egg clusters. They appear as buff-colored masses on tree trunks and stones. Destroy them by saturating with creosote diluted with kerosene.

Your Own Reminders

Week of Nov. 26–Dec. 2

December 3

Furnace Filters Need Replacing, Cleaning?

Air filters in forced-draft, warm-air furnaces clog up rapidly at this time of year. Throwaway filters demand replacement about once a month, and cleanable ones should be cleaned on the same schedule at the height of the heating season. If you have a warm-air heater, the once-a-month schedule suggests that your filters may be overdue now for attention. Dust-clogged filters make a noticeable reduction in heat output and force furnaces to work overtime.

Framed fiberglass filters usually have arrows on the edge to show which way to install them. A dust-catching adhesive is factory applied to one side of those filters, the side at the point of the arrows. Install the filter with the arrows pointing toward the heat exchanger. This permits cold air to enter the untreated face. Dust then is trapped by the adhesive on the exit side and gradually builds up through the thickness of the filter. A filter strip cut from a roll should be installed so that cold air enters the tinted side. Filters installed backwards clog up quickly and may last only half as long as they should.

If yours is a cleanable filter, better think now about tackling the job again in the recommended manner. Some home owners place a vacuum cleaner to the cold air side of throwaway filters and suck out the accumulated dust. But filter makers do not recommend the practice.

Make the final spading of ground you are preparing for a new flower bed next spring.

December 4

Prune Spring-Flowering Shrubs

You might very well start an argument with your neighbors by announcing that you intend to prune your spring-flowering shrubs now—during the dormant season. The neighbors could contend that the proper time is just after the shrubs have bloomed. Some horticulturists would agree.

But there are sound arguments for waiting until the dormant season. For that reason, the suggestion is made that you do the job now or at your convenience within the next eight weeks in the northern states. For good reasons why you should, listen to this from a bulletin issued by the Rutgers University Agricultural Experiment Station:

"The most beautiful form that most of our flowering shrubs can assume is the natural form. It is best maintained by following a renewal system of pruning, which is more easily and adequately performed during the winter. More time is available since no other garden operations demand immediate attention. With the foliage off the plant, it is possible to see the framework and make a better decision about what to leave and what to remove."

Your objective in shrub pruning should be

to encourage renewal growth from the base. Best way to do this is removal of the oldest canes to open up the center. This will admit light and air and encourage growth of new canes.

Take out dead, diseased, or weak wood first. Make your cuts as close to the ground as possible. Remove other live wood as necessary to open up the shrub. Choose the oldest trunks for removal first. Cut out any that rub others or that overhang and withhold sunshine from the plant as a whole. Don't hesitate to remove the weaker shoots of the previous year if you still haven't opened up the shrub. Cutting others back about a third will encourage side growth.

When the shrub has been opened up satisfactorily, consider whether top thinning is needed. If some stems project far beyond the others, you may prefer to remove them. If so, cut to a sound twig projecting outwards—or even back to the parent stem.

Not all spring-flowering shrubs need be pruned each year. Thinning out old wood every two or three years is about all you need to do to deutzia, exochorda, the shrub types of forsythia, kerria, kolkwitzia, physocarpus, philadelphus, stephandra, and weigelia.

Corrective thinning occasionally—no actual pruning—is enough for some shrubs. Among them: amelanchier, aronia, berberis, cydonia, cytisus, euonymus, lonicera, and viburnum.

December 5

Any Bagworms on Your Trees?

A leisurely stroll around your grounds on a mild day at this time of year can have a purpose. Examine all of your ornamental shrubs and trees for the presence of bagworms. As you stroll, look for the pointed cylindrical bags up to two inches long in which bagworm eggs overwinter. You may already have seen the bags and mistaken them for the cocoons of a moth. Pull off any that you find and burn them. If the bags are discarded on the ground, the eggs will hatch in the spring and the larvae may crawl back to the trees.

Bagworms occur in greatest numbers in the eastern half of the U.S. but only at scattered locations north of Pennsylvania, Indiana, Illinois, and Missouri. Arborvitae is a highly susceptible host, but the insect also may be found on maple, boxelder, sycamore, willow, black locust, cedars, junipers, elm, linden, poplars, oak, apple, cypress, spruce, wild cherry, sassafras, and persimmon. A heavy infestation can defoliate a tree. This can kill some evergreens.

December 6

Why Not Have an Electrical Fixit Day?

Plugs on electric lamp and appliance cords sometimes break, and the cords can become so damaged that they need replacement. If the lamp or appliance must remain in service, make the repairs without delay—for safety's sake. But if you are too rushed, at the

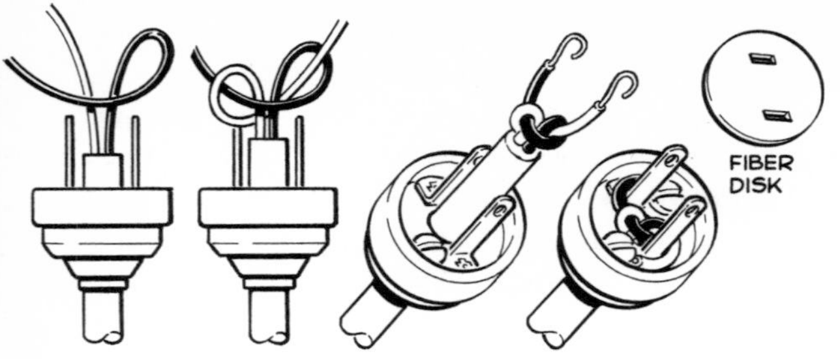

time, and have a substitute lamp or appliance, you may prefer to delay the repair and tackle several such accumulated chores on a single day.

You can buy some plugs with sharp prongs that automatically pierce the insulation and contact the two leads when you crimp the plug parts on the end of a cord. Restrict these, however, to light usage cords.

To replace a standard plug, remove the fiber protector disk from the plug cap and slip the plug cap over the end of the cord. Cut away 2½ inches of the outer covering (secondary insulation and fillers) from the cord end. Be careful not to cut the primary insulation. If the cord has a fabric covering, wind matching thread or tape around the covering to keep it from fraying.

Tie an underwriter's knot in the conductor. See the sketches. The purpose of the knot is to keep any pull on the cord from loosening the wires. If the size of cap and cord leaves no room for the knot, omit it. In this case remove only 1½ inches of the secondary insulation.

Remove the primary insulation from the last half inch of the wires. This bares just enough wire to go around the screw once without overlapping. Scrape the wires so they are bright and clean. Avoid breaking any of the fine wires. Twist each bundle of wires to the right tightly so that there are no loose ends.

Bend each conductor around a prong in a clockwise direction with the insulation covering the wires up to the screws. Fasten the wires under the screws in a clockwise direction. As the screws are tightened, the wires are tightened. Cut away excess material and replace the fiber protector disk.

December 7

> **Today in History:** A thermosetting plastic was patented on Dec. 7, 1906. It was named Bakelite after its developer, Dr. Leo Baekland.

Appliance Plug Need Replacing?

To replace an appliance plug, remove screws or clips to take the plug apart. (See sketches a and b.)

Push the spring or rubber cord-protector back on the cord. Loosen but do not remove the screws which hold the two conductor wires. Then remove the wires from the contact clamps or tubes.

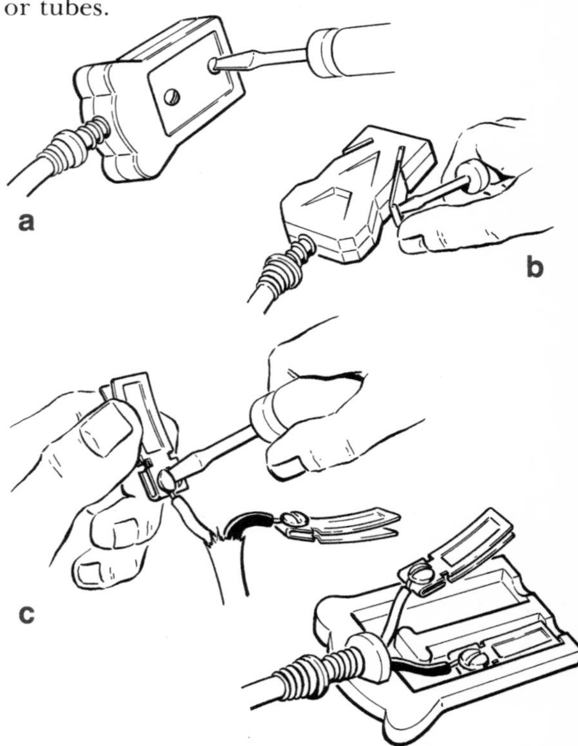

Cutting evenly across the two conductors, remove the ends of the cord to the point where the wires are covered with firm rubber insulation. If the cord is new, thread it through the cord protector and cut evenly across the two conductors.

Wrap electrical tape or thread around the cord about 2½ inches from the end to keep the outer covering from fraying. Remove ½ inch of asbestos insulation from the ends of the conductors and wrap the remaining asbestos with strong thread to keep it in place. Remove ½ inch of rubber insulation from the ends of each conductor, and check to see that the ends are cut across evenly.

Twist the wires firmly to the right and bend to form a hook. Fit the wires around the screws (sketch c) in a clockwise direction and be sure the conductors and the spring fit into the grooves. Fasten the screws firmly. Fit the plug parts together and replace the clips or screws. (Continued December 8.)

December 8

Today in History: Snow-melting pipe embedded in a sidewalk was first tested on Dec. 8, 1946 in New York City.

Electrical Cord Need Replacing?

To replace a lamp cord, disconnect the lamp from its outlet and remove shade, bulb, harp shade-holder, and bowl. Then separate the socket and remove the wires from the screws. (See sketch.)

Attach a new cord to the old cord. Then pull the new cord through the lamp and remove the old cord.

Slip the cap on the cord. On a fabric-covered cord, remove 1½ inches of the covering. With a molded conductor cord, split the two conductors apart for 1½ inches from the end. Be very careful not to cut into the wires. Tie an underwriter's or holding knot in the cord if there is room for it in the socket.

Remove ½ inch of insulation from the ends of the wires. Twist the fine wires tightly clockwise. Form hooks in ends of wires and attach to screws on body of socket.

Replace insulating shell and outer shell. Insert lamp bulb and check to see that it works.

Replacement cords for irons and other appliances are available from electrical-supply or mail-order houses. These have asbestos insulation, a rubber or plastic plug attached to one end, and two eyelets on the other end for attaching to screw terminals within the appliance. See sketch. For an iron, buy 16-gauge wire, not the smaller 18-gauge.

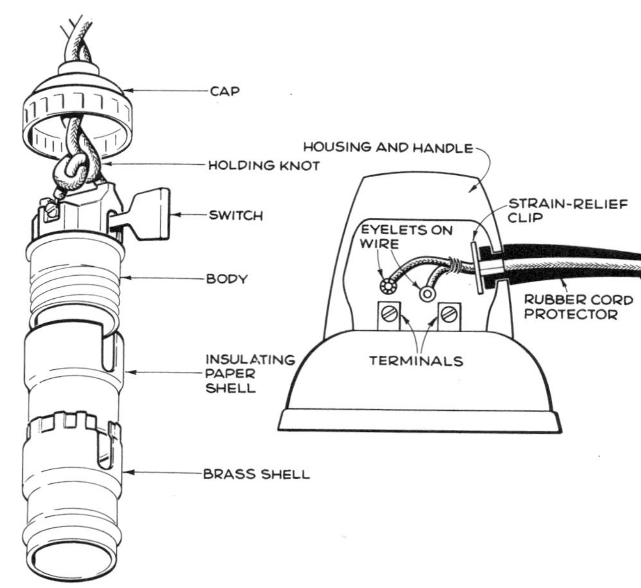

Getting at the terminals varies with the iron. On some, you must remove a cover plate or pry up the name plate. On others, the upper shell of the iron must be taken off. Unscrew the terminal screws to remove the old cord and attach the new one. On most irons, the cord is protected by a strain-relief clip. In reassembly, make sure you place it properly.

December 9

Taking Care of Electric Motors

Take time to make a list of the various electric motors throughout your home—and you may be surprised at how many you find. Some of these are permanently lubricated and need little or no attention, but there probably are others that would benefit from periodic maintenance.

Oiling is the main thing. For motors of less than one horsepower, use a light oil (SAE 10), for larger motors a slightly heavier oil (SAE 20).

Go through your home, room by room, and list every motor you find. Make a chart noting where the motor is located, the service required, the date serviced, and what was done. Some motors have instructions, especially about oiling, on the cover. If an instruction manual came with the appliance of which the motor is a part, the booklet may contain these facts.

Before working with any motor, be sure it is disconnected. Then wipe the case clean. If the motor has openings in the ends, use a vacuum cleaner to suck out dust and dirt.

If there are no instructions, remember that a very little oil goes a long way as far as motors are concerned. Motors of less than one horsepower require only three or four drops (not squirts) of oil every three or four months if the motor is used frequently. Too much oil can damage the insulation. Wipe away any excess.

If you find no oil holes, the motor probably has either sealed or greaseless bearings. Leave it alone, other than to wipe and vacuum it clean.

Today in History: Ball-bearing roller skates were patented on Dec. 9, 1884.

Christmas seals for fighting TB were first sold on Dec. 9, 1907 in Wilmington, Del.

Cleaning the kitchen fan is now probably overdue—if you follow a six-month schedule. Refer to July 21.

Kitchen paint will stay fresh longer if you leave a window slightly open to provide for ready escape for steam and moisture.

Your Own Reminders

Week of Dec. 3–9

Problem-Solving Window Shades

Window shades conventionally are mounted at the top of a rectangular window and drawn down when you want to shut out light or increase privacy. But why do it that way? Why not, for instance, mount the roller at the bottom of first-floor windows where the need for daytime privacy is constant? You then can pull the shades halfway up, have your privacy, and still have daylight coming into the room. In effect, the shade becomes a flexible cafe curtain.

Manufacturers now offer shades designed especially for bottom-up mounting. These have special brackets for sill or floor installations. Or some cords are clipped to the hem slat about three inches from each side of the shade. The cords rise to pulleys at the top of the window and then drop to a level convenient for handling. The shade is kept at the desired height by wrapping the cords around a cleat at the side of the window. Any standard shade fabric, room-darkening or translucent, can be used.

On standard windows, a bottom-up shade is sometimes used in addition to the regular shade at the top to create special decorative effects. For additional decorative interest, the shades are sometimes of contrasting colors. On a series of windows or a sectional picture window, a series of up-and-down shades of varied colors can create a dramatic geometric appearance—suggesting one of the famous paintings created by Piet Mondrian, the Dutch painter.

Bottom-up shades are a ready-made answer to light and privacy control in cathedral or other windows with slanted tops. The top hem can be cut to match the angle of the window top.

Window shades on rollers also can be installed in skylights. The cord is placed through a pulley at the end opposite the roller. Pulled taut, the cord keeps the shade flat against the skylight.

In some bottom-up installations, the shade is reversed so that the roller doesn't show from the room. This gives the shade a contemporary, scroll-like look.

December 10

Ready for a Power Failure?

Mid-winter is one of the most likely periods for storm-caused power failures. Are you prepared?

For emergency lighting, lay in a store of candles and/or flashlight batteries. You might also want to have kerosene on hand for lanterns and oil lamps.

A fireplace where you can burn wood or coal will help solve the heating and cooking problems. You will have no cooking problem, of course, if you have a gas range in the kitchen. Its oven will also help heat the room temporarily. For preparing light meals, you may also want to keep on hand a supply of canned heat, with camp-type cookers to use it in. A portable outdoor charcoal cooker may also come in handy. Use it in a ventilated area, however, not indoors.

When a power failure occurs, keep your refrigerator and freezer closed to prolong their available cooling capacity. To conserve heat in the home, open outside doors only when necessary and close shades and draperies. A power failure sometimes is a period of low voltage, when lamps glow only dimly. Low voltage can be damaging to electric motors. Therefore, it is a good idea to turn off such circuits until you are sure the emergency has passed.

When comparing prices of resilient floor tiles, be sure to consider the thickness. It should be marked on the container.

Do you get a tingling shock when you touch an electric lamp or any electric appliance? That's a sign it's unsafe; under certain conditions, the electricity could kill a member of your family. Take the lamp or appliance out of service until it can be repaired.

December 11

Today in History: A monument to the boll weevil was erected Dec. 11, 1919 by Alabama farmers. By forcing them to diversify their crops, the cotton-damaging insect soon tripled their income over the best cotton-producing year.

Frost Watch for Citrus

Better begin a frost watch now if you have a few citrus trees on your grounds. If you have only a few trees, throw a cover over them at night, remove it in the morning. On very cold nights, a lighted lantern or electric light under the cover will give needed warmth.

Many ground covers need winter protection in northern areas. After the soil freezes, probably in early December, cover semi-hardy types with a mulch such as salt hay.

December 12

Noises in Your Water Pipes?

The noise that sometimes occurs when you close a faucet is called water hammer. When you suddenly stop the water flow, its energy is expended against the piping walls. The pipes vibrate, and joints may loosen and cause leaks.

You can prevent water hammer or reduce its severity by installing an air chamber just ahead of the faucet. The air chamber can be a piece of air-filled pipe or tubing about two feet long, extending vertically from the pipe. Commercial devices designed to prevent air hammer also are available.

The air must be replenished occasionally in an air chamber, for it gradually fills with water. You can probably empty it and let in air by opening the faucet and then closing a shutoff valve beyond the air chamber. If this doesn't do it, locate a drain valve in the pipe and drain out the water.

December 13

Solving the Garbage-Can Problem

Keeping dogs and other animals from upsetting garbage cans is a problem for many people. Camouflaging the cans is another.

The illustration shows an effective way of safeguarding the cans. When you lift the hinged frame, the chain carries the lids along. You could set up this arrangement either at an outdoor site where cans are regularly stored or as part of an enclosure near the curbside pickup site.

If a fence fronts your property, you might combine this tie-down with a bit of camouflage—a short length of fence matching the regular fence and parallel to it. A fence section 40 inches long will take two cans. Place it 24 inches from the main fence, either in front or behind it. If you have no fence in front, consider planting a short hedge near the curb to hide your cans while they're awaiting pickup.

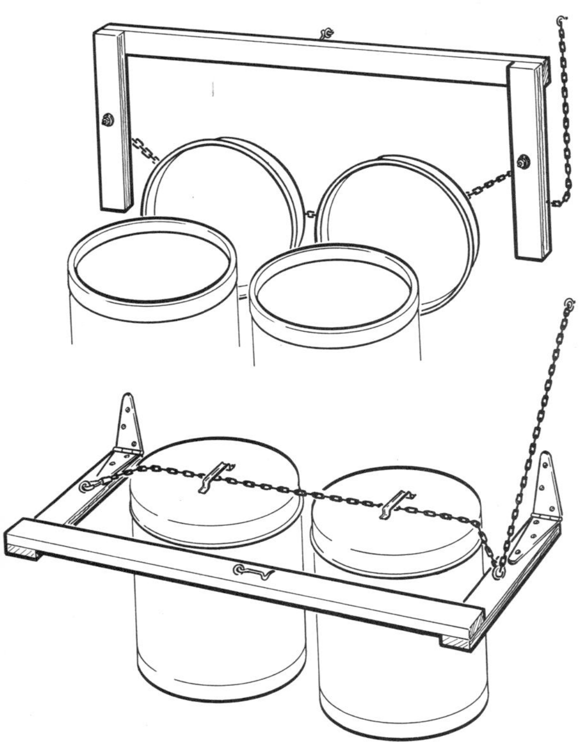

December 14

Cut Christmas Greens Now

There are two good reasons for pruning some of your evergreens at this time of year: 1, It benefits the plant in many cases; and 2, You can use the cuttings as holiday decorations.

American holly must be pruned regularly to avoid winding up with a spindly plant. Cut back the side shoots severely and you eventually will have dense growth. It is usually best, however, to leave the central leader unimpaired.

Today is not too early to cut such Christmas greens. In fact, you may find it better to do so in early December in the more northern states. Sometime during this month many evergreens begin to lose their freshness and take on drab and scraggly winter colors, often tinged with purple. Aim to cut them before they change.

You will find a difference of opinion about whether you should prune pines at this season. Some authorities caution not to do so. Reason: Long-needled evergreens, with needles in bundles of two, three, or five, cannot cover cuts made at this time of year. Pine buds are all located at the ends of the branches. Spruce, yew, holly, and most other evergreens have buds along the branches.

Shape your shrubs as you cut your greens but, except for holly, do not prune them too severely. Hide cuts by cutting just ahead of a small secondary branch. With a little practice, you will learn how to camouflage the cuts and shape the shrub at the same time. Removing branches at this time reduces the leaf surface exposed to drying winter winds. The shrub therefore will reach the growing period next spring in a healthier condition.

Store the cut greens with stems in a pail of water in the coolest part of your house. Every four or five days pour out the water, cut the stems back another inch or so, and immerse them again in fresh water. This treatment will greatly lengthen the useful life of the branches.

December 15

Today in History: The first ten amendments to the U. S. Constitution, known as the Bill of Rights, became effective on Dec. 15, 1791, after being ratified by three-fourths of the states.

Is Your Thermostat in the Right Spot?

The thermostat that controls the operation of your heating plant is sensitive only to temperature in its immediate vicinity. For that reason, its location is very important. Is it:

Too high or too low on the wall? You sacrifice efficiency if it is. Five feet above the floor is just about right for a comfortable temperature.

In a draft? Even if it's located in the current that normally comes down a stairway, it will call for more heat than a home needs. Also be sure that cold air from a frequently opened door doesn't strike it.

On an outside wall? If so, it will call for too much heat. An inside-wall location is always best. But be sure the adjoining room is heated. Even a cold inside wall would affect it.

Too near a source of heat? A radiator, register, range, fireplace, or even a lamp may cause the thermostat to turn off too soon. Because the house is cool, you'll keep turning up the heat, usually so much that heat will be wasted.

In the wrong room? For example, if you do most of your inactive sitting in a den, the living room is no place for the thermostat. The den is the room you want comfortable.

In good working order? A thermostat that lets temperature fall several degrees before calling for heat adds to fuel costs and detracts from comfort. A new one may be best. If the temperature setting on the thermostat face doesn't correspond with a thermometer, have it calibrated. Clean dust off the electrical contacts, but do not use sandpaper on them.

December 16

Choosing a Christmas Tree

Where and how do you get your Christmas tree? It is not too early to bring one home.

Why not consider selecting and cutting your own tree? Even on the fringes of urban areas you often have this opportunity. Make it a family excursion, a shared memory-building experience for the youngsters. The yellow pages of your telephone directory or the classified

section of your newspaper at this time of year will show you whether there are Christmas-tree farms within reasonable driving distance. Pack a picnic lunch and spend the day in the open. Take along a handsaw (or the pruning saw you should own anyway) and some strong cord to tie the tree to the car top if it won't go into the trunk.

Absolute freshness is a major practical advantage that you get out of cutting your own. Cut trees offered by stores and highway stands may have been harvested weeks ago. Take home the tree you have cut yourself, immerse its butt end in a pail of water, and you will keep it fresh all during the holiday season.

All types of firs, pines, hemlocks, and spruces are sometimes used as Christmas trees. Hemlocks and spruces are most prone to needle dropping and you may want to avoid them for that reason. Most of the pines will hold their needles longer.

Plant tulip bulbs now in southern and southwestern states. But remember that they won't grow well unless a period of dormancy has been simulated by keeping them at a temperature of 45 degrees for a month or six weeks.

Companion wallcover patterns are designed and colored to go together. Each is quite different from the other, and each can stand on its own merits. But each enhances the other when used in adjoining rooms.

Then copper wire strung on rustproof nails driven into the tops of shutters will discourage roosting by birds and will not be visible to passers-by.

Surplus electric cord may be concealed by hanging it on picture hooks attached to the back of the stereo or of a dressing table where a lamp is used.

Your Own Reminders

Week of Dec. 10–16

December 17

Plant Pecan Trees Soon

Plant pecan trees while they are in a dormant condition—from about December 15 to February 15. Trees planted as early as possible during this planting season will be well established, with lots of new roots, when spring growth begins. One or two trees are a fine addition to the home grounds. You get both shade and a supply of good nuts. Pecans are a suitable planting through the middle belt of the South. Winter chilling is necessary for good blossoming. For the best set of nuts, you should plant two or more trees, choosing varieties in which pollen shedding and stigma receptivity will coincide. Your county agent can tell you what varieties to plant.

December 18

Today in History: The Thirteenth Amendment to the U.S. Constitution became effective Dec. 18, 1865. It abolished slavery.

Why Rhododendron Leaves Curl Up

Don't be alarmed, at this time of the year, if you notice that leaves of a prize rhododendron have curled inward, almost forming a tube. This is normal reaction when temperatures are below freezing. Curling reduces the leaf surface exposed to drying winter winds and sun. The leaves uncurl as the temperature rises.

If evergreen leaves lose water faster than the plant roots can replenish it, the edges of the leaves will brown. The browning may cover the entire leaf if drought conditions continue for several weeks.

December 19

Today in History: Corrugated paper, patented on Dec. 19, 1871, later led to the development of corrugated cardboard shipping boxes.

Seed Bare Spots on Lawn

Are there bare spots in your lawn? Scattering seed over them at a time when snow is absent will usually give good results. Freezing and thawing will mix the seed into the soil and permit germination in early spring.

Control flower blight on camellias by beginning a spray program between December 15 and January 15 in those states where the disease has been discovered. Your extension service should have information about the procedure.

December 20

Renew Leggy Lilacs Now

A gardening chore, you might undertake at this season is renewal of lilacs that have become tall, lanky, and ungraceful. You can bring them down to the desired height by completely renewing the top. Spread the cutting over about three years. During the dormant period this winter cut down a third of the trunks to about a foot from the ground. Next winter do another third. When the shrub has been brought to a reasonable height, prune it properly each year as blossoms fade.

December 21

It's the Time of the Long Nights

The winter solstice comes at about this date and we say it marks the beginning of the season called winter.

Two solstices occur each year, one in June and one in December because the revolving earth tilts on its axis 23½ degrees as it moves around the sun. In winter, points in the Northern Hemisphere are farthest from the sun—and consequently colder.

Nights now are also the longest of the year—as long as the days are at the time of the summer solstice about June 21. The year now is at its darkest depths, and it's understandable that the ancients chose this period to revive their spirits by lighting bonfires on the hilltops. They also venerated evergreens in rites at this season as a symbol of their faith in enduring life—rites that still have a counterpart in some of our surviving Yuletide traditions.

Today in History: The first crossword puzzle appeared in the *New York World* on Dec. 21, 1913.

December 22

Prune Climbing Roses In Winter

Climbing roses may be pruned any time during the winter. But don't delay beyond very early spring. Cut out all of the oldest canes. Shorten others as desired. Except for a few ever-blooming varieties, climbing roses produce blossoms on wood of the previous season's growth.

Rambler roses may be pruned immediately after blossoming if you prefer.

Prune flowering crabapples now, during the dormant season.

Green peas and sweet and hot peppers can be planted now in the southern states for harvesting around March 1.

December 23

Rules for Holiday Safety

Keep in mind the extreme flammability of dry evergreens and take steps to avoid danger from that source. You can use fire-retardant chemicals, but keeping the evergreen stems or butts in water is still the most satisfactory method for reducing the fire hazard and needle fall.

Before you set up your tree, saw off the butt diagonally an inch or so above the original cut. Immersing the newly-slashed butt into water for a period as short as overnight will let the tree absorb some of the moisture it has lost since being taken from the forest, perhaps weeks ago. Give the same treatment to cut branches that you buy for decorative purposes. If these have been allowed to dry out, submerge them in

warm water for a couple of hours in the bathtub, washtub, or kitchen sink.

Mount a cut tree only in a holder that has a reservoir of ample size to hold a quart or more of water. Fill the reservoir at least once a day during the holiday season. Place your tree in a room that you can keep as cool as possible. Close or shut off any heat registers or radiators near

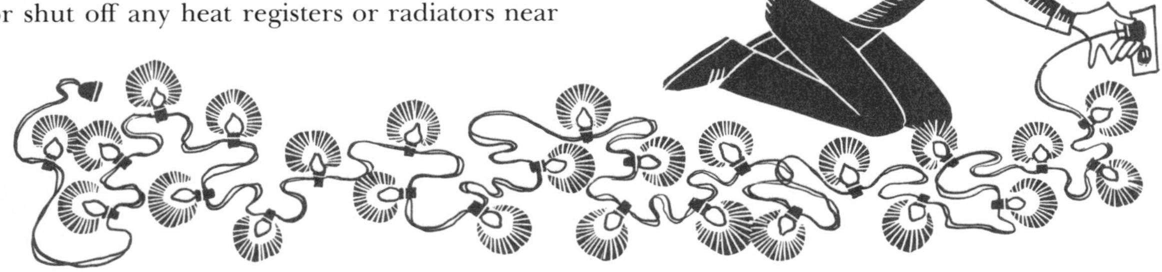

the tree. Keep it away from the fireplace, TV set, and hi fi set. Placing greenery on the mantle or around the fireplace may look lovely—but don't do it. Remember the fire hazard.

All living evergreens transpire moisture throughout the year—even in winter so you must feed plenty of water to a live Christmas tree. The burlap wrapped ball will keep the tree upright. Wrap the ball in a sheet of heavy polyethylene and pull the plastic up around the trunk. Or set the ball in a large metal or plastic wash tub, dish pan, or other large container and surround it with peat moss. Wet the ball and peat moss each day. If you wrap it in plastic, loosen the plastic from around the trunk and pour a quart or more of water over the root ball each day.

One final point about a live tree: Do not prune or otherwise damage the trunk leader at the top. If your decorations include a star or spire designed for slipping over the tip of the tree, wire it in place instead. Removing the tip might force your tree to develop a lower branch as the main trunk.

A Christmas tree bedecked with colorful ornaments and electric lights is a magical sight for any child. The lights also can be a great hazard. Each year, before you decorate the tree, take time to inspect the bulbs, sockets, and wires with great care. Check over the wires from end to end. Discard strings that show signs of breaks, wear, or deterioration. Why take the slightest chance of a dreadful electrical fire? Use strings that have individual fuses in the plugs. Keep a supply of the special fuses on hand. You twist the prongs of the male plug 90 degrees to replace a fuse.

Over the years Christmas tree lights have become relatively safe, but some are safer than others. Perhaps the least hazardous are the tiny bulbs that often are made in the shape of candles. These use less electricity and therefore burn at lower temperatures. But even so, when you place the lights—preferably in a fully sober moment—attach each bulb so it does not contact the surrounding needles or flammable decorations. Tinsel conducts electricity. For your family's safety, buy and use only products that carry a UL label. To avoid an electrical overload, use no more than ten strings of eight miniature lights (80 bulbs in all), no more than 50 regular indoor bulbs, or no more than 60 outdoor bulbs connected to a single household circuit. Never use indoor bulbs outdoors. They may not have the proper protection against rain and snow.

For safety, turn off your Christmas lights during sleeping hours and while you are absent from home.

Your Own Reminders

Week of Dec. 17–23

December 24

Where Did Santa Get His Name?

Only Americans apply this name to the roly-poly bringer of holiday gifts. In early New York, Dutch settlers called St. Nicholas *Sant Nicholaas*. When the prevailing language shifted to English, children had trouble pronouncing this name and gradually changed the spelling to what they pronounced—Santa Claus.

Try it yourself. Pronounce Sant Nicholaas aloud, varying the pronunciation until you elide the final syllables into what sounds very much like Claus.

Was St. Nicholas a mythical being? Not at all. He served as a Christian bishop in Asia Minor in the third century A.D. During his lifetime he became famous for gift giving and that reputation eventually spread to Christian nations throughout the world.

December 25

Let us pray that strength and courage abundant be given to all who work for a world of reason and understanding ❦ that the good that lies in every man's heart may day by day be magnified ❦ that men will come to see more clearly not that which divides them, but that which unites them ❦ that each hour may bring us closer to a final victory, not of nation over nation, but of man over his own evils and weaknesses ❦ that the true spirit of this Christmas Season— its joy, its beauty, its hope, and above all its abiding faith— may live among us ❦ that the blessings of peace be ours— the peace to build and grow, to live in harmony and sympathy with others, and to plan for the future with confidence.

NOTE: In recent years, thousands of persons have read these impressive words during the Christmas season in various magazines. The idea and wording for the prayer originated with officers of the New York Life Insurance Company and a copy writer for the company's advertising agency. It is reproduced here through courtesy of the New York Life Insurance Company. Copyright 1963.

December 26

Today in History: In England, this is Boxing Day, a second Christmas for tradesmen, servants, and public employees such as postmen. For years these people received gift boxes from those they served. Recently cash has usually been substituted.

A Sanctuary for the Birds

In the United States and Canada, this is an appropriate day for considering the welfare of one happy group of creatures that serve you well. The birds that visit your grounds each year make way with thousands of insects. It is a good day to consider what shrubs and trees you can plant to bring more and more birds to your neighborhood, turning your grounds into a real sanctuary. Many of the plantings that provide food and shelter for birds are ornamental as well.

You can get an informative folder from the Government Printing Office—"Conservation Plantings Invite Birds to Your Home." Also send off a note to Dutch Mt. Nursery, Augusta, Mich. 49012. Ask for price lists and folders describing berries, fruits, shrubs, and trees attractive to birds in your area. This firm specializes in such plantings and offers many that you would have difficulty locating elsewhere.

December 27

Protect Broad-Leaved Evergreens Now

Do you have azaleas, mountain laurel, or rhododendron growing between a paved walk and the house foundation? Is the exposure to the south?

These conditions are unfavorable for all the plants named because they may cause excessive loss of moisture and browning of leaves. Your first counter-measure would be to see that the plants have a chance to soak up adequate moisture during the fall and are well mulched with leaves or other organic material.

If you first become aware of the situation at this time of the year, provide a windbreak or sunshade—burlap on the sunny or windy side, or, if the shrubs are small, pile evergreen branches against them. Cut up and use your Christmas tree for this purpose when you take it down.

Eggplants can be planted now in some southern states.

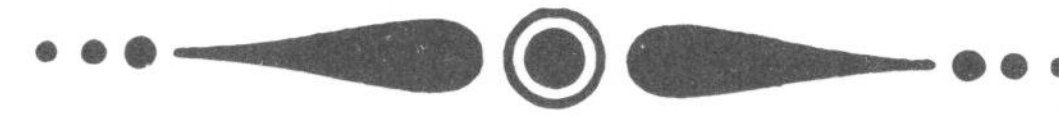

December 28

Beware of Ice Melters

Lawn areas and shrubs adjoining steps, walks, driveways, and streets may suffer from rock salt and ice-melting chemicals used at this season of the year. The salty runoff must go somewhere. An overdose of salt around roots may turn leaves or grass yellow next spring or even kill the plant.

Avoid use of such ice-melters as much as possible. Keep them from the lawn or shrubs when you can't. Instead of applying rock salt or chemicals, keep steps and walks safe with a thin coating of sand or fine gravel when ice forms. Sawdust or coal ashes are also excellent anti-skid stuff when available. Careless feet may carry any of these materials indoors, but sawdust or sand trails through the living room are easier to cure than salted grass.

Undersurfaces of a car may deposit highway and street chemicals on your driveway. From there, the salty runoff may find its way to the lawn. Have the car washed promptly when you have driven on salted roadways.

December 29

Plant Live Yule Tree Soon

In the northern states you already will have dug the hole—before freezing of the ground made digging virtually impossible. In states in the middle and southern belts you still can dig the hole.

Move the tree from the warm atmosphere of your home to a cool spot in basement or garage as soon as members of your family let you remove the decorations. Keep the ball well supplied with water.

When you are ready to plant, remove the covering you placed over the hole in the North (See October 18) to keep the soil from freezing. Loosen soil in the bottom. Bring the container of top soil from your storage spot and put in enough so that the tree is set at the same depth it grew in the nursery. Pour in a couple pails of water and let it drain away. Loosen the burlap from the trunk and remove it. Place the rest of the top soil around the tree and firm it with your foot. Then pile in the rest of your soil. Form a circular wall of soil outside the limb line of the tree. Pour in another pail or so of water. When it has disappeared, level off the soil dome and place several inches of straw mulch over the new earth. Water the tree every week or so during the first season unless you have an excess of rain.

As you put away Christmas ornaments, take the time to replace bulbs that have burned out. See if some need new fuses.

Today in history: The first major radio patent was obtained on Dec. 29, 1891 by Thomas A. Edison who claimed that "signalling between distant points can be carried on by induction without the use of wires connecting such distant points."

Four-wheel car brakes were patented on Dec. 29, 1908 by Otto Zachow and W. Besserdich, of Clintonville, Wis.

December 30

Keep a Home Diary?

Diary keeping nowadays may seem old-fashioned. That is true for conventional diaries. But what about a day-by-day record of important events in and around your home and grounds? After a few years, a home diary will become one of your most up-to-date helps in maintaining and enjoying your home and garden.

Inside the house, keep a dated record of every repair and improvement you make. Perhaps jot down there where you have stored the records and other costs of this particular home

improvement. Your home diary thus will become an important adjunct to your other home records. (See the entry for January 3.)

And don't forget those important (to you) events out in the yard and garden.

Keep a record of when prized shrubs or flowers come into bloom, when certain outdoor chores become necessary. A garden diary makes pleasant winter reading. Note the day you find the first crocus, the evening you hear the first "peepers," the dates of late spring frosts, and the first frost in the autumn. In a gardening neighborhood, your diary record in later years will keep you from responding to the competitive spirit and putting out spring plants too soon. The more years you keep a home diary, the more valuable it becomes.

The first day of the new year is the time to start it.

December 31

Today in History: The just-invented electric light was demonstrated by Thomas A. Edison in a public showing at Menlo Park, N.J., on New Year's Eve, 1879. The Pennsylvania Railroad ran special trains there. Edison received his patent the next month.

The New Year

"A flower unblown; a book unread;
A tree with fruit unharvested;
A path untrod; a house whose rooms
Lack yet the heart's divine perfumes;
A landscape whose wide border lies
In silent shade 'neath silent skies;
A wondrous fountain yet unsealed;
A casket with its gifts concealed—
This is the Year that for you waits
Beyond tomorrow's mystic gates."

—Horatio Nelson Powers (1826–1890)

"Ring out the old, ring in the new,
Ring happy bells, across the snow;
The year is going, let him go;
Ring out the false, ring in the new."

—Lord Tennyson

Resolutions for the New Year

Each year one vicious habit rooted out,
In time might make the worst man good throughout.

—Poor Richard

With the old Almanack and the old year,
Leave thy old Vices, tho' ever so dear.

—Poor Richard

Your Own Reminders

Week of Dec. 24–31

Appendix

APPENDIX A

WHAT LAWN GRASSES CAN YOU GROW?

Experts of the U.S. Department of Agriculture have found that the following grasses are suitable for lawns in the climatic regions outlined on this map:

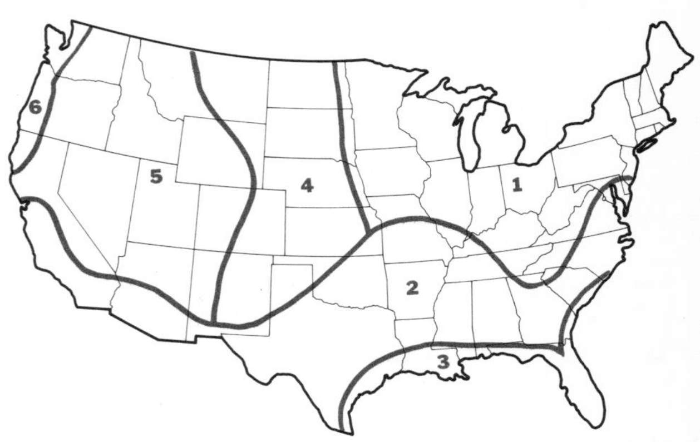

Region 1—Common Kentucky bluegrass, Merion Kentucky bluegrass, red fescue, and colonial bentgrass. In the southern part of the region, tall fescue, bermudagrass, and zoysia are suitable.

Region 2—Bermudagrass and zoysia. Centipedegrass, carpetgrass, and St. Augustine grass also are suitable in the southern part of the region, and tall fescue and Kentucky bluegrass in some northern areas.

Region 3—St. Augustinegrass, bermudagrass, zoysia, carpetgrass, and bahiagrass.

Region 4—In nonirrigated areas, crested wheatgrass, buffalograss, and blue gramagrass. In irrigated areas, Kentucky bluegrass and red fescue.

Region 5—In nonirrigated areas, crested wheatgrass. In irrigated areas, Kentucky bluegrass and red fescue.

Region 6— Colonial bentgrass and Kentucky bluegrass.

APPENDIX B

ZONES OF PLANT HARDINESS

Flowers, shrubs, and trees are often keyed to this hardiness map of North America developed by the U.S. Department of Agriculture. By referring to it, you can often determine whether a particular planting is suitable for your area.

The winter temperatures shown for each zone are based on average minimum temperatures taken from long-term weather records. The map is perhaps the most useful single guide to plant adaptability. However, other factors must be considered. Among these are soil type, rainfall, length of day, and summer temperatures.

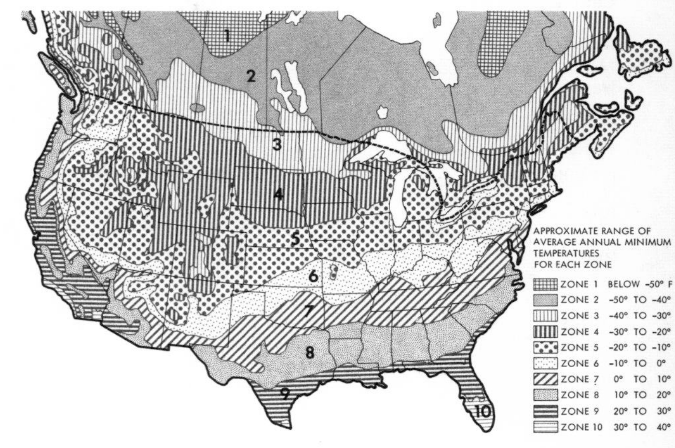

APPENDIX C

WHEN TO PLANT ANNUAL FLOWERS

Flower	Plant seed	Exposure	Germination time	Plant spacing	Remarks
			Days	*Inches*	
Ageratum	After last frost	Semishade or full sun.	5	10 to 12	Pinch tips of plants to encourage branching. Remove dead flowers.
Babysbreath	Early spring or in summer.	Sun	10	10 to 12	Make successive sowings for prolonged blooming period. Shade summer plantings.
Balsam	After last frost	.....do	10	12 to 14	
Calendula	Early spring or late fall.	Shade or sun	10	8 to 10	
Calliopsis	After last frost	.....do	8	10 to 14	
Candytuft	Early spring or late fall.	.....do	20	8 to 12	
China-aster	After last frost	.....do	8	10 to 12	For best plants start early, grow in cold-frame. Make successive sowings for prolonged bloom.
Cockscomb	.....do	.....do	10	10 to 12	
Coleus	Sow indoors anytime; outdoors after last frost.	Sun or partial shade.	10	10 to 12	
Cornflower	Early spring	Partial shade	5	12 to 14	
Cosmos	After last frost	Sun	5	10 to 12	
Dahlia	.....do	.....do	5	12 to 14	For maximum bloom, sow several weeks before other annuals.
Forget-me-not	Spring or summer; shade in summer.	Partial shade	10	10 to 12	
Four-o'clock	After last frost	Sun	5	12 to 14	Store roots, plant next year.
Gaillardia	Early spring through summer; shade in summer.	.....do	20	10 to 12	
Globe-amaranth	Early spring	.....do	15	10 to 12	
Impatiens	Indoors anytime. Set out after last frost.	Partial shade or deep shade.	15	10 to 12	
Larkspur	Late fall in South, early spring in North.	Sun	20	6 to 8	Difficult to transplant; grow in peat pots.
Lupine	Early spring or late fall	.....do	20	6 to 8	Soak seed before planting. Guard against damping-off.
Marigold	After last frost	.....do	5	10 to 14	High fertility delays bloom.
Morning-glory	.....do	.....do	5	24 to 36	Reseeds itself.
Nasturtium	.....do	.....do	8	8 to 12	For best flowers, grow in soil of low fertility.
Pansy	Spring or summer; shade in summer.	Sun or shade	10	6 to 8	Does best in cool season.
Petunia	Late fall (in South)	Sun	10	12 to 14	Start early in spring indoors. Keep cool.
Phlox	Early spring	.....do	10	6 to 8	Make successive plantings for prolonged bloom.
Pink	Early spring, spring or summer; shade in summer.	.....do	5	8 to 12	Start early in spring indoors. Keep cool. Remove dead flowers.
Poppy	Early spring through summer; shade in summer.	.....do	10	6 to 10	Difficult to transplant; start in peat pots. Make successive plantings.
Portulaca	After last frost or in late fall.	.....do	10	10 to 12	
Rudbeckia	Spring or summer; shade in summer.	Sun or partial shade.	20	10 to 14	Perennial grown as annual. Blooms first year.
Salpiglossis	Early spring	Sun	15	10 to 12	Needs supports. Avoid cold, heavy soil.

Flower	Plant seed	Exposure	Germination time	Plant spacing	Remarks
Scabiosa	Spring or summer; shade in summer.	.....do	10	12 to 14	Keep old flowers removed.
Scarlet sage	.....do	.....do	15	8 to 12	
Snapdragon	Spring or late fall	.....do	15	6 to 10	Start cool, pinch tips to encourage branching.
Spider plant	Early spring; spring, or fall.	.....do	10	12 to 14	Reseeds freely. Pinch to keep plant short. Water and fertilize freely.
Stock		.....do	5	6 to 10	
Strawflower	Early spring	.....do	5	10 to 12	
Summer-cypress	.....do	.....do	15	18 to 24	
Sunflower	After last frost	.....do	5	12 to 14	
Sweet alyssum	Early spring	.....do	5	10 to 12	Damps off easily. Sow in hills, do not thin.
Sweetpea	Early spring or late summer through late fall.	.....do	15	6 to 8	Select heat-resistant types.
Verbena	After last frost	.....do	20	18 to 24	Pinch tips often to encourage branching.
Vinca	.....do	.....do	15	10 to 12	Avoid overwatering.
Zinnia	.....do	.....do	5	8 to 12	Thin after plants begin to bloom; remove poor-flowering plants.

APPENDIX D

IMPORTANT FAMILY RECORDS AND DOCUMENTS

(Your name) ________________
Date
Revised ________________

Family Members

Name and address	Birth date	Relationship	Social Security Number

WHERE TO FIND IMPORTANT PAPERS

Paper	Where Kept	Paper	Where Kept
Adoption Papers		Income Tax Records	
Armed Forces Papers			
Auto Titles		Insurance Policies	
Bank Books		Important Receipts	
Birth Certificates		Keys, Important	
Burial Instructions		Marriage Records	
Cancelled Checks		Mortgage Papers	
Citizenship Papers		Mortgage Receipts	
Contracts		Passports	
Deeds to Property		Registration Papers	
Education Records		Safety Deposit Box	
Employment Records		Safety Deposit Keys	
Health Records (Vaccination, etc.)		Stock, Bond Certificates	
Household Inventory		Wills	

PEOPLE WHO CAN HELP IN AN EMERGENCY

	Name	Address	Phone Number
LAWYER			
EXECUTOR OF WILL			
BROKER			
GUARDIAN			
EMPLOYER			
INSURANCE AGENT			
CHURCH LEADER			

INSURANCE

Life, Health, Accident, Hospital, Income, Fire, Auto, Property, Compensation

Kind	Company Address to Contact	Name of Insured	Premium	Due Dates	Policy Number	Amount	Beneficiary

SAVINGS ACCOUNTS

Banks—Savings and Loan—Credit Union

Type of Account	Name and Address of Firm	Pass Book No.	In Whose Name(s)

INVESTMENTS

U.S. Savings Bonds

Serial Number	Purchase Price	Bond Number	Maturity Date	In Whose Name(s) and Beneficiary

Other Bonds

Name of Company or Municipality	Serial Number	Date Purchased	Purchase Price Per Bond	Maturity Date	Total Cost	In Whose Name(s)

Stocks, Mutual Funds

Company	Serial Number	Date of Purchase	No. of Shares	Cost Per Share	Total Cost	In Whose Name(s)

REAL ESTATE

Type	Location of Property	When and How Acquired	Price	Holder of Mortgage	Amount of Mortgage	Maturity Date	In Whose Name(s) and Kind of Ownership

WHAT WE OWE

Company or Person and Address	Description	Amount of Transaction	Size of Payments and Due Date	When Completed

WHAT OTHERS OWE US

Company or Person and Address	Description	Amount of Transaction	Size of Payments and Due Date	When Completed

BENEFITS AVAILABLE TO THE FAMILY

Social Security, Veterans, Lodges, Employment Pensions, Others

Type	Company or Person and Address	Enrollment Number	Information Needed to Make Claim	When Benefits Are Available	Settlement Option

OTHER FINANCIAL INFORMATION

APPENDIX E

EARLIEST DATES FOR SAFE SPRING PLANTING OF VEGETABLES

Crop	PLANTING DATES FOR LOCALITIES IN WHICH AVERAGE DATE OF LAST FREEZE IS—						
	Jan. 30	Feb. 8	Feb. 18	Feb. 28	Mar. 10	Mar. 20	Mar. 30
Asparagus[1]					Jan. 1–Mar. 1	Feb. 1–Mar. 10	Feb. 15–Mar. 20.
Beans, lima	Feb. 1–Apr. 15	Feb. 10–May 1	Mar. 1–May 1	Mar. 15–June 1	Mar. 20–June 1	Apr. 1–June 15	Apr. 15–June 20.
Beans, snap	Feb. 1–Apr. 1	Feb. 1–May 1	do	Mar. 10–May 15	Mar. 15–May 15	Mar. 15–May 25	Apr. 1–June 1.
Beet	Jan. 1–Mar. 15	Jan. 10–Mar. 15	Jan. 20–Apr. 1	Feb. 1–Apr. 15	Feb. 15–June 1	Feb. 15–May 15	Mar. 1–June 1.
Broccoli, sprouting[1]	Jan. 1–30	Jan. 1–30	Jan. 15–Feb. 15	Feb. 1–Mar. 1	Feb. 15–Mar. 15	Feb. 15–Mar. 15	Mar. 1–20.
Brussels sprouts[1]	do	do	do	do	do	do	Do.
Cabbage[1]	Jan. 1–15	Jan. 1–Feb. 10	Jan. 1–Feb. 25	Jan. 15–Feb. 25	Jan. 25–Mar. 1	Feb. 1–Mar. 1	Feb. 15–Mar. 10.
Cabbage, Chinese	(2)	(2)	(2)	(2)	(2)	(2)	(2)
Carrot	Jan. 1–Mar. 1	Jan. 1–Mar. 1	Jan. 15–Mar. 1	Feb. 1–Mar. 1	Feb. 10–Mar. 15	Feb. 15–Mar. 20	Mar. 1–Apr. 10.
Cauliflower[1]	Jan. 1–Feb. 1	Jan. 1–Feb. 1	Jan. 10–Feb. 10	Jan. 20–Feb. 20	Feb. 1–Mar. 1	Feb. 10–Mar. 10	Feb. 20–Mar. 20.
Celery and celeriac	do	Jan. 10–Feb. 10	Jan. 20–Feb. 20	Feb. 1–Mar. 1	Feb. 20–Mar. 20	Mar. 1–Apr. 1	Mar. 15–Apr. 15.
Chard	Jan. 1–Apr. 1	Jan. 10–Apr. 1	Jan. 20–Apr. 15	Feb. 1–May 1	Feb. 15–May 15	Feb. 20–May 15	Mar. 1–May 25.
Chervil and chives	Jan. 1–Feb. 1	Jan. 1–Feb. 1	Jan. 1–Feb. 1	Jan. 15–Feb. 15	Feb. 1–Mar. 1	Feb. 10–Mar. 10	Feb. 15–Mar. 15.
Chicory, witloof					June 1–July 1	June 1–July 1	June 1–July 1.
Collards[1]	Jan. 1–Feb. 15	Jan. 1–Feb. 15	Jan. 1–Mar. 15	Jan. 15–Mar. 15	Feb. 1–Apr. 1	Feb. 15–May 1	Mar. 1–June 1.
Cornsalad	do	do	do	Jan. 1–Mar. 1	Jan. 1–Mar. 15	Jan. 1–Mar. 15	Jan. 15–Mar. 15.
Corn, sweet	Feb. 1–Mar. 15	Feb. 10–Apr. 1	Feb. 20–Apr. 15	Mar. 1–Apr. 15	Mar. 10–Apr. 15	Mar. 15–May 1	Mar. 25–May 15.
Cress, upland	Jan. 1–Feb. 1	Jan. 1–Feb. 15	Jan. 15–Feb. 15	Feb. 1–Mar. 1	Feb. 10–Mar. 15	Feb. 20–Mar. 15	Mar. 1–Apr. 1.
Cucumber	Feb. 15–Mar. 15	Feb. 15–Apr. 1	Feb. 15–Apr. 15	Mar. 1–Apr. 15	Mar. 15–Apr. 15	Apr. 1–May 1	Apr. 10–May 15.
Dandelion	Jan. 1–Feb. 1	Jan. 1–Feb. 1	Jan. 15–Feb. 15	Jan. 15–Mar. 1	Feb. 1–Mar. 1	Feb. 10–Mar. 10	Feb. 20–Mar. 20.
Eggplant[1]	Feb. 1–Mar. 1	Feb. 10–Mar. 15	Feb. 20–Apr. 1	Mar. 10–Apr. 15	Mar. 15–Apr. 15	Apr. 1–May 1	Apr. 15–May 15.
Endive	Jan. 1–Mar. 1	Jan. 1–Mar. 1	Jan. 15–Mar. 1	Feb. 1–Mar. 1	Feb. 15–Mar. 15	Mar. 1–Apr. 1	Mar. 10–Apr. 10.
Fennel, Florence	do	do	do	do	do	do	Do.
Garlic	(2)	(2)	(2)	(2)	(2)	Feb. 1–Mar. 1	Feb. 10–Mar. 10.
Horseradish[1]							Mar. 1–Apr. 1.
Kale	Jan. 1–Feb. 1	Jan. 10–Feb. 1	Jan. 20–Feb. 10	Feb. 1–20	Feb. 10–Mar. 1	Feb. 20–Mar. 10	Mar. 1–20.
Kohlrabi	do	do	do	do	do	do	Mar. 1–Apr. 1.
Leek	do	Jan. 1–Feb. 1	Jan. 1–Feb. 15	Jan. 15–Feb. 15	Jan. 25–Mar. 1	Feb. 1–Mar. 1	Feb. 15–Mar. 15.
Lettuce, head[1]	do	do	Jan. 1–Feb. 1	do	Feb. 1–20	Feb. 15–Mar. 10	Mar. 1–20.
Lettuce, leaf	do	do	Jan. 1–Mar. 15	Jan. 1–Mar. 15	Jan. 15–Apr. 1	Feb. 1–Apr. 1	Feb. 15–Apr. 15.
Muskmelon	Feb. 15–Mar. 15	Feb. 15–Apr. 1	Feb. 15–Apr. 15	Mar. 1–Apr. 15	Mar. 15–Apr. 15	Apr. 1–May 1	Apr. 10–May 15.
Mustard	Jan. 1–Mar. 1	Jan. 1–Mar. 1	do	Feb. 1–Mar. 1	Feb. 10–Mar. 15	Feb. 20–Apr. 1	Mar. 1–Apr. 15.
Okra	Feb. 15–Apr. 1	Feb. 15–Apr. 15	Mar. 1–June 1	Mar. 10–June 1	Mar. 20–June 1	Apr. 1–June 15	Apr. 10–June 15.
Onion[1]	Jan. 1–15	Jan. 1–15	Jan. 1–15	Jan. 1–Feb. 1	Jan. 15–Feb. 15	Feb. 10–Mar. 10	Feb. 15–Mar. 15.
Onion, seed	do	do	do	Jan. 1–Feb. 15	Feb. 1–Mar. 1	do	Feb. 20–Mar. 15.
Onion, sets	do	do	do	Jan. 1–Mar. 1	Jan. 15–Mar. 10	Feb. 1–Mar. 20	Feb. 15–Mar. 20.
Parsley	Jan. 1–30	Jan. 1–30	Jan. 1–30	Jan. 15–Mar. 1	Feb. 1–Mar. 10	Feb. 15–Mar. 15	Mar. 1–Apr. 1.
Parsnip			Jan. 1–Feb. 1	Jan. 15–Feb. 15	Jan. 15–Mar. 1	do	Do.
Peas, garden	Jan. 1–Feb. 15	Jan. 1–Feb. 15	Jan. 1–Mar. 1	Jan. 15–Mar. 1	Jan. 15–Mar. 15	Feb. 1–Mar. 15	Feb. 10–Mar. 20.
Peas, black-eye	Feb. 15–May 1	Feb. 15–May 15	Mar. 1–June 15	Mar. 10–June 20	Mar. 15–July 1	Apr. 1–July 1	Apr. 15–July 1.
Pepper[1]	Feb. 1–Apr. 1	Feb. 15–Apr. 15	Mar. 1–May 1	Mar. 15–May 1	Apr. 1–June 1	Apr. 10–June 1	Apr. 15–June 1.
Potato	Jan. 1–Feb. 15	Jan. 1–Feb. 15	Jan. 15–Mar. 1	Jan. 15–Mar. 1	Feb. 1–Mar. 1	Feb. 10–Mar. 15	Feb. 20–Mar. 20.
Radish	Jan. 1–Apr. 1	Jan. 1–Apr. 1	Jan. 1–Apr. 1	Jan. 1–Apr. 1	Jan. 1–Apr. 15	Jan. 20–May 1	Feb. 15–May 1.
Rhubarb[1]							
Rutabaga				Jan. 1–Feb. 1	Jan. 15–Feb. 15	Jan. 15–Mar. 1	Feb. 1–Mar. 1.
Salsify	Jan. 1–Feb. 1	Jan. 10–Feb. 10	Jan. 15–Feb. 20	Jan. 15–Mar. 1	Feb. 1–Mar. 1	Feb. 15–Mar. 1	Mar. 1–15.
Shallot	do	Jan. 1–Feb. 10	Jan. 1–Feb. 20	Jan. 1–Mar. 1	Jan. 15–Mar. 1	Feb. 1–Mar. 10	Feb. 15–Mar. 15.
Sorrel	Jan. 1–Mar. 1	Jan. 1–Mar. 1	Jan. 15–Mar. 1	Feb. 1–Mar. 10	Feb. 10–Mar. 15	Feb. 10–Mar. 20	Feb. 20–Apr. 1.
Soybean	Mar. 1–June 30	Mar. 1–June 30	Mar. 10–June 30	Mar. 20–June 30	Apr. 10–June 30	Apr. 10–June 30	Apr. 20–June 30.
Spinach	Jan. 1–Feb. 15	Jan. 1–Feb. 15	Jan. 1–Mar. 1	Jan. 1–Mar. 1	Jan. 15–Mar. 10	Jan. 15–Mar. 15	Feb. 1–Mar. 20.
Spinach, New Zealand	Feb. 1–Apr. 15	Feb. 15–Apr. 15	Mar. 1–Apr. 15	Mar. 15–May 15	Mar. 20–May 15	Apr. 1–May 15	Apr. 10–June 1.
Squash, summer	do	do	do	do	Mar. 15–May 1	do	Do.
Sweetpotato	Feb. 15–May 15	Mar. 1–May 15	Mar. 20–June 1	Mar. 20–June 1	Apr. 1–June 1	Apr. 10–June 1	Apr. 20–June 1.
Tomato	Feb. 1–Apr. 1	Feb. 20–Apr. 10	Mar. 1–Apr. 20	Mar. 10–May 1	Mar. 20–May 10	Apr. 1–May 20	Apr. 10–June 1.
Turnip	Jan. 1–Mar. 1	Jan. 1–Mar. 1	Jan. 10–Mar. 1	Jan. 20–Mar. 1	Feb. 1–Mar. 1	Feb. 10–Mar. 10	Feb. 20–Mar. 20.
Watermelon	Feb. 15–Mar. 15	Feb. 15–Apr. 1	Feb. 15–Apr. 15	Mar. 1–Apr. 15	Mar. 15–Apr. 15	Apr. 1–May 1	Apr. 10–May 15.

[1] Plants.

[2] Generally fall-planted (See Appendix B)

Crop	PLANTING DATES FOR LOCALITIES IN WHICH AVERAGE DATE OF LAST FREEZE IS—						
	Apr. 10	Apr. 20	Apr. 30	May 10	May 20	May 30	June 10
Asparagus[1]	Mar. 10–Apr. 10	Mar. 15–Apr. 15	Mar. 20–Apr. 15	Apr. 10–Apr. 30	Apr. 20–May 15	May 1–June 1	May 15–June 1.
Beans, lima	Apr. 1–June 30	May 1–June 20	May 15–June 15	May 25–June 15			
Beans, snap	Apr. 10–June 30	Apr. 25–June 30	May 10–June 30	May 10–June 30	May 15–June 30	May 25–June 15	
Beet	Mar. 10–June 1	Mar. 20–June 1	Apr. 1–June 15	Apr. 15–June 15	Apr. 25–June 15	May 1–June 15	May 15–June 15.
Beans, snap	Apr. 10–June 30	Apr. 25–June 30	May 10–June 30	May 10–June 30	May 15–June 30	May 25–June 15	
Beet	Mar. 10–June 1	Mar. 20–June 1	Apr. 1–June 15	Apr. 15–June 15	Apr. 25–June 15	May 1–June 15	May 15–June 15.
Broccoli, sprouting[1]	Mar. 15–Apr. 15	Mar. 25–Apr. 20	Apr. 1–May 1	Apr. 15–June 1	May 1–June 15	May 10–June 10	May 20–June 10.
Brussels sprouts[1]	do	do	do	do	do	do	Do.
Cabbage[1]	Mar. 1–Apr. 1	Mar. 10–Apr. 1	Mar. 15–Apr. 10	Apr. 1–May 15	do	May 10–June 15	May 20–June 1.
Cabbage, Chinese	(2)	(2)	(2)	do	do	do	Do.
Carrot	Mar. 10–Apr. 20	Apr. 1–May 15	Apr. 10–June 1	Apr. 20–June 15	May 1–June 1	May 10–June 1	Do.
Cauliflower[1]	Mar. 1–Mar. 20	Mar. 15–Apr. 20	Apr. 10–May 10	Apr. 15–May 15	May 10–June 15	May 20–June 1	June 1–June 15.
Celery and celeriac	Apr. 1–Apr. 20	Apr. 10–May 1	Apr. 15–May 1	Apr. 20–June 15	do	do	Do.
Chard	Mar. 15–June 15	Apr. 1–June 15	Apr. 15–June 15	do	do	do	Do.
Chervil and chives	Mar. 1–Apr. 1	Mar. 10–Apr. 10	Mar. 20–Apr. 20	Apr. 1–May 1	Apr. 15–May 15	May 1–June 1	May 15–June 1.
Chicory, witloof	June 10–July 1	June 15–July 1	June 15–July 1	June 1–20	June 1–15	June 1–15	June 1–15.
Collards[1]	Mar. 1–June 1	Mar. 10–June 1	Apr. 1–June 1	Apr. 15–June 1	May 1–June 1	May 10–June 1	May 20–June 1.
Cornsalad	Feb. 1–Apr. 1	Feb. 15–Apr. 15	Mar. 1–May 1	Apr. 1–June 1	Apr. 15–June 1	May 1–June 15	May 15–June 15.
Corn, sweet	Apr. 10–June 1	Apr. 25–June 15	May 10–June 15	May 10–June 1	May 15–June 1	May 20–June 1	
Cress, upland	Mar. 10–Apr. 15	Mar. 20–May 1	Apr. 10–May 10	Apr. 20–May 20	May 1–June 1	May 15–June 1	May 15–June 15.
Cucumber	Apr. 20–June 1	May 1–June 15	May 15–June 15	May 20–June 15	June 1–15		
Dandelion	Mar. 1–Apr. 1	Mar. 10–Apr. 10	Mar. 20–Apr. 20	Apr. 1–May 1	Apr. 15–May 15	May 1–30	May 1–30.
Eggplant[1]	May 1–June 1	May 10–June 1	May 15–June 10	May 20–June 15	June 1–15		
Endive	Mar. 15–Apr. 15	Mar. 25–Apr. 15	Apr. 1–May 1	Apr. 15–May 15	May 1–30	May 1–30	May 15–June 1.
Fennel, Florence	do	do	do	do	do	do	Do.
Garlic	Feb. 20–Mar. 20	Mar. 10–Apr. 1	Mar. 15–Apr. 15	Apr. 1–May 1	Apr. 15–May 15	do	Do.
Horseradish[1]	Mar. 10–Apr. 10	Mar. 20–Apr. 20	Apr. 1–30	Apr. 15–May 15	Apr. 20–May 20	do	Do.
Kale	Mar. 10–Apr. 1	Mar. 20–Apr. 10	Apr. 1–20	Apr. 10–May 1	Apr. 20–May 10	do	Do.
Kohlrabi	Mar. 10–Apr. 10	Mar. 20–May 1	Apr. 1–May 10	Apr. 10–May 15	Apr. 20–May 20	do	Do.
Leek	Mar. 1–Apr. 1	Mar. 15–Apr. 15	Apr. 1–May 1	Apr. 15–May 15	May 1–May 20	May 1–15	May 1–15.
Lettuce, head[1]	Mar. 10–Apr. 1	Mar. 20–Apr. 15	do	do	May 1–June 30	May 10–June 30	May 20–June 30.
Lettuce, leaf	Mar. 15–May 15	Mar. 20–May 15	Apr. 1–June 1	Apr. 15–June 15	do	do	Do.
Muskmelon	Apr. 20–June 1	May 1–June 15	May 15–June 15	June 1–June 15			
Mustard	Mar. 10–Apr. 20	Mar. 20–May 1	Apr. 1–May 10	Apr. 15–June 1	May 1–June 30	May 10–June 30	May 20–June 30.
Okra	Apr. 20–June 15	May 1–June 1	May 10–June 1	May 20–June 10	June 1–20		
Onion[1]	Mar. 1–Apr. 1	Mar. 15–Apr. 10	Apr. 1–May 1	Apr. 10–May 1	Apr. 20–May 15	May 1–30	May 10–June 10.
Onion, seed	do	Mar. 15–Apr. 1	Mar. 15–Apr. 15	Apr. 1–May 1	do	do	Do.
Onion, sets	do	Mar. 10–Apr. 1	Mar. 10–Apr. 10	Apr. 10–May 1	do	do	Do.
Parsley	Mar. 10–Apr. 10	Mar. 20–Apr. 20	Apr. 1–May 1	Apr. 15–May 15	May 1–20	May 10–June 1	May 20–June 10.
Parsnip	do	do	do	do	do	do	Do.
Peas, garden	Feb. 20–Mar. 20	Mar. 10–Apr. 10	Mar. 20–May 1	Apr. 1–May 15	Apr. 15–June 1	May 1–June 15	May 10–June 15.
Peas, black-eye	May 1–July 1	May 10–June 15	May 15–June 1				
Pepper[1]	May 1–June 1	May 10–June 1	May 15–June 10	May 20–June 10	May 25–June 15	June 1–15	
Potato	Mar. 10–Apr. 1	Mar. 15–Apr. 10	Mar. 20–May 10	Apr. 1–June 1	Apr. 15–June 15	May 1–June 15	May 15–June 1.
Radish	Mar. 1–May 1	Mar. 10–May 10	do	do	do	do	Do.
Rhubarb[1]	Mar. 1–Apr. 1	Mar. 10–Apr. 10	Mar. 20–Apr. 15	Apr. 1–May 1	Apr. 15–May 10	May 1–20	Do.
Rutabaga			May 1–June 1	May 1–June 1	May 1–20	May 10–20	May 20–June 1.
Salsify	Mar. 10–Apr. 15	Mar. 20–May 1	Apr. 1–May 15	Apr. 15–June 1	May 1–June 1	May 10–June 1	Do.
Shallot	Mar. 1–Apr. 1	Mar. 15–Apr. 15	Apr. 1–May 1	Apr. 10–May 1	Apr. 20–May 10	May 1–June 1	May 10–June 1.
Sorrel	Mar. 1–Apr. 15	Mar. 15–May 1	Apr. 1–May 15	Apr. 15–June 1	May 1–June 1	May 10–June 10	May 20–June 10.
Soybean	May 1–June 30	May 10–June 20	May 15–June 15	May 25–June 10			
Spinach	Feb. 15–Apr. 1	Mar. 1–Apr. 15	Mar. 20–Apr. 20	Apr. 1–June 15	Apr. 10–June 15	Apr. 20–June 15	May 1–June 15.
Spinach, New Zealand	Apr. 20–June 1	May 1–June 15	May 1–June 15	May 10–June 15	May 20–June 15	June 1–15	
Squash, summer	do	do	May 1–30	May 10–June 10	do	June 1–20	June 10–20.
Sweetpotato	May 1–June 1	May 10–June 10	May 20–June 10				
Tomato	Apr. 20–June 1	May 5–June 10	May 10–June 15	May 15–June 10	May 25–June 15	June 5–20	June 15–30.
Turnip	Mar. 1–Apr. 1	Mar. 10–Apr. 1	Mar. 20–May 1	Apr. 1–June 1	Apr. 15–June 1	May 1–June 15	May 15–June 15.
Watermelon	Apr. 20–June 1	May 1–June 15	May 15–June 15	June 1–June 15	June 15–July 1		

APPENDIX F

LATEST DATES FOR SAFE FALL PLANTING OF VEGETABLES

Crop	PLANTING DATES FOR LOCALITIES IN WHICH AVERAGE DATE OF FIRST FREEZE IS—					
	Aug. 30	Sept. 10	Sept. 20	Sept. 30	Oct. 10	Oct. 20
Asparagus[1]					Oct. 20–Nov. 15	Nov. 1–Dec. 15.
Beans, lima				June 1–15	June 1–15	June 15–30.
Bean, snap		May 15–June 15	June 1–July 1	June 1–July 10	June 15–July 20	July 1–Aug. 1.
Beet	May 15–June 15	do	do	do	June 15–July 25	July 1–Aug. 5.
Broccoli, sprouting	May 1–June 1	May 1–June 1	May 1–June 15	June 1–30	June 15–July 15	July 1–Aug. 1.
Brussels sprouts	do	do	do	do	do	Do.
Cabbage[1]	do	do	do	June 1–July 10	June 1–July 15	July 1–20.
Cabbage, Chinese	May 15–June 15	May 15–June 15	June 1–July 1	June 1–July 15	June 15–Aug. 1	July 15–Aug. 15.
Carrot	do	do	do	June 1–July 10	June 1–July 20	June 15–Aug. 1.
Cauliflower[1]	May 1–June 1	May 1–July 1	May 1–July 1	May 10–July 15	June 1–July 25	July 1–Aug. 5.
Celery[1] and celeriac	do	May 15–June 15	May 15–July 1	June 1–July 5	June 1–July 15	June 1–Aug. 1.
Chard	May 15–June 15	May 15–July 1	June 1–July 1	do	June 1–July 20	Do.
Chervil and chives	May 10–June 10	May 1–June 15	May 15–June 15	(2)	(2)	(2)
Chicory, witloof	May 15–June 15	May 15–June 15	do	June–July 1	June 1–July 1	June 15–July 15.
Collards[1]	do	do	do	June 15–July 15	July 1–Aug. 1	July 15–Aug. 15
Cornsalad	do	May 15–July 1	June 15–Aug. 1	July 15–Sept. 1	Aug. 15–Sept. 15	Sept. 1–Oct. 15.
Corn, sweet			June 1–July 1	June 1–July 1	June 1–July 10	June 1–July 20.
Cress, upland	May 15–June 15	May 15–July 1	June 15–Aug. 1	July 15–Sept. 1	Aug. 15–Sept. 15	Sept. 1–Oct. 15.
Cucumber			June 1–15	June 1–July 1	June 1–July 1	June 1–July 15.
Dandelion	June 1–15	June 1–July 1	June 1–July 1	June 1–Aug. 1	July 15–Sept. 1	Aug. 1–Sept. 15.
Eggplant[1]				May 20–June 10	May 15–June 15	June 1–July 1.
Endive	June 1–July 1	June 1–July 1	June 15–July 15	June 15–Aug. 1	July 1–Aug. 15	July 15–Sept. 1.
Fennel, Florence	May 15–June 15	May 15–July 15	June 1–July 1	June 1–July 1	June 15–July 15	June 15–Aug. 1.
Garlic	(2)	(2)	(2)	(2)	(2)	(2)
Horseradish[1]	(2)	(2)	(2)	(2)	(2)	(2)
Kale	May 15–June 15	May 15–June 15	June 1–July 1	June 15–July 15	July 1–Aug. 1	July 15–Aug. 15.
Kohlrabi	do	June 1–July 1	June 1–July 15	do	do	Do.
Leek	May 1–June 1	May 1–June 1	(2)	(2)	(2)	(2)
Lettuce, head[1]	May 15–July 1	May 15–July 1	June 1–July 15	June 15–Aug. 1	July 15–Aug. 15	Aug. 1–30.
Lettuce, leaf	May 15–July 15	May 15–July 15	June 1–Aug. 1	June 1–Aug. 1	July 15–Sept. 1	July 15–Sept. 1.
Muskmelon			May 1–June 15	May 15–June 1	June 1–June 15	June 15–July 20.
Mustard	May 15–July 15	May 15–July 15	June 1–Aug. 1	June 15–Aug. 1	July 15–Aug. 15	Aug. 1–Sept. 1.
Okra			June 1–20	June 1–July 1	June 1–July 15	June 1–Aug. 1.
Onion[1]	May 1–June 10	May 1–June 10	(2)	(2)	(2)	(2)
Onion, seed	May 1–June 1	do	(2)	(2)	(2)	(2)
Onion, sets	do	do	(2)	(2)	(2)	(2)
Parsley	May 15–June 15	May 1–June 15	June 1–July 1	June 1–July 15	June 15–Aug. 1	July 15–Aug. 15.
Parsnip	May 15–June 1	do	May 15–June 15	June 1–July 1	June 1–July 10	(2)
Peas, garden	May 10–June 15	May 1–July 1	June 1–July 15	June 1–Aug. 1	(2)	(2)
Peas, black-eye					June 1–July 1	June 1–July 1.
Pepper[1]			June 1–June 20	June 1–July 1	do	June 1–July 10.
Potato	May 15–June 1	May 1–June 15	May 1–June 15	May 1–June 15	May 15–June 15	June 15–July 15.
Radish	May 1–July 15	May 1–Aug. 1	June 1–Aug. 15	July 1–Sept. 1	July 15–Sept. 15	Aug. 1–Oct. 1.
Rhubarb[1]	Sept. 1–Oct. 1	Sept. 15–Oct. 15	Sept. 15–Nov. 1	Oct. 1–Nov. 1	Oct. 15–Nov. 15	Oct. 15–Dec. 1.
Rutabaga	May 15–June 15	May 1–June 15	June 1–July 1	June 1–July 1	June 15–July 15	July 10–20.
Salsify	May 15–June 1	May 10–June 10	May 20–June 20	June 1–20	June 1–July 1	June 1–July 1.
Shallot	(2)	(2)	(2)	(2)	(2)	(2)
Sorrel	May 15–June 15	May 1–June 15	June 1–July 1	June 1–July 15	July 1–Aug. 1	July 15–Aug. 15.
Soybean				May 25–June 10	June 1–25	June 1–July 5.
Spinach	May 15–July 1	June 1–July 15	June 1–Aug. 1	July 1–Aug. 15	Aug. 1–Sept. 1	Aug. 20–Sept. 10
Spinach, New Zealand				May 15–July 1	June 1–July 15	June 1–Aug. 1.
Squash, summer	June 10–20	June 1–20	May 15–July 1	June 1–July 1	do	June 1–July 20.
Squash, winter			May 20–June 10	June 1–15	June 1–July 1	June 1–July 1.
Sweetpotato					May 20–June 10	June 1–15.
Tomato	June 20–30	June 10–20	June 1–20	June 1–20	June 1–20	June 1–July 1.
Turnip	May 15–June 15	June 1–July 1	June 1–July 15	June 1–Aug. 1	July 1–Aug. 1	July 15–Aug. 15.
Watermelon			May 1–June 15	May 15–June 1	June 1–June 15	June 15–July 20.

[1] Plants.

[2] Generally spring-planted (See Appendix A)

APPENDIX F *(continued)*

Crop	PLANTING DATES FOR LOCALITIES IN WHICH AVERAGE DATE OF FIRST FREEZE IS—					
	Oct. 30	**Nov. 10**	**Nov. 20**	**Nov. 30**	**Dec. 10**	**Dec. 20**
Asparagus[1]	Nov. 15–Jan. 1	Dec. 1–Jan. 1				
Beans, lima	July 1–Aug. 1	July 1–Aug. 15	July 15–Sept. 1	Aug. 1–Sept. 15	Sept. 1–30	Sept. 1–Oct. 1.
Beans, snap	July 1–Aug. 15	July 1–Sept. 1	July 1–Sept. 10	Aug. 15–Sept. 20	do	Sept. 1–Nov. 1.
Beet	Aug. 1–Sept. 1	Aug. 1–Oct. 1	Sept. 1–Dec. 1	Sept. 1–Dec. 15	Sept. 1–Dec. 31	Sept. 1–Dec. 31.
Broccoli, sprouting	July 1–Aug. 15	Aug. 1–Sept. 1	Aug. 1–Sept. 15	Aug. 1–Oct. 1	Aug. 1–Nov. 1	Do.
Brussels sprouts	do	do	do	do	do	Do.
Cabbage[1]	Aug. 1–Sept. 1	Sept. 1–15	Sept. 1–Dec. 1	Sept. 1–Dec. 31	Sept. 1–Dec. 31	Do.
Cabbage, Chinese	Aug. 1–Sept. 15	Aug. 15–Oct. 1	Sept. 1–Oct. 15	Sept. 1–Nov. 1	Sept. 1–Nov. 15	Sept. 1–Dec. 1.
Carrot	July 1–Aug. 15	Aug. 1–Sept. 1	Sept. 1–Nov. 1	Sept. 15–Dec. 1	Sept. 15–Dec. 1	Sept. 15–Dec. 1.
Cauliflower[1]	July 15–Aug. 15	do	Aug. 1–Sept. 15	Aug. 15–Oct. 10	Sept. 1–Oct. 20	Sept. 15–Nov. 1.
Celery[1] and celeriac	June 15–Aug. 15	July 1–Aug. 15	July 15–Sept. 1	Aug. 1–Dec. 1	Sept. 1–Dec. 31	Oct. 1–Dec. 31.
Chard	June 1–Sept. 10	June 1–Sept. 15	June 1–Oct. 1	June 1–Nov. 1	June 1–Dec. 1	June 1–Dec. 31.
Chervil and chives	([2])	([2])	Nov. 1–Dec. 31	Nov. 1–Dec. 31	Nov. 1–Dec. 31	Nov. 1–Dec. 31.
Chicory, witloof	July 1–Aug. 10	July 10–Aug. 20	July 20–Sept. 1	Aug. 15–Sept. 30	Aug. 15–Oct. 15	Aug. 15–Oct. 15.
Collards[1]	Aug. 1–Sept. 15	Aug. 15–Oct. 1	Aug. 25–Nov. 1	Sept. 1–Dec. 1	Sept. 1–Dec. 31	Sept. 1–Dec. 31.
Cornsalad	Sept. 15–Nov. 1	Oct. 1–Dec. 1	Oct. 1–Dec. 1	Oct. 1–Dec. 31	Oct. 1–Dec. 31	Oct. 1–Dec. 31.
Corn, sweet	June 1–Aug. 1	June 1–Aug. 15	June 1–Sept. 1			
Cress, upland	Sept. 15–Nov. 1	Oct. 1–Dec. 1	Oct. 1–Dec. 1	Oct. 1–Dec. 31	Oct. 1–Dec. 31	Oct. 1–Dec. 31.
Cucumber	June 1–Aug. 1	June 1–Aug. 15	June 1–Aug. 15	July 15–Sept. 15	Aug. 15–Oct. 1	Aug. 15–Oct. 1.
Dandelion	Aug. 15–Oct. 1	Sept. 1–Oct. 15	Sept. 1–Nov. 1	Sept. 15–Dec. 15	Oct. 1–Dec. 31	Oct. 1–Dec. 31.
Eggplant[1]	June 1–July 1	June 1–July 15	June 1–Aug. 1	July 1–Sept. 1	Aug. 1–Sept. 30	Aug. 1–Sept. 30.
Endive	July 15–Aug. 15	Aug. 1–Sept. 1	Sept. 1–Oct. 1	Sept. 1–Nov. 15	Sept. 1–Dec. 31	Sept. 1–Dec. 31.
Fennel, Florence	July 1–Aug. 1	July 15–Aug. 15	Aug. 15–Sept. 15	do	Sept. 1–Dec. 1	Sept. 1–Dec. 1.
Garlic	([2])	Aug. 1–Oct. 1	Aug. 15–Oct. 1	do	Sept. 15–Nov. 15	Sept. 15–Nov. 15.
Horseradish[1]	([2])	([2])	([2])	([2])	([2])	([2])
Kale	July 15–Sept. 1	Aug. 1–Sept. 15	Aug. 15–Oct. 15	Sept. 1–Dec. 1	Sept. 1–Dec. 31	Sept. 1–Dec. 31.
Kohlrabi	Aug. 1–Sept. 1	Aug. 15–Sept. 15	Sept. 1–Oct. 15	do	Sept. 15–Dec. 31	Do.
Leek	([2])	([2])	Sept. 1–Nov. 1	Sept. 1–Nov. 1	Sept. 1–Nov. 1	Sept. 15–Nov. 1.
Lettuce, head[1]	Aug. 1–Sept. 15	Aug. 15–Oct. 15	do	Sept. 1–Dec. 1	Sept. 15–Dec. 31	Sept. 15–Dec. 31.
Lettuce, leaf	Aug. 15–Oct. 1	Aug. 25–Oct. 1	do	do	do	Do.
Muskmelon	July 1–July 15	July 15–July 30				
Mustard	Aug. 15–Oct. 15	Aug. 15–Nov. 1	Sept. 1–Dec. 1	Sept. 1–Dec. 1	Sept. 1–Dec. 1	Sept. 15–Dec. 1.
Okra	June 1–Aug. 10	June 1–Aug. 20	June 1–Sept. 10	June 1–Sept. 20	Aug. 1–Oct. 1	Aug. 1–Oct. 1.
Onion[1]		Sept. 1–Oct. 15	Oct. 1–Dec. 31	Oct. 1–Dec. 31	Oct. 1–Dec. 31	Oct. 1–Dec. 31.
Onion, seed			Sept. 1–Nov. 1	Sept. 1–Nov. 1	Sept. 1–Nov. 1	Sept. 15–Nov. 1.
Onion, sets		Oct. 1–Dec. 1	Nov. 1–Dec. 31	Nov. 1–Dec. 31	Nov. 1–Dec. 31	Nov. 1–Dec. 31.
Parsley	Aug. 1–Sept. 15	Sept. 1–Nov. 15	Sept. 1–Dec. 31	Sept. 1–Dec. 31	Sept. 15–Dec. 31	Sept. 1–Dec. 31.
Parsnip	([2])	([2])	Aug. 1–Sept. 1	Sept. 1–Nov. 15	Sept. 1–Dec. 1	Sept. 1–Dec. 1.
Peas, garden	Aug. 1–Sept. 15	Sept. 1–Nov. 1	Oct. 1–Dec. 1	Oct. 1–Dec. 31	Oct. 1–Dec. 31	Oct. 1–Dec. 31.
Peas, black-eye	June 1–Aug. 1	June 15–Aug. 15	July 1–Sept. 1	July 1–Sept. 10	July 1–Sept. 20	July 1–Sept. 20.
Pepper[1]	June 1–July 20	June 1–Aug. 1	J ne 1–Aug. 15	June 15–Sept. 1	Aug. 15–Oct. 1	Aug. 15–Oct. 1.
Potato	July 20–Aug. 10	July 25–Aug. 20	Aug. 10–Sept. 15	Aug. 1–Sept. 15	Aug. 1–Sept. 15	Aug. 1–Sept. 15.
Radish	Aug. 15–Oct. 15	Sept. 1–Nov. 15	Sept. 1–Dec. 1	Sept. 1–Dec. 31	do	Oct. 1–Dec. 31.
Rhubarb[1]	Nov. 1–Dec. 1					
Rutabaga	July 15–Aug. 1	July 15–Aug. 15	Aug. 1–Sept. 1	Sept. 1–Nov. 15	Oct. 1–Nov. 15	Oct. 15–Nov. 15.
Salsify	June 1–July 10	June 15–July 20	July 15–Aug. 15	Aug. 15–Sept. 30	Aug. 15–Oct. 15	Sept. 1–Oct. 31.
Shallot	([2])	Aug. 1–Oct. 1	Aug. 15–Oct. 1	Aug. 15–Oct. 15	Sept. 15–Nov. 1	Sept. 15–Nov. 1.
Sorrel	Aug. 1–Sept. 15	Aug. 15–Oct. 1	Aug. 15–Oct. 15	Sept. 1–Nov. 15	Sept. 1–Dec. 15	Sept. 1–Dec. 31.
Soybean	June 1–July 15	June 1–July 25	June 1–July 30	June 1–July 30	June 1–July 30	June 1–July 30.
Spinach	Sept. 1–Oct. 1	Sept. 15–Nov. 1	Oct. 1–Dec. 1	Oct. 1–Dec. 31	Oct. 1–Dec. 31	Oct. 1–Dec. 31.
Spinach, New Zealand	June 1–Aug. 1	June 1–Aug. 15	June 1–Aug. 15			
Squash, summer	do	June 1–Aug. 10	June 1–Aug. 20	June 1–Sept. 1	June 1–Sept. 15	June 1–Oct. 1.
Squash, winter	June 10–July 10	June 20–July 20	July 1–Aug. 1	July 15–Aug. 15	Aug. 1–Sept. 1	Aug. 1–Sept. 1.
Sweetpotato	June 1–15	June 1–July 1	June 1–July 1	June 1–July 1	June 1–July 1	June 1–July 1.
Tomato	June 1–July 1	June 1–July 15	June 1–Aug. 1	Aug. 1–Sept. 1	Aug. 15–Oct. 1	Sept. 1–Nov. 1.
Turnip	Aug. 1–Sept. 15	Sept. 1–Oct. 15	Sept. 1–Nov. 15	Sept. 1–Nov. 15	Oct. 1–Dec. 1	Oct. 1–Dec. 31.
Watermelon	July 1–July 15	July 15–July 30				

[1] Plants

[2] Generally spring-planted (See Appendix A)

APPENDIX G

WHEN TO SEED SELECTED PERENNIAL FLOWERS

Name	Height (Inches)	Space (Inches)	Blooms	Plant Seed	Where	Germinates (Days)	Remarks
Achilla (Yarrow)	24	36	June–Sept.	Late fall, Early spring	Sun	7–14	Water seed with mist
Alyssum (Golddust)	9–12	24	Early spring	Early spring	Sun	21–28	Excellent in dry or sandy soil
Anchusa (Alkanet)	48–60	24	June, July	Spring to Sept.	Semi-shade	21–28	Refrigerate seed for 72 hours. Shade summer plantings
Anthemis (Golden Daisy)	24	24	Midsum. to frost	Spring after soil warms	Sun	21–28	Grows well in dry or sunny spot
Arabis (Rockcress)	8–12	12	Early spring	Spring to Sept.	Light shade	5	Shade summer plantings
Armeria (Sea Pink)	18–24	12	May, June	Spring to Sept.	Sun	10	Shade seedbed until plants are sturdy
Artemisia (Wormwood)	24	9–12	Late summer	Late spring to late summer	Full Sun		Grows well even in dry and poor soils
Aster (Hardy aster)	12–60	36	June	Early spring	Sun	14–21	
Astilbe japonica	12–36	24	Summer	Early spring		14–21	Plant in rich, loamy soil
Aubrieta (Rainbow cress)	6	12	April, May	Spring to Sept.	Light Shade	20	Shade plants in summer. Divide mature plants in late summer
Begonia (Hardy begonia)	12	9–12	Late summer	Summer	Shade, Moist soil	12	Propagate by planting bulblets that grow in leaf axils
Candytuft (Iberis)	12	12	Late spring	Early spring, late fall	Sun	20	Does well in dry spots
Canterbury Bells	24–30	15		Spring to Sept.	Partial shade	20	Do not cover seed. Shade seedbed in summer
Carnation	18–24	12	Late summer	Late spring	Sun	20	Cut plants back in late fall, pot, hold over winter in a coldframe.
Centaurea (Cornflower)	24	12	June to Sept.	Early spring	Sun	21–28	Remove flowers as they fade
Cerastium (Snow-in-summer)	6	18	May and June	Early spring	Sun	14–28	Rampant grower. Do not let it crowd other plants
Chinese Lanterns	24	36	Sept. Oct.	Late fall, early winter	Sun	15	Lanterns borne the second year
Columbine	30–36	12–18	Late spring, early summer	Spring to Sept.	Sun or partial shade	30	Needs fairly rich, well-drained soil
Coreopsis	24–36	30	May to fall	Early spring, late fall	Sun	5	Drought resistant. Grow as biennial
Daisy, English	6	6	All summer in cool climates		Partial shade	8	Water well in summer. Protect in winter

APPENDIX G *(continued)*

Name	Height (Inches)	Space (Inches)	Blooms	Plant Seed	Where	Germinates (Days)	Remarks
Daisy, Shasta	24–30	30	June, July	Early spring to Sept.	Sun	10	Best grown as a biennial.
Delphinium	48–60	24	June	Spring to Sept.	Sun	20	Must have well drained soil. Stake
Dianthus	12	12	May, June	Spring to Sept.	Sun	5	Best grown as a biennial
Dicenfra (Bleeding Heart)	24–48	12	Late spring	Late autumn		50	
Foxglove	48–72	12	June, July	Spring to Sept.	Sun or partial shade	20	Shade summer plantings
Gaillardia	12–30	24	Midsummer to frost	Early spring, late summer	Sun	20	
Geum	6–24	18	June, July	Spring or summer	Sun	25	Winter hardy if protected
Gypsophila	24–48	48	Early summer	Early spring to Sept.	Sun	10	Does best in well limed soil
Helianthemum	12	12	June to Sept.	Spring to Sept.	Full sun	15	Plants are evergreen
Helleborus (Christmas rose)	15	24	Early spring	Late fall, early winter	Sun	30	Refrigerate seeds for 2 months before spring planting
Hemerocallis (Day lily)	12–48	24–30	All season (various species)	Late fall, early spring	Sun or partial shade	15	
Heuchera (Coral Bells)	24	18	June to Sept.	Early spring, late fall	Partial shade	10	Grows best in a limed soil. Divide
Hibiscus	36–96	24	July to Sept.	Spring or summer	Sun or partial shade	15	
Hollyhock	72	36	Late spring to midsummer	Spring or summer	Sun	10	Does best in deep well-drained soil
Liatris (Gayfeather)	24–72	18	Summer to fall	Early spring, late fall	Sun	20	Propagate by cutting roots into pieces
Linum (Flax)	24	18	Summer	Spring to Sept.	Sun	25	Shade in summer
Lunaria (Money plant)	48	24	Summer	Early spring	Sun	10	Source of seedpods for drying
Lupine	36	36	Summer	Early spring, late fall	Sun	20	Needs good drainage. does not transplant well
Lythrum (Blackblood)	48–72	18–24	July, August	Late fall, early spring	Light shade	15	
Monardia	24–36	12–18	Summer	Spring or summer		15	Cut plants back & they'll bloom again
Penstemon	18–24	18	Summer	Early spring, late fall	Sun	10	Plant where has winter shelter
Phlox Paniculata (Summer phlox)	36	24	Early summer	Late fall, early winter	Sun	25	Refrigerate seed 1 month before planting

APPENDIX G *(continued)*

Name	Height (Inches)	Space (Inches)	Blooms	Plant Seed	Where	Germinates (Days)	Remarks
Phlox Subulata (Moss phlox)	4–5	8	Spring	Grown from stolens	Sun		Drought resistant
Plaxtycodon	24	12	Spring until frost	Spring to September	Sun	10	In fall, dig root, store in moist sand in frostfree cold frame
Poppy, Iceland	15–18	24	Summer	Early spring	Sun	10	Plant in permanent spot
Primrose	6–9	12	April, May	Late autumn, early winter	Part shade	25	
Pyrethrum (Painted daisy)	24	18	May, June	Spring to September	Sun	20	Winterkills in wet soil
Rudbeckia (Cornflower)	30–36	30	Midsummer to fall	Spring to Sept.	Sun	20	Shade in summer
Salvia	36–48	18–24	August to frost	Spring	Sun	15	
Sea Lavender	24–36	30	July, August	Early spring	Sun	15	
Siberian Wallflower	12–18	12	May, June	Early spring	Sun	5	Does very well in cool climates
Stokesia (Stokes Aster)	15	18	Sept.	Spring to Sept.	Sun	20	Shade summer plants
Sweetpea	60–72	24	June to Sept.	Early spring	Sun	20	
Sweet-william	12–18	12	May, June	Spring to Sept.	Sun	5	Grows best in well drained soil
Tritoma	36–48	18	Aug. to Oct.	Early spring, late fall	Sun	20	In north, dig and store roots
Trollius (Globe flower)	20	12	May to July	Late fall		50	
Veronica	18	16	June, July	Spring to Sept.	Sun	15	
Viola Cornuta	6	12	Summer	Spring to Sept.	Partial shade	10	Remove old flowers for all-summer bloom

APPENDIX H

PLANTING DEPTHS FOR SPRING BULBS AND HOW TALL THEY GROW

TULIP PLANTING GUIDE

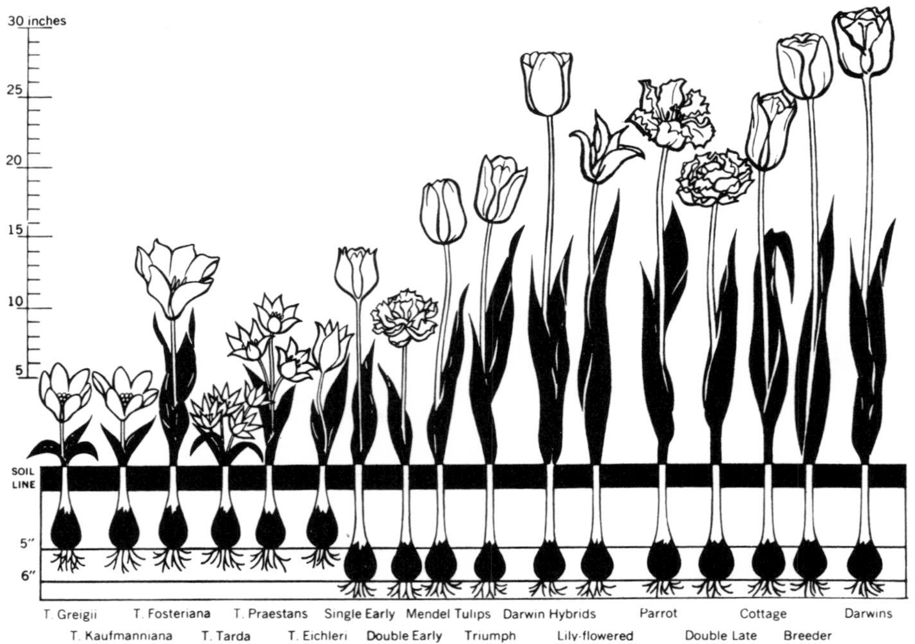

MINOR BULB PLANTING GUIDE

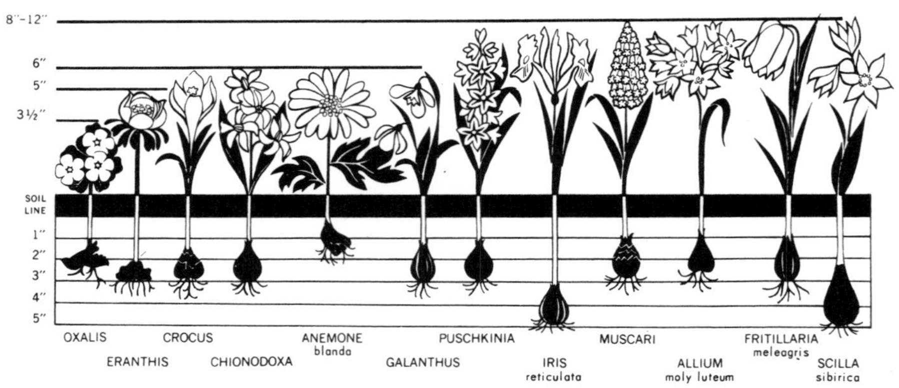

APPENDIX I

FACTS ABOUT WEIGHTS AND MEASURES

Linear Measure

12 inches = 1 foot
3 feet = 1 yard = 36 inches
5 1/2 yards = 1 rod = 16 1/2 feet
40 rods = 1 furlong = 660 feet
8 furlongs = 1 mile = 5,280 feet
3 miles = 1 league = 15,840 feet
6,080.20 feet = 1 nautical, or sea mile

Area Measure

144 square inches = 1 square foot
9 square feet = 1 square yard
30 1/4 square yards = 1 square rod
160 square rods = 1 acre
640 acres = 1 square mile
1 mile square = 1 section
6 miles square = 1 township

Cubic Measure

1,728 cubic inches = 1 cubic foot
27 cubic feet = 1 cubic yard

Surveyors' Measure

7.92 inches = 1 link
100 links = 1 chain = 4 rods = 66 feet
80 chains = 1 statute mile = 320 rods = 5,280 feet

Liquid Measure

4 gills = 1 pint
2 pints = 1 quart
4 quarts = 1 gallon

Apothecaries' Measure

60 minims = 1 fluid dram
8 fluid drams = 1 fluid ounce
16 fluid ounces = 1 pint
2 pints = 1 quart
4 quarts = 1 gallon

Dry Measure

2 pints = 1 quart
8 quarts = 1 peck
4 pecks = 1 bushel

Avoirdupois Weight

27 11/32 grains = 1 dram
16 drams = 1 ounce
16 ounces = 1 pound
100 pounds = 1 short hundredweight
20 hundredweights = 1 short ton = 2,000 pounds
112 pounds = 1 long hundredweight
20 long hundredweights = 1 long ton = 2,240 pounds

Metric System

Linear Measure

10 millimeters = 1 centimeter
10 centimeters = 1 decimeter
10 decimeters = 1 meter
10 meters = 1 dekameter
10 dekameters = 1 hectometer
10 hectometers = 1 kilometer

Volume Measure

10 milliliters = 1 centiliter
10 centiliters = 1 deciliter
10 deciliters = 1 liter
10 liters = 1 dekaliter
10 dekaliters = 1 hectoliter
10 hectoliters = 1 kilometer

Cubic Measure

1,000 cubic millimeters = 1 cubic centimeter
1,000 cubic centimeters = 1 cubic decimeter
1,000 cubic decimeters = 1 cubic meter

Weight

10 milligrams = 1 centigram
10 centigrams = 1 decigram
10 decigrams = 1 gram
10 grams = 1 dekagram
10 dekagrams = 1 hectogram
10 hectograms = 1 kilogram
1,000 kilograms = 1 metric ton

Equivalents

1 centimeter – 0.3937 inch
1 fathom – 1.829 meters
1 foot – 0.305 meter
1 hand – 4 inches
1 inch – 2.540 centimeters
1 kilometer – 0.621 mile
1 meter – 39.37 inches
1 mile (land) – 1.609 kilometers
1 mile (sea) – 1.853 kilometers
1 acre – 4,840 square yards
1 cord – (firewood) – 128 cubic feet
1 liter – 1.057 liquid quarts
1 pint, dry – 0.551 liter
1 pint, liquid – 0.473 liter
1 gram – 0.035 ounce, avoirdupois
1 kilogram – 2.205 pounds
1 ounce – 28.350 grams
1 pound, avoirdupois – 453.592 grams

EQUIVALENTS OF COMMON CAPACITY UNITS USED IN KITCHEN

Units	Fluid drams	Tea-spoon-fuls	Table-spoon-fuls	Fluid ounces	1/4 cup-fuls	Gills (1/2 cup-fuls)	Cup-fuls	Liquid pints	Liquid quarts	Cubic centi-meters	Liters
1 fluid dram equals	1	3/4	1/4	1/8	1/16	1/32	1/64	1/128	1/256	3.7	0.004
1 teaspoonful equals	1 1/3	1	1/3	1/6	1/12	1/24	1/48	1/96	1/192	4.9	0.005
1 tablespoonful equals	4	3	1	1/2	1/4	1/8	1/16	1/32	1/64	15	0.015
1 fluid ounce equals	8	6	2	1	1/2	1/4	1/8	1/16	1/32	30	0.030
1/4 cupful equals	16	12	4	2	1	1/2	1/4	1/8	1/16	59	0.059
1 gill (1/2 cupful) equals	32	24	8	4	2	1	1/2	1/4	1/8	118	0.118
1 cupful equals	64	48	16	8	4	2	1	1/2	1/4	237	0.237
1 liquid pint equals	128	96	32	16	8	4	2	1	1/2	473	0.473
1 liquid quart equals	256	192	64	32	16	8	4	2	1	946	0.946
1 cubic centimeter equals	0.27	0.20	0.068	0.034	0.017	0.0084	0.0042	0.0021	0.0011	1	1/1000
1 liter equals	270	203	67.6	33.8	16.9	8.45	4.23	2.11	1.06	1000	1

APPENDIX J

WHERE AMERICAN BUNCH GRAPES GROW

American bunch grapes can be grown in at least three fourths of the states. Areas not suitable are those with very short growing seasons or with extremely severe winters. Otherwise, you can find a variety for most climatic conditions. The accompanying map and table will guide you to the varieties suitable for your area—if you can grow them at all. (Map and data adapted from "Growing American Bunch Grapes," Bulletin No. 2123, U.S. Department of Ag.)

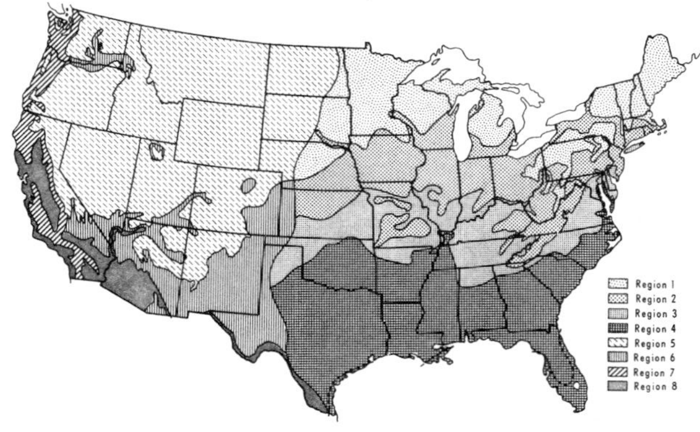

Varieties suitable for the regions shown on the map and most frequently recommended for home planting include:

Region 1,—Beta, Blue Jay, Red Amber; Region 2,—Brighton, Catawba, Concord, Delaware, Fredonia, Moore Early, Niagara, Ontario, Portland, Seneca, Van Buren, Worden; Region 3,—Brighton, Catawba, Concord, Delaware, Fredonia, Golden Muscat, Lenoir, Niagara, Norton, Portland, Sheridan, Worden; Region 4,—Blue Lake, Catawba, Champanel, Concord, Delaware, Ellen Scott, Extra, Fredonia, Lenoir, Niagara; Region 5,—Beta; Region 6,—Campbell Early, Concord, Delaware, Ellen Scott, Golden Muscat, Niagara, Worden; Region 7,—Campbell Early, Concord, Golden Muscat, Niabell, Niagara, Worden; Region 8,—Concord, Niabell.

APPENDIX K

WHEN TO PLANT VEGETABLES IN CALIFORNIA

Vegetable	N. Coast: Monterey Co. north	S. Coast: San Luis Obispo Co., south	Interior valleys: Sacramento, San Joaquin, and similar valleys	Imperial and Coachella valleys	W = warm-season crop C= cool-season crop	Moderate planting for family of four	Distance apart in row	Distance between rows without beds
ARTICHOKE[3]	Aug–Dec	Oct–Dec	......	......	C	3–4 plants	48″	60″
ASPARAGUS[3]	Jan–Mar	Jan–Feb	Jan–Feb	Feb–Apr	C	30–40 plants	12″	60″
BEANS (lima)[1]	May–June	Apr–May	May–June	......	W	15–25 ft. row	6″ bush; 24″ pole	30″
BEANS (snap)[1,2]	July May–June	Mar–Aug	Apr–May, July	Jan–Mar, Aug	W	15–25 ft. row	3″ bush; 24″ pole	30″[4]
BEETS[1]	Feb–Aug	Feb–Aug	Feb–Aug	Sept–Jan	C	10–15 ft. row	2″	24″[4]
BROCCOLI[1,3]	June–July	June–July	July	Sept	C	15–20 ft. row	24″	36″
BRUSSELS SPROUTS[3]	June	June–July	......	......	C	15–20 ft. row	24″	36″
CABBAGE[1,3]	Jan–Apr July–Sept	Oct–Feb	July, Jan–Feb	Sept–Nov	C	10–15 plants	24″	36″
CABBAGE (Chinese)[1]	July–Aug	Aug–Sept	Aug	Aug–Nov	C	10–15 ft. row	6″	30″[4]
CANTALOUPES and similar melons	May	Apr–May	Apr–May	Jan–Apr, July	W	5–10 hills	48″	72″
CARROTS[1,2]	Jan–Aug	Jan–Aug	July–Aug, Feb	Sept-Dec	C	20–30 ft. row	2″	24″[4]
CAULIFLOWER[3]	June, Jan	July–Nov	July–Aug	Sept–Oct	C	10–15 plants	24″	36″
CELERIAC	Mar–June	Mar–Aug	June–Aug	......	C	10–15 ft. row	4″	24″[4]
CELERY[1,3]	Mar–June	Mar–Aug	June–Aug	......	C	20–30 ft. row	5″	24″[4]
CHARD[1]	Feb–May	Nov–May	Feb–May	Sept–Oct	C	3–4 plants	12″	30″
CHAYOTE	......	Apr–May	May–June	......	W	1–2 plants	72″	grow along fence
CHIVES[1]	April	Jan–Feb	Feb–Mar	Nov–Jan	C	1 clump	needs 4 sq. ft.	......
CORN (sweet)[2]	Apr–July	Feb–July	Mar–July	Jan–Mar	W	20–30 ft. in 4 rows	15″	36″
CUCUMBERS	Apr–June	Apr–June	Apr–June	Feb–May	W	6 plants	24″	48″
EGGPLANT[3]	May	April	Apr–May	Feb–Aug	W	4–6 plants	24″	36″
ENDIVE[1]	Mar–July	Mar–Aug	Aug	Sept–Nov	C	10–15 ft. row	10″	24″[4]
FLORENCE FENNEL	Mar–July	Mar–Aug	Aug	Sept–Nov	C	10–15 ft. row	4″	30″[4]
GARLIC	Nov–Dec	Nov–Jan	Nov–Jan	Oct–Nov	C	10–20 ft. row	3″	18″[4]
KOHLRABI	July–Aug	Jan, Aug	Aug	Nov	C	10–15 ft. row	3″	24″
LEEK	Feb–Apr	Jan–Apr	Jan–Apr	....	C	10 ft. row	2″	24″
LETTUCE[1]	Feb–Aug	Dec–Aug	Aug, Nov–Feb	Sept–Dec	C	10–15 ft. row	head 12″; leaf 6″	24″

NOTE: Climate may vary even in small section of state. Since areas above are large, dates are only approximate.
1. Crops for a small garden.
2. Crops which, in a suitable climate, should be planted more than once.
3. Transplants used for field planting.
4. If grown on beds, plant two rows per bed with beds about 32–40 inches apart, and tops of beds 18 inches wide.

APPENDIX K *(continued)*

Vegetable	N. Coast: Monterey Co. north	S. Coast: San Luis Obispo Co., south	Interior valleys: Sacramento, San Joaquin, and similar valleys	Imperial and Coachella valleys	W = warm-season crop C= cool-season crop	Moderate planting for family of four	Distance apart in row	Distance between rows without beds
MUSTARD	July–Aug	Aug–Feb	Aug	Nov	C	10 ft. row	8″	24″[4]
OKRA	May	April	May	Mar	W	10–20 ft. row	18″	36″
ONIONS	Jan–Mar	Nov–Feb	Nov–Feb	Nov–Jan	C	30–40 ft. row	3″	24″[4]
PARSLEY[1]	Dec–May	Dec–May	Dec–May	Sept–Oct	C	1 or 2 plants	8″	24″
PARSNIPS	May–June	June–July	June–July	Oct	C	10–15 ft. row	3″	24″[4]
PEAS[1]	Jan–Aug	Aug, Dec–Mar	Nov–Jan	Aug–Nov	C	30–40 ft. row	2″	36″ bush 48″ vine
PEPPERS[1,3]	May	Apr–May	May	Mar	W	5–10 plants	24″	36″
POTATOES (sweet)[3]	May	Apr–May	May	Mar–May	W	50–100 ft. row	12″	36″
POTATOES (white)	early: Feb late: Apr–May	early: June–Feb late: Mar–Aug	early: Feb–Mar late: Aug	Jan–Feb	C	50–100 ft. row	12″	30″
PUMPKINS	May	April	Apr–June	Mar	W	1–3 plants	48″	72″
RADISH[1,2]	all year	all year	Sept–Mar	Oct–Feb	C	4 ft. row	1″	18″[4]
RHUBARB	Dec–Jan	Dec–Jan	Jan–Feb	....	C	2–3 plants	36″	48″
RUTABAGAS	July	July, Mar	July, Aug	Oct–Jan	C	10–15 ft. row	3″	24″[4]
SPINACH[1]	Aug–Feb	Sept–Jan	Sept–Jan	Sept–Nov	C	10–20 ft. row	3″	18″[4]
SQUASH (summer)	May	Apr–June	Apr–June	Feb–Mar	W	2–4 plants	24″	48″
SQUASH (winter)	May	Apr–June	Apr–June	Feb–Mar	W	2–4 plants	48″	72″
TOMATOES[1,3]	May	Apr–Aug 15	Apr–May	Dec–Mar	W	10–20 plants	See page 31	See page 31
TURNIPS[1]	Jan, Aug	Aug, Apr	Aug, Feb	Oct–Feb	C	10–15 ft. row	2″	24″[4]
WATERMELONS	May–June	Apr–May	Apr–May	Feb–Mar	W	6 plants	60″	72″

NOTE: Climate may vary even in small section of state. Since areas above are large, dates are only approximate.
1. Crops for a small garden.
2. Crops which, in a suitable climate, should be planted more than once.
3. Transplants used for field planting.
4. If grown on beds, plant two rows per bed with beds about 32–40 inches apart, and tops of beds 18 inches wide.

APPENDIX L

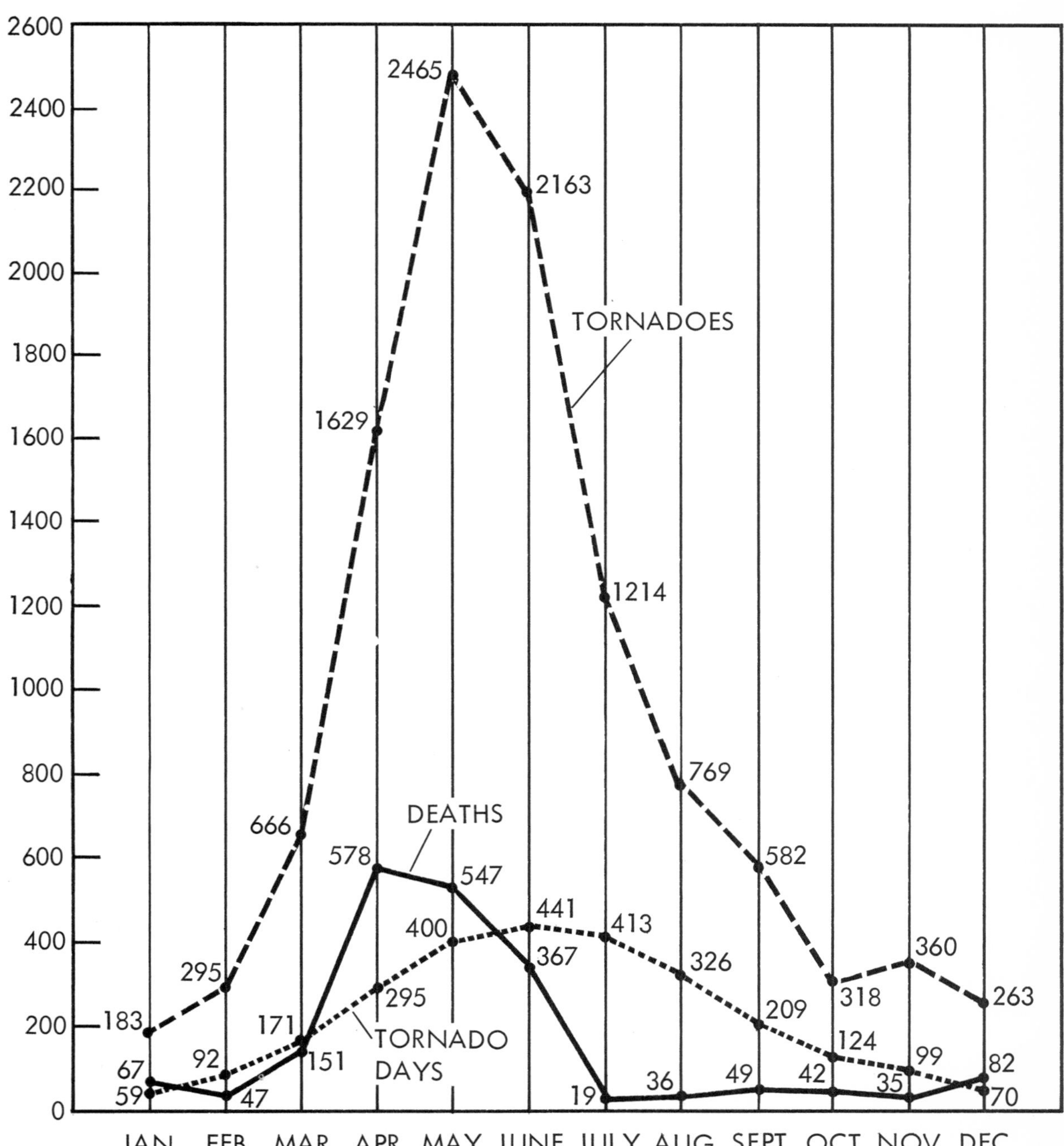
1953 - 1969
TORNADO INCIDENCE BY MONTH
2600
2400
2200
2000
1800
1600
1400
1200
1000
800
600
400
200
0
2465
2163
TORNADOES
1629
1214
769
666
DEATHS
578
547
582
441
413
400
367
360
295
326
295
318
263
183
171
209
TORNADO
DAYS
124
67
92
151
99
82
59
47
19
36
49
42
35
70
JAN
FEB
MAR
APR
MAY
JUNE
JULY
AUG
SEPT
OCT
NOV
DEC

APPENDIX L *(continued)*

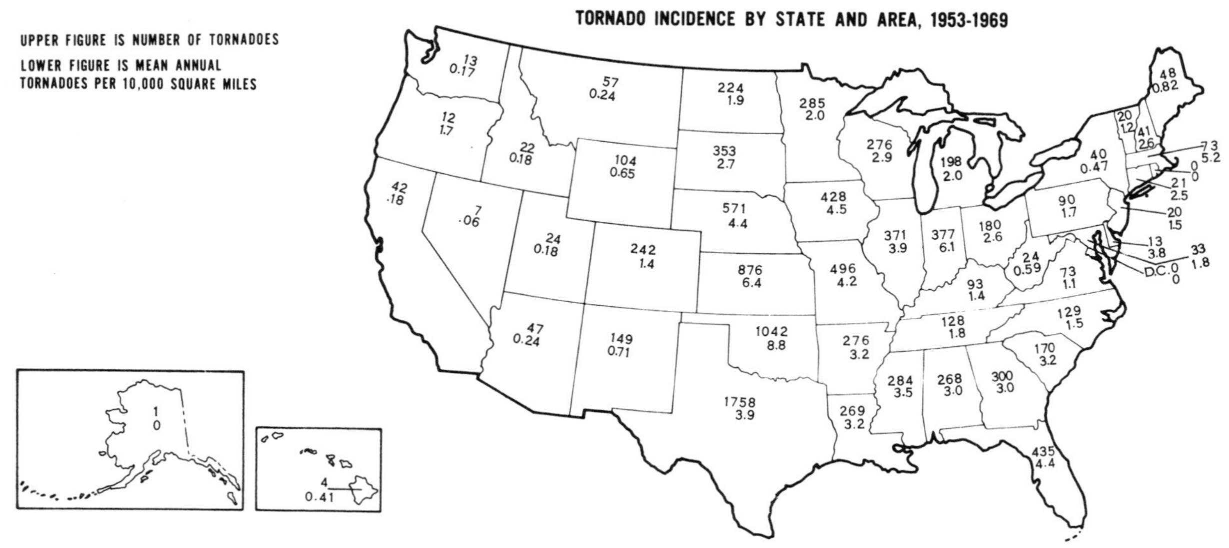

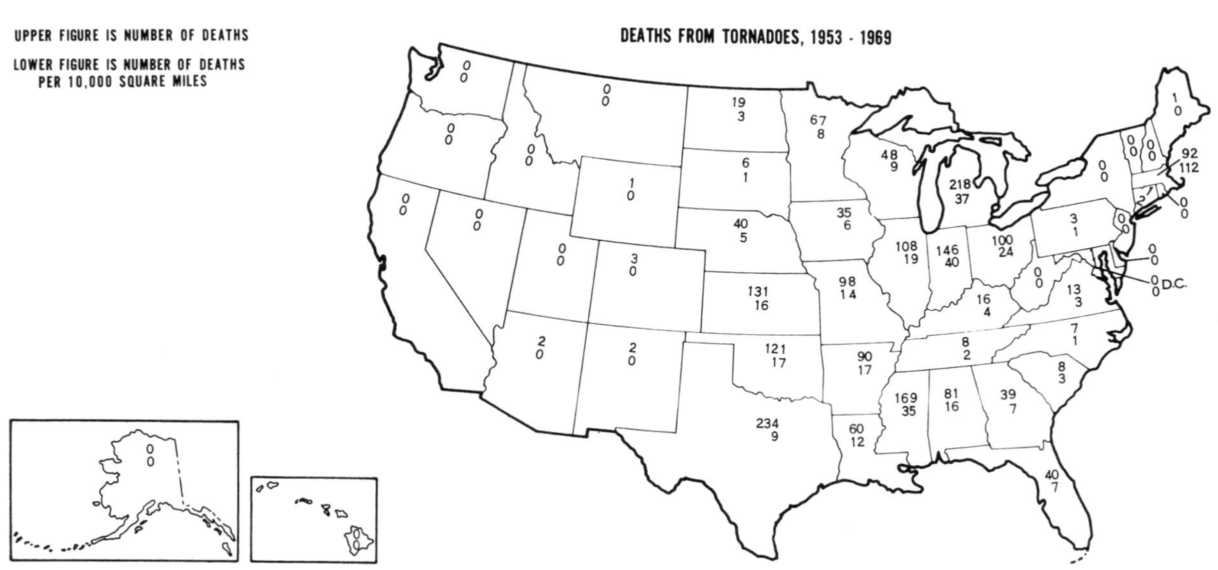

APPENDIX M

STATE EXTENSION SERVICE OFFICES

Extension services for your area usually are located in the courthouse, post office, or other government building in your county seat town. Or you can write to Director, State Extension Service, at the address below:

ALABAMA—Auburn University, Auburn 36830
ALASKA—University of Alaska, College 99701
ARIZONA—University of Arizona, Tucson 85721
ARKANSAS—University of Arkansas, Little Rock 72203
CALIFORNIA—University of California, 2200 University Avenue, Berkeley 94720
COLORADO—Colorado State University, Fort Collins 80521
CONNECTICUT—University of Connecticut, Storrs 06268
DELAWARE—University of Delaware, Newark 19711
DISTRICT OF COLUMBIA—1424 K Street NW, Washington, D.C. 20005
FLORIDA—University of Florida, Gainesville 32601
GEORGIA—University of Georgia, Athens 30601
HAWAII—University of Hawaii, Honolulu 96822
IDAHO—University of Idaho, Moscow 83843
ILLINOIS—University of Illinois, Urbana 61801
INDIANA—Purdue University, Lafayette 47907
IOWA—Iowa State University, Ames 50010
KANSAS—Kansas State University, Manhattan 66502
KENTUCKY—University of Kentucky, Lexington 40506
LOUISIANA—Louisiana State University, Baton Rouge 70803
MAINE—University of Maine, Orono 04473
MARYLAND—University of Maryland, College Park 20742
MASSACHUSETTS—University of Massachusetts, Amherst 01002
MICHIGAN—Michigan State University, East Lansing 48823
MINNESOTA—University of Minnesota, St. Paul 55101
MISSISSIPPI—Mississippi State University, State College 39762
MISSOURI—University of Missouri, Columbia 65201
MONTANA—Montana State University, Bozeman 59715
NEBRASKA—University of Nebraska, Lincoln 68503
NEVADA—University of Nevada, Reno 89507
NEW HAMPSHIRE—University of New Hampshire, Durham 03824
NEW JERSEY—Rutgers—The State University, New Brunswick 08903
NEW MEXICO—New Mexico State University, University Park 88070
NEW YORK—New York State College of Agriculture at Cornell University, Ithaca 14850
NORTH CAROLINA—North Carolina State University, Raleigh 27607
NORTH DAKOTA—North Dakota State University, Fargo 58102
OHIO—Ohio State University, Columbus 43210
OKLAHOMA—Oklahoma State University, Stillwater 74074
OREGON—Oregon State University, Corvallis 97331
PENNSYLVANIA—The Pennsylvania State University, University Park 16802
PUERTO RICO—University of Puerto Rico, Rio Piedras 00928

APPENDIX M *(continued)*

RHODE ISLAND—University of Rhode Island, Kingston 02881

SOUTH CAROLINA—Clemson University, Clemson 29631

SOUTH DAKOTA—South Dakota State University, Brookings 57006

TENNESSEE—University of Tennessee, Knoxville 37901

TEXAS—Texas A&M University, College Station 77843

UTAH—Utah State University, Logan 84321

VERMONT—University of Vermont, Burlington 05401

VIRGINIA—Virginia Polytechnic Institute, Blacksburg 24061

VIRGIN ISLANDS—P.O. Box 166, Kingshill, St. Croix 00850

WASHINGTON—Washington State University, Pullman 99163

WEST VIRGINIA—West Virginia University, Morgantown 26506

WISCONSIN—University of Wisconsin, Madison 53706

WYOMING—University of Wyoming, Laramie 82070

Index

Notes

Notes

Notes

Notes